CAMBRIDGE STUDIES IN LINGUISTICS

General Editors. W.SIDNEY ALLEN. B.COMRIE. C.J.FILLMORE
R.J.A.HENDERSON. F.W.HOUSEHOLDER. R.LASS. J.LYONS
R.B.LE PAGE. F.R.PALMER. R.POSNER. J.L.M.TRIM

Psychological reality in phonology
A theoretical study

In this series

1   DAVID CRYSTAL: *Prosodic systems and intonation in English**
2   PIETER A.M.SEUREN: *Operators and nucleus*
3   RODNEY D.HUDDLESTON: *The sentence in written English*
4   JOHN M.ANDERSON: *The grammar of case**
5   M. L. SAMUELS: *Linguistic evolution**
6   P.H.MATTHEWS: *Inflectional morphology**
7   GILLIAN BROWN: *Phonological rules and dialect variation**
8   BRIAN NEWTON: *The generative interpretation of dialect**
9   R.M.W.DIXON: *The Dyirbal language of North Queensland**
10 BRUCE L.DERWING: *Transformational grammar as theory of language acquisition**
11 MELISSA BOWERMAN: *Early syntactic development**
12 W.SIDNEY ALLEN: *Accent and rhythm*
13 PETER TRUDGILL: *The social differentiation of English in Norwich*
14 ROGER LASS and JOHN M.ANDERSON: *Old English phonology*
15 RUTH M.KEMPSON: *Presupposition and the delimitation of semantics**
16 JAMES R.HURFORD: *The linguistic theory of numerals*
17 ROGER LASS: *English phonology and phonological theory*
18 G.M.AWBERY: *The syntax of Welsh*
19 R.M.W.DIXON: *A grammar of Yidiɲ*
20 JAMES FOLEY: *Foundations of theoretical phonology*
21 A. RADFORD: *Italian syntax : transformational and relational grammar*
22 DIETER WUNDERLICH: *Foundations of linguistics**
23 DAVID W. LIGHTFOOT: *Principles of diachronic syntax**
24 ANNETTE KARMILOFF-SMITH: *A functional approach to child language*
25 PER LINELL: *Psychological reality in phonology*
    * *Issued in hard covers and as a paperback*

PSYCHOLOGICAL REALITY IN PHONOLOGY

A theoretical study

PER LINELL

Assistant Professor of Linguistics, University of Uppsala

CAMBRIDGE UNIVERSITY PRESS

CAMBRIDGE

LONDON · NEW YORK · MELBOURNE

414
L64p
114654
July 1980

Published by the Syndics of the Cambridge University Press
The Pitt Building, Trumpington Street, Cambridge CB2 1RP
Bentley House, 200 Euston Road, London NW1 2DB
32 East 57th Street, New York, NY 10022, USA
296 Beaconsfield Parade, Middle Park, Melbourne 3206, Australia

First published 1979

Printed in Great Britain by The University Press, Cambridge

Library of Congress Cataloguing in Publication Data

Linell, Per, 1944–
Psychological reality in phonology.

(Cambridge studies in linguistics; 25)
Bibliography: p.
1. Grammar, Comparative and general – Phonology.
2. Psycholinguistics. 3. Generative grammar.
4. Morphophonemics. I. Title. II. Series.
P217.L53   414   78-67429

ISBN 0 521 22234 6

ISSN 0068–676X

Contents

Prologue   xiii

1 ON PSYCHOLOGICAL REALITY
1.1 Language as a social and psychological entity   1
1.2 Attitudes to the goal of psychological reality   3
1.3 Reasons to adopt the goal of psychological reality   8
1.4 The concept of psychological reality   8
    1.4.1 Degree of representationalism   9
    1.4.2 Accessibility   12
    1.4.3 Teleology and causality: acts, rules, derivations and causal
    processes   15
1.5 Knowledge and behavior   17
    1.5.1 Introduction   17
    1.5.2 Competence vs. performance: justification for a distinction   17
    1.5.3 Competence: ability, habituality and normativity   18
    1.5.4 Grammatical competence and communicative competence   20
    1.5.5 Knowledge and rules: conventionality and consciousness   22
    1.5.6 Competence and indeterminacy   25
1.6 Methodological pluralism   27

**2 PHONOLOGY IN A MODEL OF COMMUNICATIVE
COMPETENCE**
2.1 Phonology and phonetics   30
2.2 General framework: communicative competence   32
2.3 Speakers' phonological capacities   37
2.4 Notes on speaker's competence and listener's competence   39
    2.4.1 One or two competences?   39
    2.4.2 The primacy of perception   40
    2.4.3 Speakers know more   42
    2.4.4 Different modes of listening   43
    Listening to sounds and listening to words   43
    Full comprehension of an utterance   45

3 PHONOLOGICAL FORMS AS PLANS FOR PHONETIC ACTS
3.1 Justification for the notion of 'phonetic plan'   47
3.2 Phonetic plans of words vs. complete articulatory plans of
utterances   48

3.3 The nature of phonetic plans   51
    3.3.1 Word-form invariance   51
    3.3.2 Phoneticity   51
    Non-phonological features   52
    Boundaries   52
    3.3.3 Concreteness   53
    3.3.4 Reference to careful pronunciations   54
    Careful pronunciations vs. elaborated pronunciations   54
    Arguments for the primacy of careful pronunciations   56
    3.3.5 Categoricalness   57
3.4 The existence of alternative plans   60
3.5 The role of phonetic plans in speech production   62
3.6 The role of phonetic plans in speech perception   63
3.7 Appendix: the status of the segment   65

4 PHONETIC PLANS AND LEXICAL ENTRIES
4.1 Introduction: phonetic plans vs. lexical representations   70
4.2 On lexical economy   71
    4.2.1 Economy as a metatheoretical evaluation criterion   72
    4.2.2 Memory storage and economy considerations   73
4.3 The phonological properties of lexical items   76
    4.3.1 Alternatives   76
    4.3.2 Vennemann's theory of the lexicon   76
    4.3.3. Stem and base form theory   78
    Methodological aspects   78
    Polymorphemic structures in the lexicon   78
    Input of morphological operations 1 : structural arguments 80
    Input of morphological operations 2 : substantive evidence 81
4.4 Non-phonological information in phonology   84

5 PHONEMIC CONTRASTS
5.1 Introduction   88
5.2 Arguments in favor of surface phonemic contrasts   89
    5.2.1 Identity and similarity of phonological strings   89
    5.2.2 Correctness of phonological strings   94
    5.2.3 Perceptual equivalence and the reinterpretation of deviant
    sounds   94
    5.2.4 Phonetic distinctness and surface symmetry   98
    5.2.5 Sharpening of minor allophones in lexical pronunciation 99
    5.2.6 Adaptation to secondary dialects   101
    5.2.7 Submorphemic conspiracies   102
    5.2.8 Inputs of morphological operations   103

5.2.9 Indeterminacy of morphophonemic representations 103
5.2.10 Historical change 104
Preservation of contrasts 104
The loss of non-distinctive features 105
Transition of forms to new paradigms 105
Allomorphy reduction 106
5.2.11 The transfer of allophones to new positions 106
5.2.12 Child language 109
5.2.13 Pathological speech behavior 110
Speech errors 110
Aphasia 112
Misperceptions 113
5.2.14 Divergent properties of rule types 114
5.2.15 Linguists' practice 114
5.3 Can one recognize the significance of surface contrasts without
having surface forms? 115

6 PHONOTACTICS AND PHONOLOGICAL CORRECTNESS
6.1 Introduction 117
6.2 Phonological correctness 118
6.2.1 Independence of morphophonology 118
6.2.2 Reference to careful pronunciations 120
6.3 Behavioral evidence 120
6.3.1 The adaptation of deviant forms 120
6.3.2 Reduction in fast speech 121
6.4 On capturing regularities 121
6.4.1 Conspiracies 121
6.4.2 Conditions on syllable structure 123
6.5 On some properties of phonotactic rules 124
6.5.1 Active filter function 124
6.5.2 Domain of application 126

7 MORPHOLOGICAL OPERATIONS AND
MORPHOPHONOLOGY
7.1 Introduction 127
7.2 Morphological operations: general properties 128
7.3 Morphological operations: examples 130
7.4 The unity of morphological operations 136
7.4.1 Function in speech act theory 137
7.4.2 Behavioral unity 137

7.4.3 Applicability of morphophonological rules proper 139
Derivation-specific ordering 139
Applicational dependence 140
Exceptionality of derivations with respect to rules 140
7.5 The place of morphophonology 142
7.6 Complex morphological operations 143
7.7 Morpheme identity outside morphological operations 149

8 WORD FORMS AS PRIMES
8.1 A brief recapitulation 151
8.2 Further arguments for word forms as primary units 152
   8.2.1 Syntactically 'free' forms 152
   8.2.2 Semantically 'free' forms 152
   8.2.3 Non-predictable features of meaning 153
   8.2.4 The dependence of morphs on the word form context 153
   8.2.5 Synchronic and diachronic variation and change 154
   8.2.6 Phonetic gestalts 155
   8.2.7 Intuitive plausibility 156
8.3 Refuting some counter-arguments 156
   8.3.1 The definition of word forms 156
   8.3.2 The selection of lexical forms 157
   8.3.3 The internal structure of word forms 158
   8.3.4 The loss of generalizations 158
   8.3.5 Redundancy 158
   8.3.6 What the theory does not mean 158

9 MORPHEMES AND MORPHEME IDENTITY
9.1 The nature of morphemes 160
9.2 The establishment of morpheme identity 161
9.3 Morpheme identity as a basis for reinterpretation and construction
   of forms 162
9.4 Conditions on morpheme identity 163
9.5 More on morpheme identity: inter- and intra-individual variation 164
9.6 Further consequences 165

10 TYPOLOGY OF PHONOLOGICAL RULES
10.1 Introduction 167
10.2 Functions of rules 167
10.3 Basic rule types 168
   10.3.1 Phonotactic rules 168
   10.3.2 Sharpening and elaboration rules 169
   10.3.3 Perceptual redundancy rules 170

10.3.4 Articulatory reduction rules 172
10.3.5 Morphophonological rules proper 172
10.3.6 Summary: rule types and grammatical functions 174
10.4 Properties of rules: introduction 175
10.5 Invariance and variation: obligatoriness/optionality 176
10.6 Use and validity of rules in normal regular speech 177
10.6.1 Validity as a function of speech tempo 177
10.6.2 Invocation in speech performance 178
10.7 Formal properties 179
10.7.1 Generality of rules with respect to the phonological
constitution of strings 179
Context-sensitivity 179
Conditioning 180
Generality (freedom from exceptions) 182
Transparency 183
10.7.2 Relations between inputs and outputs 185
Recoverability of inputs 185
Segment inventories of inputs and outputs 186
Requirement on feature specification changes 187
Discreteness/gradualness of change 188
10.7.3 Application within derivations 190
Stage of application within generative derivations 190
Ordering within blocks of rules 190
Applicational dependence between rules 191
10.7.4 Domain of application 193
10.8 Extensions of rule applicability beyond normal use and standard
norms 194
10.8.1 Productivity 195
10.8.2 Nativization of loan words 195
10.8.3 Transfer in foreign-language learning 197
10.8.4 Overgeneralization in child language 200
10.8.5 Linguistic games 201
10.8.6 Psycholinguistic experiments 201
10.8.7 Speech errors 202
10.8.8 Aphasia 203
10.8.9 Misperceptions 203
10.8.10 Spelling mistakes 203
10.8.11 Summary 204
10.9 Degree of consciousness 204
10.10 Relations to universal tendencies 205
10.10.1 Universality 205
10.10.2 Naturalness 206

10.11 Diachronic properties   208
10.12 Summary   210
10.13 Appendix 1: survey of properties of phonological rules   212
10.14 Appendix 2: classification of some specific rules   214

   11 THE CHILD'S ACQUISITION OF PHONOLOGY
11.1 Introduction   215
11.2 Levels of representation in adult phonology   215
11.3 Levels of representation in child phonology   216
      11.3.1 The relationship between adult norms and the forms to
      which the child is actually exposed   217
      11.3.2 The relationship between the adult's spoken forms and the
      child's perceived forms   217
      11.3.3 The relationship between the child's perceived forms and the
      child's phonetic plans   218
      11.3.4 The relationship between the child's phonetic intentions and
      his actually produced forms   219
      11.3.5 Representations and rules in young children's phonological
      competence   219
11.4 The development into adult competence   220
11.5 On children's perceptual accuracy   222

   12 ON THE FALLACY OF REGARDING MORPHEMES AS
       PHONOLOGICAL INVARIANTS
12.1 Morphemes as phonological invariants   223
12.2 The abstractness controversy in generative phonology   226
      12.2.1 Naturalness conditions   227
      12.2.2 The alternation condition   228
      12.2.3 The revised alternation condition   229
      12.2.4 The surface allomorphy condition   229
      12.2.5 'Homing in' from concrete allomorphs   230
      12.2.6 The surface phonotactics condition   232
      12.2.7 Conclusion   233
12.3 Arguments against morphemes as phonological forms   234
      12.3.1 Arguments for the primary significance of word forms and
      phonemic contrasts   234
      12.3.2 Unsupported implications for language ontogenesis   235
      Change of strategy   235
      The representation of marginal changes as basic   238
      12.3.3 Demand for excessive computing   240
      12.3.4 Morphemes as grammatical non-phonological units   241
      12.3.5 Category mistake: relations represented as 'things'   241

12.3.6 Ontological eliminability   244
12.3.7 Introspective inaccessibility   244
12.3.8 Practical inapplicability   247
12.3.9 General lack of plausible and intelligible interpretations   247
12.4 Some abstract interpretations of the notion of 'morpheme-invariant
     form'   249
     12.4.1 Morphemes as values   249
     12.4.2 Morphemes as functional information   250
     12.4.3 Morphemes as 'as-if' representations   251
12.5 Can the generative 'morpheme theory' be justified by reference to
     elegance, simplicity, coherence, etc.?   253
     12.5.1 Pragmatic success   253
     12.5.2 Coherence and explicitness   254
     12.5.3 Simplicity and elegance   254
12.6 Conclusion   255

13 THE CONCRETENESS AND NON-AUTONOMY OF
    PHONOLOGY
13.1 On the insufficiency of structuralist phonology   257
     13.1.1 Relationship between phonology and phonetics   257
     13.1.2 The concept of rule   258
     13.1.3 Autonomous phonology   258
13.2 The concreteness and non-autonomy of phonology   259
13.3 On some classical arguments against structuralist phonology   260
     13.3.1 The superfluousness of a phonemic level in a maximally
     general phonology   260
     13.3.2 The impossibility of a phonemic level in a significant
     phonology   261
     13.3.3 The non-transitivity of free variation   264
     13.3.4 Conclusion   266

EPILOGUE   268
Bibliography (and citation index)   270

Prologue

The fundamental insights of the pioneers of modern phonology have largely been lost. (Chomsky 1964:110)

The present study is the result of work in the theory of phonology pursued by myself from about 1971 through 1977.[1] My intention during the last few years has been to produce a revised version of my doctoral dissertation (Linell 1974a). However, this work has stretched out for more than three years, mainly because other duties have prevented me from indulging in it. The book that now appears is in fact almost entirely a new work, though it is of course based upon my thesis (as well as on later works: Linell 1974b, 1976a,b, 1977a,b).

To place this study in a proper perspective I would like to point out a few things about the scholarly tradition to which it belongs. My first linguistic training was in structuralist linguistics. In the late 1960s I became heavily influenced by generative transformational grammar, one reason being that this kind of process-based structuralism seemed descriptively superior to most variants of earlier item-and-arrangement grammars. But much more important was the fact that Chomskyan grammar promised to be more than merely an elegant systematization of linguistic data; it also aimed at providing a theory of covert psychological realities, i.e. the fluent speaker–listener's actual mental organization of his linguistic knowledge. This goal increased the power and relevance of linguistic theory immensely; linguistics would become much more important – in fact indispensable – for some branches of psychology, anthropology, sociology, language teaching, phonetics, aphasiology etc. However, over the years it became increasingly obvious that orthodox Chomskyan grammar was an almost complete failure in this respect. Though the theory has changed over time, most people in the field have

---

[1] The typescript of this book was completed in June 1977. A few corrections were made in April 1978.

become convinced that all variants of Chomskyan generative grammar
are psychologically invalid, for a number of reasons. Steinberg (1975)
has characterized the history of Chomskyan theory (up to the beginning
of the 1970s) as that of a movement from formalism to claims of
mentalism which actually turned out to be psychologically invalid (for
quite fundamental reasons). Thus, the original impetus for me to
inquire into the causes why Chomskyan theory failed to provide a
psychologically plausible theory was my constantly growing dissatis-
faction with the overly formalistic and 'autonomous-linguistic' approach practised by generativists.[2] This experience has apparently been
shared with many other scholars. Particularly Derwing's (1973) work has
a close affinity with mine. Both Derwing (1973) and Linell (1974a) deal
with generative phonology, and both argue that the inadequacies of this
theory should be sought among its most fundamental assumptions.[3]
Thus, I cannot agree with those numerous generativists who have
argued that many specific analyses made in works such as Chomsky &
Halle (1968) may be misguided or even absurd but that the generative
(meta) theory is basically sound.

The generative goal of striving for psychological validity is a laudable
one. Thus, I would maintain that this goal defines one out of several
other important lines of linguistic research but that the generative
means applied in the attempts to solve the problems involved are
extremely unfruitful and misguided. On the other hand, one must be
very modest in advancing alternative theories in this area. For one thing,
very little can be said about psychological reality with a reasonable
degree of certainty and confidence. One reason is the serious lack of
relevant and reliable data bearing on the problems. Therefore, any
proposals or claims made in this work have to be regarded as
preliminary. Basically, I can only argue that they seem at least
psychologically and/or behaviorally interpretable and may stand a
chance of being true.

Furthermore, very little of what is said in this work derives
primarily from original work by myself. Rather, I rely very heavily on
insights achieved in traditional and common-sense approaches to
phonology as well as in structuralist phonology and variants of
generative phonology. The fundamental ideas are quite traditional and

---

[2] I myself made some generative studies of Swedish phonology and morphology (Linell
1972, 1973a,b).
[3] Cf. also Botha 1971, 1973; Itkonen 1974; Ringen 1975 among other works.

have, in some cases, also been argued by recent 'natural' (generative) phonologists. My contribution mainly consists in trying to provide a reasonable synthesis of some of these ideas.

The title of this book is perhaps too wide, since there are many fundamental problems of phonology that I will not deal with at all. Basically, I will focus on the nature of phonological forms and phonological rules. Thus, nothing will be said on possible inventories of phonological units (segments or prosodemes) (cf. for example, such works as Hockett 1955; Trubetzkoy 1958), or on phonetic features (e.g. Jakobson, Fant & Halle 1952; Ladefoged 1971a) and their hierarchies (e.g. Drachman 1977). Also, in dealing with phonological forms and rules I will concentrate almost entirely on segmental phonology.

Relative to Linell (1974a) this work represents a shift of emphasis from a critique of generative phonology to somewhat more constructive proposals for a more adequate phonological theory. However, I will frequently contrast these latter proposals with those of *orthodox generative phonology* (henceforth OGPh), i.e. the kind of theory and practice represented by works such as Chomsky & Halle (1968), Schane (1968) and others, and a few chapters (12, 13) will deal almost entirely with OGPh argumentation. It should also be pointed out that criticisms of course also apply to other (generative or structuralist) phonological theories in so far as they share features with OGPh. I have, however, made no attempt to determine the extent to which OGPh overlaps with other theories. It is also beyond the scope of this study to trace the often rich history of the various proposals to be discussed. Interested readers may consult the excellent survey by Fischer-Jørgensen (1975).

As I have already pointed out, this work builds on the insights of an unusually great number of scholars. I hope that my references make at least partly clear the extent to which I build on the written works of others. It is more difficult to do justice to those people whose insights I have profited from in many direct discussions. Plainly, it is impossible to mention all these people here. Some, however, deserve special thanks.

Sven Öhman is beyond any doubt the one who has influenced me most during my graduate studies and also afterwards. He has been greatly inspiring and generous in letting me profit from literally countless ideas and insights propounded in teaching as well as private discussions. Some of the most fundamental points of this book originally derive from his suggestions. Obviously, I have not been able to develop all these ideas in the ways Sven would have liked. Neither he nor anyone else should be blamed for the errors I have made.

Secondly, I would like to thank Jens Allwood and Jan Anward for a great many valuable discussions which have considerably promoted my understanding of many linguistic problems. Among many others who have helped and influenced me, Raimo Anttila, W. U. Dressler, Håkan Eriksson, Greg Iverson and Fred Karlsson deserve special mention. Professor John Trim read my manuscript and made many valuable suggestions for revision. I also thank Annika Axelson for typing several manuscripts of mine.

Finally, I gratefully acknowledge the permissions by North-Holland Publishing Company (Amsterdam), Friedr. Vieweg & Sohn Verlagsgesellschaft (Wiesbaden) and Professor D. L. Goyvaerts to use material from Linell (1976a), Linell (1976b) and Linell (1977b), respectively.

1 On psychological reality

Die Sprache führt kein autonomes Dasein und existiert nur im Sprechen und im Geist der Sprecher. (Coseriu 1974: 69)

1.1 Language as a social and psychological entity

This book will deal with psychological aspects of phonology. The choice of this particular perspective is not meant to imply that there are no other legitimate and interesting aspects of phonology, or grammar in general, or that language can be exhaustively characterized in psychological terms. To make these points clear, I will try, very briefly, to define a reasonable position on these issues.

Language is both a social and a psychological phenomenon. The basic function of language is various kinds of communication between members of a social community.[1] Linguistic data are defined by social norms. The units and rules underlying data are socially shared, not private, in nature. On the other hand, the individual members of the community must have access to the rules in order to communicate or to be able to produce new, linguistically correct behavior. A language would cease to exist in at least one important sense if there were no individuals who knew its units and rules.

Anyone who wants to develop a theory of language must recognize the inherently socio-psychological nature of the object of study. However, it is evidently possible to focus on either of the two aspects. In fact, it may be possible to classify (with Ringen 1975) linguists (philosophers of language, etc.) into 'non-mentalists', who regard language primarily as an object with a social or cultural reality,[2] and 'mentalists', who regard it

---

[1] Communication defined in a sufficiently wide sense.

[2] In addition, there are of course non-mentalists who do not make any ontological assumptions at all concerning the nature of the system of units and rules underlying data. Compare the view of linguistic classification as 'hocus-pocus' (cf. Botha 1968: 107–10 for discussion and references).

primarily as an object with a psychological (mental) reality.[3] Normally, the two positions imply at least partially different opinions on the part of the analysts as to what constraints should be imposed on the theory. For example, non-mentalists would clearly prefer to rely on principles of formal simplicity, economy, etc. in the evaluation of different theories, whereas considerations of 'naturalness' (i.e. realism with respect to hypothesized properties of utterance production and recognition, memory storage, etc.) are not appealed to. Linguists with a predominantly 'social' definition of language are quite often those who prefer to pursue 'autonomous' linguistic analsis (using linguistic-structural evidence and arguments to the exclusion of so-called external evidence).[4]

If it is true, as I think it is, that a 'non-mentalist' theory of language implies that the theory is less constrained by empirical (external) evidence, this can be easily explained in terms of the following, admittedly simplified, account. The basic data, which the linguist as well as the language learner has to start out with, are of course all the specific speech acts or, in a slightly different perspective, all the various spoken or written utterances that they are faced with. Within the data, regularities and relations can be observed, units and structural properties of the combinations of units can be observed or hypothesized. Both the language learner and the linguist assume (perhaps implicitly and explicitly, respectively) that there is an underlying norm defining the linguistically relevant properties of grammatical situation-appropriate speech acts. These properties can be systematized in many ways, i.e. there are many different theories which would predict them. The non-mentalist linguist aims at the construction of a non-redundant exhaustive and consistent theory (systematization) of regularities in the social norm of language (which is *one* plausible interpretation of Saussure's *langue*). However, he does not aim at a theory of the particular way(s) in which language learners internalize *their* knowledge about the norm (mainly because he does not know very much about it).

---

[3]   Actually, this latter group should include all who look at language primarily as something possessed and used by individual speakers, rather than as a supra-individual social entity. All these need not be 'mentalists' in a narrower sense, i.e. they do not necessarily couch it in 'psychological' (phenomenological) terms. Some may treat it in terms of, say, neurophysiological states and processes only.

[4]   See Botha (1973: §3.3.1 and passim) for some discussion of internal vs. external evidence. For a tabulation of different kinds of evidence used in generative phonology, see Zwicky (1975a).

A mentalist linguist, on the other hand, is interested also in actual speakers' organization of their linguistic knowledge, and in speakers' ability – with its possibilities and limitations – to create and recreate linguistic utterances, i.e. to produce, perceive and comprehend an unbounded number of speech acts. This clearly means that the theory of language must be subject to further, 'external', conditions, i.e. it must be compatible with theories and facts concerning linguistic performance, language acquisition, linguistic variation and change, etc. as well as about properties of the human biological constitution.

To conclude, I would maintain that an exclusively non-mentalist approach to language yields a lopsided view of language. Though it is a fundamental fact that linguistic rules are social, it is equally important that speakers develop an ability to use language productively, based upon knowledge which is inferred from the publicly observable manifestations of the norm. Speakers' knowledge is established and modified in creative use. Too much emphasis on the system (norm) as such may lead to a picture of language as a closed, static system (*où tout se tient*) rather than as an open, dynamic system. Language is not so much *ergon* as it is 'Form und Potenz einer *energeia*' (Coseriu 1974: 24).[5]

1.2 Attitudes to the goal of psychological reality

Thus we see that the interest in psychological realities on the part of various individual linguists varies considerably. Often, different generations or schools of linguists differ in their attitudes. Broadly speaking, among those who tend to be anti-mentalistic (and often mechanistic, formalistic, or inclined to endorse an abstract view on language) are neogrammarians, Saussure, Hjelmslev, Bloomfield, American structuralists, Chomsky and orthodox generativists (despite claims to the contrary), whereas Humboldt, Paul, Bréal, Sapir, Ščerba, Coseriu and some 'natural generativists' tend to be more concerned with language use, psychological realism and hermeneutics ('*Verstehen*'). Perhaps, one could even discern four different attitudes to claims about psychological reality:

(1) *Radical physicalism :* One claims that there is nothing which can be meaningfully characterized as psychological which cannot be more adequately described as physical or physiological. Therefore,

---

[5] For a very perceptive treatment of these problems, see Coseriu (1974).

talking about psychological reality is nonsense. Moreover, language should be described solely in terms of overt (or non-overt) physical or physiological *events*.

This view is simply incoherent, if interpreted to mean that there is no such thing as an acquired knowledge (ability) to produce grammatical behavior, this knowledge as such being a persistent and structured cognitive state rather than behavioral events (cf. Chomsky 1975a: ch. 1). A view of type (1) may be ascribed to radical behaviorists, although upon closer scrutiny they too introduce 'intervening variables or cognitive (i.e. neurological) states'.[6]

(2)   *Pessimism*: Speakers are assumed to possess knowledge of their language, i.e. a grammar with a more or less specific organization which enables them to use their language correctly, but it is considered to be an unattainable goal to find out what properties these psychological structures have. Therefore, linguists should avoid these problems and do 'autonomous linguistics', i.e. establish linguistic generalizations by purely structural methods. (Language is seen as a system of social norms.)

This is the typical attitude of most structuralists like Hjelmslev, Malmberg, Martinet, Hockett, etc. Some structuralists actually denied that linguistic concepts, like the phoneme, have any psychological counterparts at all (e.g. Twaddell 1935), while most would probably hold that linguistic concepts may have some psychological validity though we cannot hope to find it out with the methods available for linguists. (Maybe psychologists cannot make it out either.)

The goal of psychological reality, i.e. that of accounting for the fully competent speaker's way of organizing his knowledge of his language, implies a strictly synchronic perspective, since speakers have no access to facts about the history of their languages (unless, of course, history has left clear reflexes in the synchronically present language structure). A radicalization of (2), i.e. the pessimistic attitude towards the possibility of investigating psychological realities, would therefore be to deny the possibility of writing *any* kind of strictly synchronic grammar and to claim that historical–diachronic classifications and explanations are the only truly 'scientific' alternative.[7]

[6]   Cf. my discussion (Linell 1979a) of the similarities between Skinner (1957) and Chomsky.
[7]   Compare, e.g., the formerly common denial that typological classifications may meet scientific standards of objectivity (cf. Greenberg 1973: 169–70). Martinet (1962: 39)

(3) *Moderate realism:* Speakers are assumed to have organized knowledge of their language in some specific ways. To attain explanatory adequacy, linguistic theory must strive for realism. Biological, psychological and social realities must be taken into account (cf. §1.3). However, an investigation of psychological realities cannot be pursued with purely linguistic-structural methods. Instead, many types of 'external' evidence must be exploited (whereby the relevance and reliability of this evidence must be critically examined).[8] Also, one needs plausible 'metaphysical' assumptions about the nature of language, language acquisition and use, the properties of the mind, etc. The latter should be an obvious point,[9] though the limited interest in the philosophical foundations of linguistic metatheory shows that it is not often considered to be so.

I take the view of (3) to be roughly that of, e.g., Derwing (1973)[10] and many other linguists, including myself, some of which have been or are still, in some respects, 'generativists'.

(4) *Naive optimism:* Speakers are assumed to have highly integrated and interindividually similar 'mental grammars'. Since many irrelevant factors intervene in performance the best way to determine mental grammars would then be to apply formal-linguistic methods in trying to investigate general and abstract conditions on linguistic structures.

This, of course, is Chomsky's position and hence the 'official' view of many generativists. In many respects, this kind of linguistics is an extreme form of structuralism or of 'autonomous linguistics' (i.e. a linguistics which refuses to utilize external evidence).[11] Yet, the claims

---

characterized Sapir's (1921) well-known typology as a 'nearly tragic illustration of the pitfalls of psychologism'.

[8] For this latter point, see especially Botha (1971, 1973).

[9] This is particularly stressed in Linell (1974a). See also Lass (1976: 213–20). Cf. §1.6, §12.6.

[10] Cf. also Derwing & Baker (1976).

[11] Thus, for scholars inclined to accept (3), Chomsky's 'mentalism' must appear 'formalistic' and 'dangerously unempirical' (Derwing 1973). (In fact, there is also plenty of evidence that it is psychologically invalid, see below). Incidentally, the emphasis on formal linguistic methods shows Chomsky's dependence on American structuralism. It is interesting to study his formulations in early works prior to his becoming a 'mentalist' (see Steinberg 1975 for ample excerpts). Consider Chomsky: 'The danger in the "God's truth" approach is that it sometimes verges on mysticism, and tends to blur the fact that the rational way out of this difficulty lies in the program

for psychological reality by generativists are surely meant to be taken seriously (and they should, at least for the sake of argument, be taken seriously). In fact, the claims about the as yet unknown nature of psychological reality are very strong indeed: the child is assumed to internalize a generative transformational grammar.[12] Frequently, referring to the lack of empirically supported hypotheses about psychological mechanisms,[13] scholars seem to feel free to assume that speakers have knowledge of very intricate and abstract relationships.[14] There is an obvious danger that this makes the notion of 'psychological reality' (as handled by generativists) completely vacuous and unempirical.[15]

Those pessimists (2) who oppose the 'psychologizing' of linguistic theory have some good reasons. It must be admitted that little can be known for certain in the area of the psychological reality of language and that many suggestions are simply subjective, armchair speculation. An obvious reason for being disenchanted is of course the highly cavalier

of, on the one hand, formulating behavioral criteria to replace intuitive judgments, and on the other, of constructing a rigorous account of linguistic structure and determining its implications for particular grammars' (1975b(1955): 103). What Chomsky has done since 1960 may well be characterized as a pursuit of the second-mentioned methodological line while assuming that the theory so arrived at is precisely God's truth!

[12] There is at least one point at which Chomsky in fact confesses that generative transformational grammar (or at least generative phonology) cannot be psychologically true. Consider Chomsky & Halle: 'We can therefore state our conclusion about psychological reality only in hypothetical form: *if it were the case that language acquisition were instantaneous, then the underlying forms with pre-Vowel shift representations would be psychologically real*' (1968: 332) (their italics). Usually, Chomsky and other generativists do not refer to this proviso when discussing problems of psychological reality. Moreover, 'the instantaneous model ... can very well be accepted as a reasonable first approximation' (Chomsky 1967b: 441, fn. 41). For discussion of another theory of language acquisition that may be compatible with OGPh, see §12.3.2.

[13] For this lack of knowledge psychologists, not linguists, should be blamed, according to some generativists' doctrine (cf. Derwing 1973: 278–81).

[14] Cf. for example, Lightner: 'In the absence of a major breakthrough in some field like psychology or neurophysiology, it is not clear what limits to impose on the abstractness of grammar.' Meanwhile, 'we will surely be interested in abstract grammars because these grammars will be the most interesting from a theoretical point-of-view' (1971: 524).

[15] Consider, e.g., Fromkin: 'Rather than testing each grammar to see if it is psychologically real, it seems to me that we are looking for evidence concerning the general form of grammars ... A rule of phonology is, according to this view, psychologically real if it is permitted by the general theory which places constraints on the kinds of rules and the form of rules which can occur in any language' (1975: 46–7).

manner in which many orthodox generativists have advanced mentalistic claims to the effect that the rule formulations that they, as linguists, have arrived at, most often by purely structural methods, are also the rules of *speakers'* internalized grammars (cf. (4)-type optimism). Admittedly, this is largely true also of proposals made by more 'moderate realists' (3). For example, Roberts (1976: 219, fn. 2) has pointed out that many of the arguments against abstract phonological representations are simply based on the fact that the linguists who proposed such forms have gone beyond the limits of their critical colleagues' tolerance. While I would not pretend that this critique is completely misguided, it cannot be said to be the whole truth. Arguments are also often, and should always be, backed up by a considerable amount of evidence which cannot simply be ignored. As far as the general theory is concerned, one can at least strive for a theory that is psychologically and behaviorally interpretable and that is plausible given some well-founded assumptions about the functioning of the mind. This is, in all modesty, the goal towards which the present work is directed.

While it must be conceded that one *can* argue for the standpoint of 'pessimism' (2), it must also be pointed out that most, if not all, linguists seem to impose *some* constraints on their linguistic descriptions which, I would claim, have to do with their intuitive feeling of what is psychologically acceptable or not. Malmberg who shares the aversion of structuralists towards 'psychologizing'[16] in the discussion of linguistic structure objects to the proposal to represent prevocalic [ʃ] sounds in some Swedish dialects as /rs/ or /sr/ which are possible analyses since neither *[rs] nor *[sr] occur prevocalically on the surface. Moreover, the /sr/ solution could be subsumed under the 'mirror effect'; prevocalic clusters tend to be reversed with respect to postvocalic clusters.[17] Malmberg's (1969) motivation is that 'this interpretation is inadmissible and is opposed to an elementary principle of phonemicization; one should not impose upon language a structure type, the only instance of which is the type which is created by the interpretation'.[18] However, why does he accept this constraint, when it excludes the formulation of a possible generalization ('the mirror effect')? Obviously because it seems

---

[16] For example, Malmberg (1969: Öhman 3, fn. 1).

[17] There are reasons to represent postvocalic [ʂ, ʃ] as /rs/ in the dialects concerned. The solutions discussed have been suggested by Elert (1957), and Witting (1959).

[18] My translation of Malmberg's Swedish manuscript (1969: Elert 2).

intuitively wrong; there is no reason to assume that speakers internalize a non-functional rule reversing /sr/ clusters to /rs/ clusters (and a rule /rs/ → [ʃ/__V) (or in general: abstract analyses which have no reasonable behavioral motivation whatsoever).

1.3 Reasons to adopt the goal of psychological reality

To provide a theory of the speaker's organization of linguistic knowledge is of course a goal in itself. From a methodological point-of-view, one may wish a theory to make strong claims and thus to be easily susceptible to falsification. If so, a 'mentalistic' theory is preferable to a 'non-mentalistic' one (cf. Botha 1968: 103), since there are many more data which could falsify the former one (cf. §1.1). More important, however, is the fact (also indicated in §1.1) that one cannot arrive at a plausible overall understanding of the nature of language, its structure and functions, without considering the psychological aspects. For example, conditions on the production and perception of strings may explain why certain syntactic structures are excluded, while others are preferred (cf. for example, Anward 1979). Linguistic changes may be explained by the possibilities that different groups of speakers (who have, perhaps, been exposed to qualitatively and quantitatively different sets of data) make different perceptual analyses of the same linguistic data.[19] The kind of linguistic theory needed in the description and explanation of language acquisition, foreign language learning, speech performance (including, e.g., speech errors and aphasia) must of course be psychologically adequate. Moreover, if we want linguistics to be of value for cognitive psychology (as proposed by Chomsky 1968) and if we want linguistic knowledge and behavior to be used as a 'window to the mind' (Lashley 1951), then one can hardly use a linguistic theory which is not psychologically and behaviorally interpretable and plausible.

1.4 The concept of psychological reality

Problems connected with psychological reality concern not only the lack of reliable empirical data. The concept of 'psychological reality' as such is fraught with a number of problems of interpretation. I will briefly mention some of these problems.

---

[19] Cf. for example, the theory of abduction of Andersen (1973).

1.4.1 *Degree of representationalism*

A 'psychologically real' grammar is supposed to be a theory of covert psychological abilities underlying speakers' linguistic practice. It concerns the speakers' knowledge of the socially endorsed rules that define correct linguistic behavior. Clearly, a psychologically adequate grammar must meet the following conditions:

(a) To the extent that the conventions of the language are determinate, it must generate all and only the grammatical utterances of the language[20] and assign to these their correct pronunciations, meanings and grammatical properties.

(b) In doing so it must reflect the competent speaker's way of organizing his knowledge of his language. That is, the *internal structure* of the grammar must *be isomorphic to* the speaker's *underlying psychological structure* with regard to individuation (what different forms, in particular what different lexical units, there are), properties of the forms, relations between and generalizations over the forms, derivative capacity (what forms can be derived and what the properties and interrelations of these are).

This means, for example, that the phonology of a lexical unit must be represented in the grammar in such a way that the properties of the psychologically real form are systematically reflected. If, e.g., the word *pipe* is grammatically represented as /pīp/ (cf. Chomsky & Halle 1968),[21] i.e. as a feature matrix with three columns and certain feature specifications for each column (defining the segments of /p/ and /ī/), the internal isomorphy condition (b) amounts to a claim that there is a psychologically real structuring (at some level) such that it contains precisely three segments, the first and last of which are identical in type, the second of which *is* actually [+vocalic, −consonantal, +high, −back, +tense, etc.] while the first and third ones *are* actually [−vocalic, −sonorant, −voiced, +anterior, −coronal, −continuant, etc.].

I will give one example more. An English speaker may note that there are numerous cases of regular morphophonological vowel alternations in English, such as [aî]–[ɪ] (*divine – divinity*), [ı̂j]–[e] (*serene – serenity*), [êı]–[æ](*sane–sanity*). Orthodox generative phonology expresses this by

---

[20] The utterances which the speaker considers to be correct in the language.

[21] Here, and in subsequent discussions of Chomsky & Halle (1968), I disregard the fact that they consider English long tense vowels (e.g. in *pipe*, *meat*) to be underlying tense (e.g. ī, ē/ etc.) rather than long (i.e. /i:, e:/ etc.).

setting up morpheme-invariant underlying forms and deriving the surface vowels by rules. However, this theory is not just an arbitrary way of expressing a regular morphophonological relation (one kind of description out of several possible alternatives); much more is claimed. When, for example, *sane* [sêɪn] is represented as /sǣn/ (Chomsky & Halle 1968: 178ff) and the surface vowel is derived by rules (vowel shift, diphthongization), the internal isomorphy condition (b) above means that *sane has actually* in a real mental world (the memory?) a low, non-diphthongized vowel (not a non-high, non-low diphthongized vowel), and that the rules have *some* kind of counterpart in the mental processes needed in the production or perception of the sound shape corresponding to *sane*.

Two grammars may of course be equivalent with respect to condition (a),[22] while only one of them tries to meet (or succeeds in meeting) condition (b).[23] Only the latter is a true *representational model* of the covert mental reality.[24]

---

[22] Such grammars are 'weakly equivalent' (Bach 1964: 159) or 'extensionally equivalent' (Quine 1970, cf. Chomsky 1975a: 179ff).

[23] Actually, several grammars may be psychologically valid, cf. §1.5.6, p. 25, fn. 58.

[24] To simplify the matter considerably, we may distinguish two different opinions as to the nature of a theory and its entities and processes and their relations to the world. (Actually, we are here classifying several opinions into two groups.) According to one conception, usually referred to as *realism* (e.g. Botha 1968; Harré 1972) or *representationalism* (cf. Bunge 1964), the theoretical entities and processes refer to real (though most often non-observable or inaccessible) entities and processes which are assumed to stand in a causal relation to the observable phenomena. Thus, the theory would depict or represent an inaccessible reality (cf. Bunge 1964: 234). The other way of looking at theories, called *fictionalism* (Harré 1972), *instrumentalism* (Botha 1968), *constructivism* (Wartofsky 1968) or even *black-boxism* (Bunge 1964), claims that the theory with all its components is merely a useful fiction which expresses generalizations over or relationships between the observable phenomena. Then, the theory is just 'a more effective tool for summarizing and predicting observations' (Bunge 1964: 234). The theoretical entities are only 'imaginary constructs which we invent to aid our understanding' or are used 'to name characteristic configurations of observed properties economically' (Wartofsky 1968: 283). Naturally, we must admit several types of theories, from the completely fictionalistic ones to those which are almost totally representational. That is, 'a realist does not maintain that *every* hypothetical entity exists' (Harré 1972: 90) (my italics).

The discussion of representationalism vs. fictionalism of theories as summarized here is usually confined to theories of natural sciences. By 'theory' we would then understand a system of theoretical, i.e. non-observable, entities and processes (*explanans*), which underlie (generate) the observable phenomena to be explained (*explananda*) (cf. Hempel 1966: 77). However, one may make use of the distinction in discussing '*Verstehen*' theories of the human sciences too, in which theoretical concepts explicate relations and properties of, say, a cognitive (cultural, linguistic, etc.) system of

However, there are quite different opinions as to what degree or in what sense a grammar can be or should be a representational model of psychological realities. These different views are clearly discernible within generative linguistics. To begin with, Watt (1970), Ringen (1975) and others have distinguished between a *strong* position (Watt's 'correlation hypothesis', Ringen's 'strong mentalism') (Katz 1964; Whitaker 1969 and others) according to which every aspect or detail of the theory is assumed to be isomorphic to some psychological (or neurological) counterpart, and a vaguer *weak* position (Watt's 'derivational theory of complexity',[25] Ringen's 'weak mentalism') according to which the relationship between the theoretical grammar model and the speaker's internalized knowledge is more indirect. Some levels of representation are assumed to be psychologically valid (e.g. phonetic, morphophonological (i.e. underlying morpheme-invariant), surface syntactic, deep syntactic), and some significant relation between length of grammatical derivation and performance parameters such as perceptual complexity and ease of production[26] is assumed to exist. This position, which is presumably the most popular one, only forces the linguist to claim that *some* aspects of his theory mirror psychological structures.[27]

Many generativists have gradually retreated to even weaker claims than those of the 'derivational theory of complexity' (DTC). Thus, e.g., Fodor, Bever & Garrett (1974)[28] argue that most of the psychological experiments carried out in order to test the psychological validity of generative transformational grammars have, if they have been successful at all, demostrated the validity of the linguistic taxonomy of sentences provided by the grammar rather than the reality of the means employed to generate this taxonomy, i.e. the grammatical operations

primary 'atheoretical' knowledge (*explicanda*) (cf. Itkonen 1974). A representationalist would then require the theory to be in accordance with people's conscious experiences as well as behavioral application of their knowledge.

[25] Cf. also Fodor, Bever & Garrett (1974:32off and passim).

[26] Cf. Fodor & Garrett 1966: 141; Kiparsky 1968a: 171; Watt 1970. For a recent statement, see Fodor (1976: 152) who argues, in effect, that the 'internal language' of semantic representations, in which 'messages' are couched, must not be too abstract with respect to syntactic surface structure, since otherwise sentence understanding would involve too much computing.

[27] However, Steinberg (1975) argues that Chomsky's (inconsistently stated) assumptions of psychological validity for *only some* aspects entails that the whole theory is psychologically invalid.

[28] Cf. (1974: 234, 241, 263, 273 and passim).

involved in derivations (cf. DTC).[29] Obviously, the weakest claim
possible is to say that only the *output* of the grammar relates to
psychological reality, i.e. the strings generated are those which are
judged as 'correct' by the speakers. Such a theory meets only condition
(a) above (a 'formalistic', as opposed to 'mentalistic', theory in
Steinberg's (1975: 219) terminology).

Some may argue that the present account does not do justice to
Chomsky's subtle arguments on the nature of grammatical competence
and the kind of psychological reality involved. While I can concede to
this partly, I also think that Chomsky's various explications have often
been vague and/or partly inconsistent (see Derwing 1973; Steinberg
1975). Of course, if generativists prefer to make only very weak or empty
claims about psychological validity (as Chomsky has sometimes done),
then there is no point in discussing them. On the other hand, to the
extent that OGPh will be discussed in this work I will assume that at
least an interpretation of the type DTC is intended by them. It is
beyond any doubt that such claims have been frequently made, so I will
not be beating a dead horse. For example, the ardent discussions of what
conditions constrain possible underlying forms (§12.2) and of what are
the correct morpheme-invariants in the various specific cases would be
inexplicable and meaningless, unless these underlying morpheme-
invariants are assumed to be real forms (and there is hardly any question
that the nature of their reality is assumed to be psychological).

1.4.2 *Accessibility*

Obviously, there are mental phenomena which cannot be investigated
by introspection and which are normally not or never conscious to the
individual. Linguistic structures and rules are normally not conscious to
the speaker–listener, and the question arises whether it is reasonable to
assume that they can be made conscious. Chomsky has argued that the
psychological realities of language need not be introspectively accessible
or even intuitively plausible. 'Any interesting generative grammar will
be dealing, for the most part, with mental processes that are far beyond
the level of actual or *even potential* consciousness; it is quite apparent
that a speaker's reports and viewpoints about his behavior and his
competence may be in error' (Chomsky 1965: 8) (my italics). 'The
greatest defect of classical philosophy of mind . . . seems to me to be its
unquestioned assumption that the properties and content of the mind

[29] Cf. also Fodor (1976: 110).

are accessible to introspection' (Chomsky 1968: 22). Similar statements can be found in the works of Chomsky's associates.[30] Chomsky has several times expressed doubts about the relevance and reliability of introspective evidence.[31] There are also indications that some generativists would claim that the real nature of the internalized grammar is inaccessible to introspective reflection *in principle*, and that reflection leads to an artificial and fallacious conception of grammar.[32]

On the other hand, one may argue that Chomskyans have taken this stand vis-à-vis introspection simply because intuitive and introspective judgments hardly endorse their kind of grammatical model.[33] In fact, the arguments that linguistic competence would be systematically inaccessible seem quite dubious to me. The use of language is typically carried out consciously by speakers who have specific communicative intentions in mind and who are often capable of explaining these intentions, e.g. in cases of misunderstanding. Though conscious attention is normally not paid to the phonological and grammatical aspects of behavior, speakers and listeners may become conscious of at least some of these aspects in cases of difficulties or failures of pronunciation and comprehension. If a word is mispronounced by a speaker, he will often make conscious efforts to execute his articulatory plans properly.[34] Listeners may also detect and react to other speakers' violations of very subtle phonological rules. Indeed, the conventionality of linguistic rules implies some measure of consciousness (see §1.5.5).

It is true that such awareness does not pertain directly to grammatical categories and rules and that speakers are typically unable to explicate the abstract features of their language. However, speakers do have some intuitions about properties of acts (such as pragmatic or semantic equivalence, syntactic well-formedness, situation-appropriateness) and grammar concerns such properties of or conditions on meaningful, conscious acts. Therefore, grammar too has to be analyzed much in the

[30] For example, Katz 1966: 179–81; Fodor 1976: 52–3.
[31] Cf. Chomsky 1957: 93–4, 1964: 56–9, 1965: 19, 1969: 82.
[32] This artificial and misleading 'knowledge' about language would in general be more 'superficial' than is real grammar. As for phonology, this may imply that the analyst (erroneously) comes up with a 'taxonomic' or 'autonomous' phonemics rather than the correct 'systematic' phonology (generative phonology). There are some indications in the literature which may be used as justifications for this speculation of mine (cf. S. Anderson 1973: 11, and pp. 246–7).
[33] Thus, this is just another aspect of the non-empiricalness of Chomskyan 'competence', cf. Botha 1971, 1973; Derwing 1973; Linell 1974a; Steinberg 1975.
[34] Cf. Allwood (1976: 16).

same language as the acts and their molar properties. Thus, I would argue that language must be explicated in a 'phenomenological' (rather than 'psychoanalytic') metalanguage (cf. Allwood 1976: 12), i.e. the analysis can be performed at a 'molar' level[35] without necessarily making any specific assumptions about neurophysiological or other unconscious causal mechanisms.

I hasten to add a few remarks. I am of course not claiming that the neurophysiological basis (reality) of linguistic abilities should be analyzed phenomenologically or that it would be non-existent. However, next to nothing is known about 'neurolinguistic' structures, and detailed proposals about psycholinguistic realities cannot be made on this level today. This, of course, is not to deny that whatever facts can be established in this field must be taken into account also by a psychological (phenomenologically-based) theory.[36]

Secondly, I would not deny that there are interesting data about the organization of language to be uncovered by a psychoanalytic approach. For example, associational structures of the lexicon may be a case in point. However, I do not see any reason to include phonological representations and rules in the domain of application of psychoanalytic methods.

Finally, I am not arguing for an entirely introspective or intuitive approach to grammar. On the contrary, I believe that using only introspection and common-sense arguments would provide an extremely shaky basis for a theory of linguistic competence, especially if we consider unreflected and immediate judgments and reactions by laymen (which may be highly dependent on various irrelevant factors). However, in many cases, intuitive judgments and common-sense-based views can be argued, corrected, and refined by means of critical discussion among experienced language users.[37] In fact, such activities are not qualitatively different from the *Verstehen* approach used by specialists,[38] and this is something indispensable in the social sciences. However, there are obviously many areas left where this approach is not

[35] This point has been made by several authors. Cf. for example, Fodor, Bever & Garrett (1974: xiii). For some general considerations, cf. Taylor (1970: 63ff).

[36] See Linell (1978a).

[37] Cf. for example, Harré & Secord (1972: especially ch. 6).

[38] It would be wrong to consider such assessments of linguistic structures as similar to reports of sensations in simple psychophysical experiments (as suggested by Ringen 1976).

enough and where all sorts of behavioral and other evidence is badly needed. Thus, I plead for a methodological pluralism (§1.6).

1.4.3 *Teleology and causality : acts, rules, derivations and causal processes*

A speaker's grammatical knowledge is concerned with phonological, morphological, syntactic, semantic, pragmatic conditions that must be met in correct linguistic behavior. These conditions are not causally related to the speech events. Rather they enter a teleological explication of speech acts. Linguistic behavior can be explicated in terms of 'practical syllogisms' (von Wright 1971; Itkonen 1974). Thus, one may explicate a person A's act of uttering 'p' as follows (cf. Itkonen 1974: 300):

> Given that A and B (the listener) know the rules for the use of language L (and that they comply with general conditions on communication, e.g. Grice's (1975) maxims):
> A intends that B knows that p
> A intends that B recognizes that A intends that B knows that p
> A considers that he will not achieve his intentions unless he utters 'p'
> _____
> Therefore A sets himself to utter 'p'

Within a teleological theory of linguistic communication the concepts of *action* and *act* are of fundamental importance. Actions may be defined simply as behaviour governed by intentions, and acts are a subclass, i.e. units of behaviour which are, often consciously, directed towards a certain well-defined goal (end state).[39] When communicating, both speakers and listeners perform actions and acts (Allwood 1976).

A speaker's act of communicating a message involves many instrumental (sub)acts and subroutines (§2.2). I will use the term *operation* for some types of such subacts. In particular I will talk about *morphological operations*, i.e. acts in which the speaker constructs specific word forms (this is one area where phonology is relevant, see ch. 7). Acts and operations are supposed to be real units of behavior, something that speakers, and listeners, actually do, or can do. However, these behavioral units must be explicated in phenomenological or linguistic terms, since we cannot today provide a causal theory of how they are actually implemented in the central nervous system.

---

[39] For discussion of concepts like 'action' and 'act', see e.g. von Wright (1971); Nordenfelt (1977) and references in fn. 41 overleaf.

What is the status of grammatical and phonological *rules*? Among the speaker's intentions are also his intentions to follow such rules, we may argue. Are rules, then, also subacts or processes in behavior? In my opinion the answer must clearly be negative. At least this is true if we use the term '(phonological) rule' to refer to phonological regularities in the usual way. (My use of the term 'rule' will be extensionally identical to this traditional use, although some intensional (connotative) aspects of my interpretation may be different from some current (e.g. generative) interpretations.)

I propose that 'rules' be understood as properties of or as conditions on linguistic strings or the underlying constructing operations. Thus, some rules may be regarded as conditions on, e.g., morphological operations (e.g. morphophonological rules proper (MRPs), which refer to changes that have to be performed as aspects of morphological formation patterns, see chs. 7, 10), whereas other rules are best understood as conditions on phonetic strings (e.g. phonotactic rules, see chs. 7, 10).[40]

Thus, rules must not be conceived of as acts or behavioral events. It follows that they must not be treated as causal processes. In fact, it would be conceptually rather naive to equate rules and causally efficient processes.[41] Yet, this is sometimes done, at least implicitly, by some generativists, particularly those advocating a 'strong mentalism' (e.g. Katz 1964), which amounts to paramechanism.[42] Some phonologists have suggested that phonological structures, derivations and rules, or rule applications, be regarded as causal processes, e.g. as neurophysiological commands to the articulators (cf. Drachman 1972; Schnitzer 1972; Kehoe & Whitaker 1973). However, generative rules simply relate phonological representations of various kinds, some of which may, at best, refer to psychological structurings, and they are ipso facto not necessarily anything but corresponding formulas. While it is true that there must be causally efficient processes in speech production and perception, and that many aspects of speech are habitual and automatized (i.e. not always consciously intended or monitored), it

---

[40] It is much easier to see how rules can be socially shared and socially acquired if we conceive of them as (language-specific) conditions on vocal behaviour rather than as, say, unconscious mental processes.

[41] Similarly, it would be a category mistake to confuse, e.g., reasons and causes; these types of concepts provide explanations of different kinds. Cf. for example, Taylor 1970; Harré & Secord 1972; Allwood 1976: 14ff.

[42] Cf. Linell (1974a: 14ff, 1979a).

would be too simplistic to take some isomorphy between causal process and rule for granted.[43] Moreover, our knowledge of the 'neurology of language' is extremely coarse, far from sufficient for determining the possible brain correlates of specific details of grammars (cf. also §1.5.5–6).

1.5 Knowledge and behavior

1.5.1 *Introduction*

In developing theories of complex behavior philosophers and psychologists have generally made some kind of fundamental distinction between dispositions to behave, and behavior itself, or between abilities and manifestations, or between knowledge and the use of knowledge, competence and performance, theory and practice. These concepts are certainly not construed in the same way by all scholars. Even if we consider only, e.g., the use of the concepts of 'competence' and 'performance' *within* Chomskyan generative linguistics and its variants, we will find quite important differences. A penetrating analysis of these and the other concepts mentioned is far beyond the scope of this study. However, since some kind of distinction is evidently needed, I will briefly consider a few points related to them in this section.

1.5.2 *Competence vs. performance : justification for a distinction*

It is sometimes remarked (e.g. Fodor, Bever & Garrett 1974: 1ff) that, e.g., theories of perception, action and memory must involve (mutually dependent) theories of two different sorts, i.e. theories about the concepts and conceptual systems involved in perception, etc., and theories about how these concepts are employed in actual behavior (perceptual integration, behavioral organization, memory recall). For example, perception involves recognizing that some specific stimulus falls under a certain concept, and performing an action involves integrating one's behavior in such a way that the rules constituting the action type are fulfilled.

Similarly a theory of linguistic (verbal) communication would involve two mutually dependent theories, i.e. a theory of language structure with its units (e.g. lexical items with their semantic, syntactic, phonological and other properties and interrelations) and rules, and a

---

[43] For further comments on the notion of 'rule', and on the distinction 'phonological rule' vs. phonetic (articulatory, physiological) process, see §1.5.5 and §10.6.2.

theory of how language users put their knowledge of language structure into use. Thus, we get some kind of a competence/performance distinction. The question is how this distinction should be conceived of.

Language is an abstract system of units and rules, since it obviously does not consist of the various concrete utterances made by specific speakers in specific situations. Rather, language is abstracted (abduced)[44] from such data (given the inherent properties of the mind). This abstraction can conceivably be made in different ways; there are different descriptions compatible with linguistic primary data, as every linguist knows all too well. In view of the fact that language is more or less socially shared, one may be tempted to treat it as an abstraction, a supra-individual 'third world'[45] phenomenon, possibly characterized by properties of simplicity, economy, etc. (cf. §1.1). (This conception of 'competence' comes in fact very close to Chomsky's.) However, we are not interested in just *any* kind of linguistic description that is compatible with data. We are concerned about that specific way (or those ways) of organizing linguistic knowledge that speakers actually use. This puts additional conditions on our theory of 'competence' (§1.1) which, as we will argue, forces us to adopt a model of language which will be quite concrete, redundant and not fully integrated (at least relative to the abstract, non-redundant and closed systems postulated by many structuralists and generativists).

1.5.3 *Competence : ability, habituality and normativity*

One of the metaphysical (i.e. general) axioms to be adopted in this work is that there is a very close relationship between a speaker's linguistic competence and his actual communicative performance. Theories of language structure, linguistic competence and linguistic performance must, accordingly, be very closely related. Competence is largely practical know-how; one knows how to use language for various communicative (and, possibly, other) purposes.

One way to characterize the relation between a speaker's competence and his actual performance would be to say that they are related as potentiality vs. actuality, as what he *can do* vs. what he *actually does*. However, in that case potentiality must not refer to what is physically (or, for that matter, mentally) possible for the speaker to do, because he

---

[44] In the sense of Ch. S. Peirce (cf. Anttila 1972a: 196ff).

[45] On abstractions as ontologically real entities of a 'third world', see e.g. Popper (1972).

can produce all sorts of intended or unintended performance errors (violations of rules). That is, normativity also enters the concept of competence; linguistic knowledge is knowledge of norms (conventions, rules) for what *should be done*. Thus, competence would be concerned with what the speaker–listener implicitly 'knows', or assumes, to be correct in his language. In actual performance there are lots of deficiencies, and the speaker–listener often recognizes that these deficiencies are errors or due to linguistically irrelevant factors. Thus, disregarding such linguistically uninteresting things as hiccoughs, sneezes, effects of intoxication, false teeth and food in the speech apparatus, etc., we will find many speech errors (slips of the tongue), syntactic inconsistencies and errors due to incomplete knowledge of the language. Naturally, we are normally interested primarily in finding out the knowledge and abilities of a maximally competent speaker, i.e. something which constitutes a norm that is seldom reflected in all respects in actual performance.[46]

However, things are more entangled than this. There will always be a complex interaction of ability, habituality and normativity in the concept of competence, especially when we are considering the competences of speakers who are *not* maximally competent. If a certain speaker always produces utterances exhibiting a certain regular pattern, which is wrong according to the social norm (something which even the speaker himself may know although he cannot help violating the putative norm all the time), should we not say that this regularity belongs to the speaker's active competence? Clearly there are such cases. Moreover, speakers' assumptions of what they should do (the norm) may be mistaken. Norms sometimes change when the actual habits change. On the other hand, there are cases in which speakers actually know more, in *some* respects, than they can carry out in performance. (This is perhaps most typical of children learning their language, cf. ch. 11.) But speakers may also sometimes perform correctly without knowing how to do it (!); they may occasionally produce grammatical utterances, e.g. by means of imitation, without actually being able to construct, or understand, them.

[46] However, we will still be concerned with knowledge that could reasonably be ascribed to actual human speakers. Thus, we will not entertain a version of Chomskyan competence which is idealized beyond all reasonable limits. See for discussion Cazden 1967; Campbell & Wales 1970; Hymes 1971, 1972; Mehan 1972; Öhman 1972, 1976; Rommetveit 1972; Derwing 1973: ch. 8; Linell 1974a: 19–25; Steinberg 1975, and others.

By way of conclusion, when we speak of performance, we are concerned with what speakers, and listeners, actually do, but when we speak of competence, we seem to be concerned with several aspects at once, what speakers and listeners are able to do, what they habitually do and, above all, what they should do. How, and to what extent, these factors should enter a description depends on, among other things, the scope (a whole linguistic community sharing a standard language, a particular group of speakers, a specific individual) and the purpose (e.g. describing actual habits or defining an abstract norm) of the study in question.

1.5.4 *Grammatical competence and communicative competence*

We are interested in determining what kind of grammatical knowledge a speaker–listener must be assumed to possess in order to perform the 'basic linguistic capacities' (Bever 1970), i.e. to produce, perceive and comprehend an unbounded number of utterances formulated in the language,[47] and also to exercise metalinguistic abilities such as to judge utterances, words, sound strings, etc. with respect to, e.g., grammaticality, synonymy, similarity in meaning and form, etc. As regards phonology, I will return in §2.3 to the question what this means more exactly.

It seems reasonable to assume that a speaker's communicative and grammatical competence, and his actual communicative performance are very closely related (§1.5.3). A speaker's grammar is shaped and constantly modified by his continued experiences of language in use, i.e. mostly by his own linguistic practice which involves hypothesis formation (concerning what might be correct use) and testing, trials and errors, etc. The basic function of language is communication in social contexts. This view of linguistic competence is therefore in accordance with Wittgenstein's (1953) argumentation against the possibility of a 'private language'. Language and the knowledge of language are logically inseparable from the use of language which is subject to social rules (cf. Itkonen 1974: 50–67).

It is also reasonable to assume that speakers' *intuitions* about linguistic structures, and their meaning and use, which are also primary data for a theory of competence, are based on their communicative experience. Such an assumption is by and large empirically supported (cf. Stich

---

[47] This means that the speaker–listener can produce and comprehend not only all or most grammatical utterances, but *also* a wide range of ungrammatical utterances.

1975: 102).[48] Linguistic knowledge concerns what you can *do*, i.e. speech acts, language games, etc., and grammatical and other conditions on these acts. Of course, there is no *logical* necessity that speakers' knowledge is dependent on their abilities to perform, but I will assume that any point of incongruence between what a speaker allegedly knows and what he can do (or habitually does) must be specifically argued for.

This of course means that grammatical competence must be thought of as something that is rather different from Chomsky's 'competence'. The latter concept, disregarding all inconsistent and mutually contradictory characterizations by Chomsky himself and his followers, involves a very high degree of idealization, which in fact makes it psychologically invalid and immune to falsification, i.e. testing by empirical data of real speakers' psychology and behavior (cf. especially Derwing 1973: ch. 8; Steinberg 1975).[49] Rather, our notion

---

[48] However, one may legitimately ask whether the 'intuitive' grammar which a person, presumably a linguist, comes up with as a result of penetrating reflection over his language is really the *same* grammatical knowledge that the naive speaker unconsciously utilizes in behavior. In a slightly different way we could ask: Suppose we construct a P-grammar, i.e. a competence grammar based on observations of speech performance (NB: this is not a description of performance) and an I-grammar, i.e. a systematization of all those grammatical structures and generalizations that emerge as a result of the speaker's intuitive evaluation of his language. What would the relationship between the two descriptions presumably be? Different standpoints are clearly discernible. One could, e.g., argue that they are essentially identical (e.g. because speakers are presumably incapable of spontaneously developing I-grammars which do not have a firm basis in their P-grammars) or that the I-grammar is relatively independent (e.g. because intuitive appreciations concern grammatical structures abstracted from all conditions of use). My answer would be that there is *one* grammar, but what is normally utilized in performance is only the concrete part (first-order knowledge) while introspection is most often concerned with higher-order knowledge. In introspective reflection about grammar (something which is frequently done by linguists), many regularities seem to be 'discovered' and 'internalized' without ever having played any role before, not even in 'passive' aspects of (decoding) competence. However, there is a dialectic relationship between the concrete and abstract parts of grammar.

[49] In fact, though Chomsky's competence is said to be embodied in an idealized speaker's mind, the idealization involved is so great that Chomsky's mentalism boils down to some kind of 'non-mentalism' (cf. §1.1). Thus, though this may not be intended by Chomsky and his associates, a Chomskyan competence model could be assigned several non-mentalistic and completely reasonable interpretations, e.g.
(i) a model of *la langue* as the idealized supra-individual linguistic norm of a linguistic community (described in a manner that meets high requirements of completeness, simplicity and economy, cf. Linell 1974a: 21–2), or
(ii) a pandialectal model, in which the structural relationships between related dialects are stated in a maximally integrated way (cf. Bailey 1972; St Clair 1973). Such a pandialectal grammar is not psychologically valid, cf. §5.2.6. See also references on p. 19, fn. 46.

of 'competence' is similar to proposals by Hymes (1971, 1972) and others.

1.5.5 *Knowledge and rules : conventionality and consciousness*

Among many other terms which are used by contemporary linguists in many different and often unclear ways are the terms 'knowledge' ('know', etc.; 'the speaker *knows* the rules of his language') and 'rule'. I will not attempt to perform a conceptual analysis of their various uses, merely point out that there are problems to be solved in this area.

The traditional philosophical distinction regarding 'knowledge' is that between *'knowledge that'* (e.g. theoretical and conscious knowledge of facts) and *'knowledge how'* (e.g. practical ability to do something). As far as speakers' 'grammatical knowledge' is concerned, it is definitely most akin to 'knowledge how', i.e. speakers know how to use their language (according to implicit norms). Chomsky (e.g. 1969) has argued that speakers' knowledge is neither 'knowledge that' nor 'knowledge how', but rather something in between: 'implicit or *tacit* knowledge'. There are some facts speaking for this position. Thus, linguistic rules are, at least partly, *constitutive* for the behavior, not merely regulative (Searle 1969: 33ff).[50] Certain rules are conscious, and perhaps taught and learnt explicitly, e.g. rules for the selection of speaking style, specific words, etc. Any language learner probably realizes that it is not enough merely to be understood, there are rules for what counts as correct which go far beyond that (departures from rules are recognized as 'errors', 'mispronunciations', 'foreign accent', etc.). Speakers are generally willing to believe that there are rules even if they do not know what the rules are (cf. Black 1962: 166). Itkonen argues that speakers may have knowledge 'without quite realizing it', but it is usually possible to guide them into knowing the existence of the rules (1974: 180–1, 188–9). However, it is rather difficult to define exactly what rules are 'knowable', i.e. potentially amenable to consciousness. Wang (1968: 707) has pointed out that 'when we say, somewhat metaphorically, that a speaker "knows" the phonology of his language, we are in fact using the verb "know" to cover many types of awareness'. In other words, some aspects of 'grammatical knowledge' are more unequivocally 'knowledge how' (cf. §10.9). One may, as Chomsky (1975a: 164ff) has suggested, avoid the term 'know' altogether in discussing speakers' competence.

---

[50] For a critique of this distinction see Allwood (1976: 28ff).

However, I will continue to use it – following the tradition – though in some cases the term 'ability' will be preferred to 'knowledge'.[51]

Closely connected with the terminological problems concerning 'knowledge' are those of 'rule'. In fact, the semantics of this term are even more entangled, since it has several very different uses. Its basic sense in traditional linguistics, as well as in the theory or philosophy of social psychology and sociology, is that of a norm which people follow in performing actions and which is conscious to them to at least some extent, and which may be more or less explicit. However, the term 'rule' is also used in various 'degenerate' senses in which it is almost synonymous with 'regularity in behavior' or 'generalization about matters of fact'.[52] Moreover, in contemporary linguistics the term 'rule' has acquired at least two other and rather different connotations. On the one hand, it has been associated with the notion of 'mathematical rule', e.g. a 'rule' for deriving theorems from axioms or simply 'a formal operation which converts one formally defined string of symbols into another well-defined string'.[53] On the other hand, it has been associated with the concept of 'causally efficient (neurophysiological) process' (e.g. Katz 1964). This latter interpretation is particularly troublesome, since we must take pains not to assume a priori that rules of grammar are isomorphic to processes (§1.4.3).

In this work, I will deliberately continue to use the term '(phonological) rule' much like in contemporary phonological theory, i.e. in referring to phonological regularities of particular languages. In addition to what was said in §1.4.3, I would like to emphasize that, in my conception, rules must be associated with *conventionality*. A phonetic regularity may correspond to a phonological rule, only if some measure

---

[51] For discussion of the notion of 'knowledge of grammatical rules' see e.g. Harman 1967; Chomsky 1969, 1975a; Nagel 1969; Schwartz 1969; Searle 1969; Quine 1970; Ganz 1971; Derwing 1973: 251–8; Itkonen 1974.

[52] See especially Black 1962: 109–15, 133; Ganz 1971: 128–9; and also Winch 1958; C. Taylor 1964; R. Taylor 1966; Harré & Secord 1972; Itkonen 1974; Allwood 1976: 28ff, who all argue that rules and rule following are necessary concepts in a theory of human behavior.

[53] Cf. Chomsky (1961: 'On the notion "rule of grammar"'). Obviously, rules in this sense can also be related to norms, since each rule would be a norm for a correct derivation of one structure from another. However, these rules are obviously not norms of primary linguistic behaviour. Rather, such rules and metarules (e.g. evaluation measures, §4.2.2) constitute norms for the grammarian's behavior when he is practising linguistic (generative) analysis. I owe this point to Sven Ohman.

of arbitrariness obtains.[54] This means that, by definition (cf. §2.1), no phonological rule is a natural necessity, i.e. it is never entirely predictable from the inherent properties of the speech and hearing organs and the central nervous system. Each specific rule could have been otherwise; it is a matter of historical accident that rules and rule systems are precisely the way they are in each specific language. This is not to deny that many rules have a natural phonetic basis. However, all properties of sound signals which are necessary and purely 'mechanical' consequences of the biological limitations will by definition be excluded from phonology (§2.1). Thus, all rules are language-specific[55] and learned in at least some respects.

Closely related to conventionality is potential consciousness. Since all rules are, at least partly, language-specific and hence learned, the speaker who knows them must have been aware, at some level and stage of development,[56] that the rule is followed by other speakers. Yet, we have argued that speakers seem to be unconscious of many rules and aspects of rules. However, in one area a certain consciousness reveals itself; speakers may always become aware of *violations* of rules (§1.4.2).

Thus, we see that consciousness must be important in grammatical competence. Yet, Chomsky and his associates do not seem to agree with this (§1.4.2). Fodor (1976: 52–3) even argues that the distinction between conscious states and processes of the mind (where the agent has some awareness of what he knows, feels or does) and processes that happen to and in the nervous system and that are often not accessible to consciousness, is neither 'frightfully important' nor 'relevant to the purposes of cognitive psychology'. It may certainly be true that the distinction between conscious and unconscious processes is not important in a psychological model of the actual physiological processes going on in the nervous system of an individual during thinking, speaking, listening, trying to understand, etc. But a model of grammatical and communicative competence is *not* a model of these processes, as we have argued several times above. Thus, I maintain that for a theory of communicative competence the distinction between conscious and unconscious *is* important.

---

54 See Allwood (1976: 25, 35, and passim).

55 Which does not exclude the possibility that several languages may happen to have partly the same rules.

56 For a speaker to have learned a rule, it may suffice that he has once, at a particular stage of development, attended to (the effects of) the rule. For substantiation of this point, cf. §2.4.2.

1.5.6 *Competence and indeterminacy*

It has often been contended by Chomsky, and of course by many other linguists, that the grammar (i.e. speakers' competence) is under-determined by the 'primary linguistic data'. Data can be analyzed in many ways and are, consequently, compatible with many grammars. Chomsky, however, argues that there is only one (psychologically valid) true speakers' grammar (of which a generative transformational grammar is a theory). To 'explain' how speakers arrive at this particular grammar, Chomsky invokes the notion of an innate highly specialized *faculté de langage* (Language Acquisition Device).[57] To my knowledge, Chomsky has never given any detailed arguments why speakers must be assumed to possess the same unique grammatical competence;[58] it is simply adopted as an axiom (thus not subjected to empirical investigation). In fact, there is of course abundant evidence that speakers

---

[57] Chomsky also has other reasons to assume this innate capacity, but all can be argued against. For some comments, see §12.3.2.

[58] Chomsky (1975a: especially 183ff) does present one argument, namely that theories are always underdetermined by data and since we assume in physics that there is only one (causally efficient) true theory, we must assume the same for linguistics, and all other sciences. This, I think, is a fallacious argument, which shows the insufficient appreciation by generativists of the metascientific status of linguistics, and human sciences in general (cf. Itkonen 1974). Chomsky's claim can be argued against on several accounts. For one thing, a theory of grammatical competence is not a theory of causally efficient forces in behavior. Rather, it concerns knowledge of conditions on meaningful intentional acts, and relations between such conditions (cf. §1.4.3).
Theories in natural sciences, on the other hand, are theories about causal mechanisms which explain events as ('mechanical') necessary consequences of these mechanisms. Of course, one may construe a Chomskyan competence theory as a theory of neurophysiological (causally efficient) mechanisms (cf. for example, Katz 1964). This is indeed what Chomsky (1975a) sometimes alludes to (e.g. 186), though such a view seems hard to reconcile with other statements of Chomsky's to the effect that competence is only very indirectly related to performance (see e.g. Steinberg's (1975) excerpts). Anyway, one must not confuse a theory of competence with a theory of causal mechanisms (§1.4.3), and, by all standards, it is entirely premature to speculate about their mutual relationship or about the neurophysiological correlates of specific grammatical details (as one must, if one has to discuss the merits of one specific 'neurophysiologically interpreted' competence theory over another). Notice, by the way, that Chomsky's 'uniqueness argument' would not go through, even if we make the debatable assumption that competence theories (grammars) are models of brain structures. Suppose we have two grammars, or grammar fragments, which, when applied to the same set of data, make two different (at least partially contradictory) analyses. Then, there is nothing (except empirically unsupported speculations trying to motivate linguistic economy, §4.2.2) which excludes the possibility that both grammar fragments are neurophysiologically implemented in the brains of different speakers or, for that matter, in the brain of the same speaker.

do *not* develop identical competences. We all know that linguistic variation is legion, and without that we would not be able to explain either the whole range of interindividual variation in linguistic skill or the historical changes of languages. There *are* many areas of indeterminacy in the data. Thus, differences between speakers' grammars are hardly due only to the fact that individual speakers have been exposed to partially different subsets of the data belonging to the language as a whole. (For example, even for the same speaker there may exist conflicting rules or grammar segments.) It would be absurd to regard all the 'idiolectal grammars' as referring to *separate* dialects or languages;[59] one has to admit that a language is a 'structured (orderly) heterogeneity' (Weinreich, Labov & Herzog 1968: 151) and that this also holds, though not to the same extent, for the individual speakers' knowledge of the language.

Of course, not all parts of a language and its grammar are equally unstable or equivocal. Naturally, people's intuitions and grammatical competences are most uncertain or vague when applied to complex and/or unusual linguistic constructions. Thus, abstract and/or peripheral rules and units would generally be more amenable to divergent treatments by speakers. But also well-established rules of morphology and phonology (cf. English plural formation, Haber 1975) or syntax (cf. English verb agreement, Morgan 1972) may be quite indeterminate when applied to unusual cases. McCawley (1976: 157), referring to Morgan and Haber, argues that speakers have a grammatical '"core" system, which covers a wide range of normal cases, plus strategies ("patches") for handling cases that are not covered by the "core" system'.[60] It thus seems that any adequate theory of linguistic competence must assign a certain range of fuzziness to the grammar, its components, units and rules.

[59] Cf. the '"my dialect – your dialect" gambit' as discussed by Botha 1973: 217–19; Stich 1975, and others.

[60] Compare in this context Ross' (1973) fuzzy grammatical categories. Compare also, as for the semantics of words (especially everyday concepts such as *tree, run, red*), the quite plausible theory that one knows what some referent stereotypes (exemplars) are like and that one follows the strategy of classifying less typical instances under a certain concept if they can be judged as sufficiently similar to the stereotypes in form and function (e.g. Fodor 1976: 96, 153 and passim). A certain measure of arbitrariness and accidence will of course characterize the application of such a strategy.

1.6 Methodological pluralism

In my subsequent treatment of problems of psychological reality in this book, I will have to leave many loose ends and fuzzy areas, which will probably prove to be less satisfactory to those readers who would have preferred to get a stronger theory. However, though psychological reality is at the heart of linguistic theory (§1.3), it seems to be wise to leave many questions open. We know by now (cf. Botha 1973; Derwing 1973, 1975; Linell 1974a; Steinberg 1975) that most claims for psychological validity made by generativists and others have not been supported by empirical evidence or general plausibility. Linguistic-structural solutions have often been presented as stating *the* rules of the language in question, without there being any relevant and reliable evidence in support (§1.2). Instead, we can say [61]

(a)   that there are in general many more different theories ('solutions') available which are compatible with the data than is usually admitted by linguists (cf. §1.5.6),

(b)   that for some of these solutions it is very difficult, sometimes next to impossible, to find a plausible psychological interpretation,[62] but

(c)   that many of those solutions which are directly discarded by generativists as 'complex', 'uneconomical', 'insignificant', etc. cannot be a priori excluded, in particular since reliable data and plausible hypotheses about linguistic performance and psychological realities have generally not been seriously considered.[63]

In the light of this, there is surely reason to be modest in one's claims. My purpose is to suggest some hypotheses which seem to be at least behaviorally interpretable and plausible, and to adduce some evidence indicating that at least some of them are indeed true and psychologically valid.

There is a great need for more data pertaining to psychology of linguistic structures. In our attempts to gather such data we should try many ways, i.e. both hermeneutic methods of trying to explicate and understand linguistic behavior and natural-science-inspired methods of observation, hypotheses-and-testing, etc.

Hermeneutics sets the limits of what the theory must account for, e.g. in making explicit the role of the communicative agent and in defining

[61] See Derwing (1975) for discussion and illustrations.
[62] See discussion of aspects of OGPh in this book (particularly ch. 12).
[63] Concerning the role of simplicity considerations, cf. §4.2.

the notion of 'correct speech act' and its reflections on the levels of phonology, morphology, syntactics, semantics and pragmatics. Thus, Chomsky is right in that 'there is no way to avoid the traditional assumption that the speaker–hearer's linguistic intuition is the ultimate standard that determines the accuracy of any proposed grammar, linguistic theory, or operational test . . .' (1965: 21). (Yet, generativists have not at all understood the role of hermeneutic *Verstehen* methodology in linguistics (Itkonen 1974, 1976; Ringen 1975), in spite of the fact that it has a long and respectable tradition.)[64] I have already given some reasons why linguistic analysis must largely rely on a 'phenomenological' approach (§1.4.2–3).

The hermeneutic approach, however, has its obvious limitations. There are many aspects of linguistic structure and behavior which are not directly amenable to conscious awareness and introspective assessments.[65] As I have explained in Linell (1976c), the following areas belong to this category:

(a)   metaprinciples of grammar

(b)   more or less universal tendencies, e.g. markedness relations in phonology, morphology, syntax, etc., which may be assumed to be explainable by constraints on man's biologically determined equipment

(c)   processes of perception and language acquisition (both of which involve clearly hypothetico-deductive components)

(d)   other aspects of language use which are beyond the speaker's conscious control

(e)   variation within speech communities or between different stages in the historical developments of languages, neither of which can be part of the mind of a single speaker unless of course they are directly accessible through his/her experience of the use of language.

Thus, adopting a methodological pluralism would reflect the fact that language and language use (and other aspects of human minds and behavior) can be experienced both 'from inside' (the agent's or participant's perspective) and 'from outside' (the observer's perspective). The former perspective corresponds more or less to the hermeneutic approach of immanent reflection and phenomenological analysis; the

[64] See Anttila (1976c).

[65] Of course, one can *speculate* on all sorts of things.

latter implies observation, experimentation and objective hypothesis testing. Man is both a rule-following social being and a biologically determined organism.[66]

[66] Cf. Linell (1976c: 92–3).

2 *Phonology in a model of communicative competence*

2.1 Phonology and phonetics

This book will try to develop parts of a model of phonology. However, before this can be done, we should perhaps ask ourselves what phonology actually is about. What kind of reality are we concerned with? Are we dealing with abstract knowledge or with the physical nature of articulatory behavior and acoustic signals? What is the relationship between phonology and phonetics?

The history of phonology shows that different schools and scholars have provided rather different answers to such questions. Perhaps everyone can agree that phonology deals with the sound signals of languages and that it does so from a linguistic, rather than a physical, point-of-view. But beyond this opinions are quite divergent. A rather common approach is to define the phonology of a language rather narrowly as the system of functionally relevant sound distinctions or of distinctive units (phonemes) where each unit is defined by its relations to the other units. Some structuralists have been reluctant to deal with the phonetic substance of phonemes at all, whereas others are more interested in phonetic realities. Another area of disagreement is the relationship between phonology and morphophonology.[1]

What definition of phonology one adopts will depend on what goals are set up. In our case we will strive not only to meet linguistic-structural standards; if possible, we also want our model to be psychologically and behaviorally adequate (ch. 1).[2] From this point-of-

[1] For a comprehensive survey of trends in phonological theory, see Fischer-Jørgensen (1975). For surveys of the most recent trends in generative phonology, see e.g. Bailey (1976) and the introduction of Goyvaerts & Pullum (1975).

[2] Since these latter goals will no doubt lead to a model that is less tight, 'simple', general, etc. than are some purely structural phonologies, some people will obviously argue that such a model simply does not meet *linguistic* standards (i.e. 'linguistically significant generalizations' are not captured). For some viewpoints on such arguments, see §1.1–3.

view many structuralist approaches focus too narrowly on only linguistically relevant (distinctive) units (the 'form' of language). Considering the range of variation and change of languages it seems impossible that the synchronic language system could be realistically pictured as a maximally integrated closed system. For example, it is implausible, and in many cases dangerously aprioristic, to assume that one particular structural model of language, e.g. one which is constructed on the basis of exclusively structural arguments and considers the 'distinctive' units (features or phonemes) to form a closed system separated from 'predictable' units (features and allophones), is psychologically adequate.[3]

My approach will emphasize the close relations of phonology to phonetics. Phonology is concerned with the *linguistic* aspects of *sound* structure and articulatory and perceptual *behavior*, or, if you will, speaker–listeners' knowledge about the language-specific use of sound signals. If phonology is *language-specific phonetics*, it should account for all those rules which have to do with the sound structure of what is regarded as phonologically and grammatically correct or acceptable idiomatic speech. Such a phonology must, in principle, be able to specify all those phonetic details – all 'extrinsic allophones' – that contribute to defining idiomatic pronunciations.[4] For example, reductions in fast or casual speech would clearly be a matter of phonology, since such reduction is subject to many language-specific conditions. In §2.3 I will make a preliminary analysis of speakers' phonological capacities.

Thus I will assume that phonology is intimately connected with phonetics. For example, we must often go to phonetics to find *explanations* of phonological regularities. In general, I assume that psychology is closely related to behavior; grammatical knowledge is primarily knowledge of rules for correct *use*, and psychological capacities primarily concern what you can *do* in behavior (§1.5.4).[5]

---

[3] Note that OGPh often takes such an aprioristic attitude with respect to claims of psychological reality (§1.2). See Derwing (1973) and below.

[4] For discussion of the 'limits of phonology' and the distinction between 'intrinsic' and 'extrinsic' allophones, see Tatham 1969; Ladefoged 1971b; Mansell 1973b; Morin 1974. Personally, I doubt that an absolute distinction between intrinsic and extrinsic allophones can be maintained, but this difficulty will be ignored here. For some discussion of the definition of 'rule' as opposed to, e.g., mechanical process, see §1.4.3, §1.5.5 and §3.5.

[5] This holds for at least 'first-order' knowledge and abilities (§2.3).

As for the relation of phonology to morphophonology, this is also a matter which should not be decided upon a priori or by stipulation. A careful consideration of the facts clearly suggests that the major part of morphophonology belongs to morphology rather than to phonology proper (see below, especially ch. 7).

2.2 General framework: communicative competence

A theory of speakers' linguistic competence must explicate what speakers must know in order to communicate linguistically their various intentions in different kinds of situations. Thus, communicative intentions of the parties involved are a prime concept (§1.4.3). The basic unit of analysis of linguistic communicative behavior may be language games, speech acts or the like (e.g. Allwood 1976). Games or acts, or utterances which constitute their behavioral manifestations, are subject to various conditions:

> PHONETIC–PHONOLOGICAL: utterances must meet certain conditions of pronunciation defined by the phonetic plans of lexical items and syntactic structures utilized (furthermore, reduced forms must meet conditions defined by rules for articulatory reduction)
>
> MORPHOLOGICAL: word forms used must be formally appropriate expressions of the categories involved
>
> SYNTACTIC: word forms must be organized into larger units (macrosyntagms, sentences, etc.) subject to conditions on word order and prosody
>
> SEMANTIC: utterances must meet requirements defined by the utterer's aims regarding reference and predication, primary and presupposed information, etc.
>
> PRAGMATIC: utterances must be situationally appropriate, i.e. they must meet conditions having to do with what kind of situation-specific meanings the utterer wants to communicate (what kind of communicative act he wants to perform). At this level, the interplay with general principles of communication (e.g. agent-hood, rationality) comes in (e.g. Grice 1975; Allwood 1976).

Conditions or rules of these types seem to me to be the basic 'knowledge' speakers need in order to be able to produce, perceive and comprehend linguistically formulated communicative acts. However, there are reasons to assume that speakers also have – probably to a varying extent – 'higher-order' knowledge about systematic relations between different lexical items (e.g. in terms of morpheme identity, cf. §9.5) or between different speech acts (utterances, sentences, etc.) or parts of such units, e.g. formal-syntactic relationships (transformational relations) and semantic relationships (properties and relations such as those of paraphrase, equivalence, synonymy, semantic similarity and difference, analyticity, syntheticity, ambiguity, entailment, pre-supposition, etc.). A basic mistake of generative grammar is its total integration of this paradigmatic or 'higher-order' knowledge with the basic knowledge of conditions on speech acts (cf. above), thus making the latter necessarily and crucially dependent on the former. This point will be argued in some detail with respect to phonology below (§12.3.2.2).

Let us now narrow down our perspective and speculate a little over a speaker's act of producing a sentence, or some comparable unit.[6] We recall that uttering a sentence is part of a superordinate speech act or language game. We assume that speakers are 'active' in their sentence construction; what they do is successively to construct and realize expression plans as necessary parts of such meaningful acts (cf. §1.4.3).[7] The act of producing a sentence is of course a very complex act which comprises several different component acts and/or operations. Disregarding details, we assume that the speaker starts with an *intention to communicate a certain message*, and, perhaps, to communicate it in a specific way, using for example some specific linguistic *style*. The intention itself of course depends on various external and internal stimuli present in the situation. The speaker's communicative

---

[6] The following account has, at least partly, been inspired by ideas that have been proposed by Sven Öhman (cf. Öhman 1975).

[7] This active theory should be compared to the paramechanistic view which may be suggested by the generative competence model (e.g. Lakoff 1971) in which the speaker sets up a semantic representation which subsequently runs through all the transformations, sometimes picking up a couple of lexical items from the lexicon, and in which the whole derivation is brought to an end by a phonological component which transforms sequences of abstract morphemes to phonetic representations (which may be thought of as instructions to the articulators). In this picture the only constructive element in communication consists in setting up a 'semantic representation' (in many ways very abstract) whereas the rest of the sentence 'generation' is some kind of deterministic process that 'happens' to speakers *qua* speech-producing automata. The so-called mentalism of Katz (1964) actually implies a (para)mechanistic view on linguistic competence and performance. Cf. Linell (1979a).

intention(s) will govern his selection of the lexical building blocks and the various operations to be used in modifying and combining these lexemes. The lexical building blocks are, as I will argue (chs. 4, 7), concrete expressions, such as stems, word forms and (lexicalized) phrases, of course associated with their specific semantic and grammatical properties. The operations which are applied to the basic expressions have both a semantic function and a grammatical manifestation (such as inflection, word order, prosody, etc.). That is, the operations are double-sided; they construct both a semantic representation and an expression. The latter may be thought of as an expression plan for the grammatical–phonetic structure of the sentence. However, the operational structure of sentences is more complex than this; the primary, semantically functional operations may involve subsidiary or secondary – semantically more or less empty – operations on the expression side. Morphological operations (ch. 7) typically belong to this latter category.

Let us discuss a simple example. Suppose that a Swedish-speaking person wants to communicate the message 'The cat is drinking the milk' (Swedish: *Katten dricker mjölken*). Perhaps this sentence is uttered in a situation where in fact a cat can be observed drinking milk. If the cat is perceptually focal, or otherwise central in the universe of discourse at the particular point of time when the message is communicated, the speaker will draw from his lexicon an item which matches his percept semantically, e.g. the word *katt* (the uninflected indefinite singular form), and – in the unmarked case – make this subject of the sentence. If the particular referent (the cat in question) is assumed to be obvious to the listener, the speaker will – again in the unmarked case – apply the definitivization operation to this word, thus getting *katten* (def. sg.). Making *katten* subject and topic of a sentence implies that the speaker has to operate on this to form a sentence with a predicate part, which will express the rheme to be communicated. In doing so, the speaker is forced to find – by some kind of subroutine – a verb; Swedish grammar requires finite verbs to come second in all main clauses (except questions and imperatives). Thus, he has to retrieve *dricka* (or the stem /drikk/ which may be the lexicon form). Finite verbs always have to carry the overt expression of tense, mood, etc. Therefore, another morphological operation has to apply at this stage to give the present tense form, *dricker*. Similarly, another morphological operation is called for to yield the object *mjölken*, etc. The expression string thus constructed may be thought of as a plan for the articulation of a certain phonetic signal. The plan may be construed as a set of conditions that the phonetic realization must fulfil; it thus represents a certain level of phonological abstraction (see §3.2). In the specific situation the plan may be realized (executed) in various ways having to do with tempo and speaking style. For example, the word *katten* may be pronounced with an ending [ən] or with a single syllabic [n̩], the /t/ may be more or less unaspirated or even unreleased, etc.

The sentence formation process also gives a *semantic representation* of the sentence. Note that this representation is not the same as the intention or intended meaning. For one thing, it often happens that the speaker, after uttering something, feels that he has not succeeded in expressing what he wanted to communicate, i.e. there is a discrepancy between the semantics of the linguistic expression produced and the intended meaning. Secondly, and more importantly, a sentence has very often implicit and non-literal interpretations which are not part of its literal semantic representation. For example, its intended speech act status (illocutionary force) may be at variance with its overt form. A statement may, e.g., be intended as a question or a request. (Perhaps, the utterance *Katten dricker mjölken* was intended as a suggestion to the listener to remove the cat from the milk bowl, since the milk was to be reserved for the hedgehog.) In such a case, the proper *situational interpretation* of the sentence token (utterance) (which in its turn should of course match the intended meaning, if the speech act is to be entirely successful), cannot be inferred by simply finding a straightforward (literal) interpretation of the semantic representation (=structural meaning). Rather the speaker's communicative intentions may be said to include the strategy of conveying the intended meaning by using a sentence, the structural (literal) meaning of which the listener is supposed to use for inferring the actually intended meaning. Compare, in this context, Grice's (1975) conversational implicatures. However, in the case of a simple declarative or narrative speech act, the structural meaning may be thought of as a set of conditions which govern the listener's search for an interpretation of the sentence in the particular situational context. Öhman (1975) has argued that the structural meaning functions as a *perceptual plan* for the listener; (thus there would be a certain parallelism with the expression side where operations also yield entities of 'plan' type, 1975: 329).[8]

---

[8] For some further suggestions concerning the comprehension of utterances, see §2.4.4.2.

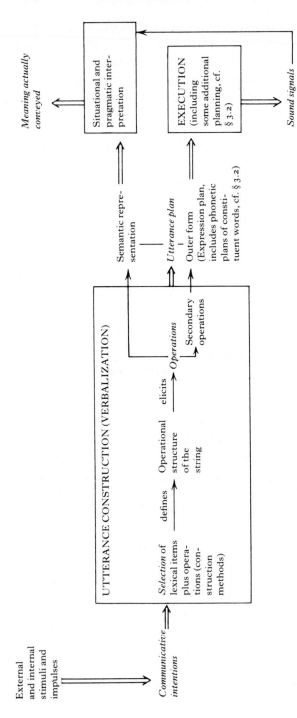

Fig. 2.1

What has now been proposed may be summarized as in fig. 2.1.

This scheme must not be interpreted so as to imply some sort of absolute temporal sequence of subacts such as intention, plan construction (with its various subroutines) and execution. Rather, the speaker is active at many levels simultaneously; he does not have to postpone partial execution until the plan of the whole utterance has been completely constructed. However, certain temporal necessities hold. For example, to produce a correct noun phrase the speaker must normally make up his mind what head noun and preposed modifiers should be used before the execution is started (at least this is true of languages with NP-internal agreement). Postposed modifiers, such as certain relative clauses, may be added to the plan later on. Similarly, by choosing a certain sentence subject the speaker is committed to selecting certain predicate phrase constituents, whereas other complements may be decided upon (or omitted altogether) later, etc.

We have seen that the formal side of utterance construction yields an expression plan for the sentence. I will assume that this involves, among other things (cf. §3.2), phonetic plans of the various word forms arranged in a surface-syntactic pattern (i.e. in a certain linear order and with a certain prosodic pattern). Central to my conception is the distinction between the *construction* of the expression plan and its *execution*.[9] Phonological regularities, which will be the subject matter of this work, come in at three different places in our theoretical framework:

(a) as aspects of *morphological operations*, i.e. those subordinate acts in which 'word forms' are created (ch. 7)

(b) in defining conditions on the structure of phonetic plans (chs. 3, 6)

(c) in accounting for variation in the execution of plans.

Note that morphophonology, which according to OGPh belongs to phonology, will be treated as aspects of morphological operations, i.e. as belonging to the construction phase in utterance production.

2.3 Speakers' phonological capacities

A speaker's language-specific phonetic (i.e. phonological) capacities seem to include roughly the following:

[9] These notions are basically derived from the work of Öhman (1975).

Phonological knowledge/abilities of competent speakers:	Principal grammar-theoretical analogues:
(a) Knowledge how to pronounce the specific words	
(i) the properties defining the linguistic identity of the words (types underlying all tokens)	phonological forms = phonetic plans (primarily of lexical items)
(ii) the totality of properties defining the most careful pronunciations	fully specified articulatory plans for careful pronunciations
(iii) more or less general strategies or rules of reduction	articulatory reduction rules
(b) Ability to perceive pronunciations differently (at different levels of detail)	perceptual redundancy rules
(c) Knowledge of general conditions on phonological–phonetic structure (conditions on pronounceability), manifested in e.g.	phonotactic (or phonotactically motivated) rules or constraints
(i) ability to judge the phonological correctness of strings	
(ii) ability to construct new forms meeting the conditions	
(iii) ability to adjust foreign words so that they conform to the conditions	
(d) Knowledge how to form new phonetic plans (word forms) from lexical structures	morphological operations

The abilities referred to in (a–c) all concern knowledge of surface forms, and relations between different pronunciations and percepts of surface forms along reduction scales. In (d) something more is involved. As I have already argued (§2.2), morphological operations belong to the construction phase of utterance production and not to phonology proper.

All the capacities (a–d) seem necessary, though in different ways, for the speaker–listener to produce, perceive and comprehend grammatical speech, i.e. they belong to his/her *basic linguistic capacities* (cf. Bever 1970). Some, particularly (ci), are involved in his/her metalinguistic capacity to judge the phonological correctness of forms (ch. 6).

In addition to this, peripheral correspondences, such as 'via rules' for certain regularities involved in non-productive allomorphy (see §7.7) may be set up. This is often the result of more or less systematic reflection over the linguistic data, something which is professionally practised by linguists.[10]

The various kinds of phonological knowledge/abilities mentioned here are taken to be facts that a theory of phonology must account for (i.e. explicate or explain). Of course, one could include other abilities as well, but it seems to me that those would be implied by the ones mentioned. For example, an important point, neglected in OGPh, is speakers' intuitions for what are variants of the *same pronunciation* of a certain form (i.e. pronunciations differing in their degree of casualness) vs. *different pronunciations* of a given form (e.g. [âɪðə] vs. [iːðə] *either*). The former variations are often not conscious to the speaker, whereas the latter are (see §3.4).

2.4 Notes on speaker's competence and listener's competence

2.4.1 *One or two competences?*

In contemporary linguistic metatheory there is a controversy whether one should distinguish a 'speaker's competence' from a 'listener's competence' or not.[11] Though this problem cannot be treated here, I will assume that there *is* a unitary competence to be used in encoding as well as in decoding. An obvious argument for this can be based on the fact that, in the normal case, the *same* person alternatingly takes the role of the speaker and the role of the listener. There can be no 'speaker's competence' which is not heavily influenced by the way listeners operate, and vice versa. This, of course, does not imply that there are no variations with regard to what extent a person utilizes different parts of his grammatical knowledge *qua* speaker and *qua* listener (cf. for example, Straight 1976).

However, we will assume that a fully fluent person's competence is biased towards the production aspect, since speakers apparently have to know more than listeners (§2.4.3–4), in spite of the fact that a person's receptive competence is developmentally prior to his productive competence (§2.4.2).

[10] Cf. here p. 21, fn. 48 and § 1.5.6.
[11] In a recent monograph, Vandamme (1972) argues for competential dualism. For some comments, see Eliasson (1975a). Cf. also Straight 1976; Teleman 1977.

2.4.2   *The primacy of perception*

There are some reasons for regarding perception as primary with respect to speech production. For example, it is trivial that one must be able to perceive something, normally by means of auditive perception, in order to acquire language. The child must be perceptually capable of discerning a structure in the sound signals in order to imitate that structure articulatorily. It is well-known from observations of child language and the general behavior of children that the perceptual structuring capacity develops faster and earlier than the capacity for articulatory differentiation. Therefore, it is evident that perception primarily determines what will count as phonologically equivalent or identical. Later too, phonological identity or equivalence seems to be matched by perceptual identity rather than articulatory identity. The same perceptual impression may correspond to several different articulations (but see below). Consequently, phonological equivalence can not be expressed in articulatory terms exclusively. (The traditional mainly articulation-based phonetic terminology is somewhat misleading since phonological analysis is primarily based on perception, cf. Ladefoged 1967: 51ff.)

Other observations may also support the claim for the primacy of perception. People comprehend many more words, constructions and dialectal variants than they are capable of actively producing. It also seems possible for a person to decide whether another speaker's pronunciation of a foreign dialect or language is idiomatic or not, although he himself may be unable to speak the dialect without an accent. This has been used as evidence against the motor theory of perception (Jakobson & Halle 1956: 34; Jakobson 1968: 18). A more extreme case is Lenneberg's (1967: 305–9) patient who developed a complete comprehension of English in spite of his congenital anarthria.

Though these arguments for the primacy of perception are quite strong, there are also arguments which would rather speak for the primary importance of speech production in determining constraints on people's phonological competence.

One of these latter arguments is a very general one. It is sometimes contended that speech production is the only truly creative activity in the individual's linguistic behavioral repertoire. Speech recognition would be more passive and 'parasitic' on the ability to produce speech. But then one forgets that linguistic creativity (at least its rule-consistent aspects) on the production side presupposes a previous abduction of structures from the input linguistic data provided by perception. Novel productions are merely the overt sign of this abduction (cf. Anttila 1972a: 197ff).

Another argument seems somewhat stronger. Öhman (1975) has pointed out that in everyday life we often comprehend (identify) sounds in terms of the mechanical events which produce them (cf. for example, the sound of a tea cup put down on the saucer, the crash of two colliding cars, etc.). It is suggested that this also applies to speech sounds; acoustic events are heard in terms of their underlying articulatory acts and receive their identity thereby. Though this is a very interesting proposal, one may doubt that articulatory events, relatively unobservable and unconscious as they are, may play such a decisive role. Nevertheless, it *is* plausible to argue that what one can perceive in speech recognition is not independent of what one can produce in speech production. In this context we may recall Troike's (1969) findings from perception and repetition tests that speakers are often unable to perceive distinctions in other dialects, such as *pin – pen, horse – hoarse*, if they do not make these distinctions in their own speech.

An interesting problem, which may raise some doubts about the explanatory force of auditive perception only, concerns the selection by a speech community of *one* articulation out of several perceptually equivalent ones. It is sometimes claimed (e.g. Jakobson, Fant & Halle 1952: 31) that labialization and pharyngealization may result in identical acoustical events. Yet the members of most speech communities happen to choose one and the same articulatory method. This seems to be an embarrassing problem. However, one may suspect that such 'equivalent' articulations do not, after all, lead to quite identical acoustic results. Possibly, there are subtle differences to be perceptually registered by the child. The question is related to another problem brought to attention by Labov (1972). He gathered evidence for the so-called 'fallacy of the minimal pair' by showing that speakers may consistently keep apart articulatorily and acoustically distinct but highly similar sounds without being able to discriminate between them perceptually when they are presented to them in minimal pair tests. Labov (1972: 1,118ff) showed that speakers of a British community consistently kept their dialectal pronunciations of *two* and *toe* apart without being able to tell which was which when presented with tape recordings of their own speech. The same situation was found for pairs like *line – loin, vice – voice* in another linguistic community. It is to be suspected, according to Labov, that such 'formally' but not perceptually identifiable phonemic contrasts are much more common than we usually believe.[12]

G. Drachman (pers. comm.) has suggested an explanation why such cases are possible. Thus, young children may be able to make very fine perceptual differentiations and then let their distinct perceptual structurings determine distinct articulations. The articulatory habits thus achieved are retained through life while the ability of perceptual discrimination is diminished. If this explanation is correct, it means that the theory of phonological structurings as perceptually defined (§3.3.5) must be specified in an interesting way. A speaker need no longer be capable of making *all* types of perceptual structurings which underlie his knowledge of the phonological forms of his language which determines his speech performance. It suffices that at some period in his linguistic development he has been able to make these perceptual structurings.

By way of summary, though the receptive capacity is undoubtedly logically and developmentally prior to the productive capacity, it may be argued that the perceptual habits which finally crystallize in the mature speaker–listener closely match what he is able to produce. (However, the competition between rival theories of speech perception is certainly not settled yet, cf. Studdert-Kennedy 1976.) Moreover, if we leave phonology proper and consider grammatical competence as a whole, including morphology and morphophonology, I will argue that our competence model must be speaker-biased (§2.4.3).

2.4.3 *Speakers know more*

In a certain sense it is the speaker who cares about grammaticality. He has to know all the rules for constructing a grammatically (syntactically, morphologically and phonologically) correct utterance. The listener, on the other hand, may rely on recognition of certain surface properties and then use various sorts of short cuts to infer the intended meaning of the utterance. (There is evidence that this is the case, cf. §2.4.4.2.) Moreover, the listener need not be able to use actively all the words and grammatical operations involved in order to recognize the meaningfulness and grammaticality of other people's utterances. Therefore, it

---

[12] For further examples and discussion, see Labov, Yaeger & Steiner (1973: ch. 6). It may perhaps be argued that Labov's results are due to the vague instructions given to the participants.

seems that what may suffice for a successful recognition and comprehension is not always enough for a successful production. This, of
course, is in accordance with general insights in the psychology of
learning. It also fits everyday experience of language use that one's
'passive' competence covers more than one's 'active' competence; e.g.,
one may understand a foreign dialect or language quite well without
being able to speak it.[13] Furthermore, it casts some light on the fact that
children regularly comprehend more complex structures than they can
produce (e.g. Fraser, Bellugi & Brown 1963; cf. also § 2.4.2). Also, data
on the acquisition of morphology indicates that children first simply
know the canonical surface forms for the various morphological
categories, which is enough for perception, and only later acquire the
exact morphological operations of the language. For example, Derwing
& Baker's (1976) experiments on the formation of plurals of English
nonsense words showed that children (even up to the age of seven to
eight) responded very often with zero when the singular ended in a
sibilant, and particularly so if this was /z/ or /s/. The explanation must be
that in such cases the singular forms already meet the surface condition
characteristic of plurals, namely that they end in a sibilant (cf. Linell
1976a: 20–1).

2.4.4 *Different modes of listening*

It seems to be a valid generalization that in speech recognition an
incomplete computing at lower levels is a prerequisite for successful
results at higher levels. I will briefly discuss a couple of aspects of this
claim.

2.4.4.1 *Listening to sounds and listening to words.* Speech recognition
does not normally involve the perception of sounds merely as sounds
but rather the 'direct' recognition of words (phrases, etc.) and their
meanings. Chomsky further argues: 'it is well-known that intelligibility
is preserved under gross phonetic distortion, which may be completely
unnoticed when grammatical constraints are met; and brief exposure to
an unfamiliar dialect is often sufficient to overcome unintelligibility or
even an impression of strangeness ...' (1964: 99–100). One should note
that Chomsky uses these facts to conclude that it is not a concrete
phonetic representation of speech that is linguistically significant but

---

[13] These differences obviously also depend on the ways in which long-term memory is
made accessible in speech production and recognition.

rather a higher-level representation, i.e. that of morpheme-invariants.[14] However, this argumentation of Chomsky's is not conclusive. What seems clear is that higher-level grammatical information intervenes in speech perception. It fulfils a function as a guiding principle or condition on the perceptual process and determines together with situational predictabilities and the high phonetic redundancy of the speech signal the correct phonological structuring even in the presence of much noise. Thus, for the purpose of linguistic identification we do not *need* all phonetic data.[15] But it does not follow from this that phonological structurings must be abstract or that concrete sound shapes are superfluous. (Nor is it true that 'meanings' are tied to abstract morphemes, cf. for example, §4.3.3.2.) Instead, we can agree with Polanyi about speech perception that we are only subsidiarily conscious of the sounds and focally conscious of the totalities, the meaningful words. Speech perception follows the schema of 'tacit inference' (or 'tacit knowing') (1969). The sounds have the function of 'pointing to' the words as the integrated units of a higher level. (One of the characteristics of Polanyi's tacit inference is that the integrated totality possesses emergent properties which do not belong to its component parts or its 'clues'.)

Polanyi points out that if one focuses on what is normally subsidiary, i.e. in our case on the phonetic properties, then one loses the integration and everything becomes unintelligible. The parts are 'externalized' and become 'external objects without functional meaning' (1969: 216). This is exactly what happens when one listens to the sound shape proper of a word and repeats this over and over again. The word then turns into funny sounds.

We therefore admit that sound shapes have only a subsidiary function (in the sense of Polanyi) in the process of understanding utterances. We recognize words 'directly' on the basis of sound shapes, normally with the aid of guesses about semantic and syntactic properties of the utterances. But sound shapes are the object of study of phonology. And even if they are subsidiary, i.e. not consciously attended to, they are not linguistically irrelevant. Most facts speak for a conception of phonological structurings as concrete and phonetic. It would be a queer logic

---

[14] Chomsky uses the term 'systematic phonemic representation'.

[15] In fact, we cannot identify every phoneme in normal speech recognition, because that would involve a rate of identification which 'overreaches the temporal resolving power of the ear' (Liberman et al. 1967: 432).

to argue as if the existence of abstract morphemes were some kind of consequence of the fact that phonological–phonetic properties have a subsidiary function in the perception of meaningful speech.

2.4.4.2 *Full comprehension of an utterance.* The recognition and comprehension of an utterance can, for our present purposes, be analyzed in the following simplified manner. Suppose someone utters, say, *There is a burglar in the kitchen.* This utterance can then be understood at several levels:

(a)   *Recognition of words.* The listener must recognize at least most of the words used by the speaker. This is presumably done on the basis of some, but only *some*, phonetic properties of the speech signal and his own semantic and situational expectations.

(b)   *Recognition of structural meaning.* On the basis of the words and some cues pertaining to the syntactic structure, the listener computes the structural meaning of the utterance, i.e. what conditions a reference situation must fulfil provided it is correctly characterized by the sentence used (cf. §2.2). In my example there must be someone who fulfils the conditions for being characterized as a burglar, there must be a locality characterizable as a kitchen, the specific kitchen referred to must be known or evident to the listener, and the person referred to as a burglar must be in the kitchen at the moment of the speaker's uttering the sentence.

(c)   *Assignment of a situational interpretation.* In normal linguistic communication, it is not enough to have understood the structural meaning of the utterance. The listener must also find out what specific extralinguistic situation the speaker actually refers to, what specific properties of this reference situation he points to and what he wants to communicate about it. We may argue with Öhman (1975) that the structural meaning functions as an instruction or a perceptual plan for the listener in searching for the situational interpretation (cf. §2.2).

(d)   *Inferences from the interpretation.* Often the full comprehension of the communicative context of an utterance involves more than this. For example, the situation interpretation may, in the case of 'indirect' speech acts, involve other pragmatic factors, such as non-literal interpretation (cf. Grice 1975), invited inference (e.g. Geis & Zwicky 1971) and other implicit meanings. Furthermore, the listener may be expected by the speaker to respond to his speech act by some kind of action, linguistic (e.g. answering a question) or non-linguistic (e.g. trying to capture the burglar). In other words, it is usually not enough to understand the propositional content of the utterance. Often the listener must also understand *what* the speaker means by uttering it and *why* he does so (cf. Allwood 1976; 98–100).

I am not suggesting that listeners actually go through all these stages. Rather, they try to get to the intended situational interpretation as swiftly as possible. There is evidence that listeners do not pay attention to the form of utterances in listening; a more detailed computing on these levels is only carried out in cases of failures of finding plausible situational interpretations.[16] In fact, a full comprehension of the intended meaning of a speech act or a text may be seriously impeded if the listener invests too much energy in attending to phonological or syntactic properties.[17]

Thus, it seems probable that a listener uses short cuts and strategies to avoid focusing on grammatical and phonological aspects. The speaker, on the other hand, must obey these grammatical and phonological conditions, although he may sometimes allow himself a rather careless (casual) phonetic execution. (Otherwise, listeners may object to his deviant grammatical performance.) These considerations makes it probable that the grammatical competence concerning especially syntax and morphology (which includes morphophonology) is speaker-biased; it is speakers who need it most.

[16] E.g. Bransford & McCarrell (1974). Cf. facts about memory retention in Johnson-Laird 1970; Bransford, Barclay & Franks 1972.

[17] By now it also seems clear that so-called analysis-by-synthesis models of speech recognition (Halle & Stevens 1959; Stevens 1960. Cf. also Fodor, Bever & Garrett 1974: 307–8, 390–3) are too complex and empirically unsupported. These models, if founded on generative grammar and generative phonology, are based on the assumption of the crucial interaction of highly abstract structures, i.e. syntactic deep structures and morpheme-invariant phonological forms, in precisely those areas which seem to be less important in recognition.

3 *Phonological forms as plans for phonetic acts*

> Wenn man *rot* (Russ. род) in der bedeutung 'gattung' ausspricht, hat man angeblich die *absicht*, ein *d* auszusprechen. Man könnte ebenso gut behaupten, dass ich die absicht habe, *m* und *n* auszusprechen, wenn ich *seeleute* sage. (Collinder 1938)

3.1 Justification for the notion of 'phonetic plan'

As is well-known, there is a great deal of phonetic variation between different pronunciations of word forms by the same speaker or different speakers. For example, the English word *winter* can be pronounced in many ways; /w/ pronunciations may vary in consonantal friction and rounding, the /i/ pronunciations in tongue height and nasalization, the /n/ may be clearly segmentalized or more or less merged with the syllabic peak (/i/), the /t/ may be tense, even aspirated [tʰ], or it may be realized as a glottal stop or as a flap, the /ər/ may be segmentalized into a (perhaps [r]-colored) [ə] plus a more or less clear [r]-sound, or there may be just one syllabic segment with both vocalic and retroflex features, etc. In reality there are many more minute variations possible. Yet, speakers invariably intend to pronounce the same word form (*winter*), they know that the different tokens are instances of the same invariant word form, indeed as speakers we typically *believe* that the pronunciations *are* the same all the time (at least as long as they all belong to the same dialect), and as listeners we tend to perceive different variants as phonetically identical, or at least as less dissimilar than they actually are. And of course, there are many physical properties which *are* similar or identical in all the tokens. I take these as facts to be explicated by a theory of phonology. This can be done by assuming that for each word form there is (at least, cf. §3.4) one *phonetic plan* which is psychologically central and defines the phonological identity of the word form in question.[1] In speech production the speaker intends to realize this plan (§3.5) and in speech perception the listener tries to reinterpret the speaker's phonetic intentions into the perceived speech, i.e. he tries to figure out what word forms the speaker planned to articulate (§3.6).

3.2 Phonetic plans of words vs. complete articulatory plans of utterances

A theory of (goal-directed) behavior needs the concept of *plan* for behavioral units (acts, operations etc.) to account for the *equivalence* of various physical manifestations. The plan (intention, goal) is what is constant, while manifestations vary.[2] As a special case a theory of phonetic behavior needs the notion of phonetic plan.

By 'phonetic plan' I mean a plan to perform a certain type of phonetic act, i.e. to produce a sound signal with certain specific (phonetic/ phonological) properties. Thus, I assume that for each word form there is (at least, cf. §3.4) one phonetic plan that specifies its phonological identity. In other words, I follow the tradition in assuming that only certain properties of phonetic events (sound signals) are linguistically relevant. These properties define the intended linguistic status of all the tokens of a certain word form (the type defined by the plan), and they may be supposed to distinguish the phonetic plan involved from other possible phonetic plans. It is an empirical question to find out exactly what these linguistically relevant properties are in the various individual cases and whether they may be characterized in terms of general principles. There is evidence, however, that phonemic contrasts are important for determining them (§3.3 and ch. 4).

Of course, the phonetic plans of the words involved in a particular utterance specify only some aspects of the utterance in question. Thus, we must carefully distinguish phonetic plans from *complete (fully specified) articulatory plans* of particular utterances. The latter involve much more:

---

[1] In Linell (1974a) I used the somewhat clumsy term 'psychologically central invariant structuring' (PCIS) instead of 'phonetic plan'. I have also sometimes used the term 'articulatory plan' in this sense. I now prefer 'phonetic plan', since some scholars are inclined to understand 'articulatory plan' as 'fully specified articulatory plan of an utterance' (see §3.2). For further discussion of phonetic plans, see Linell (1979b).

[2] Cf. for example, Hebb's (1949) analysis of 'motor equivalence'. See also Miller, Galanter & Pribram (1960).

(a) There must be a prosodic plan for the utterance. (Prosodic plans are obviously very important but will not be considered in this book)

(b) The pronunciation plan must be specified down to all extrinsic allophonic details. It is assumed that these details are not part of the phonetic plans but may be predicted by general rules (in my framework: perceptual redundancy rules, §10.3.3)

(c) The degree of articulatory accuracy to be used must also be planned (at least to some extent).

Thus, using the general framework sketched in §2.2, we assume that the speaker first has to construct the expression plan of the utterance (which is the output of a complex multi-level construction activity). This plan includes the phonetic plans of words, a syntactic plan (for word order) and a prosodic plan. To be able to execute the phonetic behavior, some additional planning is needed. All allophonic details must be specified by filling in predictable properties and by assigning a certain level of articulatory accuracy.

Thus, the actual execution of specific utterance tokens (or the precise physical nature of specific speech signals) can be fully explained only if we can pinpoint *both* the fully specified articulatory plans, which would probably correspond to some kind of patterns of neurological inner-vations, *and* the various universal boundary conditions that follow from the biologically determined characteristics of the speech apparatus. This is what one needs in a causal model of phonetic behavior. I assume, however, that a teleological theory of phonetic behavior is also necessary (§1.4.3), and here the notion of phonological form (alias phonetic plan) will be crucial. (Moreover, we need phonetic plans also for deriving the fully specified articulatory plans, as has already been suggested.)

My notion of 'phonetic plan' is quite close to notions like '*Lautabsicht*' (used in early phonological theory from de Courtenay (1895) on), and recently Donegan & Stampe (1978) have used the term 'phonological intention' in approximately the same sense. Nevertheless, some will most certainly object to using the term 'plan (for phonetic behavior)' in the way recommended here. Thus, e.g., Trubetzkoy (1958: 37) rejected the notion of '*Lautabsicht*' as a possible interpretation of the concept of phonological form on the grounds that the intended sounds are not phonemes but allophones. In our wording, he would probably think of '*Lautabsichte*' as fully specified articulatory plans. However, terms like 'plan' or 'intention' (*Absicht*) may perfectly well be used when we consider only the linguistically relevant properties of the intended signals. In fact, this is the most reasonable and straightforward interpretation of the terms; the linguistic identity of the words used is what matters most in communication and hence also in speakers' planning of communicative acts.[3]

The theory of phonetic plans gives us a nice way of making sense of the notion of 'phonological representation' (or 'phonological form'), which is such a central term in traditional phonological theory, and we can thus explain the role of phonology in actual phonetic behavior. Compare this with the classical structuralist way of talking about phonological forms as social values or abstractions (what Trubetzkoy's arguments led to) which leaves us largely in the dark (cf. §12.4).

Furthermore, our theory will put very strong abstractness conditions on phonology. Though abstractness/concreteness is a relative matter (§3.3.3), one may argue that phonetic plans have to be concrete; although plans for behavior are not always executed (or executed only partially), they have to be executable. They should be describable in terms of the agent's practical know-how,[4] which should have manifested itself repeatedly in his behavior.[5] Thus, I argue that phonetic plans may not contain feature specifications which would *always* be contradicted when the behavior, corresponding to the plans (forms) in question, is actually carried out. In other words, phonological representations (=phonetic plans) are phonetic representations.[6]

---

[3] Consider another example of human intentional behavior. Suppose a tennis player intends to pass his opponent by striking a backhand cross. Then we would conceive of his plan for this act as including the specifications that could distinguish this kind of shot from other possible shots that the player might choose instead. It would be odd to conceive of his plan as specifying all the innervations needed for bringing about all the required movements of muscles, joints, etc., given that the player has a certain point of departure for his action.

[4] We are talking here about a fully mature, competent speaker, cf. end of §2.4.2, ch. 11.

[5] Otherwise the notion of plan or intention would become completely vacuous (cf. for example, Allwood 1976: 15). One may of course make the quite different claim that in phonology, and linguistics as a whole, we are dealing with subconscious intentions or causes, much as in psychoanalysis. Cf. §1.4.2 for a rejection of this position.

[6] Of course, we cannot demonstrate by proof that phonological forms cannot be very abstract, e.g. such that they are contradictory to actual phonetic behavior as is often the case with OGPh type forms. However, it is easy to show the absurdities involved in such proposals.

To take an illustrative and very typical example, Chomsky & Halle (1968) postulate a vowel shift rule which obligatorily switches feature specifications for all vowels in English. A segment with a phonetic feature value $[\alpha F_i]$ is supposed to be phonologically

3.3 The nature of phonetic plans

3.3.1 *Word-form invariance*

Invariant morphemes are not phonetic entities, as they are conceived of in, e.g., orthodox generative phonology (OGPh). Therefore, phonetic plans cannot be associated with morpheme-invariants. Instead, they are associated with 'concrete forms', i.e. word forms (or possibly stems or morphs, i.e. parts of word forms). That word forms are the proper 'domain' of phonetic plans will be further argued in ch. 8.

3.3.2 *Phoneticity*

Obviously the assumption that phonological representations are phonetic representations has a number of implications as to what kind of features may be part of them.

structured as $[-\alpha F_i]$; thus, *mite* [máit] would be phonologically /mīt/, and *meet, meat* [mīt] would similarly be /mēt/ and *mate* [méit] similarly /mǣt/. They discuss 'exchange rules' (cf. §10.10.2) at several places (1968: 256–9, 355–7) and conclude that 'exchange rules ... should be no more restricted than other types of phonological rules' (259. Cf. also Kiparsky 1965: 12ff). Some scholars have indeed argued that such rules may be involved in speech production. Drachman (1972) argues:

'... a train of processes for a given segment or segment-sequence in phonology does not result in a corresponding train of overt motor activity. Rather, only the segment-representations available at the output of the final process can be the basis for signals to the appropriate cranial nerves and thus commands to the speech tract ... let me illustrate with an unambiguous example: thus, in "divine" neither the underlying /ī/ nor any intermediate stage, but only the final output /āi/ is responsible for a signal for tongue-movement. The claim remains, that is, that the discharge to the final common command path (the cranial nerves) is under the control of the central neuron representing a particular linguistic segment. But there is a special constraint on the system that scans the space-pattern of the central system (cf. Lashley 1951); *excitation is suspended until the entire process-train has been scanned* (1972: 6) (my italics). Thus, in speech production we would go through an entire – and sometimes very long – and real derivation 'in vain' before any neural command to the speech organs can be triggered. Drachman (1972) claims that we can find analogues in the neurophysiology of certain lower animals to certain mechanisms, which seem to be needed in order to explain speech production, but he admits that 'it is difficult to find any analog in the lower systems for precisely this last quality, viz. the constraint "excite the final output only"' (1972: 6).

Chomsky & Halle (1968: 256) seem to base their argument for the reality of exchange rules, and hence for the reality of phonological forms absolutely violating the invariance condition, on the fact that we do not need all phonetic data to identify the words of an utterance. Compare, in this context, McCawley's (1974) pertinent comments: 'CH gratuitously assume that changes without information loss [e.g. as in the English vowel shift case] always impair intelligibility less than changes with information loss [e.g. when all vowels are replaced by only one vowel, cf. Chomsky & Halle 1968: 256: 'it is well-known that intelligibility is only moderately affected in normal everyday speech even when all vowel contrasts are eliminated and a single vowel is made to stand in their

3.3.2.1 *Non-phonological features.* The phoneticity of plans means that they should be specified entirely in phonetically-based phonological features (like the features of Jakobson, Fant & Halle 1952; Jakobson & Halle 1956; Chomsky & Halle 1968; or Ladefoged 1971a) to the exclusion of all other kinds of features such as morphological and lexical features (e.g. [+foreign], [+Latin] or Chomsky & Halle's (1968: 223 and passim) Romance /k/ and /d/, written as /k^d/ and /g^d/, where 'd' means 'derivable'), rule features and other diacritic features. On the other hand, such features may of course be associated with forms in the lexicon; see the discussion of morphophonological and other features in §4.4. It is important to distinguish properly between information which is part of phonological forms and other information which may be needed in deriving, i.e. constructing, phonological forms (§4.4, §7.3, ch. 13).

3.3.2.2 *Boundaries.* Are grammatical boundaries present in phonetic plans? After all, word forms, and sometimes morphs, are recognized as units of phonetic behavior, and boundaries between such units are often phonetically manifested. One can therefore argue that boundary features be interpreted as cover features for those phonetic properties

place'] an assumption which is directly contradicted by Miller's experiments in which speech where front and back vowels had been interchanged was found practically unintelligible but became quite easy to understand when played through a filter which removed the locus of the front–back distinction (the second formant): I am sure that anyone who has heard tapes of speech whose spectrum had been reflected around an axis of 1500 Hz finds it immeasurably harder to understand than filtered speech. [cf. Blesser 1969] Evidently speakers find it easier to fill in missing information (which they do anyway in their normal use of language) than to correct "wrong" information, and some changes without information loss do impair intelligibility' (McCawley 1974: 73–4).

One may in this context add the general remark that it is rather absurd to claim the possibility of a semiotic system in which the allegedly 'real' and relevant expression features of certain signs are always contradicted by their actual manifestations 'on the surface'. Suppose, for example, that in the ordinary system of traffic signal lights, the different lights are reinterpreted so that the function of green ('go') is taken over by the yellow light, and similarly that of yellow ('wait') by red, and that of red ('stop') by green. Then there has occurred a chain of shifts; the different 'meanings' have changed their expressions. It would be nonsense to claim that 'go' is still signalled by green (though it is 'manifested' as yellow), that 'wait' is signalled by yellow, etc. Yet, Chomsky & Halle (1968) do claim that [aɪ] is still phonologically /ī/, [ij]/ē/, and [êɪ]/æ/ in contemporary English phonology!

For other arguments concerning the English vowel shift rule and the underlying forms implied by it (as described by Chomsky & Halle), see the various articles in Goyvaerts & Pullum (1975).

which may constitute the manifestations of the intended or recognized boundaries.[7] Of course, grammatical boundaries (e.g. morph boundaries) which cannot be phonetically manifested should *not* appear in phonetic plans. It has been suggested (Nyman 1977: 180) that grammatical boundaries could be eliminated from phonological forms altogether, since they are never directly relevant for phonological processes. Instead, we would have syllable boundaries. It is quite clear that many phonological processes are defined relative to syllable boundaries (cf. for example, Basbøll 1974, 1977b; Hooper 1976), and also that, in careful speech, grammatical boundaries, in as far as they are phonetically manifested, coincide with syllable boundaries (while in more casual styles syllable boundaries are moved according to natural syllabification processes). However, Nyman's proposal could be accepted only if *all* phonetically manifested boundaries coincide with syllable boundaries. I do not think that this condition is met.[8] For example, under emphasis there may be length differences between Sw. *valls* [val::s] (gen. of *vall* 'wall') – *vals* [val:s] ('waltz'), *vällt* [vɛl::t] (supine of *välla* 'to well') – *vält* [vɛl:t] (supine of *välta* 'to upset') etc.; thus, the morph boundary before the /t/ or /s/ ending is signalled through the lengthening of the stem-final consonants, without the endings constituting syllables of their own (cf. also §3.3.5).

3.3.3 *Concreteness*

The proposal that phonological representations be thought of as phonetic plans will, as we just noted, entail assumptions of concreteness. However, plans are set up on the basis of perceptually abstracted information and hypotheses about the underlying realities behind other speakers' articulatory behavior. What guarantee is there that perception is not based upon principles which may in fact make the plans quite 'abstract'? The answer is of course that there is no such guarantee but that, in the light of the many arguments to be given, it seems extremely implausible. Perception involves abduction (hypotheses-and-testing)

[7] The use of unitary boundary features may be perceptually justified, since the manifestation of the higher level (grammatical) boundary may be a non-analyzed whole at the level of phonetic plans. Similar justifications have been advanced for other phonological cover features, e.g. [+syllabic] (Cf. Ladefoged 1971b). Cf. also Lass (1976: 186–97).

[8] In addition, grammatical categories may of course influence the applicability of articulatory reduction rules (§10.7.1.2), but this is irrelevant to the present discussion, since no one suggests that grammatical categories are part of phonological forms.

but there is no reason to believe in those very intricate analysis-by-synthesis strategies presupposed by the OGPh theory (Halle & Stevens 1959; Stevens & Halle 1967; Chomsky & Halle 1968: 24; Chomsky 1969: 52). For one thing, OGPh is based upon the theory of morphemes as phonological invariants, which is entirely unmotivated (see chs. 9, 12). Moreover, it would presuppose very special acquisition devices (as are indeed postulated by Chomsky); well-known human capacities of discrimination, generalization and regularity extraction from the physically present environment would not suffice at all (cf. Derwing 1973: 201, 310; Braine 1974, etc.). I will return to these issues repeatedly below.

Thus, we can characterize plans as 'concrete'. However, concreteness is a relative matter, and we could just as well argue that plans are 'abstract', i.e. abstract with respect to the actually occurring phonetic manifestations. There are two sources of this abstractness. Thus, though the same word form may be pronounced and perceived at many levels of accuracy, I will argue that there is evidence for assuming:

(a) that the phonetic plan refers to the most *careful pronunciation* that the speaker is acquainted with (§3.3.4, §3.4)

(b) that the phonetic plan is not a fully specified plan (of the most careful pronunciation) (§3.2); rather it is *categorical* and specifies only some perceptually fundamental features (from which other feature specifications can be deduced) (§3.3.5).

3.3.4 *Reference to careful pronunciations*

There are several good reasons to assume that phonetic plans refer to some kind of careful pronunciations (see §3.3.4.2). However, before I can go into these matters, the notion of 'careful pronunciation' needs some clarification.

3.3.4.1 *Careful pronunciation vs. elaborated pronunciation.* It appears

that one can pronounce 'carefully' or 'exactly' in at least two different ways or with two different aims in mind.[9] Thus, I will distinguish between *careful pronunciation* (in a restricted sense) and *sharpened* or *elaborated pronunciation*.

On the one hand, speakers can try to pronounce the words carefully in order to keep the different words (with their different meanings)

---

[9] I am indebted to Håkan Eriksson for making me aware of this.

phonetically distinct. This happens, for example, in a situation where a speaker is aware of the fact that a certain word can be mistaken for another, phonetically very similar word. Then, the speaker may deliberately try to avoid the possible neutralization with the other word(s), thus making his pronunciation(s) distinct.[10] This is what I shall mean by 'careful pronunciation'. As I will argue below, phonetic plans concern these careful pronunciations.

On the other hand, one may sometimes want to articulate *the sounds* of the various words pronounced very clearly and distinctly. This may be done without any particular attention to the meanings of the words, i.e. one does not primarily aim at keeping different *words* distinct. In fact, this kind of sound-focusing articulatory accuracy often leads to sharpening of certain sound types (allophones) and to neutralizations of phonemic distinctions. I will refer to such pronunciations as sharpened or elaborated pronunciations.

A few examples are necessary. Consider, e.g., the French words *nier* 'deny' and *briller* 'shine'. Clearly, these words are phonologically distinct in that *nier* ends in /ie/ and *briller* in /ije/. In careful pronunciation this distinction is brought out (and the words are also reduced in fast speech in different ways). However, in elaborated pronunciation *nier* becomes [ni·'je·], i.e. the /i/ is lengthened and a hiatus-breaking [j] is inserted, thus making the word rhyme with *briller*. As another example, compare Swedish *snabbt* (neuter form of *snabb* 'quick') and *slappt* (neuter form of *slapp* 'sloppily'). These forms can be kept distinct, i.e. [snab̥ːt] vs. [slapːt]. Obviously, this distinction must be present in the respective phonetic plans. However, in lexical pronunciation, or when a speaker wants to articulate the sounds very clearly, [b̥] in *snabbt* may be sharpened, thus becoming [p], and the two words will rhyme (cf. §5.2.5).

Thus, in overprecise, elaborated pronunciations there may apply certain *sharpening processes* which in fact neutralize distinctions which are present in other (careful, and also in reduced) pronunciations in connected speech (and hence *also* part of the phonetic plans). Sharpening rules often affect word-final segments, and apply most probably in pronunciations of isolated word forms, or when the word is

[10] I disregard here the fact that this is often not the most effective way of making oneself understood in situations of possible misunderstanding. It may be better to avoid the problematic words altogether, or to explain what one has in mind by means of circumlocutions or references to spelling distinctions and the like.

stressed, perhaps contrastively, and/or is phrase-final. German (or Dutch) final tensing seems to be a case. Here, word-final obstruents are devoiced and tensed ('sharpened', cf. 'verhärtet'), so the distinctions /p/ ↔ /b/, /t/ ↔ /d/, /k/ ↔ /g/, /s/ ↔ /z/ are neutralized. Yet these distinctions are, or may be, present in more reduced forms in connected speech, as shown by Kohler (1977).[11]

Some of the sharpening rules are conventionally restricted to certain speaking styles, e.g. recitation of poetry. I will discuss these rules in §10.3.2.

One should be aware of the fact that careful and elaborated pronunciations are not always easy to distinguish in actual speech performance. Careful pronunciations may be difficult to elicit; it is difficult to get a speaker to pronounce carefully *all* the details of the sound shape of a word form in one and the same realization. Note that something similar applies to the listening process; it seems impossible to attend to all phonetic properties of the pronunciation of a word at the same time.

Finally it must be emphasized that maximally careful pronunciations need not be, and are very often not, the most frequent or normal pronunciations of the word forms involved. On the contrary, they will often be somewhat artificial and pedantic, particularly perhaps in languages that have heavy stresses and thus normally a great deal of reduction (e.g. English, Danish, Russian). In such cases, it may be that speakers may even construct full-vowel plans which are virtually never realized as such.[12]

3.3.4.2 *Arguments for the primacy of careful pronunciations.* The hypothesis that phonetic plans refer to maximally careful pronunciations can be justified on different grounds:

(a)   It seems to fit intuition. When speakers are asked to give the pronunciation of a word form, they tend to give it in its most articulated form, since giving a reduced rendition would leave out

---

[11] Note that I am talking about tensing in German, not devoicing, which occurs syllable-finally; cf. §10.7.2.3:(9). It should be pointed out that if Kohler is correct, I have given an inaccurate account of this German case in earlier works (Linell 1974a: 92–4; 1974b: 209–10, also 1976a: 12–14).

[12] Something like this has been argued for Russian by Derwing 1973: 191ff; Braine 1974: 290 and Darden 1976: 111–12, for Palauan and English by Schane (1974: 300), and for Breton by Dressler (1972a). Possibly, such abstractness may be due to conventional orthography.

some parts of the knowledge they have. (Note however, that certain details of phonetic plans are sometimes not completely carried out in 'lexical pronunciations' (when word forms are pronounced in isolation) §3.3.4.1).

(b) One can derive reduced variants from the maximally segmentalized variant, but not always vice versa, since some articulatory reduction rules are neutralizing.

(c) In perception, there seems to be a common process of reinterpreting more structure into the perceived phonetic signals than is actually present in reduced speech (§3.6). Likewise, speakers seem to believe that they articulate more carefully than they actually do (cf. §3.5).

(d) People's intuitions about what are phonologically permissible, i.e. pronounceable, forms in the language are clearly based upon careful pronunciations (see §6.2.2).

(e) There is also behavioral evidence that conditions on careful pronunciations sometimes have interesting consequences for the nature of reduction, whereas conditions on some level of reduced pronunciations have no such status (cf. §6.3.2).

(f) In practice, most traditional, structuralist and generative discussions of the phonology of languages have, often implicitly, been restricted by and large to careful pronunciations, which indicates that linguists have taken these to be *the* phonetic data of the language.

3.3.5 *Categoricalness*

It is well-known that perception tends to be categorical. We tend to perceive *structures* in the physical environment, where variation and continuancy are more typical than structure, invariance and discreteness. Often, perceptual categories ('things', 'properties', 'processes' to speak in everyday-language terms) are functional in some way; something is perceived as an entity because it is useful to single it out as an entity. There is no reason to think that the perception of speech and the assignment of linguistic structure are different; rather, it is commonly assumed that there is *more* structure and categoricalness in language and speech than in other areas. For a person to develop a phonetic plan of a certain word form, it is necessary first to assign perceptually a structure to the speech signals in which he hears the word being realized by other speakers. Thus, I assume that phonetic plans are perceptually defined (§ 2.4.2). There are reasons to suspect that they are not fully specified for all the phonetic details of the corresponding manifestations:

(a)   not all properties are linguistically relevant
(b)   perception *in general* is categorical (cf. above)
(c)   there is no need to assign properties which are entirely predictable from other properties (cf. however, below)
and, most importantly:
(d)   there is evidence from, e.g., perception experiments, child language, historical changes of languages, etc. that not all features are attended to to the same extent.

As for the crucial question of exactly *how* phonetic plans are structured, it is hard to propose any definite answers. However, there seems to be strong evidence that *surface phonemic contrasts* (between careful pronunciations) are very important in this context (ch. 5). On the other hand, we must be careful not to assume aprioristically that some particular, purely structurally defined notions of phonemic contrast, distributional constraints, economy, symmetry of inventories, etc. are exclusively relevant for speakers' phonetic plans. For example, a good case can be made for a certain *redundancy* in lexical items (§4.2.2). Thus, there may be limits to the applicability of argument (c) above, i.e. that predictable properties are absent from phonetic plans. Quite a few features are predictable or redundant (in a strictly structural sense), especially if we are allowed to use non-phonological information in deriving (predicting) them.[13] Some of these predictable features may well be present in phonetic plans. A good example is word stress, which in many languages is largely derivable from the morphological and syllabic structure of the forms involved. It is however difficult to imagine a phonetic plan without any, prosodic pattern at all. In fact, there is evidence that the prosodic patterns of words are stored in the memory; people often recall the prosody better than the segmental structure of words (cf. the so-called tip-of-the-tongue phenomenon, Brown & McNeill 1965).

As another case for a certain redundancy in phonetic plans, consider length of vowels and consonants in Swedish, which is partly predictable from stress and the segmental structure of morphs. The location of

---

[13] And of course even more so if underlying forms are made very abstract and, hence, also more easily manipulated.

stress is also largely predictable (Linell 1972). However, there is no agreement as to the proper description of these facts.[14] In Linell (1974b: 214–5) I argued for a particular interpretation of a solution that is basically that of Eliasson & La Pelle (1973); assuming that consonant length in morphs with only one postvocalic consonant (e.g. *vis* 'wise' /vis/ vs. *viss* 'certain' /vis:/ (or in a different notation: /viss/)) is non-predictable, we can formulate the following two rules:

(1) IF:

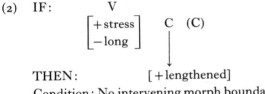

THEN: [+long]

Conditions: An underlyingly long consonant is equivalent to two consonants with respect to this rule. C must be [−son] if followed by a sonorant, cf. Eliasson & La Pelle (1973)

(2) IF:

$$\begin{bmatrix} V \\ +\text{stress} \\ -\text{long} \end{bmatrix} \quad C \quad (C)$$

THEN: [+lengthened]

Condition: No intervening morph boundary

From a purely structural point-of-view, this type of solution minimizes redundancy in the underlying phonological forms.[15] However, it is quite abstract, (Eliasson & La Pelle (1973) in fact assume that length is never underlyingly present, i.e. neither in vowels nor in consonants, which is only possible given the assumption of underlying geminates) and some would prefer to have vowel length unpredictably present (underlying) in phonological representations (e.g. *vis* /vi:s/ vs. *viss* /vis/ or /vis:/) (cf. most classical structuralists, e.g. Witting 1959, 1977). Indeed, there are good arguments that both stress and vowel length are

[14] For discussion of the regularities involved, see Elert 1970; Linell 1972, 1974b, 1978b; Eliasson & La Pelle 1973; Bannert 1974; Hellberg 1974; Karlsson 1977; Witting 1977.

[15] For arguments in favor of this solution, see Eliasson & La Pelle (1973). One of my reasons for accepting a modified version of this theory in Linell (1974b) was the apparent need for two degrees of consonant length (cf. examples in §3.3.2.2), which would here be accounted for in terms of underlying length and allophonic lengthening derived by (2). However, if, instead, vowel length is considered to be present in phonetic plans (cf. p. 60), these distinctions in consonant length can be predicted, given the location of morph boundaries (cf. §3.3.2.2).

very important features in speech production and perception (e.g. Bannert 1974; Witting 1977). Consonant length, on the other hand, is less clearly marked phonetically and is traditionally regarded by most analysts as allophonic. This solution is also supported by evidence from transfer in foreign languages, slips of the tongue, etc. (Linell 1978b). The assumption that vowel length is present in the phonetic plans of Swedish words means that some redundant features are specified there (for example, vowel length is predictable in a stressed syllable if no consonants follow, e.g. *bi* 'bee' /bi:/).[16] The general conclusion would be that predictability alone is not necessarily a sufficient condition for removability from phonetic plans.[17]

3.4 The existence of alternative plans

So far I have argued that there is only one phonetic plan for each semantically and grammatically specific word form, in spite of the fact that such a form can be pronounced in many ways, e.g. at several levels of articulatory accuracy. I have assumed that this plan refers to a maximally careful pronunciation. However, things are not so simple. There are words which seem to have several distinct careful pronunciations, and for which the speaker presumably has alternative plans stored.

Some typical examples of such words are the following. Some function words have at least two forms, one strong form and one weak, most often clitic, variant, e.g. French *moi*, /mwa/ *toi* /twa/ etc. vs. *me* /mə/, *te* /tə/ etc. Though phonologically related, such forms must be assumed to be different lexical entries, i.e. they have different phonetic plans. Sometimes, words have distinct pronunciations in natural spoken language and in formal 'spelling pronunciations', e.g. Sw. [mɛj:, dɛj:] etc., vs. [mi:g, di:g] etc. for *mig*, *dig* ('me, you'). (These all belong to the standard language; I will consider dialect mixtures below.) Furthermore, in cases of 'phonemic' (as opposed to 'allophonic') variation, e.g. Engl. [ì:kənɔ́mɪks] vs. [èkənɔ́mɪks] *economics*, [i:ðə] vs.

---

[16] Our solution implies that we have a rule for vowel length (which is considerably less general than (1)), which should be regarded as a phonotactic rule stating predictable, though still present, properties of phonetic plans (§10.3.1), and two rules for consonant length, one stating the obligatory lengthening of consonants after short stressed vowels (a perceptual redundancy rule?, cf. §10.3.3) and perhaps one for extra lengthening under emphasis (a sharpening rule?). See Linell (1978b).

[17] Cf. also discussion in §4.2, §5.2.3 and §10.3.1–3.

[âιðə] *either*, Sw. [çans, çaŋs, ʃans, ʃaŋs] *chans* 'chance', etc., variants are normally perceived as distinct pronunciations rather than variants of the same pronunciation (§5.2.1). Accordingly, these should presumably also be assigned distinct phonetic plans.

The greatest problems, however, arise in cases of speakers who master several related dialects. Such speakers are very common in modern industrialized states. Most typical is the speaker who knows his own vernacular (primary dialect) and the official standard language, but sometimes speakers know several non-standard dialects too. Sometimes, the primary vernacular simply represents a more casual and reduced level of pronunciation, and in such cases the learning of standard forms mainly implies that the speaker becomes acquainted with more careful and segmentalized pronunciations. This would then mean that the standard language pronunciations determine his new phonetic plans and talking casual dialect would simply mean that the speaker uses a reduced, relaxed way of only partially realizing these plans. One may argue that this description fits cases like distinct $[t^h]$ vs. [d] in relation to [D] of flapping dialects (*writer, rider*), or $[V\{^n_m\}]$ of Standard German in relation to $[\tilde{V}]$ of Bavarian dialects (*Bahn* [ba:n] vs. [bã:]). However, very often the situation is not so neat. On the contrary, there are reasons to assume that words may get alternative phonetic plans, one for each style or dialect, and that ad hoc adaptive rules are set up for the relations of the secondary dialect to the primary one (§5.2.6).

Unfortunately, there is a large number of boundary cases, the proper analysis of which is uncertain. Take such a common case as the use of different *r*-manifestations, i.e. apical versus uvular or postvelar types, by different speakers (usually but not necessarily belonging to different dialectal groups) of the same language. [r] and [R] types are undoubtedly perceptually similar, which of course is the reason why they are so often functionally equivalent in languages, and it does not seem unmotivated to assume one common representation (/r/) in phonetic plans. At the same time, [r] and [R] must of course be different in speakers' fully specified articulatory plans; they are also reduced in casual speech in quite different ways. However, the language-specific choice of either apical or uvular *r* may sometimes have quite far-reaching repercussions on many phonological processes. Thus, e.g., the occurrence of apical *r* induces alveolarization of dentals in Swedish (a very typical feature of the phonology of the standard language), whereas the uvular *r* of many southern Swedish dialects does not. Considering the fact that alveolarization ('supradentalization') is often obligatory in many words of many Swedish dialects (see §10.6.1), one may, contrary to what was suggested earlier, be inclined to consider the feature [+apical] to be part of the phonetic plans.

To summarize, there are several problems in determining under what conditions different (alternative) phonetic plans have to be postulated. One problem has to do with what factors determine the structure of phonetic plans. At least in some cases (cf. the different *r*-sounds), we may be obliged to impose, in addition to *perceptual equivalence* (supposedly responsible for the categoricalness of plans), a condition of *articulatory homogeneity* (homorganity) of behavioral manifestations.

Furthermore, we do not know under what linguistic and sociolinguistic conditions related dialects are integrated in speakers' competences, and to what extent they may exist distinct from each other, sometimes with adaptive rules accounting for new, often hypercorrect, creations in the secondary dialect. Of course, dialectology has always been and remains a dilemma for structuralists (Dahlstedt 1970). The generative integrated pandialectal model is not psychologically valid (see §5.2.6); facts are much more chaotic. Unfortunately, no principled solution is at hand.

3.5   The role of phonetic plans in speech production

The concepts of phonetic plan and fully specified articulatory plan (in the technical senses adopted in §3.2) are both necessary in an explanatory theory of meaningful grammatical behavior (§2.2). It is worth noting that the planning and monitoring of allophonic details (cf. fully specified articulatory plans of utterances) must also be described in teleological terms. Thus, the pronunciation of an utterance, i.e. the correct execution of an articulatory plan, means that the speaker has to coordinate and time a considerable number of different gestures which must be integrated in such a way that an acoustic signal with a certain intended structure results, and this intended (perceptually defined) structure defines the phonetic and articulatory plans. To perform this, the various motor commands needed for the different gestures must be triggered at different points in time, and this sequence and timing of cerebral events does not correspond in a simple manner to the sequence and timing of the intended articulatory movements and acoustic segments (cf. Lenneberg 1967: 98ff). Thus, we see that the planning of phonetic events is a complicated matter[18] which necessitates a teleological account.

Needless to say, a teleological theory of phonetic behavior must be compatible with facts and theories about causal mechanisms in speech production (cf. §1.4.3). Moreover, there are certainly differences in the degrees to which intentions enter at different levels of the planning process. This is implicit in my theory; conscious intentions are more central at the level of phonetic plans where certain specific words are selected and constructed, and where the speaker must care about keeping these words distinct from other words that could have been selected instead. The full specification of allophonic details, on the other hand, may be assumed to be a much more automatic process. In the phonological model, this is reflected by the fact that perceptual redundancy rules (§10.3.3) automatically fill in predictable features given that certain distinctive properties are present in the phonetic plans. Similarly, the type of articulatory 'reduction' occurring in the actual manifestations can largely be predicted from factors like lack of time, deficient articulatory control (as a consequence of, e.g., nervousness, intoxication, fatigue), inattentive monitoring, cognizance of situational redundancy (the situation may be such that the listener has a good chance to identify the words even if they are pronounced sloppily) or simple laziness, all of which may cause the speaker not to attain, or not to care about trying to attain, a careful pronunciation. However, some conscious planning may enter the execution process too (§3.2); speakers do select their general speaking style. Moreover, the fact that allophonics and articulatory reduction are characterized by many language- (or dialect-) specific details implies that they can be attended to and intentionally governed in some way or another (see ch. 10).

3.6 The role of phonetic plans in speech perception

As Kim (1971: 76) has remarked, 'the area of speech perception is in obscure limbo'. For this reason, I will not make any specific proposals here but only contribute a few observations and speculations pertaining to phonetic plans (see also §2.4). We have already assumed that phonetic plans have a perceptual genesis (§3.3.5). Thus, in acquisition,

---

[18] That articulatory events in speech behavior cannot be explained in terms of simple associative sequential processes is of course well-known in phonetic theory, at least since Lashley (1951).

perception and articulatory intentions are in general ahead of the child's actual articulatory performance (ch. 11). But what role can phonetic plans possibly play in normal speech perception of a competent adult language user?

It seems to me that one can listen to speech sounds in at least two different ways: either simply as sounds, trying to hear the actual phonetic properties that there are, or as meaningful speech composed of words belonging to a language that one knows, i.e. normal speech perception. The first-mentioned ('observer's') approach[19] is of course very difficult to adopt; as is well-known, even when we listen to a foreign language, we cannot entirely avoid being influenced by the perceptual (phonological) habits of our own language. But a child has to register very fine phonetic details in order to acquire an idiomatic pronunciation. He must reach down to register all 'extrinsic allophones' (Tatham 1969); 'a speaker must know ... enough about his language so that there is nothing other than purely automatic, non-linguistic features remaining unexpressed' (Ladefoged 1971b: 53). This presupposes that the child is able to adopt more of a 'phonetic' way of listening.

However, in normal speech perception we adopt 'an agent's' perspective, i.e. in a way we try to take the role of the speaker in an attempt to find out what (words) the speaker could possibly have intended to say. There are two interesting properties of this way of listening:

(a)   it must *not* focus on phonetic properties, but

(b)   the listener generally believes afterwards that he has heard more phonetic structure than was actually present in the physical signal.

In §2.4 I discussed some aspects of (a), noting that conscious attention to the sound structure (which is basically the 'observer's attitude' of above) means that we lose the possibility of immediately recognizing the meaning of the message. What interests us now is (b), since it is there that phonetic and articulatory plans may come in. Thus, it seems to be a fact that listeners are not aware of the very wide range of reduction that actually characterizes many people's normal speech. Indeed, it is a commonplace in the psychology of perception that 'in situations where a subject is presented with insufficient sensory input to provide a

---

[19] Cf. Witting's (1962: 246) concept of 'echoist attitude'.

comprehensible pattern . . . he typically . . . *fill(s) in* the missing information by analogy with his previous experience in similar situations' (Derwing 1973: 209, fn. 1, his italics.)[20] Thus, when listeners are exposed to reduced variants of words in normal communicative situations, they often tend to ignore this reduction and believe that they heard much more fully articulated words in spite of the fact that several sounds and syllables may have been missing.[21] It is somewhat unclear, however, whether the reinterpretation of more structure into signals actually characterizes the process of normal speech perception in itself, or whether it characterizes recall from short-term memory, i.e. what happens when listeners are afterwards asked what words and sounds they heard just before. Whatever the truth is, the phenomenon of reinterpretation may be taken as evidence that phonetic plans have some function in perception and/or recall too. We know that there are arguments for assigning a maximally segmentalized structure to plans (§3.3.4),[22] and the assignment of a similarly rich structure in perception or recall may be explained by the theory of listeners taking the role of speakers, a theory which is well argued for on independent grounds (cf. Mead 1950).[23]

3.7 Appendix: the status of the segment

Of the many questions that could be raised concerning the organization of phonetic plans I will select one for a brief consideration, i.e. the status of segments. Are segments units of plans, or are rather syllables primary? Another possibility is to conceive of plans for word forms as holistic structures. I will review a number of arguments here.

Let me begin by pointing out a difference between features and segments. Segments seem to be the smallest parts that may be observed as 'wholes' (as 'things', if you will). In *see* [si:j] we can perceive two or perhaps three segments which may be looked upon as 'things'. But features like the acuteness or palatality of /i:/ or the stridency of /s/ can hardly be described as anything but properties of the perceived entities.

---

[20] For discussion of this phenomenon, see e.g. Neisser (1967: 108–10, 196).

[21] This can be easily established as a fact if e.g. the listener gets the opportunity of listening carefully, perhaps several times, to tape-recorded speech. He will then detect the discrepancy between what he originally thought that he heard (or, simply, what he in fact heard) and what was actually there to be heard. Cf. Warren (1970).

[22] As for evidence pertaining to misperception and perceptual reinterpretation of deviant phonetic signals, cf. §5.2.13.3.

[23] For a more comprehensive discussion of plans see Linell (1979b).

Therefore, it may be misleading to regard the segments or phonemes merely as sums of their features (simultaneous feature complexes), as in OGPh.[24] The segment, 'the thing', has an emergent gestalt property which cannot be derived from the separate properties.

An argument for the assumption that speakers manipulate segments rather than features in speech production can be derived from observations of slips of the tongue. For example, metatheses, anticipations and perseverations of whole segments are common (see Fromkin 1973). Moreover, all speech errors seem to result in segments and segment combinations that are possible in the language in question. Thus, e.g., in English errors, there never emerge voiceless nasals. If features did play an independent role, one might expect that they could be combined into such ungrammatical segments too.[25]

Dahl (1974b: 59) observes that the reduction of morphemes to mere feature complexes seems to be inconsistent with well-supported assumptions of limitations on the human information-processing systems. Thus, the identification of a morpheme would necessitate a recognition of a large number of binary feature specifications in a very short time, something which seems impossible. Rather, he argues, the information must be coded in terms of larger chunks such as segments. However, this argument is weakened by the fact that just a small fraction of the phonetic information is necessary for successful understanding in normal speech perception (§2.4.4), but it adds to the plausibility of segments *or* (NB) larger units as significant entities.[26]

I have proposed that segments *may* be observed as things, which does not necessarily mean that they normally *are* regarded so. In fact, there are several arguments against the psychological reality of an exhaustive analysis of sound shapes in terms of segments. It is primarily larger sound shapes such as word forms or morphs which are observed in the sound signals. Such forms, but not single segments, carry meanings and are communicative units, which, in all probability, adds to their

[24] Cf. Halle 1962, 1969; Chomsky & Halle 1965: 106–10, 119, 1968: 335–40; Harms 1968: 1.

[25] Fromkin comes to the opposite conclusion. She argues that slips like *bang the nail* → *mang the mail*, *pedestrian* → *tebestrian* exemplify substitutions involving single features; nasality, voicing, etc. (Fromkin 1973: 224–5). However, such slips could also be analyzed in terms of substitutions of whole segments, these substitutions being conditioned by the properties (features) of the segments.

[26] Dahl (1974b) also gives other arguments for the segment. In addition, he shows that Chomsky & Halle (1968), contrary to their own claims, do ascribe some significance to segments.

individuality and thingness. Actually, segments may also be conceived of as properties rather than component parts of the words. For instance, the degree of segmentalization varies among different manifestations of the same word; a feature is sometimes only part of a segment but sometimes realized as a segment of its own. Retroflexion of coronals in Swedish may, e.g., be segmentalized as an independent /r/-segment ([bœ(ː)rd] *börd* 'birth, descent') in overprecise speech as opposed to the more common pronunciation ([bœːɖ]) where it is just a feature (here of [ɖ]). In American English the retroflexion of vowels may also be pronounced as a more or less distinct [ɚ]-segment. In slow and careful speech of many languages a postconsonantal liquid or glide may be realized in such a way that an extra vowel segment emerges, as for example in Sw. *blomma* [bəlùmːa], *kruka* [kərʉ̈ːβka], Engl. *Christ* [kr̩ˈraist, kəˈraist], *sweet* [suˈu̯iːt], *beaut* [biˈi̯uːt]. In Polish /ɲ/ before a stop is often preceded by a glide, e.g. *słońce* [su̯oĩntse], *hańba* [xaĩnba] (Andersen 1972: 36, 39, 40). The examples may easily be multiplied. Moreover, simple segments which occur in the speech of one speaker may often be perceptually interpreted by other speakers, with perhaps another linguistic background, as several segments (perceptual segment splitting), or conversely, several segments may be interpreted as a single unitary segment (perceptual segment fusion) (cf. Andersen (1972) for more data and discussion).

The absolute status as units or 'things' in phonological structurings of segments or phonemes may thus be questioned on the basis of data concerning variations in the pronunciation and perceptual structuring of words. In this context we may also take into consideration the numerous phonetic investigations which seem to show that syllables rather than phonemes or segments are articulatory primes or perceptual decision units. There is an extensive research in this field (cf. Kozhevnikov & Chistovich 1965; Laver 1970; Studdert-Kennedy 1976 and references there). Data on coarticulation support syllables as articulatory units (Kim 1971). Furthermore, stutterers usually stutter, and babblers babble in terms of syllables, not in terms of segments. False starts cannot be corrected before at least one syllable has been emitted (cf. Kim 1971: 61–6). Metatheses in slips also involve syllables, and their parts, as domains; onsets shift with onsets, nuclei with nuclei, codas with codas, never do, say, syllable onsets shift with codas. Furthermore, it has been shown that many phonological regularities (of phonotactic and other natures) may be best formulated within the domain of syllables (Vennemann 1972b; Basbøll 1974, 1977b; Hooper 1976), which also speaks for the syllable as a phonological prime.[27]

Savin & Bever (1970), and similarly Foss & Swinney (1973), have produced other kinds of evidence against the segment as an independent fundamental unit in speech perception. They conducted experiments in which listeners were asked 'to monitor a sequence of nonsense syllables for the presence of a certain linguistic unit, either a phoneme or a syllable, and to respond as quickly as possible when they heard it. The results show(ed) that subjects respond consistently faster when given syllable targets to listen for than when given phoneme targets' (Savin & Bever 1970: 295). The experiments thus showed that phonemes can be identified only after 'some larger linguistic sequence (e.g. syllables or words) of which they are part' (299). Similar experiments by Ahlgren (1975) indicate that word forms, rather than syllables, are the proper decision units in these experimental tasks. Thus, it seems as if phonemes are, so to speak, derived from larger units rather than vice versa. That is, phonemes are segmental properties of syllables or word forms rather than basic units, the mere sums of which constitute syllables and word forms.

Would it then be motivated to deny all psychological reality for segments (phonemes)? No, this seems impossible in the light of all the arguments about phonological systematicity and regularities, many of which cannot be formulated without segments or features, and introspective plausibility which have been advanced by phonologists. Savin & Bever (1970) claim that the reality of phonemes is not based on perception or articulation, but they do think that phonemes are necessary units in a psychological theory of language. They advance as behavioral evidence for phonemes 'the occurrence of alphabetic writing systems, the existence of rhyme and alliteration in non-literate poetry, the natural existence of segmental phonemic spoonerisms and the innumerable well-attested historical changes in language that are described very simply in terms of phonemes and only clumsily and arbitrarily without them' (1970: 301). Bever summarizes: 'Phonemes are "psychologically real", but their level of conscious reality is *derived* from the primary acoustic/articulatory speech unit, which is the syllable' (1977: 179, his italics). Most probably, the ability to segment speech in terms of sound segments is reinforced, in some cases even

[27] Of course, syllables have occasionally been assumed to be phonological primes by scholars of other convictions, cf. for example, Firthian phonology (Firth 1957).

caused, by the process of learning to read (cf. Savin 1972).[28] However, it is also premature to think that the perceptual reality of *larger* phonetic units, e.g. syllables, is proved by the reported experiments, since one may reasonably argue that the difficulties of identifying single segments in perceptual experiments has to do with the fact that phonological details do not arise in focal consciousness in normal perception (cf. McNeill & Lindig 1973).

By way of summary, I would say that the segmental analysis, which is nearly always taken for granted in phonology,[29] is not self-evident. Segments may be perceived as units, but such an analysis is probably *partly* a result of cultural traditions (alphabetical writing, the tradition of talking about sound structure in terms of 'sound types', etc.). There are several facts which speak for the perception of morphs and word forms as phonetic gestalts. In fact, this is precisely what may be expected, given that (morphs and) word forms are communicative and grammatical primes (see especially ch. 8).

[28] Note also that many children have considerable difficulties in learning to read. It takes a long time and much effort before they 'break the code', i.e. discover the phonemic principle underlying alphabetical writing. This would not be expected, if segments were evident elements in natural speech perception.

[29] There are of course some exceptions, such as the Firthian tradition in phonological analysis (e.g. Firth 1957). Cf. also the recent suggestions by Goldsmith (1976).

4 *Phonetic plans and lexical entries*

No language is tyrannically consistent. All grammars leak.
(Sapir 1921: 38)

4.1 Introduction: phonetic plans vs. lexical representations

In ch. 3 I have argued for the necessity of the notion of 'phonetic plan' in a theory of phonology. I have also argued that when we speak about 'the phonological form (structure, representation) of an utterance', we should interpret this expression as referring to the phonetic plan(s) underlying the actually manifested speech signal. Accepting these arguments does *not*, however, imply that phonetic and articulatory plans must be regarded as the *only* kinds of representations of linguistic expression units that may be necessary in phonology. It is *very important to distinguish between phonetic and articulatory plans*, i.e. specifications (of some particular kind, see ch. 3) of the phonetic behavior that the speaker intends to produce, *and lexical representations*, i.e. the totality of the memory-stored phonological and other (i.e. grammatical, semantic) information that is needed for the speaker to construct the phonetic plans. In fact, it is quite clear that the set of possible phonetic plans is not extensionally identical to the set of lexical representations. This is obvious for at least two reasons. First, it seems clear that the speaker has *not* stored all possibly occurring (i.e. constructible) phonetic plans as ready-mades in lexical memory (§ 4.3). Secondly, it is very often the case that the construction of phonetic plans for certain grammatical forms cannot be performed without access to non-phonological lexical information (§ 4.4), and such information is by definition *not* included in the phonetic plans (i.e. the phonological forms) associated with those items which *are* stored in the memory.

In this chapter I will discuss the *phonological aspects of lexical items (lexemes)*. Though I will argue that there *is* evidence that the phonological parts of lexical representations are indeed the phonetic plans of the forms involved, I must stress again that this in no way follows from what I have said so far. Thus, one might perhaps still argue for, e.g., abstract morpheme-invariant (morphophonemic) forms as lexical items. Even if perceptually defined phonetic plans are crucial in articulation, perception and short-term storage (ch. 3), we could still argue that lexical long-term storage involves considerably restructured forms. Moreover, as Hooper has remarked, 'there is no evidence of constraints on what sort of forms may be stored, but only constraints on what sort of forms may be pronounced and perceived, and these affect what is stored' (1975: 556).

It is tempting to think of mental representations of sound gestalts as perceptual 'images' (*'Lautvorstellungen'*) or copies of auditive impressions, and also to argue that these images are stored in the memory. However, there are several conceptual difficulties with such a view.[1] Rather, we should choose more neutral terms and talk about lexical information (semantic, syntactic, morphological, morphophonological and phonological) which allows the speaker–listener to construct phonetic plans. (These may perhaps give rise to conscious *'Lautvorstellungen'* but it is not contended that the construction of 'perceptual images' is necessarily involved in every act of speech production or speech perception (cf. §2.4).) However, I will argue that there *is* some evidence for a very close relation, perhaps even isomorphy, between the lexicalized information about *sound* structure and phonetic plans (§4.3).

4.2 On lexical economy

In OGPh argumentations it is often emphasized that long-term memory must store lexical information in a maximally economic (or 'simple') manner. It is also assumed that the relevant 'simplicity' measure can be characterized in purely linguistic-formal terms. Such general assumptions have led generativists to believe that abstract morphemes have a mnemonic reality.

Arguments of this type seem to be important in OGPh type theories and should be carefully analyzed. However, before we can do that (§4.2.2), we will have to make a short digression to discuss the status of evaluation criteria in metascience (§4.2.1). Their status in generative

---

[1] See in particular Pylyshyn (1973), and also Fodor (1976: 179ff) and Linell (1979b).

linguistics is somewhat confused, since some generativists apparently want to motivate their plea for formal simplicity of competence theories by reference to the allegedly economical functioning of the mind, which amounts to a rather special conception of the role of simplicity in theory-building.

4.2.1 *Economy as a metatheoretical evaluation criterion*

Simplicity (also termed economy, parsimony, Occam's razor) is commonly assumed to be a reasonable evaluation criterion for theories. However, it can hardly be the most important criterion. Most philosophers of science would probably agree that it applies only if there are two or more theories which are equivalent in other respects, more specifically with regard to (i) *exhaustiveness* (both theories cover the same data); (ii) *verisimilitude* (both theories could, according to all available relevant and reliable evidence, be true theories of the data);[2] (iii) *coherence* (both theories are internally coherent and non-contradictory); and, possibly, (iv) *theoretical fit* (both theories are compatible with other, more general or more specific, theories which are known, or assumed, to be true). It goes without saying that two theories are equivalent in all these respects only very seldom. And simplicity never overrides the other criteria (except perhaps, when, for some pedagogical or other practical purpose, a simple theory of some limited area is desired). Consider, for example, exhaustiveness. Obviously, a theory T_1 that covers only a limited set of data (D_1) may often be simpler than a theory T_2 that covers a more extensive set of data (D_2) ($D_1 \subset D_2$). For example, D_1 could be a set of linguistic-structural data (e.g. generalizations concerning contrast and free variation, co-occurrence and other distributional constraints, semantic or grammatical relatedness, etc.), whereas D_2 could comprise D_1 plus a set of 'external' data concerning, e.g., diachronic developments, diatopic variation, psychological and behavioral properties of structures. Clearly, T_1 may well be 'simpler' than T_2, but it would be very odd to prefer T_1 to T_2 on this ground, at least as long as T_1 (or some suitable revision: T_1') has not been shown to cover D_2 as well. Similarly, simplicity could hardly outweigh validity (cf. (ii)). One could not possibly prefer a theory which is demonstrably invalid just because it is 'simple' (or 'elegant', 'interesting').[3]

---

[2]   I.e. the theories have so far not been falsified and seem to be equally plausible.
[3]   Nevertheless, some generativists come close to this. Cf. for example, §12.5.3.

Obviously, simplicity is a very reasonable evaluation criterion which we should certainly not dispose of. But since it must be subordinate to other criteria, it will, in practice, be of very limited importance, once theories are sufficiently developed. In addition, it is often a moot point what should be meant by 'simplicity'. Thus, in modern natural science it is hardly a central notion (cf. Bunge 1963; Harré 1972, etc.); simplicity is a difficult thing! A prolific recent discussion in linguistic theory has also shown the problems in arguing for particular simplicity criteria in linguistics.[4]

Ultimately, the simplicity criterion is based on a metaphysical assumption that Nature is simple. Thus, it does not involve an empirical argument. However, in contemporary linguistic theory there seems to be a common opinion that simplicity of linguistic structure may be empirically motivated. The argument is, as I suggested earlier, that the lexicon and the grammar are maximally economical *because* the memory (and various mental functions involved in speech processes) are, or have to be, simple and economical. (Actually, the latter is simply taken for granted; the claim is never, as far as I know, substantiated.) This way of reasoning is obviously quite different from the usual way of using economy in theory-building and needs to be scrutinized. Thus, I will argue (§4.2.2) that there is no empirical evidence whatsoever for a structure of the mind such that it would support the OGPh type of simplicity of phonological structures.[5]

4.2.2 *Memory storage and economy considerations*

It is rather obvious that the generative assumptions of the economical functioning of the mind are speculative and aprioristic. How, for example, do we know what is considered as simple or economical by the memory or the brain? Which way of storing information is least burdening for the brain? Indeed, why must the brain economize at all? Is it not large enough to admit of 'uneconomical storage'? Such problems are never approached in generative discussions where it is simply taken for granted that it *is* more simple and economical to store a morpheme-invariant form plus information about what happens to this form in various contexts (rules for deriving different phonetic forms) than to

[4] Cf. Braine 1967: fn. 6; Chomsky & Halle 1968: ch. 9; McCawley 1968b; Postal 1968; Wang 1968; Zimmer 1969; Kiefer 1970: 79f; Wurzel 1970: 11–14, 267ff; Linell 1972: 4–9; Chen 1973a,b; Derwing 1973: 135–55, 243–7 Hale 1973: 409ff.
[5] The same holds for generative syntax, although this point will not be argued here.

store concrete forms (phonetic plans) plus information about their various interrelations. That is, it is supposed, e.g., that /divi:n/ plus rules (cf. §1.4.1) is more simple than /divain/, /divin(iti)/ plus rules. The claim is usually based on some way of counting the feature specifications needed in the lexicon and the rule system in the different solutions (Halle 1959; McCawley 1968a: 47–52). But there is no empirical evidence that gross feature countings – even if these could be performed in a consistent and non-arbitrary manner, which seems unlikely – are a realistic simplicity measure of memory storage. Even if 'brute' feature counting is supplemented with some refinements in terms of marked-ness considerations (cf. Chomsky & Halle 1968: ch. 9 and other references given, p. 73, fn. 4) it is highly dubious that such quasi-*quantitative* measures are really decisive. It seems quite reasonable to assume that also qualitative properties of the stored information are essential. And even more importantly, 'economy' is not just a matter of *storage*; the information must also be easily *retrieved* (cf. Derwing 1973: 154, fn. 2). From a functional point-of-view, a redundant lexicon, in which there are many paths of associations between items and in which, consequently, information can be retrieved in many ways, would be more useful than a non-redundant one. Indeed, there is evidence that speakers can search for information in the memory by several parallel strategies.[6] Furthermore, if word forms are stored, rather than abstract morphemes, we would benefit from the concreteness in that the amount of computing necessary in both speech production and speech recognition would, most probably, be drastically diminished (cf. §12.3.3). And, in fact, modern theories of the human memory[7] do not assume that long-term memory storage is subject to any limitations in terms of quantity. The capacity of the brain to store large numbers of items seems very great, if not unlimited. There should be no problems as far as word forms as lexical items are concerned (cf. also Sampson 1970: 620; Braine 1974: 297). Thus, contrary to OGPh claims, there is every reason to suppose that abstract non-redundant storing methods would be quite 'expensive'. Speech recognition probably involves many parallel strategies on different linguistic levels (and a fair amount of guess-work), rather than complex analysis-by-synthesis mechanisms

---

[6] This seems to agree with assumptions of, e.g., processing shortcuts, heuristic routines, parallel derivations, multiple retrieval and matching mechanisms within fields like artificial intelligence and speech understanding.

[7] See works like Tulving & Donaldson 1972; Murdock 1974.

operating on abstract underlying representations.[8] Hörmann argues that 'speech perception is geared more towards a high degree of security of communication than towards a maximal exploitation of channel capacity' (1971:68).

Of course, a concrete theory assuming that word forms (phonetic plans) occur in the lexicon need not imply that *all* word forms, or all allomorphs of morphemes, are lexicalized (§4.3), just as the existence of rules does not necessitate *removing* from the lexicon all allomorphs in favor of unique morpheme-invariants. Several possibilities exist. In fact, it is conceivable that we have both several forms *and* rules, or that we have many rules some of which may make conflicting analyses of data.[9] In any case, the problem of the brain's functioning is an empirical

---

[8] Cf. p. 74, fn. 6.

[9] The idea of maximal integration and economy in grammar and lexicon is an integrating element of the structuralist conception of language (*langue*) as a *closed* system (*où tout se tient*). According to general systems theory (e.g. von Bertalanffy 1968; Emery 1969) closed systems are generally ascribed stability, equilibrium, integration and an economical way of functioning. Such systems, the models of which are usually fetched from mechanical systems or living organisms, have often been used in psychological and sociological theory. But it has also been claimed that many problems of psychology and sociology are better regarded as problems of *open* systems. A speaker's grammatical competence is such an open system into which new elements can be introduced without being fully integrated. Hence a certain instability and certain conflicts may characterize the system. The concomitant adaptivity to new situations – also a characteristic of open systems – is an inherent property of language (cf. Anttila 1972b, Coseriu 1974). Sapir (1921: 38) formulated the same insight in his famous words 'No language is tyrannically consistent. All grammars leak'. This means that linguistic theory must 'break down the "down-traded" identification of structuredness with homogeneity' and realize that language is 'a structured (orderly) heterogeneity' (Weinreich, Labov & Herzog 1968: 101, 151). Very few generativists have explicitly abandoned the assumption of a more or less monolithic, completely integrated closed system as a model of linguistic competence (but cf. Bever 1970: 196; Klima 1972: 59–60; Hale 1973: 457). Yet, it seems plausible that different grammar fragments coexist in the same speech community and even in the same speaker's mind and that the same data can sometimes be given conflicting though presumably psychologically valid analyses (cf. §1.5.6). Note that the notion of the same integrated grammar occurring in the minds of all speakers of a completely homogeneous speech community (cf. Chomsky 1965: 3) makes many historical changes incomprehensible. 'Each historical change would have to be conceived of as a willful distortion of the inherited pattern, which would be absurd' (Andersen 1969: 828). Furthermore, if speech communities were homogeneous, changes would have to occur throughout the entire community at one and the same time which we know they do not (cf. Itkonen 1974: 315). Instead, historical change presupposes variation. 'Competing regularities' within grammars in the community may often be a characteristic and a source of historical changes (Wang 1969; King 1975). There are also various kinds of evidence, e.g. from dialectology (Luelsdorff 1971; St Clair 1973), linguistic games (Sherzer 1970), psycholinguistic

issue, and nothing in terms of economy, generality or naturalness must be taken for granted. The little evidence that there is clearly seems to support the assumption of a redundant lexicon of concrete lexical items (§4.3).[10] With regard to generativist simplicity considerations, one must say that they are, after all, purely formal and *not* empirical (in any reasonable sense of the word). Derwing aptly concludes that 'transformationalists are simply convinced that their opinions [concerning simplicity and naturalness] . . . are essentially correct, though there is no empirical evidence in support of their convictions' (1973 : 153).

4.3 The phonological properties of lexical items

4.3.1 *Alternatives*
We assume that a speaker's grammar must contain certain lexical building-blocks and various grammatical operations to be applied to these building-blocks when utterances with certain intended phonological, syntactic and semantic–pragmatic properties are constructed. What properties do lexical items have? In particular, what are their *phonological* properties? There seem to be three principal possibilities:

The lexicon contains:

(a) all phonetic plans of surface forms with which the speaker is acquainted   cf. proposal by Vennemann (1974b)

(b) a subset of phonetic plans of surface forms (stems and/or base forms)   most favored alternative in 'traditional' accounts

(c) entities that are more abstract than phonetic plans of surface forms, e.g. morpheme-invariants.   proposed by, e.g., OGPh

4.3.2 *Vennemann's theory of the lexicon*
The alternatives of §4.3.1 are given in the order of 'decreasing redundancy'. The (c) alternative is the one I am arguing against

experiments (Zimmer 1969: 11–12; M. Ohala 1974) and observations of productivity (Skousen 1975a: 200–2), which all support the idea of different grammars in the speech community. We also know that there are many structural regularities which are easily identified in a 'purely linguistic-structural' analysis but which are seldom or never part of the native speakers' internalized grammars (e.g. Hsieh 1970; Skousen 1975b, see also §4.3.3.4). See also p. 238, fn. 26.

[10] Not surprisingly, Chomsky denies this: 'Plainly, one can draw no conclusions from the

throughout this book, and (b) is the one being propagated. Presently I will consider Vennemann's[11] 'maximally redundant' proposal according to which virtually all word forms, plus idiomatic phrases and sentences, are stored in the speaker's lexicon. In this theory, entire paradigms are listed in the lexicon, and the regularities of paradigms are captured by rules 'which function entirely as redundancy rules for forms already registered in the lexicon, and as generative rules only when unknown words are adapted to the lexicon, or new words are created by a speaker' (Vennemann 1974b: 349). 'The generative use of the rules [would be] limited to the spontaneous creation of new words and their analysis, the adaptation of foreign words, and pathological application (speech errors)' (369).

I find this theory quite unrealistic. It hardly fits the intuitive experience of sentence production to say that word forms are not created, 'formed', but rather drawn from a lexicon of ready-made forms. Hesitation phenomena, introspection over slow, controlled speech, etc. are better explained in a theory with productive morphological processes. There are numerous cases, when speakers undoubtedly know, i.e. have stored, correct (maybe irregular) forms, but still now and then spontaneously produce incorrect forms according to productive (regular) patterns. This situation is perhaps most typically exposed in foreign language performance, but the same phenomenon also occurs in slips and aphasia (e.g. forms like *knowed*, *haved* in English slips, cf. Fromkin 1973: 28, 266) and in young children's performance. Vennemann could of course argue that in such cases the memorized forms have simply become temporally inaccessible. But when it comes to speech errors, his position is more endangered. Vennemann argues that morphological rules are applied in speech errors but not in correct speech production. However, there are extensive regularities in slips (Fromkin 1973) which must be due to some regular processes. Speech errors are not committed on purpose; rather we must assume that there are productive processes going on in *normal* speech and that it is these processes which go wrong in slips.[12]

lack of any substantive theory of memory or learning' (1975a: 231–2, fn. 3). Of course, absolutely no definite conclusions can be drawn, but I would contend that most people in the field would agree that to the extent that *anything* can be said, this very definitely speaks against Chomsky's proposals.

[11] Also espoused by Rudes 1976; Leben & Robinson 1977, and others

[12] In cases where extensive experimental tests on morphological rules have been carried out Vennemann's position is not confirmed (Haber 1975; Derwing & Baker 1976).

4.3.3   *Stem and base form theory*

What evidence is there for the (b) alternative, which is adopted in this work and which is also the traditional one?[13] Recall that this theory assumes that, in cases of productive patterns, only certain word forms ('base forms') or *parts* of word forms (stems) are stored.[14] (Besides, many larger structures, i.e. phrases,[15] are of course also stored. In cases of irregular and non-productive patterns, suppletion must be assumed, cf. Hudson 1974.)

4.3.3.1   *Methodological aspects.* First, it should be pointed out that if the word form theory (b) is an empirically viable alternative, then there are purely metatheoretical reasons to prefer it to the abstract morpheme theory (c). For in a theory of phonology we would surely prefer descriptions and explanations in terms of pronunciations and percepts of sound signals, and plans, rules, etc. pertaining to observable behavior, since these are entities of which we have some independent understanding. By contrast, if we build our theories upon abstract morphemes and morphophonological rules, the psychological and behavioral interpretation of which is poorly or not at all understood, we get explanations of a formal and not very substantial kind (cf. Botha 1971; Linell 1974a: 148–9).[16] Indeed, the concept of 'morpheme' as a phonological invariant is fraught with methodological and conceptual difficulties (see §12.3).

4.3.3.2   *Polymorphemic structures in the lexicon.* The view that the speaker's lexicon consists only of separate morphemes is contrary to both semantic and morphological facts. There have to be many polymorphemic structures stored as units. Thus, it is a typical property of most derived words and compounds that their meanings are *not* completely predictable from the meanings of their constituent morphemes. For example, a *blackbird* is not just any bird which is black. There is hardly any difference in meaning between the Swedish verbs *titta* 'to look' and *kika* 'peep, have a look' which can account for the

---

[13] Vennemann (1974b: 354) claims that his position (cf. §4.3.2) is quite traditional, something which I find hard to believe.

[14] I will not discuss the choice between base forms and stems here. See Linell (1976b: 7–8) for some discussion. Cf. also Matthews (1974).

[15] For some properties of lexicalized phrases, see Anward & Linell (1975).

[16] Some generativists do not seem to appreciate this point at all. Compare, e.g., the statements by Lightner (1971) quoted on p. 6, fn. 14.

difference between *tittare* 'voyeur' or 'TV spectator' (i.e. a human agent) and *kikare* 'binoculars' (i.e. an instrument). Independent occurrences in the lexicon of constituent morphemes are out of the question in the case of *cran-* (*cranberry*), *cray-* (*crayfish*) type morphemes. Furthermore, the applicability of many non-productive derivational patterns is not predictable. That is, speakers must simply know that the deadjectival nouns related to Sw. *lång* 'long', *svår* 'difficult', *varm* 'hot' and *fet* 'fat' are *längd, svårighet, värme* and *fetma* (instead of the productive types **långhet, *svårhet, *varmhet, *fethet*). There is no point in, e.g., arguing that *fetma* does not occur in the lexicon and that, instead, *fet* would be marked as [+ma − Deriv.]. Sometimes, derived or compounded forms have phonological and/or morphological properties other than the base word. Thus, Sw. *tapetsera* 'paper (walls)' (v.) contains an inexplicable /s/ (the expected form would be **tapetera*), *snickra* 'do carpentry work' has an /r/ which is missing in *snickare* 'carpenter' (cf. *ockra* 'practise usury' − *ockrare* 'usurer' both with the /r/), *bagare* 'baker' a /g/ instead of /k/ as in *baka* 'bake', etc. In French, *héros, Hitler* contain an *h aspiré*, but this is not true of *héroïne, hitlérisme*, etc. Thus, the *h aspiré* cannot be an invariant property of the root morpheme. Often, base words exhibit an irregular morphology but words derived from them do not; Sw. *land, länder* 'country, countries' but *trädgårdsland, -ø* 'garden plot, plots', Fr. *dire, dîtes* 'to say, you say (2. pl. pres.)' but *contredire, contredisez* 'contradict' (for some speakers) (many more examples in Kiparsky 1974). There is clearly a tendency for irregular morphological features of words to get eliminated in derivatives but the specific cases are not predictable by rule; the regular behavior must be known about the specific derivatives as units in their own right.[17]

It should also be mentioned that these linguistic arguments have been corroborated by psychological experimental results. Thus, e.g., Kintsch summarizes:

The purpose of the series of studies presented here was to decide how derivable words are represented in episodic memory. The results were quite unambiguous; it appears that derived nouns (abstract nouns and agent nouns) as well as derived verbs (verbs of saying and verbs of causation) are stored in memory as lexical items in their own right, and are not necessarily decomposed either in comprehending or in memorizing sentences. (1974: 240)

Thus, there are many cases of polymorphemic structures in the

[17] This passage is taken, with slight modifications, from Linell (1976b: 5–6).

lexicon. There is no reason why their phonological structure should be given in terms of concatenated morpheme-invariants, i.e. in unnecessarily abstract forms. But if *these* units are lexically stored as surface forms, there is no reason why other forms should be otherwise stored, i.e. at a much more abstract level of representation, since no particularly important *phonological* differences between these categories exist.

4.3.3.3 *Input of morphological operations I : structural arguments.* The next argument for concrete word forms as lexical items goes as follows. Properties of many productively generated (inflected, derived or compounded) forms are predictable if morphological operations operating on other word forms or stems produce the forms in question[18] but *not* if operations applying to single root morphemes are assumed to produce them. Examples of this are legion in Indo-European inflectional morphology. Consider, e.g., the inflection of Spanish verbs of the *-ar* and *-er* conjugations:

(1)	*-ar-*: Pres. ind.	Pres. subj.	*-er-*: Pres. ind.	Pres. subj.
Sg. 1.	*tomo* 'I take'	*tome*	*como* 'I eat'	*coma*
2.	*tomas*	*tomes*	*comes*	*comas*
3.	*toma*	*tome*	*come*	*coma*
Pl. 1.	*tomamos*	*tomemos*	*comemos*	*comamos*
2.	*tomáis*	*toméis*	*coméis*	*comáis*
3.	*toman*	*tomen*	*comen*	*coman*

Here it is quite obvious that the roots are /tom/ and /kom/ respectively. From these, the correct indicative and subjunctive forms cannot be derived, unless of course they are marked as, e.g., [+a-Conj] and [+e-Conj] or the like. What one needs to know is some specific word form, e.g. 3. sg. pres. ind. (*toma, come*) or the infinitive (*tomar, comer*), or part of a word form (e.g. a stem *toma-, come-*).

Examples like this can easily be multiplied. In morphological theory, they are normally used in arguing for a 'word-and-paradigm' model (cf. Matthews 1974).

Elsewhere (Linell 1976a,b, 1977a) I have discussed several other cases where one needs information about base word forms, not only about morphemes, to derive other forms. A very illustrative case concerns the tonal accents of compounded words in the Malmö dialect of Swedish,

---

[18] The nature of morphological operations will be discussed in ch. 7.

where the accent of the whole compound can be predicted only if one knows the accent of the left constituent, i.e. the accent this constituent has (would have) when (if) it occurs (were to occur) as a separate word form. On the other hand, the accent is *not* predictable from abstract morpheme-invariant forms, unless these are marked with ad hoc diacritics (Linell 1976a: 271–4). As another example, consider Danish imperative formation which is considered to apply to infinitives rather than stems (= root-morphemes). In our model this is only natural. But Anderson (1975) is puzzled by this and similar examples, because they seem to show the necessity of a phonological rule preceding a morphological rule in a derivation of his OGPh type model, where the lexicon is assumed to contain morpheme-invariants. Anderson's and our derivations of the imperative of *bade* 'to bathe' are given here as (2) and (3) respectively:

(2)   Morpheme-inv. repr. of infinitive 'to bathe': /bad + e/[19]
       Phonological rule: /ba:d + e/ (lengthening)
       Morphological rule: /ba:d/ (imperative formation)
       Phonological rule: /ba:ʔd/[20] (stød-insertion)

(3)   A morphological operation gives /ba:ʔd/[20] from the inf. /ba:de/[21]
       The operation can be analyzed as follows:
       Operand: /ba:de/
       Morpholexical rule: /ba:d/ (imperative formation)
       Phonotactic rule (stød): /ba:ʔd/[20,22]

4.3.3.4 *Input of morphological operations 2 : substantive evidence.* The structural evidence brought forward in §4.3.3.3 is not logically conclusive, since one *could* argue that instead of simply using base forms as operands, as we suggested, the speaker could be hypothesized to use abstract morphemes supplemented with all those ad hoc diacritic markings that would be necessary to generate the correct outputs. Therefore, it is important to note that there is rich empirical evidence that speakers *do* use concrete word forms, not abstract morphemes, as operands of morphological operations. In fact, they do this *also* when the abstract morphophonemic 'solution' involves *no* diacritic markings

[19] The vowel is underlyingly short because of the morpheme identity with *bad* [bæð] 'bath' (n.).
[20] /d/ is pronounced as [ð].
[21] For discussion of the analysis of morphological operations, see §7.2–3.
[22] The lengthening rule would also be a PhtR valid for the lexicalized infinitive.

but the concrete 'solution' *does* involve diacritic markings of operand forms.

A paradigm case is Maori passive formation as discussed by Hale (1973). Hale gives the following examples of active and passive verb forms in Maori:

(4) *awhi*   *awhitia*   'to embrace'
     hopu   *hopukia*   'to catch'
     aru   *arumia*   'to follow'
     tohu   *tohuŋia*   'to point out'
     mau   *mauria*   'to carry'
     wero   *werohia*   'to stab'
     patu   *patua*   'to strike, kill'
     kite   *kitea*   'to see, find'

Hale depicts two solutions to the descriptive problem of accounting for passives, i.e. the 'phonological alternative' and the 'conjugation alternative'. The first of these would set up the following underlying morphemes: /awhit/, /hopuk/, /arum/, /tohuŋ/, /maur/, /weroh/, /patu/, /kite/. The morphological rules can then be stated in purely phonological terms:

$$(5) \quad \begin{cases} \text{Pass} \rightarrow \text{-ia} \;/\; C \;+\; \underline{\quad} \\ \qquad\qquad \text{-a} \;\;/\; V \;+\; \underline{\quad} \end{cases}$$

All you need now is a consonant deletion rule which deletes the final consonant when it is immediately followed by a word boundary:

$$(6) \quad C \rightarrow \varnothing \;/\; \underline{\quad} \; \#$$

The other descriptive alternative, 'the conjugation alternative', assumes that the uninflected active forms are underlying stems and that these stems must be diacritically marked for which passive ending they take (/tia/, /kia/, /mia/ etc.).

Every sound generativist would of course prefer the 'phonological' solution (which is in fact 'morphophonological') to the morphological one. Generations of students have been taught that a phonological solution is always — so the theory says — simpler, more significant, correct and elegant (more such honorific adjectives could be enumerated) than a solution which uses diacritic features. However, it appears that there is ample evidence that the psychologically correct solution is the 'conjugation alternative' in the Maori case! I restate only some of Hale's points: (i) nominal stems can often be used as verbal stems in spontaneous discourse; if so, they always take /-tia/ in the passive; (ii) derived causatives always take /-tia/ in the passive even if the basic verb belongs to another conjugation; (iii) compound verbs derived by incorporating a noun from an adverbial phrase take /-tia/ in the passive; (iv) borrowings from English take /-tia/; (v) in general, /-tia/ can be used when the conventional passive termination for a given verb is not remembered. (See Hale 1973: 417.) It is interesting to note that much of this evidence is 'external', having to do with productivity and similar things. Such evidence is evidently needed in most cases if we want to rule out psychologically incorrect solutions. (In the Maori case, there is some marginal 'purely structural' evidence which indicates that the phonological alternative cannot be maintained. Kiparsky (1971: 593) observes that a phonological solution can handle cases like the simple verb *mau ~ mauria* vs. the derived causative *whakamau ~ whakamautia* only in a very clumsy way.) The Maori facts indicate rather beautifully that what speakers do is to operate on the concrete word forms (in this case, the active forms), not on abstract morphemes, and these operations consist, if possible, in the mere addition of affixes to these forms.[23]

The Maori case is not isolated.[24] In fact, it seems quite typical. The historical developments of languages involving analogical levelings can only be explained if we assume that surface forms are stored in the lexicon. For example, Vennemann (1974a) has adduced evidence that Kisseberth's (1969) well-known analysis of Yawelmani vowel harmony and echo verbs, which is structurally well-motivated although it involves positing abstract, absolutely neutralized distinctions, must be rejected in favor of a concrete and less general analysis involving diacritic markings.[25] Other examples can be found in, e.g., Hudson (1974) (Ethiopian Semitic languages) and Skousen (1975b) (French and Finnish); for example, Skousen shows that historical changes and children's perturbations of French irregular verbal inflections are explicable if speakers are assumed to operate on concrete word forms and concrete stems but *not* if they are hypothesized to start out from abstract morphemes à la Schane (1968). I will review yet another illustrative example in §4.4.

[23] The account of Hale's data is taken in extenso from Linell (1976a: 276–7).
[24] For quite similar facts from Kekchi, see Campbell (1974: 274–5).
[25] See Kisseberth's and Vennemann's respective rules for suffix harmony in Yawelmani quoted as (8a,b), p.184–5.

In addition to the evidence from historical developments and from the normal productive use by competent speakers (cf. the Maori case), we can adduce evidence from, e.g., child language and speech errors to show that properties of unmarked word forms, rather than of abstract morphemes, tend to generalize to other forms. Thus, in Linell (1976a: 275–6) I have discussed some data produced by an aphasic person studied by both Schnitzer (1972) and Kehoe & Whitaker (1973). This patient produced, e.g., the following forms in a reading test:

(7)	Item	Correct pronunciation	Produced pronunciation	Cf. base word
	pronunciation	[prənʌnsīyéyšən]	[prōwnāwnsīyéyšən]	*pronounce*
	clarification	[klærəfəkéyšən]	[klærəfāykéyšən]	*clarify*
	logician	[lajišən]	[lájəkən]	*logic*
	variety	[vəráyəti]	[vǽrətīy]	*vary*
	domesticity	[domestísitīy]	[dōwmést̬əktīy]	*domestic*
	satisfaction	[sætəsfǽkšən]	[sætəsfəkéysən]	*satisfy*
	relaxation	[rīylækséyšən]	[rīylǽksən]	*relax*
	pathological	[pæθəlájikəl]	[pæθálajikəl]	*pathology*

As can be easily seen, the pronunciations of the base forms appear only slightly distorted as parts of the produced forms for the derived words.[26] That is, the data are given a simple explanation in our concrete theory, whereas OGPh type explanations in terms of wrong underlying morpheme-invariants and misapplied rules (see Schnitzer 1972; Kehoe & Whitaker 1973) are extremely far-fetched (see also §5.2.13.2 and Linell 1974a: 143–6).

By way of conclusion, there is evidence that speakers do accept the redundancy involved in a word-form-based lexicon. This is in fact what should be expected, given a general consideration of the conditions on memory and data-processing functions (§4.2.2).

4.4 Non-phonological information in phonology

It is quite clear that there are numerous productive morphological operations in languages where you cannot derive (all) word forms *only* from the phonological surface form of any single base form or stem. If

---

[26] It may be mentioned that the patient's productions conformed to the 'correct' stress patterns much better when the test items were made-up nonsense words of the same length and complexity as the items in (7). That is, the patient had more difficulties when she happened to know the differently stressed underived forms (see Kehoe & Whitaker 1973: 275). This further indicates the correctness of the concrete theory.

we do not rely on suppletion in all those cases, more information is needed; morphological, morphophonological, diacritic. However, whereas OGPh integrates this information with phonology so as to create abstract morpheme-invariants, perhaps by means of abstract phonological segments, diacritic use of phonological segments, etc.[27] (cf. §13.2), I argue that it is supplied as lexical markings on lexicalized phonetic plans (§4.3.3.4). In OGPh, features which are motivated only on the basis of morphophonological alternations between forms are considered to be 'phonological' and are integrated into underlying forms. My approach to phonology includes the constraint that a phonological representation must not contain feature specifications that can never be realized in the pronunciations of the word from in question (see §3.3.1). This precludes the use of abstract morphophonemic forms. Instead, I propose that morphophonological features be considered as diacritic markings (though they are non-arbitrarily related to the phonology of the forms).

As an example, consider Finnish words like *käsi* 'hand' (*vesi* 'water', *vuosi* 'year', etc.) which show oblique forms such as *käden* (gen.), *kättä* (part.), *kätenä* (ess.). The alternations involved here are not automatic and not productive (except in some morphological contexts) in contemporary Finnish (Paunonen 1973; Karlsson 1974b; Skousen 1975a,b), but the rules involved are still quite general, and virtually no generativist analysis of Finnish fails to set up the underlying form /käte/ (and similarly for other words of this type) (cf. references in Skousen 1975b: 56, fn. 11 and passim). In my theory, this would be an impossible phonological representation of the uninflected form, since it posits properties of the phonetic plan which can never be realized as such (i.e. /t/ and /e/). Instead, we would give the phonological structure as /käsi/. However, from this form alone the oblique forms cannot be generated; the rules involved are non-productive morphophonological rules proper (cf. ch. 10), and the productive paradigm type is *lasi* 'glass' – *lasin* – *lasia* – *lasina* (Karlsson 1974b: 54). Let us assume however, at least for the sake of discussion, that speakers *can* form oblique forms, type *käden*, given base forms like *käsi*. In fact, there is dialectal data that some new words have joined this type (Skousen 1975b: 72), and many speakers may inflect new words according to this pattern in jokes.[28]

[27] For a generative critique of such abstract devices, cf. Kiparsky (1973a).
[28] Fred Karlsson (pers. comm.). The /t/ → /s/ rule is possibly productive in the preterite formation of certain verbs, see §7.3.

Given this, to account for the fact that /käsi/ is inflected *käden, kättä,* etc., we must mark its phonological representation with morphophonological markings: / k ä s i / (or / k ä s   i /).   An alternation feature

$$\text{/ k ä } \underset{\underset{\text{t e}}{\displaystyle\wr\,\wr}}{\text{s i}} \text{ / (or / k ä } \underset{\underset{[-\text{cnt}][-\text{high}]}{\displaystyle\wr\,\wr}}{\text{s}} \text{   i /)}$$

$\sim[\alpha F_i]$ is to be interpreted as follows:

(8)   As part of a morphological operation the segment marked as $\sim[\alpha F_i]$ changes its phonological specification to $[\alpha F_i]$ in contexts where this value is permitted by the phonotactic rules of the language.

Thus, $/ \text{ k ä } \underset{\underset{[-\text{cnt}]\ [-\text{high}]}{\displaystyle\wr\,\wr}}{\text{s i}} /$ means that /käsi/ will be turned into /käte-/ as

part of morphological operations (in contexts where /t/ (or its weak grade /d/) and /e/ are phonotactically permitted). Note that the morphophonological markings are *not part of* the phonological structure (phonetic plan) of /käsi/. Rather, they govern the morphophonological behavior of this form. In OGPh, however, the corresponding features are integrated into the underlying phonological form of the morpheme (= /käte/).

One may of course propose that there is no difference apart from pure notation between our $/ \text{ k ä } \underset{\underset{\text{t e}}{\displaystyle\wr\,\wr}}{\text{s i}} /$ and OGPh /käte/. I would, however,

argue that there is. (Though everything of course depends on how we interpret these linguistic formulas.) Thus, I would suggest the following implications, some of which involve clearly different empirical claims.

Our theory assumes that the nominative singular, being the unmarked form, is lexicalized, that its phonological structure is /käsi/ (just as *lasi* is /lasi/) and that speakers know about this form that it alternates with /käte-/ (while /lasi/, with no morphophonological features, is non-alternating). OGPh, on the other hand, claims that the lexical form of *käsi* is /käte/ with /t/ rather than /s/ (just as *koti* 'home' (*kodin*, etc.), *neiti* 'miss' (*neitin*, etc.) are /koti/, /neiti/, etc.). Our theory gives *käsi* as $/\text{käsi}/\underset{\text{te}}{\displaystyle\wr\,\wr}$

and *lasi* as /lasi/, thereby indicating that *käsi* is the marked, irregular type, while *lasi* is the regular type. OGPh depicts both types as equally complex (/käte/, /lasi/); only the derivations of surface forms show a difference in complexity. External evidence of various kinds clearly supports my concrete theory. Thus, new words tend to join the *lasi* type. Children tend to eliminate the alternations in the marked types, thus inflecting *käsi* as *käsin, käsiä* (Kauppinen 1977). There is no tendency for *käsi* to become [käti]. In jokes, student jargon, etc., the nominative singular of *lasi, viini* 'wine', etc. is never changed, while oblique forms may be (*viintä* 'some wine' (part.) instead of normal *viiniä*)[29] (cf. Germanic languages, where speakers sometimes change oblique forms of weak verbs into strong ones in jokes). These facts seem to indicate that semantic-syntactically unmarked forms (e.g. nom. sg. of nouns, infinitive or 3 sg. pres. of verbs) are used as operands in morphological operations (§4.3.3). Nothing of this is predicted by the OGPh theory. Often, one would in fact expect the opposite changes to occur, if OGPh were true.[30]

Thus, I argue that my theory and OGPh do make different claims about psychological realities in cases like the Finnish one (which can be thought of as quite typical). On the other hand, it may be difficult to find any empirical difference between our /käsi/ and a true suppletion

$$\underset{\text{te}}{\overset{\text{≀≀}}{}}$$

alternative which lists two entries for *käsi*, namely the nominative singular /käsi/ (as the primary form) and the oblique stem /käte-/ (this seems to be a plausible interpretation of the theory underlying most traditional grammars of Finnish).[31] One reason for *not* treating the relationship between /käsi/ and /käte-/, etc. as true suppletion (as, e.g., *go* vs. *went*) is however, that it is after all partly regular, which speakers presumably do not fail to discover.

---

[29] I am indebted to Fred Karlsson for these and other facts about Finnish.

[30] There are of course additional difficulties with OGPh. Instead of simply saying that the phonetic and articulatory plans of *käsi* end in /si/, OGPh theoreticians would have to say that the speaker starts out with /te/ but that no articulatory commands may be elicited until several rules have operated (cf. p. 51, fn. 6). Similarly, we assume that speakers hear /si/ in *käsi* by perceiving phonetic properties, while an OGPh analysis-by-synthesis would require that /si/ is reinterpreted (synthesized) by the listener's assumption that what is actually involved is /te/!

[31] There are obvious similarities between my ~[αF$_i$]-descriptions and Hudson's (1974) suppletion theory for non-productive alternations. I have not had access to Hudson (1975a), but judging from Hooper & Rudes (1977) his theory is akin to mine.

5 *Phonemic contrasts*

5.1 Introduction

In most phonological theories from Courtenay (1895) and through the history of phonology up to the 'Chomskyan revolution' and the breakthrough of OGPh, the *phoneme* was considered to be the most fundamental theoretical entity in phonology. Then Chomsky (1964) and Halle (1959, 1961) launched their attacks on the 'autonomous phonemic' level,[1] and ever since, generativists, except for some dissenters starting with Johns (1969) and Schane (1971), have regarded the phoneme as dead.[2] However, some recent papers have argued that perhaps Chomsky's and Halle's arguments were not quite as devastating as generativists believed (see ch. 13).[3] In this chapter I have collected arguments and evidence indicating that the notion of 'surface phonemic contrast' is indispensable in phonological theory.

Before I proceed to this task, a few provisos may be appropriate. Thus, I will not argue for a return to, say, post-Bloomfieldian phonemics with its excesses in structuralist classificatory arrangements. Some simplistic concept of the 'autonomous phoneme' as a class of phones or a redundancy-free phone will not do. Within an approach in which rules and processes are central and in which also relations between different speech styles are considered, emphasis will necessarily be shifted. As Chomsky (1967a: 113) has remarked, even though phonemic contrasts are important, it does not follow that we have to set

[1] However, note that many phonologists would not accept the 'autonomous phoneme' in the form that was attacked by generativists.

[2] For example, Bailey writes: 'What few (less than a dozen) predictions, trivial or non-trivial, can be wrung out of this now ancient artifact [i.e. the phoneme] all seem to be wrong – not least those involving linguistic change and psychological validity' (1976: 14–15, fn. 6). Bailey gives no argument for his claim.

[3] From the point-of-view of the sociology of scientific research, I find it quite remarkable that a few arguments (Chomsky, Halle) could convince a majority of a whole generation of phonologists that some of the most fundamental insights of previous scholarship were completely misguided.

up one unique level of representation where all and only phonemic contrasts can be directly read off. However, I will argue that there *are* many kinds of evidence for the importance of surface phonemic contrasts in a model where phonetic plans (chs. 3, 4) are fundamental entities.

It should also be pointed out that in as far as the subsequent considerations will support the classical phoneme, the arguments involved are concerned with the abstractness of phonological forms rather than with the size of phonological primes. Thus, I will *not* commit myself to any proposal to the effect that the organization of phonological strings can be adequately and exhaustively accounted for in terms of *segments* to the exclusion of features and syllables (cf. §3.7).

5.2 Arguments in favor of surface phonemic contrasts

Note that generative arguments against the phonemic level (ch. 13) presuppose that the adequate model of phonology is one in which *morphophonemic* (morpheme-invariant) representations are mapped by rules directly onto more or less narrow *phonetic* representations of more or less careful pronunciations. Of course, such arguments are deprived of most of their force if it is correct as I argue (chs. 8, 9, 12) that *there are no morpheme-invariant forms*. Furthermore, I have shown (ch. 3) that there is evidence for the reality of phonetic plans, which – from a generative point-of-view – are entities at an intermediate level of abstraction. In this chapter, I will adduce arguments and evidence specifically for the primary importance of surface phonemic contrasts in defining this level of representation.

5.2.1 *Identity and similarity of phonological strings*
Speakers seem to be able (§2.3) to classify utterances as being either repetitions or non-repetitions of each other, i.e. as being either the same or different, in spite of the fact that virtually all utterances are, at least in some minute details, physically different. Phonemic theory was developed to account for the distinction between *contrast* (phonological non-identity) and *free variation* (phonological identity in spite of phonetic variation). In my theory, I will talk about different vs. identical phonetic plans.

However, it is clear that there are two kinds of free variation in the pronunciation of words, sometimes called 'allophonic' and 'phonemic', respectively. In the former case, the utterances are in phonetic free variation but are grammatically, lexically and phonemically identical, e.g. variations in aspiration in *sit* (e.g. [sɪt] vs. [sɪtʰ]). We assume that there is one single phonetic plan in such cases. Variations are perceived by listeners (if they are perceived at all) as variations in speaking style, articulatory force, etc. In the other type of variation there is grammatical and lexical but *not* phonemic identity; examples are Engl. [ɪ̂jkənɔ́mɪks] – [èkənɔ́mɪks], Engl. *direct* [dâɪrékt] – [dɪrékt], Sw. *chans* 'chance' [çans] – [ʃans] – [çaŋs] – [ʃaŋs] (some of these are slightly substandard), Sw. *genial* 'ingenious' [jɛni·(j)á:l] – [ʃɛni·(j)á:l]).[4] Such variations are perceived by native listeners as distinct pronunciations, which seems to be due to the fact that English / ɪ̂j / and /e/, or Engl. /âɪ/ and /ɪ/, or Sw. /ç/ and /ʃ/, /n/ and /ŋ/, /j/ and /ʃ/ make up surface contrasts in other words of the language. I will have to assume distinct phonetic plans for such items (§3.4).

My theory, as well as traditional phonemic theory, can account for the empirical fact that there is a clear difference between 'phonemic variation'[5] and 'phonetic variation'. Though Postal (1968) explicitly argued that OGPh can account for contrast versus free variation, it cannot distinguish the two kinds of free variation, as Weitzman (1972) has observed; 'phonemic' variation would be handled by some optional rules just like 'phonetic' variation. Hence, OGPh would have to be supplemented with some device to handle surface phonemic contrasts (cf. Mansell 1973a; Linell 1976a). The same conclusion follows from other arguments to be given below.

If we consider the problem of speakers' judgments of identity and similarity of phonological strings in general one may conclude that something like surface phonemes crucially interferes, whereas morphophonemic structures are completely irrelevant.[6] It is of course somewhat trivial to assert that sounds which belong to the same phoneme are perceived as similar or identical, since phonetic (perceptual and articulatory) similarity is a criterion used in phonemici-

---

[4] Note that these cases are different from examples like [ɪnkʌm] ~ [ɪŋkʌm] where the [n] ~ [ŋ] alternation can be attributed to different levels of articulatory accuracy, cf. §13.3.3.

[5] Sometimes, 'phonemic variation' seems to be general for a substantial number of lexical items. Consider, e.g., the variation between /u(:)/ and /o(:)/ in certain foreign words in Swedish (Linell 1973a: 35–7).

[6] Compare the completely analogous argument concerning phonological correctness (§5.2.2, ch. 6).

zation. However, it is not trivial that depending on whether a phonetic difference has a potentially meaning-differentiating function or not, listeners tend to increase (vs. not increase or even decrease) the *perceived* difference, and this may in turn influence their own articulatory differentiation (§5.2.4).

In any case, it is clear that sounds which are derived from the same morphophoneme are perceived as similar or equivalent only if they also belong to the same phoneme. Conversely, sounds which have identical phonemic representations are perceived as similar also if they are derived from different morphophonemes. Thus, the vowels of Swedish *grov* ([gru:v], morphophon. /grov/ 'coarse') and *grövre* ([grø:vrə), morphophon. /grov + re/, comp. of *grov*) are clearly not perceived as similar, whereas those of *hög* ([hø:g], morphophon. /høg/ 'high') and *högre* ([hø:grə), /høg + re/, comp. of *hög*) are. The Swedish forms *lett* ([lɛt:], morphophon. /led + t/, supine of *leda* 'lead'), *lett* ([lɛt:], /le + t/, supine of *le* 'smile') and *lett* ([lɛt:], /lett/ 'Latvian' (n.)) are all perceived as homophonous despite the morphophonemic differences. Such examples may easily be multiplied ad nauseam.[7]

As yet another example, let us compare two languages which are alike on the morphophonemic level but quite different on the surface phonemic level. Consider sequences of nasal vowel and voiceless stop in French, e.g. [tɛ̃:t] *teinte* 'hue, tint', [gʁɛ̃:p] *grimpe* 'climbs', and American English, e.g. [kæ̃:t] *can't*, [kæ̃:p] *camp*.[8] In both these cases,[9] the nasal vowels correspond to sequences of oral vowel plus nasal consonant on the morphophonemic level at least if we accept the standard OGPh analysis of the French facts (cf. Schane 1968, 1973; Dell 1970, etc.), and for both languages OGPh would posit entirely homologous phonological rules for deriving the nasal vowels. Yet nasal vowels, e.g. /ɛ̃/, have the status of independent segment types in the intuition of French speakers, whereas Americans generally perceive nasal vowels, e.g. /æ̃/, merely as variants of oral vowel plus nasal consonant, e.g. /æn/ (or /æm/, /æŋ/). The difference is typical and

---

[7] Sapir, often referred to as a 'pioneer' in phonology by generativists (cf. Chomsky 1964: 95, 108–9), claims that the naive native speaker perceives /e/ in *led* (from the verb *lead*) and /e/ in *lead* ('plumbum') as psychologically different (Sapir 1933). It is not clear whether Sapir actually means that they are 'heard' differently. His term is 'not psychologically homonymous' (Mandelbaum 1949: 52, fn. 8).

[8] Such examples are discussed by Chomsky (1964: 82). For data, see Malécot (1960).

[9] I disregard here other occurrences of nasal vowels in French and American English. The argument is an adapted variant of one used by Hutchinson (1972: 32).

important. It illustrates the relevance of phonemic contrasts and the importance of differences between distinct types of phonological rules (ch. 10). That is, in French the nasalization rule has a morphophonological function; it gives rise to segments which constitute phonemes of their own (also in careful pronunciation), cf. contrasts like [tɛ̃:t] *teinte* – [tɛ:t] *tête* 'head', [gʁɛ̃:p] *grimpe* – [gɛ:p] *guêpe* 'wasp'.[10] In American English, on the other hand, nasalization is an articulatory reduction rule relating, e.g., the pronunciation [æ̃] to alternative pronunciations in very careful speech, i.e. [æ̃n, æn] (*can't*), [æ̃m, æm] (*camp*), [æ̃ŋ, æŋ] (*rank*); in overprecise pronunciation [æ̃] is not a separate phoneme (only in causal speech words like *can't – cat, camp – cap* form minimal pairs). Note, furthermore, that there are other structural differences between English and French. 'Contrasts' between nasal vowel and oral vowel are possible only before voiceless stops (in casual speech) in English, whereas in French contrasts occur in many contexts (and in all speaking styles). In English, the underlying nasal is recoverable,[11] but that is not always the case in French (Schane 1971 : 515).

The native speaker's intuition for phonological identity vs. non-identity (and similarity vs. dissimilarity) can of course be checked in perceptual tests or by direct questions. It also reveals itself in, e.g., spelling practice and rhyming. Orthographic errors usually deviate from the often abstract norm in the concrete direction. Rhymes are also a rich source of evidence. There is no doubt that almost all types of common rhymes are built upon phonetic and phonemic identity or similarity. On the other hand, rhyming words are often morphophonologically heterogeneous. Steinberg (1971: 6) cites examples like *night, kite* (according to Chomsky & Halle (1968) underlyingly /nixt/ and /ki:t/ respectively), and *sign, divine* (Chomsky & Halle (1968): underlyingly /sign/, /divi:n/). In Swedish dialects where the reflexes of morphophonological /e/ and /ɛ/ have merged phonemically, we frequently get rhymes like *sett* (/se +t/ [sɛt:] supine of *se* 'see') – *klätt* (/klɛ +t/ [klɛt:] supine of *klä* 'dress'), *veta* 'know' – *äta* 'eat', *spel* 'play' – *själ* 'soul', etc. One might argue that ordinary rhymes are 'allophonic' or 'phonetic' rather than 'phonemic'. For example, rhymes in Swedish *-är* must of course contain precisely the [æ] allophone of the /ɛ/ phoneme. But this follows from the fact that this allophone is conditioned by the following

---

[10] Actually, the synchronic motivation for deriving nasal vowels by rule is quite weak (cf. Picard 1974; Tranel 1974).

[11] Cf. however p. 186, fn. 27.

/r/. Of course, rhyming allophones always belong to the same phoneme, but they need not represent the same morphophoneme.[12]

Thus, rhymes and other principles of metric organization are often built upon the speaker's intuitions for phonological similarity on a concrete level. But poetry is also often performed by 'professional' poets as a highly skilled and artificial work with linguistic material, and we cannot be sure that the principles utilized in metrics are 'natural' with respect to the 'naive' speaker. Just like orthography, metric organization may be 'irregular' from the point of view of natural and synchronic phonology; it may be based on principles which were natural for the language of an earlier historical period. This would be the most natural explanation of the 'abstract' metric principles which sometimes occur in folk poetry and elsewhere. Examples of orally traded folk poetry based on 'abstract' metrical principles are discussed by e.g. Kiparsky (1968c) (metrics in the Kalevala),[13] Kiparsky (1972b) (metrics in the Rigveda) and S. Anderson (1973) (Old Norse Skaldic verse).[14] I do not know whether the above-mentioned explanation is possible in these cases.[15] In any case, the two generativist authors show that the phonological

---

[12] Compare, e.g., as for Swedish [æʈ:] *tvärt* ('abruptly', morphophon. /...ɛr + t/ related to *tvär* [tvæ:r]) ↔ *offert* ('offer' (n.) morphophon. /...er + t/ related to *offerera* /e/ [e] 'offer' (v.)).

[13] Kiparsky (1968c) argues that 'the metrical correctness of a line depends on its form at a certain cutoff-point in the derivation' (143), two rules below the morphophonemic representation but well above the phoneme level. Kiparsky also notes numerous homonymous words which are never metrically equivalent (144). There are also cases where a syllable is metrically short 'although it is long both morphophonemically and phonetically' (144).

[14] Anderson shows that some phonemically non-equivalent vowels (a/ö, e/ɸ, i/y) rhyme in Skaldic verse. Thus, Anderson ascribes to early Skaldic poets an 'unconscious skill' 'guided by the more abstract components of the grammar' (1973: 11). Anderson argues furthermore that Snorri Sturluson's later explicit norms for creating verse, which were based on something like taxonomic phonemics, 'lost sight of' these abstract–phonological regularities (11). It seems as if Anderson means that Snorri's reflecting over the grammar results in a less natural and less significant phonology, i.e. taxonomic phonemics (cf. §1.4.2).

[15] Cf. however Kiparsky (1968c: 145). Kiparsky maintains that poets could not continue to create 'correct' poetry if there were no synchronic basis for the abstract principles in the form of morphophonological processes. This is an interesting hypothesis, though it may be questioned in the light of the fact that speakers may correctly use irregular orthographies lacking every kind of synchronic morphophonological support. That is, speakers can very well learn complicated principles that are completely ad hoc. It would be interesting to know the nature of the metrical errors made by less skilled Kalevala or Skaldic poets. Do these deviate from the norm in the direction of more concrete representations?

representation underlying metrics in these cases is not as abstract as the underlying morpheme-invariant forms.

5.2.2   *Correctness of phonological strings*

Speakers are also able (§2.3) to make judgments of correctness (well-formedness) or pronounceability, i.e. whether arbitrary phonetic strings would be possible (words) in their language. Such judgments also apply to surface forms and are obviously independent of assumptions of morphophonemic representations. As we will see (ch. 6), there are also other arguments for phonotactic rules as applying at a surface level, more specifically the level of careful pronunciations. It may be that arguments for phonotactics do not support surface phonemic contrasts, rather than simply phonetic representations, in the first place. However, if there is a valid distinction between phonotactic constraints and perceptual redundancy rules (§10.3.3) they may in fact do this too.

5.2.3   *Perceptual equivalence and the reinterpretation of deviant sounds*

It was suggested earlier (§2.4.4, §3.6) that there are different modes of listening to speech. Clearly, a very high precision of perception is needed in order to observe all those details which are necessary in the specification of idiomatic pronunciations. But I also argued that perception tends to be categorical (more so than articulation),[16] and that there is some basis for arguing that phonetic plans need not be fully specified for all phonetic details (§3.3.5). Similarly, classical phoneme theory is based on the assumption that though there are great, maybe infinite, variations in actual speech performance, speaker–listeners typically 'believe' that words are made up by segments drawn from a small inventory of types ('phonemes').[17]

The theory that phonetically distinct sounds are perceptually identical or equivalent at some level implies that some features of sounds are perceptually more important than other features, the latter thus being subordinate, less conscious and perhaps derivable from the first-

---

[16] Cf. Labov (1971). See §3.6.

[17] It is interesting to note that it is possible to understand synthetic speech consisting of only stable invariant segments (Sven Öhman, pers. comm.). Coarticulation effects are not needed, except of course, for the speech to sound 'natural' and idiomatic. Thus, there may be *some* validity to two of the principles underlying conventional phonemicization, those of complete reduction to segments and minimization of the number of postulated segment types. Cf. however, §3.7.

mentioned. The subordinate features would be more or less systematically ignored in normal listening. For example, in Swedish or English the aspiration of voiceless tense stops may be such a subordinate feature. Thus, there would be some motivation for the structuralist distinction between 'distinctive' vs. 'predictable' ('concomitant', 'redundant') features. However, structuralists have probably somewhat over-emphasized the sharpness of this distinction. For example, what features are central (important, distinctive) may vary for different speakers. This can be seen in historical phonology; if a group of speakers start to interpret a new distinction as fundamental, and if the articulatory productions later reinforce the results of these new perceptual habits, a phonological change has occurred.[18] There are also other kinds of data (e.g. from child language, transfer in foreign-language learning, psycholinguistic experiments) showing that different speakers, and especially those who have an incomplete command of the language in question, may make different categorical structurings of the same words. For example, Swedish children, and probably children learning other similar languages, who have not yet acquired the proper pronunciation of /r/, may all be able to produce /d/, /l/ and /j/ freely and distinguish these units from each other and from /r/ in perception, yet some of these children substitute [d] for /r/, others [l] for /r/, and still others [j] for /r/ in their speech production. This seems to show that (i) not all features of the strings perceived (here: the /r/ manifestations) are attended to (abstracted) in perception; and (ii) that different individuals make different selections of distinctive features.[19] Similarly, when we listen to speech in a foreign language, different individuals will extract different sets of features as central or 'distinctive' (especially so if the individual listeners have different primary languages).

In discussing the supposedly gross structure of phonetic plans with regard to maximally specified structurings we have so far mainly considered perception of the 'same' sound occurring repeatedly in the same phonetic environment. But there are other aspects of the categorical nature of perception. It seems evident that there are phonological identifications of phonetically (articulatorily) *distinct* segments in *different* positions. Thus, despite some phonetic differences

---

[18] Cf. Andersen's (1973) notion of 'abductive change'.

[19] Yet, it seems reasonable to assume that within a sufficiently stable speech community with little variation in canonical (careful) pronunciations there are also considerable similarities between the perceptual habits of different fluent speakers (cf. §2.4.2).

there seems to be perceptual identity between, e.g., the first segment of Engl. *top* and the last segment of *pot* and vice versa. Such identifications are obviously made on the basis of phonetic similarity. Yet, some (e.g. Bailey 1970: 683) have argued that phonological identification crucially involves morphophonemic identity. That is, the [pʰ] of *prePare* and the [p] of *preParation* are considered as phonologically identical because they are morphophonemically identical. This is obviously nonsense; could not a speaker recognize [pʰ] and [p] as phonologically identical in morphologically unrelated words like *prePare* and *proPagation*?

If speech sounds are classified in terms of a limited number of types, it follows that deviant sounds are necessarily interpreted as variants of these types,[20] and that the exact nature of the deviance is not attended to. I think this implication is corroborated by countless observations of the reactions of speakers to aberrant features.[21] If, e.g., a person is a lisper, especially in a language with no (inter)dental non-strident fricatives (/θ/), then his lisp is interpreted just as a peculiar rendition of /s/, not as a sound of the same status as, e.g., [s]. Similar examples of reinterpretation can be drawn from observations within the areas of child language, transfer in foreign language performance, loan word adaptation, etc. Let me give a few pieces of anecdotal evidence from child language. I remember vividly that as a child I used to pronounce *oerhört* 'enormously' (a word with a rather opaque morphological structure) as [uːvəhœʁt] (instead of [uːʁhœʁt]) and that this pronunciation was repeatedly corrected. Apparently I had heard the [β] which occurs after long [uː] in Swedish (especially before another vowel) and identified this sound fragment with /v/, an interpretation which was underlying my pronunciation. Similarly, in some data collected from my sons' speech (at the age of three to four) I note reinterpretations such as [v] for the rather uncommon diphthongal off-glide [u̯] ([klavm̩] for [klau̯n] *clown* (loan-word) and similarly [v] for [u̯] in English words such as *hallo* (pronounced by my son as [hæləv]) and *Brown* ([bravn])).

In the adaptation of foreign loans we can identify exactly the same processes. For example, English [w] is reinterpreted and pronounced as [v] /v/ in Swedish; *vajer* [vájər] for Engl. *wire, whisky* [vískɪ], *show* [ʃɔvː]. In Finnish, we find Sw. [b, d, g] rendered as [p, t, k]; *pankki* (cf. Sw. *bank*), *parakki* (cf. *barack*), *tanssi* (cf. *dans*), *tohtori* (cf. *doktor*), *kaasu* (cf.

---

[20] One should probably add: Unless the phonetic discrepancy is very great.
[21] Cf. also perceptual reinterpretation in dichotic listening tests (§5.2.13.3).

gas), *kulta* (cf. *guld*).[22] At least for monolingual speakers, foreign language adaptation is approximation to the phonetic and phonemic system of one's own language (see §10.8.2). A similar point is made by Householder:

Speakers can *repeat* (not just *mimic*) new words. This kind of repetition implies a systematic analysis of the sound system *without any possible reference to deep morphophonemic potential* (hence not Chomsky's systematic phonemic level) and without the kind of detail which permits international phoneticians to discuss similarities and differences between sounds in different languages (hence not Chomsky's systematic phonetic level). Indeed one point emphasized by early investigators was that what is phonetically identical in two languages (say [x] in French and German) may be at this immediate repetition level quite different (say /r/ in French but /x/ in German). (1966: 99–100)

Householder, in other words, argues that speakers have a 'phonemic competence' which cannot be accounted for on either of the levels of morphophonemics or narrow phonetics.

Most cases of language-internal perceptual equivalence, i.e. that which is supposed to underlie the categoricalness of phonetic plans, concern sounds which represent different degrees of strength of what seems to be one and the same articulatory unit. Such strength variations may occur in the same position as a consequence of different articulatory accuracy (prominence), e.g. the different strengths of apical /r/: [r], [ɾ], [ɚ], r-coloring of adjacent vowel or consonant, or even zero manifestation (cf. Eriksson 1974), or be dependent on the differences in articulatory energy typical of different positions.

However, there are other cases of perceptual equivalence which obtain between articulatorily more heterogeneous sound types. Such cases are often not internal to the same dialect but concern relations between related dialects (or also quite different languages) and represent a problem for the theory of phonetic plans, and for every theory of phonology (see §3.4). In general, I am inclined to argue that there is one common phonetic plan but, of course, different fully specified articulatory plans in the case of apical /r/ and uvular /R/ and in other such cases[23] of articulatorily heterogeneous but presumably perceptually equivalent sounds (see §3.4, §10.3.3).

To return to the main line of argument, I have argued that surface

[22] However, learned words are now normally incorporated into Finnish without any change of /b, d, g/, e.g. *baletti, diftongi, gabardiini*.
[23] For some examples, see Jonasson 1971; Linell 1973a: 43–5.

phonemic contrasts are relevant for determining perceptual equivalence, which in turn is one important factor in determining phonological forms (=phonetic plans). However, it is an empirical issue to find out exactly how much information (structure and features) is included in such plans, and it would be wrong to conclude a priori that there is *nothing* but strictly phonemic (structurally non-predictable) features. For example, the condition of articulatory homogeneity proposed in §3.4 might add some specifications. There are also other reasons to believe that phonetic plans are *not* characterized by absolutely minimal redundancy (see §4.2.2 for some general considerations). Some major allophones may well be present. Consider, e.g. /ç/ and /x/ in German or /ø/ and /œ/ in Swedish. Sometimes, these may indeed form marginal minimal pairs, e.g. *Kuhchen* [kuːçən] and *Kuchen* [kuːxən] in German, *mör* [mœːr] 'tender' and *mö(e)r* [møːr] 'virgins' in some variants of Swedish. Similarly, we may distinguish Russian /i/ and /ɨ/, and /e/ and /ɛ/, although these sounds never contrast (if a [±palatalized] contrast is assumed for consonants), and /e/ and /ɛ/ occur in comparable positions only marginally ([m'iɫə] 'friendly' – [miɫə] 'soap', [k'etɔ̀ɫ] 'salmon' (instr. sg.) – [kɛtɔ̀ɫ] 'to this one' (fem.), [gʌr'el'i] 'they burnt?' – [gʌr'ɛl'i] 'to the mountain?'). Darden (1971: 329–30) claims that such contrasts must be postulated also at the underlying phonological level for some diachronic developments to become explicable. Korhonen (1969) has invented the term 'quasi-phoneme' for such units, which, according to normal distributional criteria, are allophones but still seem to be on their way to becoming phonemes. Indeed, they are open to competitive analyses; they are allophonic if we take grammatical boundaries into consideration (which speakers undoubtedly do in most cases) but marginally phenomic if we exclude grammatical factors (cf. also § 10.3.3).

5.2.4 *Phonetic distinctness and surface symmetry*

It is natural that different distinctive sounds in a language tend to be as phonetically dissimilar as possible (the principle of maximal differentiation of phonological units). This is a regularity which must be explained in terms of phonemes rather than morphophonemes, since morphophonemes often merge phonetically. It is well-known that languages having more than one phoneme within a certain limited phonetic class, e.g. sibilants, laterals, high front vowels, etc. tend to make these clearly different from a 'neutral' phonetic type in that class.

Languages lacking a /ʃ/ phoneme (opposed to /s/) often have a [ʃ-colored ('thick' or acoustically flat) /s/, i.e. [sʲ]. Compare, e.g., Finnish, Greek or Spanish (only one sibilant phoneme) to, for example, Swedish or French (two voiceless sibilant phonemes, clearly kept apart as strident, non-flat [s] and flat, 'hushing' [ʃ]). Or one could compare, say, German /l/ [l] (non-sharp, non-flat) to the two phonetically clearly distinct lateral phonemes of Russian, /l/ [ɫ] (flat, very 'dark', velarized) and /l'/ [ʎ] (sharp, palatalized). English has only one 'plain' /s/, whereas Arabic also has a very 'flat' (pharyngealized) /ʂ/ and Russian a very 'sharp' (palatalized) /s'/.

It seems reasonable to argue that surface phonemic contrasts contribute considerably to reinforcing phonetic differences. In fact, there are cases reported in the literature, in which a phonetic distinction has been sharpened after (or simultaneously with) its becoming distinctive. Thus, in the Granada variant of Spanish where the laxing of vowels is part of a morphological rule ([AltOʰ] *altos* as opposed to [alto] *alto*, [sElvA] *selvas* as opposed to [selva] *selva*, [kOr:E][24] *corres* as opposed to [kor:e] *corre*) the distinction between tense and lax vowels is reportedly much greater than in those Spanish dialects in which laxing is merely conditioned by a following [h] (aspirated /s/) (Hooper 1974: esp. 166, 1976: 37).

It is also clear that the tendency to keep phonemes apart may explain constraints on phonological change, as has been eloquently argued by Martinet (1955). Recently, the generativist Schane (1971) 'rediscovered' this (cf. §5.2.10).

It should be added that some major allophones, i.e. sounds that are not 'real' phonemes, must be taken into account in a discussion of phonetic distinctness within the 'phonological space' (cf. Dressler 1977b: 15, 52). Some major allophones are phonetically quite different, and partly context-independent; in fact, such allophones ('quasi-phonemes') tend to develop into real phonemes (§5.2.3).

5.2.5 *Sharpening of minor allophones in lexical pronunciation*
When speakers are asked to pronounce the sounds of words in isolation as clearly and carefully as they possibly can, certain substitutions are bound to occur. Sounds are, as it were, 'sharpened' (§3.3.4.1). Contextual weak (reduced) variants tend to be substituted with 'strong allophones', i.e. the major variants normally occurring only in strong

[24] [A, E, O] stand for lax, lowered counterparts of [a, e, o].

positions, e.g. under stress (for vowels) or initially in stressed syllables (for consonants). For example, in English or Swedish a syllable-final, less aspirated or even unreleased [t] in, e.g. *fooтball* (Sw. *foтboll*) will become a strongly aspirated [tʰ]. Some phonologists, e.g. the Russians Ščerba and Gvozdev, according to Halle (1963), have used the isolation pronunciations for words, or even single sounds, as a means to elicit and thus determine the fundamental variants of phonemes.[25]

Isolation pronunciations introduce some problems which, however, are quite interesting in the light of our present discussion. In isolation, and under very strong emphasis, people often sharpen or elaborate sounds beyond what can occur in normal connected speech. For example, if a Swedish obstruent cluster contains at least one inherently voiceless obstruent, the whole cluster becomes voiceless by assimilation. Thus, lax voiced obstruents, especially stops, become voiceless but not tense in natural speech. Thus, adjectives like *snabb* 'quick' [snab:, snab̥:][26] and *vig* 'nimble' [vi:g, vi:g̥][26] have the neuter forms *snabbt* [snab̥:t] and *vigt* [vi:g̥t]. The [b̥] and [g̥] are obviously positional variants of /b/ and /g/, contrasting with tense [p⁽ʰ⁾] and [k⁽ʰ⁾] (*slappt* 'sloppy', *vikt* supine of *vika* 'to fold'). However, in isolation pronunciations [b̥] and [g̥] are typically sharpened, i.e. tensed, to [p⁽ʰ⁾] and [k⁽ʰ⁾],[27] thus causing a neutralization at this particular level of speech. In this case, the sounds are thus transferred to phonemic units, to which they do not normally belong. However, what this phenomenon seems to show is that speakers tend to eliminate sound types (here: lax voiceless stops) which are specific for certain positions and, as it were, deviant from the inventory of major types, something which thus has a great deal in common with other eliminations of deviant sounds (§5.2.3).[28]

[25] According to Fischer-Jørgensen (1975: 330), Halle's account is typical only of Gvozdev.

[26] Devoicing is optional word-finally.

[27] Actually, there is a rule of assimilation operating within lexical items in Swedish (*jakt* [jak(:)t] related to *jaga* /ja:g(a)/, *gudstjänst* [gèt:sçénst] related to *Gud* /gʉ:d/ etc.) which both devoices and tenses stops. This rule might be considered to be a morphologically conditioned PhtR (cf. §10.3.1) valid only for (all monosyllabic and some polysyllabic) monomorphemic items, derived words and a few compounds (plus the neuter form of *hög* 'high', i.e. *högt* [hœk:t], and some other inflected forms). It should be distinguished from the ordinary devoicing rule which applies over boundaries and does *not* involve tensing (e.g. *låg* 'low', neuter form: [lo:gt]). For discussion of both rules, see Hellberg (1974: 144–7).

[28] As a similar example, consider Lehmann's (1953) observations of hypercorrections in Texas speech such as [bɪtʰər] for *bidder*. The flap [D], a segment type which does not belong to the underlying inventory, was sharpened to [tʰ] and thereby (in this case) assigned to the wrong phoneme.

5.2.6 *Adaptation to secondary dialects*

If one makes independent analyses of a number of different but closely related dialects within an OGPh framework, one will very often come up with quite similar, if not identical, morphophonemic representations (since dialects often share many abstract, morphologized regularities), while the dialects may often be phonemically and (especially) phonetically quite different.[29] Assuming for the moment that morphophonemes are psychologically real, consider what this might mean for a person who speaks a dialect in which there are, say, two distinct morphophonemic sources for one phoneme (i.e. the morphophonemes have merged phonetically (at least in some positions)), and who tries to learn a related, secondary dialect in which the phonetic (and phonemic) reflexes of these two morphophonemes are distinct. OGPh predicts that there will be no particular problem for the speaker to keep the two phonemes distinct, since they are morphophonemically distinct in his own dialect. But this is not what typically happens. Instead, the speaker seems to be guided by the *phonemic* system of his own dialect; the counterparts of the single phoneme (phone type) in that dialect are treated alike in the secondary dialect. Wurzel (1977) has shown this on German material. For example, in Standard German, /x/ is replaced by /ç/ in palatal contexts, cf. alternations such as *bach* [bax] – *bäche* [bɛçə], *loch* [lɔx] – *löcher* [lœçər]. In some dialects of Upper Saxony the corresponding pattern is [x] – [š], e.g. [bax] – [bešə], [lox] – [lešər]. Both Standard German and the Saxon dialect also have non-alternating /š/ in e.g. *falsch, fleisch, wäsche*, etc. Obviously, Saxon [š] in [bešə] and [š] in [vešə] are morphophonemically distinct (though phonemically merged). In Standard German, they are distinct, both morphophonemically and phonemically. Now, what typically happens when Saxons learn the prestige language as a secondary dialect is *not* that only [š] alternating with [x] (i.e. morphophonemic /x/) is replaced by [ç] (as the OGPh framework would predict). Instead, all instances of [š], i.e. the whole

[29] In OGPh-based dialectology, this is one of two approaches (Campbell 1971: 192–5, 1972), practised by e.g. Becker 1967; King 1969: 29–9. Another approach is to assume that speakers revise their underlying forms so that they are *made* identical for reasonably closely related dialects that the speaker knows (i.e. understands) (Bailey 1972). According to both these generative approaches, related dialects generally have common underlying forms (and the differences between dialects are due to their having partly different rules, or the same rules differently ordered), and these forms are what *explains* the mutual understanding of speakers with different dialects (Bailey 1972). See, e.g. Halle 1962: 343–4; Chomsky 1964: 100; Stevens & Halle 1967: 94; Chomsky & Halle 1968: 49, 54; Ureland 1972: 105.

phoneme, in the appropriate context (after consonants and front vowels) tend to be replaced by [ç], i.e. we also get e.g. [veçə] for *wäsche*.

Wurzel's facts are quite typical for *hypercorrections*. A speaker's adaptive rules for secondary dialects are of the form A → B/C where A is a *surface* unit, not a morphophoneme, of the primary dialect, and B is the postulated counterpart in the secondary dialect.[30] Thus, in Black English, *pin* and *pen* are both pronounced *pin*.[31] Yet, some OGPh theoreticians (cf. fn. 29) would assume that *pen* and *pin* have different underlying forms (presumably /pen/ and /pin/ respectively) since they are pronounced differently in Standard English, and that Black English has a rule that raises /e/ to /i/ in *pen*. However, when Black English speakers try to adopt Standard English, hypercorrections often occur and both *pin* and *pen* are pronounced as [pen].[32]

5.2.7 *Submorphemic conspiracies*

In Swedish, the [ç]-sound (which is also a (surface) /ç/ phoneme) may have two kinds of morphophonemic sources: (i) /k/ (before non-back vowels); and (ii) /tj/ or /kj/ (before any vowel in principle) (cf. Sigurd 1970; Linell, Svensson & Öhman 1971: 99–103; Eliasson 1973). (There is often indeterminacy as to the right underlying morphophonemic representation, although it can be uniquely determined in some cases (see Eliasson 1973).) Eliasson also points out that there is a 'submorphemic' conspiracy around the /ç/ phoneme which is independent of the morphophonemic sources. Thus, there is a substantial number of verbs with some kind of pejorative connotation beginning with /ç/, e.g. (morphophonemic source /k/:) *kinka* 'whimper', *kitslas* 'be hyper-critical, unfair', *kivas* 'quarrel', *käbbla* 'bicker', *käfta* 'jaw' (v.), *kälta* 'nag', *käxa* 'nag', (morphophonemic source /tj/ (or /kj/):) *tjabba* 'nag', *tjafsa* 'jabber', *tjalla* 'peach against', *tjata* 'nag', *tjattra* 'jabber', *tjoa* 'be noisy', *tjura* 'sulk', *tjuta* 'howl, cry'. It is no doubt a significant generalization about language that words which are semantically similar in some respect sometimes cluster around some preferred invariant phonological units ('submorphemic regularities').[33] Fudge argues that words which are 'expressive', 'notably onomatopoeias, movement verbs,

---

[30] Thus, such adaptive rules are *not* integrated so that the most simple pandialectal grammar results. Adaptive rules are often phonetically unnatural and may be a source of 'crazy' rules.

[31] St Clair (1973) (data from Luelsdorff 1971).

[32] St Clair (1973) also offers some more arguments against OGPh type dialectology.

[33] For a list of such submorphemic conspiracies in English, see Bloomfield (1933: 245).

and words with pejorative, jocular, or intense connotations, have a
tendency in a wide range of languages to be associated with peculiarities
of phonological structures' (1970: 164), and that the relevant phonological properties are phonetic. In our Swedish example the relevant
phonological units are clearly phonemic, not morphophonemic, a fact
which speaks for the psychological reality of phonemes.

5.2.8 *Inputs of morphological operations*

What are morphophonemic representations good for? They are set up to
account for regularities among morphologically or morphemically
related forms. Conceivably, the most important function of morphophonological rules would therefore consist in being applied in the
derivation of new word forms. Therefore, if one can argue that the
inflection and formation of words necessarily presupposes the existence
of morphophonemic forms, we might be forced to adopt an OGPh type
theory. However, a careful analysis of inflection and word formation
processes reveals that the input forms must be surface forms rather than
morpheme-invariants. Quite often, the phonemic (rather than the
morphophonemic) properties of input forms determine the properties of
outputs. For discussion of this point, see §4.3.3–4, §4.4, chs. 7, 8.

5.2.9 *Indeterminacy of morphophonemic representations*

In OGPh, morphophonemic representations are the basic entities in a
phonology that is assumed to be psychologically valid. However, the
exact morphophonemic representations of various specific words can
often not be determined on the basis of structural data. Language
structure often does not provide any clue as to which of several possible
underlying sources for a certain segment is the 'correct' one for the
specific word.[34] This situation has been discussed for /ç/ and /ʃ/ in
Swedish by Eliasson (1973), for /ŋ/ in Swedish by Eliasson (1977) and
for /ʒ/ in Ukrainian by Darden (1971: 232). Eliasson argues that in cases
where abstract forms are underdetermined, one should prefer more
concrete (e.g. surface phonemic) representations (which are 'inferable'
from the phonetic data, cf. Eliasson 1977). This, then, would constitute
still another argument for phonemic rather than morphophonemic
forms.[35]

---

[34] Sometimes, but not always, a principle like 'In cases of underdetermination, choose the
simplest (most natural) underlying form' may be of some help.

[35] Of course, there may be points of indeterminacy concerning phonemic forms too, but
this indeterminacy seems less dangerous, particularly if one adheres to phonetic
properties.

Though I argue for phonological representations as being phonetic representations, I do not think that the indeterminacy argument is too strong. Thus, there is in fact no compelling reason why there must be one unique 'solution' to the various problems in the description and explanation of the grammar of a given language. In fact, many historical changes and synchronic situations must apparently be analyzed in terms of competing regularities (Wang 1969). Data often indicate that different speakers do make different generalizations, though they may be confronted with largely the same data.[36] In the case under discussion, one could also argue that indeterminacy is desirable, since then there is nothing that forces the speaker to find precisely one uniquely correct solution.[37]

5.2.10 *Historical change*

Most phonological changes directly concern phonetic realities, i.e. relations between percepts and pronunciations of words. Although many of these changes cannot be explained in isolation from grammatical and morphophonological conditions (e.g. Anttila 1972a: 81–4) (and some changes of course directly concern morphophonology, cf. §10.11), there are no convincing indications that diachronic facts might necessitate an OGPh type model.[38] However, I will not consider the various general problems of historical phonology here.[39] Instead, I will call attention to some scattered problems of historical phonology which seem to indicate the importance of surface phonemic constraints.

5.2.10.1 *Preservation of contrasts.* Some scholars, particularly Martinet (1955, and other works) have argued that the phonetic transposition of

---

[36] Consider, e.g., child language acquisition, where variation is great (Ferguson & Farwell 1975; Kiparsky & Menn 1977). This variation can hardly be entirely reduced to the fact that different children have actually been confronted with different data sets.

[37] See also Derwing 1973: 173, fn. 1; Roberts 1976. In general, one may suggest that the common search for uniquely correct solutions in grammar theory *may* reveal an insufficient appreciation on the part of the analyst of the differences between the subject matter of natural sciences and human sciences. Cf. §1.5.6.

[38] Some of Halle's (1962) and Kiparsky's (1965, 1968a) most celebrated cases in which it was claimed that morphophonemically distinct but phonetically (and hence phonemically) identical segments may be kept distinct by speakers over time, have actually turned out to be based on insufficient data (cf. Linell 1974a: 126–30).

[39] For relevant facts and theories, cf. Weinreich, Labov & Herzog 1968; Wang 1969; Labov, Yaeger & Steiner 1973.

phonological systems is subject to conditions of preserving (surface) phonemic contrasts by constantly keeping phonemes apart in the 'phonological space' (cf. §5.2.4).[40] For an illustrative example, compare Martinet's (1955: 86ff) discussion of the vowel system of the Hauteville dialect.[41] Recently, Labov (1975) has claimed that his studies of chain shifts in progress support the view that whole phonemes, not single allophones, move together.[42]

5.2.10.2 *The loss of non-distinctive features.* In an attempt to provide a place for the phoneme in generative phonology, Schane (1971) showed with examples from widely different languages that certain diachronic phenomena like the loss of marked phonological features occur, or at least tend to occur, only in contexts where no surface contrast depends on them. One of Schane's examples concerns the development of nasalized vowels in French. In Middle French, vowels were nasalized before nasal consonants [bɔ̃n, bɔ̃nte, bɔ̃nə]. Subsequently, the nasal consonant was dropped except before vowels [bɔ̃, bɔ̃te, bɔ̃nə]. This gave rise to a surface contrast between nasal and oral vowels (e.g. [bɔ̃] *bon* 'good' – [bo] *beau* 'beautiful') except before nasals, where the nasalization of the vowel was still synchronically conditioned by the nasal consonants [bɔ̃nə] *bonne* 'good' (fem.). Later on, the marked feature of nasalization was dropped in this context; [bɔnə] (*bonne*). Schane argues, on the basis of this and similar examples,[43] that speakers' recognition of the contrasting function of sounds may impede changes that occur in the languages from applying in precisely the contrastive contexts.[44]

5.2.10.3 *Transition of forms to new paradigms.* Darden (1971) brings up an interesting case from Russian indicating that some forms resulting from the transition of certain nouns from one declension to another can be explained only if we assume that the lexical representations of base

[40] For a generative critique, see Kiparsky 1968a: 184–5; King 1969: 191ff.
[41] A summary of this can be found in Fischer-Jørgensen (1975: 46).
[42] Cf. however, Dressler (1971: 346).
[43] Schane considers denasalization in French, depalatalization in Rumanian, delabialization in Romance, palatalization and labialization in Nupe, and palatalization in Japanese.
[44] For some discussion of Schane's theory, see Mansell (1973a); and Linell (1976a: 267–9).

forms reflect surface phonemic contrasts. Thus, in Russian the loss of jers led to a contrast between palatalized and non-palatalized consonants; e.g. *tat'* 'thief' came to end in a palatalized /t'/ (≠ /t/). Here, an OGPh analysis might retain underlying /ĭ/ (jer) in the nominative (/tat + ĭ/) and let rules first palatalize the /t/ and then delete /ĭ/ (cf. Lightner 1965), but this cannot explain the fact that *tat'*, after shifting its declension, behaves as a soft stem (genitive *tat' ä*, not *tata* as we would have expected if the solution with stem-final /t/ were correct).[45] Thus, this example supports the hypothesis (§4.3.3) that surface phonemic contrasts are part of the lexicalized phonetic plans of base forms which serve as operands of morphological operations.

5.2.10.4 *Allomorphy reduction.* Schane (1971) is not the only example of a generativist's returning[46] to pre-generative insights such as the significance of allomorphs and surface contrasts. Thus, Kiparsky (1971, 1972a) has argued that the minimization of intraparadigmatic variation between surface allomorphs ('paradigm conditions') is an important factor conditioning phonological change. (Of course, this is what has traditionally been treated in terms of analogical leveling and/or Systemzwang.) Kiparsky's theory seems to imply, as Karlsson (1974a: 27) points out, a recognition of the significance of surface forms. Obviously, minimization of allomorphy cannot be expressed at the underlying morpheme-invariant level, since there are no allomorphs there. Moreover, we are not concerned with narrow phonetic allomorphy; every morpheme shows phonetic allomorphy, and there is no trend towards eliminating this largely unconscious allomorphy. Instead, the relevant type of allomorphy must apparently be formulated on a roughly phonemic level.

5.2.11 *The transfer of allophones to new positions*
The following argument, which is based on diatopic rather than diachronic facts, may be seen as a complement to the Schane type argument (§5.2.10.2). I will be concerned with variation patterns of [ʃ]-sounds in Swedish dialects. In Swedish, [ʃ]-sounds may have two

---

[45] Cf. *brat* 'brother', gen. *brata*, vs. *kon'* 'horse', gen. *kon'ä*. For further discussion, see Hudson (1975b: 215–16).

[46] It should be pointed out that this retreat is usually disguised by the use of a new terminology.

different types of morphophonological sources, i.e. (i) /rs/, which in the standard language is pronounced [ʂ] (a product of 'supradentalization');[47] and (ii) various other sources *not* containing /r/, the phonetic reflex of which is [ɧ].[48] In the latter case various abstract sources, such as /sj/, /sk/, /stj/, can be assumed for some items, but in general the structural evidence for them is extremely weak; Eliasson (1973) argues that in most cases the underlying representation should be simply /š/. For the sake of simplicity, I will refer to the two structural units as /rs/ (i) and /š/ (ii) (thus disregarding the marginal differences that can be identified morphophonologically within the second group). /rs/ only occurs medially and finally in words or morphemes, never initially. /š/ can occur in any position (the items with final /š/ are foreign loans, e.g. *page* 'page-boy', *garage* 'garage', *beige* 'beige'). The only contexts where a phonemic contrast could occur are medial and final positions. In some dialects, there are minimal pairs, e.g. *pars* /pa:r+s/ pɑ:ʂ] gen. of *par* 'pair' – *page* /pa:š/ [pɑ:ɧ] 'page-boy', *lårs* /lo:r + s/ [lo:ʂ] gen. of *lår* 'thigh' – *loge* /lo:š/ [lo:ɧ] 'lodge', *fars* /fars/ [faʂ:] 'farce' – *krasch* /kraš/ [kraɧ:] 'crash' (n.), *kursa* /kʉrs + a/ [køʂ:a] 'sell out' – *kuscha* /kʉša/ [køɧ:a]'keep down, browbeat'. However, in many dialects the distribution of [ʂ] and [ɧ] is not so straightforward relative to the morphophonological representations. Elert (1970: 75–6) distinguishes four dialect types, which could schematically be described as follows:

(I = initial position, MF = medial or final position)

		Morphophonological unit:	
		/sj/	/rs/
Dialect 1			
('main standard	I:	ɧ	–
variant')	MF:	ɧ	ʂ
Dialect 2			
(southern Sweden)	I:	ɧ	–
	MF:	ɧ	ʀs

[47] [ʂ] may also be the reflex of a single underlying /s/, if there is at least one more dental intervening between the triggering /r/ and the /s/, e.g. *barns* /barn+s/ [bɑ:ɳʂ] (gen. of *barn* 'child').
[48] For a phonetic characterization of this velarized [ʃ]-sound, see, e.g., Malmberg (1968: 94–7); Elert (1970: 75). I disregard all the phonetic differences between dialectal variants of the [ɧ] ([ʃ]) type sounds, since these are immaterial to my arguments.

Dialect 3[49]

I:	ɧ	–	[ɧ] also medially
MF:	ʂ	ʂ	before stressed
			vowel, otherwise
			[ʂ] general in non-
			initial position.

Dialect 4[49]

I:	ʂ	–	[ʂ] is the only
MF:	ʂ	ʂ	occurring type.

There is however (to the best of my knowledge), no dialect type 5:

*Dialect 5	I:	ʂ	–
	MF:	ɧ	ʂ

If it is true, as I believe it is, that the non-occurrence of dialect 5 is a necessary and not an accidental gap, what is the explanation? We cannot explain the non-occurrence of [ʂ] in initial position by reference to the fact that /rs/ is impossible there, since in dialect 4 [ʂ] does occur initially. Moreover, if we were to accept the generative hypothesis that closely related dialects have the same underlying morpheme-invariant forms (§5.2.6), no structural explanation would be found at the underlying level. (Incidentally, it makes no difference whatever underlying morphophonemic sources, including /ʂ/, we may assume as substitutes for /š/ in different dialects; only /rs/ is excluded (in initial position it would violate quite general morpheme structure conditions of Swedish, in other positions there would not be any motivation for it).) Rather, the correct explanatory principle seems to be: [ʂ] can be (but need not be) the [ʃ]-sound in initial position (i.e. a realization of /š/) *only if* there is *no (surface) phonemic contrast* medially or finally (the only positions where such a contrast could emerge). Moreover, since this case seems quite typical, one may even formulate a general principle: If /x/ and /y/ are distinct morphophonemes, and /x/ only occurs in the context Z whereas /y/ is more generally distributed, we can never have realization rules of the following kind:

$$x \to a, \text{ and } y \to \begin{cases} b \ / \ Z \\ a \end{cases} \quad \text{(i.e. in the context Z there would be a surface phonemic contrast } /a/ \leftrightarrow /b/.)$$

[49] There may still be a marginal phonetic reflex of the /š/↔/rs/ contrast in these dialects, i.e. in the vowels of words like *depesch* /-eš/ [-ɛʂ:] 'dispatch' vs. *kommers* /-ers/ [-æʂ:] 'commerce'.

That is, a rule y → a/W (≠ Z) is possible only if the morphophonological difference between /x/ and /y/ is neutralized phonemically wherever it occurs (i.e. in the context Z). Thus, the possibility of occurrence of certain sounds in some positions may be dependent on the presence or absence of phonemic contrasts in other positions. Obviously, this also has implications for what directions diachronic changes may take (§5.2.10).

5.2.12 *Child language*

I will deal with children's acquisition of phonology in a separate chapter (11). In this context, I would only like to bring attention to a small piece of evidence uncovered by Ingram (1975). He argues that surface contrasts play a role in children's development of phonology in that children may be aware of a contrast though they are incapable of realizing it correctly. In this situation, at least some children invent various strategies to circumvent the difficulty, thus trying to keep their surface forms distinct. 'When the child's phonological processes would result in a homonym pair, two ways are used to avoid the loss of contrast: (i) the use of alternant pronunciations for one or both forms, or (ii) the use of unique phonological processes and contrasts, i.e. ones that are not used for non-homonymous pairs' (1975: 288). These unusual processes include metatheses, [ʔ]-substitution, transfer of contrast from vowel to consonant, etc. Some of Ingram's examples are summarized below (291).

Words in surface contrast[50]		Form predicted by the child's usual rules
(a) *plane*	[me]	*[pe]
plate	[pe]	
(b) *arm*	[ma]	*[a]
hot	[a]	
(c) *out*	[æʔ]	*[æ]
hat	[æ]	
(d) *hat*	[ak]	*[at]
hot	[at]	
(e) *milk*	[nək]	*[mək]
Mark	[mək]	

[50] The data except (a–c) come from different children.

5.2.13   *Pathological speech behavior*

5.2.13.1   *Speech errors.* Slips of the tongue comprise various types of substitutions, permutations, omissions and additions of single phones, groups of phones and syllables. It seems evident that they can be described in terms of reorganizations of phonetic plans. Units of such plans, i.e. roughly 'phonemes', are being substituted and permuted under influence of other parts of the utterance plan under construction.[51]

Many errors can only be explained with reference to grammatically conditioned processes. Thus, slips constitute important behavioral evidence that the construction of phonetic plans is subordinate to other operations (cf. §2.2). For example, grammatical units such as derivational and inflectional affixes may be permuted:

(1)   Sw. *det ortodox*T *Chomsky*ANSKA → *det ortod*ANSKT *Cho . . .*
'the orthodox Chomskyan things'
(from an unpublished corpus of mine)

(2)   Engl. *He made a lot of money* INstallING *telephone*s → *He made a lot of money* INtelephonING *stall*s
(Garrett and Shattuck, quoted in Fodor, Bever & Garrett 1974: 432)

In the following example from my corpus there is an interchange of different morphologically (or lexically) conditioned allomorphs of the Swedish plural morpheme:

(3)   Sw. *två dagar i rad*   → *två rader i dag*
'two days in (a) row'   'two rows in (a) day'

(This example would, in my theory, show the reality of morphological operations (ch. 7). The Swedish plural operation involves different morpholexical subrules (for *-ar, -er, -or, -n*, etc. cf. Linell 1972).)

Another type of grammatical conditioning is involved in the following segmental errors:[52]

(4)   *bloody students* [blʌdij stuwdənts] → [blʌdənt stuwdijz]
(Fromkin 1973: 27, 230)

(5)   *an eating marathon*   → *a meeting arathon*
a history of an ideology → *an istory of a hideology*
(231)

---

[51] For data, see papers in Fromkin 1973. Also Bond 1969; Roberts 1975.
[52] More examples, Fromkin (1973: 258–60).

The interesting feature of (4) is the final [z], instead of [s], which we could have expected if this was a simple case of segment transposition. The sequence [js] is possible in English as in *peace* [pijs], *mice* [majs], *face* [fejs]. However, as Fromkin points out, '[ij + s] cannot occur when the final sibilant represents the plural morpheme' (1973: 230). She therefore concludes that the morphophonological representation of the plural morpheme accounts for the /z/ in [stuwdijz]. (In *students* it becomes voiceless by a phonological rule.)

In (5) we find the alternation *a/an* according to the rule of the indefinite article. The distribution of the *a/an* cannot be explained solely in phonetic terms, since [ə] plus vowel is a possible English sequence, e.g. as in *America is, Rosa and I* (1973: 231).

Fromkin, faithful to her OGPh theory, interprets examples of this type as evidence that 'segmental errors' involve the transposition of morphophonemes at the morpheme-invariant level.[53] However, a more reasonable theory is to assume that slips involve more concrete units of phonetic plans. All speech errors give rise to sound sequences which are possible according to the surface phonotactic rules or constraints (PhtRs) of the language (cf. Fromkin 1973: 229). Some such constraints are grammatically conditioned (see ch. 10) (phonology is not 'autonomous', cf. ch. 13). The rules involved in (4, 5) above may all be regarded as such grammatically conditioned PhtRs.

Most scholars, both structuralists (see some contributions to Fromkin 1973) and post-structuralists (e.g. Bond 1969: 305; Roberts 1975; cf. also Stampe 1972: 42–3) agree that production errors support the reality of phonemes, rather than more abstract segments. Fromkin is a notable exception,[54] although she too is cognizant of 'concrete' alternatives. An 'abstract' theory might be supported if there were cases in which typically morphophonemic or other non-surface structures, i.e. ones which could not appear normally at a 'phonemic' level, are manifested, or are necessarily presupposed in the explanation of slips. The only obvious case in Fromkin's (1973) data from English and German[55] which suggests something like this, involves the split of English [ŋ]:

---

[53] Note that even if some grammatically conditioned slips could be explained in terms of permutations of morphophonemes in morpheme-invariant forms, this would by no means solve all problems. Thus, e.g., (3) above involves different lexically conditioned allomorphs (/ar/ vs. /er/, cf. Linell 1972), which cannot be predicted from (morpho)phonological representations.

[54] Also Celce-Murcia (1973).

[55] The German data are from Meringer (1908).

(6)   *cut the string*   → [kʌnt ðə strɪg]
      Springtime for Hitler → *sprig time for hintler*
      swing and sway   → [swĩn] *and* [sweig]
      (1973: 21–2, 223)[56]

Fromkin interprets these data as evidence that the abstract source /ng/ proposed for English [ŋ] by, e.g., Sapir (1925) and Chomsky & Halle (1968), is psychologically real and that errors 'provide "behavioral" support for the English rule ... g → ∅/N__#. Since the [g] emerges if the nasal is deleted or transposed during speech production, the /g/ must be present at some stage in the production process' (1973: 22).

However, [ŋ] may simply be a phonetically less coherent segment type, more easily amenable to disintegration than [m] and [n].[57] If so, one would not have to assume that there exists an abstract underlying sequence /ng/ for English words like *string*, *spring*, etc. If, on the other hand, the split of [ŋ] in English is really dependent on the *phonological* structure of English, one would expect [ŋ] not to split in languages where it is an underlying phonological unit. In the absence of the relevant data the issue cannot yet be settled.

5.2.13.2 *Aphasia*. The phonology of aphasic aberrations would also be potentially relevant in determining the abstractness of speakers' internalized phonological forms. Some generativists (e.g. Weigl & Bierwisch 1970; Drachman 1972; Schnitzer 1972; Kehoe & Whitaker 1973, and others) have indeed used aphasic data in arguing for the psychological validity of OGPh type representations and rules. Drachman (1972) discusses two aphasic pronunciations of *degradation* and *practicality* with the same vowels and stress patterns as in the respective underived forms *degrade* and *practical*[58] and comments: 'It seems that distinctly non-surface processes of English [i.e. abstract–phonological rules] are being suspended or misapplied, and *must then, it follows, be accessible during the act of speech*.' (Drachman 1972: 13) (my italics). Schnitzer (1972) and Kehoe & Whitaker (1973) similarly interpret aphasic errors in terms of wrong morphophonemic forms (of OGPh type) and misapplied rules, thus arguing that their data constitute evidence for OGPh. However, the validity of OGPh does not

[56] For more examples, see Fromkin (1973: 250).
[57] A fact which would also be reflected in its less consolidated place in the phoneme system of many languages.
[58] There are many more examples of this type.

follow from the fact that the aphasic aberrations can be described in terms of such a model; observational facts can be generated by an infinite number of false theories. OGPh explanations are extremely weak, since the hypothetical constructs of the theory (e.g. morpheme-invariants) are largely empirically uninterpreted (or even uninter-pretable, cf. ch. 12) and are therefore open to uncontrolled manipulation and adjustment by the analyst. Moreover, the explanations offered by Schnitzer and others are extremely far-fetched (Linell 1974a: 144–6).

In fact, data given by the authors mentioned clearly suggest an explanation in terms of surface forms and operations applied to such forms (see §4.3.3.4).[59] As far as other kinds of phonological errors of aphasia are concerned (which do not involve relations between forms (morpheme identity)), we get a rather mixed picture. There are some regularities which resemble those of ordinary slips (which speak for surface-phonemic forms, §5.2.13.1) but many aphasic deviations consist of cluster simplifications[60] and paradigmatic substitutions (e.g. /r/↔/l/, /s/ ↔ /f/, /b/ ↔ /d/, etc.) in which there are no obvious sources for the substitute segments in the phonological structure of the strings involved. In fact, aphasia may involve sounds or sound combinations which are not permitted in the language, neither on a phonemic nor on a more abstract level of representation (e.g. Dressler 1973d). Apart from the fact that deviant substitutions usually involve phonetically similar sounds, substitutions seem rather random. It seems difficult to use such data as evidence for or against hypotheses about normal language-specific phonological forms and rules.

5.2.13.3 *Misperceptions.* Garnes & Bond discuss regularities within a corpus of misperceptions ('slips of the ear'), i.e. cases of listeners 'hearing something that does not correspond to what a speaker said' (1975: 214). The results match at most points those of studies of production slips, i.e. the patterns perceived conform to the phonotactic patterns of the language. The same is, moreover, true of the types of perceptual reinterpretation occurring in so-called dichotic listening, in which a person is fed with two simultaneous but partially different stimuli in his two ears; listeners usually synthesize their impressions into perceived strings that meet the phonotactic rules of the language. For instance, if an English speaking person hears [gab] in one ear and

---

[59] Drachman's examples fit the same mould.
[60] Cf. for example, Wurzel & Böttcher (1977).

[lab] in the other, the [g] and [l] stimuli being exactly simultaneous, he will perceive [glab], not *[lgab] or any other phonotactically impossible sequence (cf. Cutting 1975).

5.2.13.4 *Summary*. Speech errors and misperceptions are seemingly always in accordance with phonotactic conditions on the structure of phonetic plans. Thus, they also indirectly support the importance of phonemic contrasts (cf. §5.2.2).

5.2.14 *Divergent properties of rule types*
Within an OGPh type theory, a system of phonological rules map morpheme-invariant (morphophonemic) representations onto allophonic representations, without there being any significant phonemic level in between. The rules involved are all assumed to be similar in form and function, e.g. there would be no significant differences between 'early' rules (which would correspond to traditional morphophonemic rules mapping morphophonemic forms onto phonemic forms) and 'late' rules (which could correspond to traditional allophonic rules mapping phonemic forms onto phonetic representations).[61] However, a careful consideration of the properties of phonological rules does indeed show that there are many important formal and behavioral differences between phonological rule types. In particular, morphophonological rules proper, i.e. rules which are motivated *solely* to account for morphophonological alternations, (§7.2, §10.3.5) are quite different on a large number of accounts (indeed, they should not be regarded as living phonological rules at all). Thus, the considerations of ch. 10 will show that there *are* arguments for a bipartition of OGPh 'phonology' into morphophonology and phonology proper. This automatically supports the significance of surface-phonemic representations.[62]

5.2.15 *Linguists' practice*
As a final point, which is less important but quite revealing, consider the

---

[61] Some generativists do single out low-level detail rules as a special category (e.g. King 1973: 567–8), but these rules are *not* the same as traditional allophonic rules.

[62] Lately, generativists too have begun to recognize differences between rule types which would indirectly imply recognition of phonemes. For instance, Kiparsky's (1973b) introduction of the distinction between opaque and transparent rules implies a recognition of the distinction between morphophonology and phonology (Crothers & Shibatani 1975: 507).

fact that even linguists who deny the significance of surface phonemic contrasts theoretically, nevertheless obey some rules in their practical linguistic analyses which suggest that they do ascribe some importance to these contrasts. Thus, as some generativists point out themselves,[63] though an OGPh analysis *in theory* proceeds from morphophonemic representations (via various intermediate forms) right down to narrow phonetic representations, in actual OGPh practice, derivations are usually never pursued that far. In fact, the output forms of OGPh derivations are roughly phonemic (rather than allophonic) representations. Schane says:

So long as generativists do not generate a narrow phonetic representation, their rules will generate explicitly a broad phonetic representation, which, implicitly, is a representation of surface contrasts. It can be no mere coincidence, then, that the output of a generative phonology is so often almost amazingly identical to a classical phonemic representation. This similarity ought to be disconcerting to generativists, since, if anything, it corroborates a phonemic type representation in spite of claims to the contrary. (1971 : 520)

5.3 Can one recognize the significance of surface contrasts without having surface forms?

In view of the arguments of §5.2, it seems inevitable to recognize the linguistic, as well as psychological and behavioral, significance of surface phonemic contrasts. The obvious conclusion would seem to be that phonology should be based on surface forms rather than abstract morpheme-invariants, especially so since there are other arguments for surface forms (see chs. 3–8). However, OGPh may perhaps accommodate phonemic contrasts without giving up the overall structure of the model. In fact, Postal (1968: 18, 22) did admit the importance of contrast vs. free variation but suggested that this does not mean that one must be capable of reading off contrasts (vs. free variation) at one particular level. Instead, it is possible to deduce, or derive, contrasts, given the underlying forms and the rule system. Later, Mansell (1973a) proposed that OGPh should be extended by some device of this kind, i.e. constraints on derivations, to account derivatively for contrasts. Contrasts would be accounted for, not in terms of relations between (surface) forms, but rather in terms of rule interaction within derivations. In Linell (1976a) I argue that Mansell's theory would be

[63] E.g. Schane (1971 : 519–20).

utterly complex and implausible from a psychological or behavioral point-of-view. Furthermore, it is *impossible*, if our arguments (chs. 8, 9, 12) are correct that there are no morpheme-invariants (which would serve as the fundament of an OGPh type theory).

6 Phonotactics and phonological correctness

6.1 Introduction

I have already (§2.3) argued that speakers have an ability to distinguish admissible (correct, well-formed) phonological structures from structures which are non-admissible (incorrect) or, at least, less admissible, 'foreign' or deviant in their language. This ability manifests itself behaviorally in that speakers tend not to pronounce 'foreign-sounding' elements in their deviant phonetic form; instead, they either refuse to use these elements or they change them so that they conform to (or at least, conform more to) native phonological patterns. Furthermore, most speakers are able to pronounce judgments concerning the relative correctness (nativeness) of different phonological–phonetic strings. An adequate theory of phonological competence must therefore have means to define and explain the properties of correct phonological forms vs. incorrect or deviant forms. Traditionally, this is handled in phonological theory by context-free rules, which define the set of admissible segments (cf. paradigmatic redundancy), and context-sensitive rules, which define admissible strings of segments, i.e. phonotactic patterns (cf. syntagmatic redundancy). This distinction crucially presupposes the significance of the *segmental* make-up of strings. As was noted in §3.7, some doubts concerning the complete justification of this assumption may be raised. Yet I will, as elsewhere in this book, assume that it has a sufficient basis as a convenient and workable idealization.

In this chapter I will mostly be concerned with restrictions on admissible strings, i.e. *phonotactic* constraints. Traditionally, phonotactic constraints have been formulated as conditions on phoneme combinations within word forms (or parts of word forms, i.e. morphs of various types) (cf. for example, Sigurd 1965). However, OGPh proposes instead that phonotactic conditions must concern underlying morpheme-invariants, i.e. the generative–phonological lexical entries (Chomsky & Halle 1968: 380). Later critics, e.g. Shibatani (1973), have argued that, contrary to Chomsky & Halle's assertions, speakers' judgments of phonological correctness are built upon surface phonotactics (i.e. the traditional position). Shibatani argues that generative phonology must have both underlying morpheme-structure (MSCs) and surface structure constraints (SSCs). Others, e.g. Clayton (1976), argue that only the latter are necessary.

In this chapter I will summarize arguments to the following effects:

(i)   phonological correctness must be defined in terms of restrictions on concrete word forms, and more specifically,

(ii)   such restrictions concern the structure of careful pronunciations, i.e. they refer to phonetic plans as conceived of in ch. 3,

(iii) there is both psychological and behavioral evidence for (ii),

(iv)   arguments for generative MSCs are misconceived. (MSCs are of course impossible in my theory which denies the existence of abstract morpheme-invariants, see ch. 12.)

6.2 Phonological correctness

6.2.1 *Independence of morphophonology*

Judgments of phonological correctness cannot be based on morphophonemic strings. This follows from the following simple argument. Consider the fact that a typical situation in which a speaker is faced with the task of deciding whether a certain word is phonologically correct is when he is confronted with an item which so far did not belong to his lexicon. If such a word cannot be analyzed in terms of already known morphemes, then its OGPh type underlying form would often be impossible to determine, and hence, according to Chomsky & Halle (1968), the grammaticality of the word form would not be decidable. Still speakers *can* make such judgments of grammaticality. Obviously the OGPh theory is wrong; these judgments are made on the basis of phonotactic conditions on concrete phonetic strings (cf. also Shibatani 1973: 95; Sommerstein 1974: 73).

Estimations of phonological correctness are more or less 'purely phonological' (cf. §5.2.1–3) except for the fact that speakers may know that certain surface forms are phonologically admissible only if they belong to some specific morphological category or have a certain morph structure. Thus, a Swedish nonsense form like *pàmmer* (tone 2) is a phonotactically perfect word in Swedish, but it cannot be an adjective, a neutral noun[1] or a verbal present tense form. For these morphological classes there is a phonotactic constraint for forms with the kind of segmental structure exemplified above which only admits of tone 1 (e.g. *pámmer*). Thus, we have to allow for certain kinds of morphologically conditioned phonotactic constraints (see ch. 7, §10.7.1.2). Of course, having such surface conditions sensitive to grammatical conditions is quite different from claiming that morphophonology is relevant for the definition of phonological correctness.

That morphophonology is irrelevant for the estimation of phono-logical correctness is clear from other considerations too. There is no difference between the ways in which we experience words involved in morphophonological alternations and words *not* involved in such alternations, as far as their phonological well-formedness is concerned. Likewise, judgments of phonological similarity or identity are based on surface forms (careful pronunciations); it makes no difference if some words are alternating and others not, or indeed if some words actually exist whereas others do not (cf. §5.2.1–2). Thus, there are no intuitively perceptible differences in the ways in which the following three kinds of Swedish word forms are structured phonologically:

(a) alternating existing words: [le:d] *led* (e.g. imp. of *leda* 'to lead', thus related to [lὲd:ə] *ledde*, pret. of *leda*), [sὸ:nər] *söner* 'sons' (related to [so:n] 'son'), [çὲmpa] *kämpa* 'to fight' (related to [kamp] 'fight' (n.))

(b) non-alternating existing words: [ʃe:d] *sked* 'spoon', [bὸ:nər] *böner* 'prayers' (plural of [bø:n]), [dὲmpa] *dämpa* 'to moderate'

(c) non-existent words (nonsense-words): [fe:d], [vὸ:nər], [ʃὲmpa].

Moreover, there are strings which are possible on an underlying morphophonemic level but impossible on a surface level. Such strings would be deemed as ungrammatical by speakers, which again shows that it is the latter level that matters. For example, German speakers would reject [ra:d] as non-German, though this is an actually occurring morpheme-invariant in German (/ra:d/ *Rad* 'wheel, bicycle') (Shibatani 1973).[2] Similarly, *[tjø:l] and *[bɔng], etc. are impossible in Swedish,

---

1 There are two neutral nouns of this type with tone 2, namely *papper* and *siden*.

2 It does not seem to matter that there is a bound morph [ra:d], e.g. in *dem Rade* [dəm ra:də] (dat. sg.). Note that the [d] in such forms belongs to the following syllable, where it is followed by a vowel.

though there may be good reasons to set up morphophonemic forms such as /tjø:l/ and /bɔng/ in an OGPh description of Swedish (e.g. Linell, Svensson & Öhman 1971).

6.2.2 *Reference to careful pronunciations*

Thus, we can safely argue that intuitions about phonological correctness (cf. 'pronounceability') are based on phonetic forms. More precisely, these intuitions seem to be based on careful pronunciations. That is, in casual speech there may in fact occur types of phonetic segments and segment combinations which would, if presented in isolation, be considered as deviant or phonologically impossible by speakers. For example, [# tsn-] would be judged as un-English by English speakers, yet something like this occurs in [tsnɒt], a common pronunciation of *it's not* (Brown 1977: 71), [# fst-] is not a possible initial cluster in Swedish, yet [fstó:ɾɨ] is a very common rendition of *förstår du?* 'do you understand?', a long vowel before a velar nasal is deemed as incorrect in German (*[me:ŋ]), yet we have often pronunciations such as [le:ŋ] for *legen*. Examples of this type are hardly atypical. Thus, we may assume that intuitions about phonological correctness are based upon phonetic plans as proposed in ch. 3.

6.3 Behavioral evidence

6.3.1 *The adaptation of deviant forms*

Quite often language users are confronted with forms which are perceived as phonologically deviant in their own language. Such forms tend to be restructured in both speech perception and speech production so that they conform fully, or at least, to a greater extent, to the phonotactic patterns of the language. Words of (or from) foreign languages are almost invariably changed, at least by monolingual speakers, into forms that satisfy, or at least, deviate less from, the phonotactic conditions of the mother tongue. Thus, loan word adaptation is primarily phonetic approximation, plus sometimes preservation and transposition of surface phonemic contrasts of the lending language (if this is possible within the phonemic system of the borrowing language). Thus, phonotactic rules, and other true phono-logical rules, apply productively to loans, whereas morphophonological rules proper (§7.2.3), morphophonemic forms and conditions on such forms play no role (see §10.8.2).

Other cases of correcting or adjusting deviant forms are quite similar. Perceptual reinterpretation is a case in point (§5.2.3). The outputs of morphological operations always obey the phonotactic generalizations (§7.3). Moreover, speech errors and products of linguistic games also show the productivity of these rules, while morphophonological rules proper are irrelevant throughout (§10.8.7–9).

6.3.2 *Reduction in fast speech*

The phonetic structure of fast or casual speech is often different from that of very careful speech; new segment types and combinations appear (§6.2.2). Vowels are omitted, which gives rise to new consonant clusters, which in their turn are often reduced or simplified. However, a very interesting finding in Gårding's (1974) study of consonant cluster reduction in Swedish casual speech is that syllable-final consonants are transposed to the next syllable if and only if thereby a syllable-initial cluster is created which would be permissible also on the level of careful pronunciations, i.e. according to the phonotactic constraints of the language (in our model). Such clusters then turn out to be *immune to reduction*, while other types of clusters are obligatorily or optionally reduced. I interpret this preservation of syllable-initial clusters as an interesting piece of evidence that at least some of the structures defined by constraints on careful pronunciations have a substantial significance also for speech behavior at other phonostylistic levels.

6.4 On capturing regularities

Though it is clear that not all detectable linguistic regularities are significant from a psychological or behavioral point-of-view (ch. 1), it may be worth pointing out that there are surface-phonotactic generalizations which seem to be important but which cannot be captured in an OGPh type phonology.

6.4.1 *Conspiracies*

A frequently occurring type of 'lost generalization' in OGPh which has also been prominent in the theoretical discussion among generativists, is that of 'conspiracies', i.e. cases where different (morpho)phonological rules 'conspire' to conform to certain preferred phonotactic patterns (e.g. Kisseberth 1970; Ross 1972). In fact, the postulation of such a conspiracy reveals the failure on the part of OGPh to state the unity of a single phonotactic generalization. The failure seems to be inherent in the generative-phonological model which forces the analyst to select certain unique morpheme-invariant forms and to formulate morpho-phonological rules with a certain direction, rather than to formulate natural conditions on pronounceability of forms. A classical example concerns Swedish consonant clusters of the type obstruent-plus-sonorant (and some of type sonorant-plus-sonorant, e.g. /lr, nl, mr/) which occur between vowels but not word-finally and before consonants, where they must be split up by an epenthetic /e/, e.g. sing. *fågel* 'bird' – pl. *fåglar*, sing. *nỳckel* 'key' – pl. *nỳcklar*, *tápper* 'brave' – *tàppra* (infl. form), *slàmra* 'to rustle' – *slámmer* 'rustle' (n.). Here, most generative descriptions have set up underlying forms of different types, with or without unstable vowels (to make the tonal accents predictable), and two morphophonological rules (epenthesis and syncope) which seem to be the same rule in two variants applying in opposite directions in complementary contexts.[3] To avoid this awkward solution, Eliasson (1972) proposes only one rule (syncope). However, this is done at the cost of setting up a number of imaginary underlying forms.[4] Since there are reasons to regard the phonotactic generalizations as primary and the specific structure of the morphological operations as secondary (phonotactic constraints rather than morphophonological rules determine constraints on outputs of operations, cf. §7.3, Linell 1976b: 20–1), we would instead want to state the phonotactic generalization involved, possibly in the form of a complex but unitary if–then condition:

(1)   IF: $\text{X C}_i \begin{bmatrix} \underline{\qquad} \\ -\text{stress} \end{bmatrix} \left\{ \begin{matrix} r \\ l \\ n \end{matrix} \right\} \text{Y}$

THEN: (a) $\text{e if Y} = \left\{ \begin{matrix} \# \\ C \end{matrix} \right\}$

(b) $\emptyset \text{ if Y} = \text{V}$

Conditions: X contains a stressed syllable and no word boundary. C_i is one of the consonants occurring first in the type of clusters under consideration. (For further details, see e.g. Eliasson 1972.)

[3]   Cf. Teleman 1969; Eliasson 1972; Linell 1972; Hellberg 1974.

[4]   E.g. /muskul/, /fabul/, /nobil/ for *muskel* 'muscle', *fabel* 'fable', *nobel* 'noble' (1972: 185). Eliasson (1972: 183, fn. 13) also suggests the possibility of positing /koper/, /kober/, /ragel/, etc. for the roots of *kopra* 'copra', *kobra* 'cobra', *ragla* 'stagger' (in which the /e/ never surfaces).

This would handle the alternation involved in the forms in question (cf. the examples given above). (In some cases the unstable vowel is not /e/, e.g. *sommar* 'summer' – *somrar* (pl.), *gammal* 'old' – *gamla* (infl. form), *morron* 'morning' – *mornar* (pl.), *djävul* 'devil' – *djävlar* (pl.), but then the vowel is always present in the lexical base form.[5] (1) covers all possible cases of productive application of the phonotactic generalization.)

It seems to me that this sort of complex phonotactic constraints which can be applied 'in either direction' may be needed rather often. Thus, in Finnish consonant gradation one may need to go from either the strong grade to the weak grade *or* vice versa by having some phonotactic constraint like the following (simplified):

(2) IF: $V \ C_x \ V \ Y$ (C_x is a consonant or consonant cluster subject to gradation.)

THEN: (a) strong grade if $Y = \#$

(b) weak grade if $Y = C \begin{Bmatrix} C \\ \# \end{Bmatrix}$

(Some morphological contextual conditions must be added, cf. Karlsson 1974b.)

The generative straitjacket has normally forced analysts to start from inputs in the strong grade irrespective of whether or not the lexical base form has strong grade on the surface. Karlsson (1974b: 100), on the other hand, has to formulate two rules, gradation and inverted gradation, which seems unnecessary in the framework proposed here. 'Bidirected' phonotactic if–then conditions represent a possibility which should be further explored.

6.4.2 *Conditions on syllable structure*

Basbøll (1974) has provided a detailed discussion of the nature and structure of syllables with special reference to Danish. Among other things, he discusses at which level the regularities in the distribution of different segment types (defined in terms of features, cf. also Basbøll 1977a) within syllables should be formulated. It turns out for Danish that this level is a surface level rather than a morphophonemic (or some other kind of remote abstract) level of representation. More specifically, it is a level of very careful ('overprecise') pronunciations, something

---

[5] Words like *titulera muskulös, nobilitet*, etc. (Eliasson 1972) must be assumed to be separate lexical items for independent reasons (cf. §4.3.3.2).

which supports the hypothesis of having phonetic plans pertain to careful pronunciations, as has been proposed in this work (ch. 3, §6.2.2).

6.5 On some properties of phonotactic rules

6.5.1 *Active filter function*

Phonotactic conditions (or rules) are a natural type of generalizations about phonological structures; they are directly extractable ('transparent', §10.7.1.4) from the surface patterns of careful pronunciations. They may be regarded as defining the notion of 'pronounceability in language L', where 'pronounceability' of course does not refer to what is physically possible for the speakers to pronounce. Rather, we are concerned with what speakers 'believe are restrictions on pronunciations' (Bjarkman 1975: 71). In fact, the rules in question are often not descriptively true of more reduced forms, although speakers are usually unaware of this (§6.2.2). Derwing talks about phonotactic generalizations as 'representing a set of articulatory habits which speakers of a language have acquired, over time, as a result of constant practice' (1973: 215). (Such a characterization would, however, cover other types of (true) phonological rules too and serves mainly to distinguish these rules from morphophonological rules proper, cf. §10.3.)

Phonotactic generalizations have been pictured here as conditions or constraints on correct phonological strings, or more exactly, phonetic plans. However, they cannot simply be regarded as static (positive or negative) conditions on a finite set of existing forms. They have a projective character, governing new forms too. Thus, (i) neologisms are made to conform to them; (ii) outputs of morphological operations are subject to them; and (iii) foreign words, which sometimes violate them, tend to be restructured so as to agree fully, or at least, to a greater extent, with the constraints. These points, especially (ii) and (iii), show that phonotactic conditions must be construed as active if–then conditions which map certain inadmissible forms onto admissible ones. Thus, rather than simply throwing out ungrammatical forms[6] they transform

---

[6] Exceptionally one encounters such negative 'static' conditions too. One example would be the condition which prohibits the formation of neutral forms of certain Swedish adjectives, e.g. *rädd* 'scared', *fadd* 'insipid', *lat* 'lazy'. For some discussion of these, see Eliasson (1975b). Another example might be the non-existence of the 1. sg. present forms of certain -*at'* verbs in Russian (**lažu*, **deržu*, **muču*, **erunžu*, etc.) as discussed by Halle (1973: 7). For various formal types of 'conditions' on phonological strings, see Stanley (1967).

the unacceptable strings (be these foreign words or structures generated by grammatical rules) into forms conforming to the conditions. Consider as a simple example German final tensing.[7] This cannot fruitfully be construed as a negative condition (3) but should be formulated as an if–then condition (4):

$$
(3) \quad * \begin{bmatrix} -\text{son} \\ +\text{vce} \\ -\text{tns} \end{bmatrix} \# \qquad (4) \quad \text{IF:} \quad \begin{array}{c} [-\text{son}] \# \text{ (simplified)} \\ \downarrow \end{array}
$$

$$
\text{THEN:} \quad \begin{bmatrix} (-\text{vce}) \\ +\text{tns} \end{bmatrix}
$$

A rule like (3) would correctly fail to accept e.g. [za:g] as a possible German form without, however, telling what we should have instead; for instance, when we derive the imperative singular from *sagen* (by a morphological operation, cf. §7.3), this rule does not prevent us from getting e.g. [za:ŋ] instead of [za:k] by changing the feature specification for [son] rather than for [tns] (and [vce]). (4), on the other hand, predicts the correct form /za:k/. The if–then character of most phonotactic generalizations is therefore obvious (cf. also Matthews 1972; Derwing 1973: 215;[8] Shibatani 1973; Sommerstein 1974). Some call these generalizations 'conditions', or 'constraints' (e.g. Shibatani 1973), while others prefer the term 'rule' (e.g. Sommerstein's (1974) 'phonotactically motivated P-rule'). The former term finds some motivation in that phonotactic generalizations are defined at a certain level (intralevel rules, §10.7.2.3), while the term 'rule' is motivated because they (may) convert (ill-formed) strings onto other (correct) strings. I will use both terms, though with a certain preference for 'phonotactic rule' (PhtR) (§10.3.1). The relationships of PhtRs to other kinds of rules will be treated in considerable detail in ch. 10 (concerning the role of PhtRs in morphological operations and morphophonological alternations, see ch. 7).

---

[7] We disregard here the fact that this rule seems to belong to a special type, 'sharpening rules' (§10.3.2).

[8] Derwing explicates his conception of phonological rules as 'phonotactic generalizations' as follows: 'I assume that each such "rule" has two essential parts: (1) a statement of the particular "impossible" or "outlawed" sequences of elements which the habit has produced and (2) a statement of the particular "instruction" to be followed whenever an asterisked sequence of this sort is "submitted" by the lexicon for articulation' (1973: 215). Incidentally, I find this characterization partly inadequate, since it is a typical property of a phonotactic rule, as opposed to a morphophonological rule proper, that the 'outlawed' string is *not* defined in its structural description (§10.7.2.3).

6.5.2 *Domain of application*

In the theory proposed here, phonotactic rules concern surface forms, whereas OGPh, on the other hand, characterizes restrictions on admissible phonological strings as morpheme-structure constraints (MSCs) at the morpheme-invariant level. Note that this theoretical disagreement seems to involve claims about two rather different properties of phonological correctness conditions, i.e. their level of abstractness and their domain of application. That is, OGPh claims that conditions are defined at the abstract morphophonemic level and that the domain of conditions is the morpheme rather than concatenated *strings* of morphemes (e.g. the underlying representation of whole word forms). Our theory claims that conditions pertain to careful pronunciations at the surface level. But note that we do *not* claim that all conditions have the same domain. On the contrary, while many conditions seem to be defined for whole word forms, there are obviously many others which have *parts* of concrete forms, such as morphs, stems or syllables as their domain (see §10.7.4). Some scholars who have recently defended MSCs against SSCs (surface structure constraints)[9] apparently confuse the two issues.[10] What can be demonstrated is that some correctness conditions have *morphs* (perhaps roots) (morphologically defined parts of surface forms) as their domain. However, it does not appear to be true that these conditions must be defined in terms of abstract morphophonemic forms.

[9]   See Kaye 1974; Morin 1975; Dressler 1977b: 54. Cf. also Clayton (1976: 302, fn. 7).
[10] Admittedly, this is also true of Hooper (1975: 556 and passim) who seems to deny the significance of morphs. Cf. also §3.3.2.2.

7 Morphological operations and morphophonology

7.1 Introduction
I have now developed the main features of a model of phonology in which:

(a)   the phonological identity of phonetic strings is defined by phonetic plans of constituent word forms[1]

(b)   phonetic plans are plans for phonetic behavior, pertaining to careful pronunciations

(c)   surface phonemic contrasts have a function in characterizing the nature of phonetic plans

(d)   the lexicon contains a set of such phonetic plans (together with grammatical information about the forms).

So far, very little has been said about morphology, morpheme identity and morphophonology, i.e. those parts of language which are in the focus of interest in OGPh. In chapters 7–9 this will be done (see also ch. 12 which contains a critique of the treatment of morpheme identity in OGPh). Though problems of morphology and morphophonology are closely interrelated with phonology, I will argue that they should be handled outside phonology proper, rather than in one comprehensive 'phonological' component as in OGPh.[2]

---

[1]   I have not treated the prosodic properties of phrases, clauses and sentences. These, of course, represent a completely different dimension in phonology, which should be considered in its own right, for both phonetic and grammatical–functional reasons.

[2]   Chomsky & Halle (1968) relegate some aspects of morpholexis and suppletion to a 'readjustment component' between syntax and phonology. In a European variant of generative morphology (Bierwisch 1967; Kiefer 1970; Wurzel 1970; Linell 1972) morpholexis and part of morphophonology are treated in a morphological component, but here too most of morphophonology belongs to the phonological component. For another position, rather close to what is proposed in this book, see Dressler (1977b).

7.2 **Morphological operations: general properties**

As far as morphology is concerned, the most important aspect of a speaker's communicative competence is his ability to form new word forms, or, in my terminology, to construct new phonetic plans (i.e. plans which are not lexically stored). Such productive morphological processes are most central in inflection, but they are obviously important also in what has traditionally been called 'word formation', i.e. derivation and compounding.

I will use the term *morphological operation* to refer to the kind of linguistic act in which a speaker constructs a new word form on the basis of other (in most cases) lexicalized forms.

Note that *operations* are supposed to have the following properties (cf. §1.4.3):

(a)   they are (a subtype of) acts, i.e. they lead to a certain intended goal (in this case, that of constructing word forms with certain intended properties, §7.4.1)

(b)   as acts they are real behavioral events, i.e. actions that are, or can be, performed by speakers. Some evidence that morphological operations are real subacts in the construction of utterances will be briefly discussed in §7.4.2. Recall that rules are not acts; rather some rules may be seen as conditions on or aspects of acts or operations (§1.4.3 and below)

(c)   they transform one formally defined object into another such object (cf. the mathematical notion of operation). In the case of morphological operations, these objects are supposed to be phonetic plans.

In ch. 4 I argued that lexical forms, which serve as operands of morphological operations, are surface forms, i.e. base forms or stems. This means that a morphological operation can be seen as an analogical inference schema of the following format:

(1)   If there is a form X (the operand) with the semantic, syntactic and lexical properties α_1, α_2, α_3 ... and the phonological properties φ_1, φ_2, φ_3 ..., then there must also be a form Y (the resultant) with the semantic, syntactic and lexical properties β_1, β_2, β_3 ... and the phonological properties ψ_1, ψ_2, ψ_3 ...

For example, if we have English singular forms such as /wʌg/, /blik/,

/mʌz/, etc., the pluralization operation predicts that there have to be corresponding plural forms: /wʌgz/, /bliks/, /mʌzɪz/.

A morphological operation corresponds fairly well to the traditional idea of extension by regular *analogy*. As is well-known, the concept of analogy has been in disrepute in OGPh (ever since Kiparsky 1965).[3] One of the generative arguments has been that traditional grammarians often failed to define conditions on regular (i.e. rule-governed) analogies as opposed to sporadic analogies. Obviously, we must define the properties of regular analogies (alias morphological operations), e.g. English plural formation. Apart from this and perhaps a few other points, however, the rejection of the concept of analogy has been unfortunate.[4] There is evidence that the model of 'analogically' extending a relation between surface forms is more realistic than the OGPh account of morphological productivity in terms of derivations from abstract morpheme configurations to surface forms (§4.3.3). Furthermore, there are important differences between the interaction of morphophonological rules (within morphological operations) and that of phonological rules proper (outside morphological operations) (see §7.4, ch. 10), something which is entirely obscured in OGPh.

A morphological operation is a rule-governed formation pattern. To account for its regularity we must define it in terms of general properties of input and output forms (α_{1-n}, β_{1-n}, φ_{1-n}, ψ_{1-n} of (1) above). To account for the expression side it may be analytically necessary to discern different aspects of the change effected:

(2) *Aspects of a morphological operation :*

CORE: Morpholexical rule(s)

DEPENDENT PART: Morphophonological changes

Morphophonology is seen in the traditional way as concerning those phonological adjustments which, according to the rules of the language, are dependent consequences of a morphological or syntactic change of expression, the latter being defined by the morpholexical core. As should be well-known, it is important to distinguish between two types of morphophonological alternations, and, correspondingly, two types of rules with morphophonological effects:

---

[3] Cf. also King 1969: 127–34; Kiparsky 1974.
[4] See also J. Ohala 1974a; Skousen 1975a; Anttila 1976a.

(3)   *Types of rules with morphophonological effects:*

(a) Phonotactic constraints on phonetic plans (= phonotactic rules, PhtRs)	valid for all surface forms, whether participating in alternations or not
(b) (Non-phonotactically motivated) morphophonological rules proper (MRPs)	needed solely for the purpose of taking care of certain morphophonological alternations

Phonotactic rules have already been discussed in ch. 6. A thorough discussion of different types of phonological rules will be given in ch. 10.

7.3 Morphological operations: examples

I will now proceed to a discussion of a number of actually occurring morphological operations, thereby focusing on their general principles, in particular the role of phonotactic rules (PhtRs) and morphophonological rules proper (MRPs).

As a first example, consider English regular plural formation. This is a case where the basic facts seem clear. Yet, a considerable number of theoretical interpretations of the facts have been proposed.[5] Without pretending that the ultimate solution has been found I give here the interpretation which seems, after all, most probable (cf. Derwing & Baker 1976; Linell 1976b: 14–16):

(4)   (a) Morpholexical rule: Plural → /z/

  (b) PhtR I: $\varnothing$ → I (or [ə]) between sibilants

  (c) PhtR II: z → s after voiceless obstruents

More exactly, (4c) and (4b) can be formulated as follows:

(4c)   IF: $\begin{bmatrix} -\text{son} \\ -\text{vce} \end{bmatrix}$ + $\begin{matrix} [-\text{son}] \# \\ \downarrow \end{matrix}$

  THEN: $[-\text{vce}]$

(4b)   IF: $\begin{bmatrix} -\text{son} \\ +\text{cor} \\ \alpha\,\text{strid} \\ \alpha\,\text{del rel} \end{bmatrix}$ $\begin{matrix} \varnothing \\ \mid \\ \downarrow \end{matrix}$ $\begin{bmatrix} -\text{son} \\ +\text{cor} \\ \alpha\,\text{strid} \\ \alpha\,\text{del rel} \end{bmatrix} \#$ [6]

  THEN: I

---

[5] See esp. Miner 1975; Zwicky 1975b; Derwing & Baker 1976.

[6] Fricatives are assumed to be [+del rel]. For discussion of alternatives, cf. Zwicky 1975b; Linell 1976b: 15.

(4c) is a language-specific variant of a universal condition that obstruent clusters agree in voicing. (Among its language-specific details is the progressiveness of the assimilation.) (4b) is a PhtR which seems to apply also in English speakers' nativization of loan words (Shibatani 1972:115).

Given (4) we get the following sample derivations:

(5) Operands: /dʌk/ (*duck*)   /eg/ (*egg*)   /fɔks/ (*fox*)

    Morpholex. (4a): dʌk + z   eg + z   fɔks + z

    PhtR (4b):   fɔksɪz

    PhtR (4c):   dʌks

    Outputs: /dʌks/   /egz/   /fɔksɪz/

In this analytical description the operation proceeds in different steps. However, this is only a descriptive technique justified if we want to discern the different aspects of the operation. In reality, the operation is a unit; given inputs such as /dʌk/, /eg/, /fɔks/, the speaker immediately comes up with (infers) the correct plurals /dʌks/, /egz/, /fɔksɪz/. The intermediate representations in the derivations have no psychological reality at all. That is, the only phonological forms there are, are the inputs (operands) and outputs (resultants). Note especially that the structures generated by morpholexis, which would more or less correspond to OGPh type underlying forms, are not genuine forms. They are only a convenient way of stating that plurals are formed by concatenating the singular forms (/dʌk/, /eg/, /fɔks/) and the plural /z/, or, to put it in more adequate terms, by operating on the singular forms adding /z/ as a marker of the operation.

It follows from what has just been said that PhtRs are considered to be integrated aspects of the operations. While one may quarrel about this in the case of PhtRs which exist in the grammar also as independent rules (e.g. (4b)) (cf. §7.5), the degree of integration is more obvious in the case of MRPs. However, before proceeding to cases involving MRPs, let us consider a few other examples involving only PhtRs.

Take Turkish plural formation first:

(6) (a) Morpholexical rule: Plural → /l V r/
                              [+low]

(b) PhtR (Suffix harmony): IF: $\begin{bmatrix} +\text{syll} \\ \alpha\,\text{back} \end{bmatrix}$ C_0 $\begin{bmatrix} +\text{syll} \\ -\text{ROOT} \end{bmatrix}^7$
↓

THEN: $[\alpha\,\text{back}]$

A few sample derivations:[8]

(7)　Operands:　/göz/ 'eye'　/kɨz/ 'girl'
　　　(6a):　　　göz + lVr　kɨz + lVr
　　　(6b):　　　gözler　　　kɨzlar

It may be debated whether the plural should be represented with an archiphoneme $\begin{bmatrix} V \\ +\text{low} \end{bmatrix}$ rather than with, say, /a/.[9] If we opt for the archiphoneme solution, PhtR (6b) obligatorily applies in all derivations involving the plural operation. Thus, it is closely tied to the operation (and similarly to other Turkish morphological operations in which it occurs). Moreover, (6b) is not a completely general PhtR, since it refers to morph category membership (suffix rather than root). Such morphologically conditioned PhtRs constitute a somewhat vague category lying between true MRPs and general PhtRs. As another example of a morphologically conditioned PhtR, consider Swedish /n/-deletion:

(8)　IF:　　　X $\begin{bmatrix} V \\ -\text{str} \end{bmatrix}$ n + t # (X contains a stressed syllable)
↓
　　　THEN:　　　∅

There is no general constraint in Swedish excluding / − V̌nt # / forms (cf. for example, *fórint* (Hungarian currency), names like *Créscent*, *Víncent*, etc.). Rather, (8) applies only to neuter forms of adjectives and participles.[10] Thus, it is completely dependent on the morpholexical rule which adds /t/ within the neuter-forming operation. Some derivations:

---

[7]　This formulation is due to J. van Marle (paper given at the third Phonologie-Tagung, Vienna, Sept. 1976).

[8]　The forms generated here are nominative forms. As for the generation of oblique and more complex forms, cf. §7.6.

[9]　In general, I find arguments for archiphonemes in lexical representations rather weak, but this case concerns a marker of an operation (i.e. a grammatical morpheme) rather than an operand.

[10]　Thus, either the rule must contain the + boundary specification, or it must refer to these morphological categories.

(9) Operands: /fi:n/ 'fine'   /va:ken/ 'awake'
     Morpholex.:   fi:n + t   va:ken + t
     PhtR (8):   va:ket
     Outputs: /fi:nt/   /va:ket/

Note again that (8) is considered to be part of the whole neuter-forming operation, though, of course, it is not included in the morpholexical core and applies only to a subset of input forms (those ending in $-Vn\#$). Thus, an intermediate representation such as
$$[-str]$$
/va:ken + t/ is no real phonological form.

My next examples will involve true MRPs, i.e. rules which are *only* needed for handling the morphophonological alternations between forms related in terms of morpheme identity. Let us suppose that speakers are able to form nouns from adjectives according to the *divine – divinity* pattern in English.[11] The corresponding operation would then involve at least three aspects (not formalized here):

(10) (a) Morpholexical rule: Add /iti/ to the adjective
      (b) Morphophonological part:
           (i) Trisyllabic laxing: IF: $VC_0VC_0V\#$ (cf. Chomsky
                                                            & Halle
                                           $\downarrow$ 1968:180)
                            THEN: $[-tns]$
                (C_0V could also be given as S ($=$syllable))
           (ii) Vowel shift, which is an MRP regulating the connections
                within pairs of vowels: /áî/ $\sim$ /I/, /î̂j/ $\sim$ /e/, /éî/ $\sim$ /æ/, etc.
                Since a vowel has to become lax according to (10bi) this
                rule states *which* lax vowel should be selected

The derivation of *sanity* would be analyzed as follows:

(11) Operand: /séîn/
      Morpholex.:   séîn + iti
      (10bi):   seniti
      (10bii):   sæniti

Once more, /séîn + iti/ or any other intermediate representation is not the phonological form of *sanity*. Rather, it simply says that /sæniti/ may

---

[11] There is evidence that at least some speakers can do this, cf. Moskowitz 1973; J. Ohala 1974a.

be constructed from /sêin/ and /iti/. Recall that one must distinguish the phonological form from the information that may be needed for the construction of the same form (§4.1).

The trisyllabic laxing rule (10bi) may be thought of as a formerly general PhtR which now displays an increasing number of exceptions (e.g. *obese – obesity*). Vowel shift (10bii) is a rather typical example of an MRP. It is *not* phonotactically motivated; its input structures would be phonotactically correct in English. For example, /seniti/ would be a perfectly acceptable noun in English. However, it does not happen to be the noun connected with *sane*. A few other properties of the vowel shift rule may be worth while pointing out. Thus, it seems to be applicable in both directions; thus, you can get a lax vowel given a tense one (e.g. *sanity – sane*) *or* vice versa (e.g. *variety – vary*). (Within their OGPh framework Chomsky & Halle (1968: 187ff) were forced to give the rule a unidirectional formulation, from tense to lax.) Furthermore, the vowel shift rule must be sensitive to the condition that a quantity change (e.g. (10bi)) is also included in the morphological operation in question. This supports the contention that vowel shift is not a rule functioning independently of other rules in the grammar. In fact, it is often true of MRPs that they are *applicationally dependent* on other rules, i.e. they apply correctly only if they are allowed to 'look back' at previous stages of the derivation to see if some other specific rule(s) has (have) applied (or sometimes, has *not* applied) (see §7.4.3.2, §10.7.3.3). This fact supports the view that the whole operation, within which applicational dependencies hold, is the proper unit and that MRPs are not independently living phonological rules.

The /t/ → /s/ assibilation in Finnish is another example of an MRP, notoriously misrepresented as a phonological rule by generativists (§4.4). The only productive operation in which this rule occurs as an aspect is preterite formation of certain verbs, e.g. *tunte-* 'to feel' – *tunsi* 'felt' (3. sg.), *rakenta-* 'to build' – *rakensi*, *tietä-* 'to know' – *tiesi*, etc.

Thus, the derivation of *tunsi* goes as follows:

(12) Operand: /tunte-/[12]
      Morpholex.:   tunte + i
      MRP (e-drop):   tunti
      MRP (assib.):   /tunsi/

So far we have seen no cases of operands involving morphophono-

---

[12] I assume here without proof that the lexical form is the present stem /tunte-/.

logical markings (§4.4). Let us therefore give also the derivation of Fi. gen. *käden* from nom. *käsi* 'hand'[13] as compared to *lasin* from *lasi* (the examples discussed in §4.4):

(13) Operands: /käsi/ (cf. §4.4)   /lasi/ 'glass'
                         ⁊⁊
                         te

   (a) Morpholex.:   käsi + n   lasi + n
                         ⁊⁊
                         te

   (b) MRP (i) s→t:[14] kätin   –
       (interpretation of   ⁊
       ∼[t] marking)   e
       MRP (ii) i→e:[14] käten   –
       (interpretation of
       ∼[e] marking)
       PhtR (Consonant   käden   –
       gradation)[15]
       Outputs   /käden/   /lasin/

Here we find another example of a complete applicational dependence between rules of the same morphological operation; a form which undergoes (bi) *always* also undergoes (bii) (though not vice versa). Like all MRPs, (bi) and (bii) should be considered as synchronically unmotivated complications of the paradigm. As such they have a tendency to be lost without the disappearing of the morphological operations (cf. the productive type *lasi – lasin*, §4.4). In fact, the desirability of distinguishing the simple case of *lasi – lasin* and the complex case of *käsi – käden*, or, in general, of displaying the degree of complexity of operations, provides a reason for an analytic split-up of operations in different aspects. (Analogously, we may resolve segments in terms of features to show the relative similarity between segments, without committing ourselves to the view that features rather than segments are psychological primes.)

As a final example, consider diminutive formation of Russian nouns. If the nominal stem ends in a velar (/k,g,x/),[16] this is turned into a

---

[13] However, this pattern is hardly productive in the normal sense. However, in jokes, student jargon, etc. the pattern may possibly be extended (see §4.4).

[14] These rules, if they are rules, are inversions of the historically original ones. See Karlsson (1974b) for arguments.

[15] In fact, consonant gradation is also becoming an MRP, cf. Karlsson 1974b; Skousen 1975b.

[16] Or /c/.

palato-alveolar (/č, ž, š/). This rule, sometimes called 'transitive softening', is often represented as a phonological rule by generativists,[17] though it is a clear MRP occurring in some operations of derivational morphology.[18] Thus we have nouns and diminutives such as *stroka* 'line' – *stročka, doroga* 'road' – *dorožka* 'rails', *jabloko* 'apple' – *jabločko, uxo* 'ear' – *uško, petux* 'cock' – *petušok*, and with iterative diminutivization *kniga* 'book' – *knižka – knižečka*, etc. Some derivations in gross outline:[19]

(14) Operands: /petux/   /kniga/   /jabloko/
      Morpholex.:[20]   petux + k   knig + ka   jablok + ko
      MRP (trans.
      softening):   petuš + k   knižka   jabločko
      PhtR (mobile
      vowel insertion): petušok
      Outputs:[19]   /petušok/   /knižka/   /jabločko/

Though transitive softening occurs in a number of operations (cf. fn. 18), it seems hard to treat it as a PhtR. Thus, it is not possible to formulate it in phonological terms. Nor does it apply before all derivational affixes, e.g. not before the denominal adjective suffix *-in* (*suka* 'bitch' – *sukin* (**sučin*) 'of a bitch'). I will return to this rule in §7.4.3.3.

7.4 The unity of morphological operations

An important difference between the present theory of morphological formation processes and the corresponding OGPh devices is that our morphological operations are assumed to be psychological and behavioral wholes, whereas OGPh seems to postulate no such holistic properties of derivations; instead, independent 'phonological' rules happen to be applied in derivations, these derivations being clearly

[17] E.g. Lightner (1965); Coats (1970).
[18] Besides in diminutive formation in /-(V)k, -ka, -ko/ it seems to be productive in e.g. formation of abstract *-(e)stvo* nouns (*bitnik* 'beatnik' – *bitničestvo, levak* 'leftist' – *levačestvo*), formation of agent nouns in *-nik* (*kol'aska* 'side-car' – *kol'asočnik, luk* 'bow' – *lučnik*), formation of adjectives in *-n(yj)* (*dorožka* 'rails' – *dvuxdorožečnyj*), formation of *-it'*-verbs (*levak* – *levačit', mor'ak* 'sailor' – *omor'ačit'*, cf. older types *suxoj* 'dry' – *sušit', sluga* 'service' – *služit'* 'serve'). I am grateful to Nils B. Thelin for providing me with the Russian data.
[19] The interaction of stress rules is ignored here.
[20] Exactly how the morpholexical part has to be analyzed will not concern us here.

secondary entities. What arguments, then, can be said to support the unity of morphological operations?

7.4.1 *Function in speech act theory*

I have argued that speakers use language for certain conscious communicative purposes; they perform actions (§2.2). Morphological operations form a natural part of a speech act theory. Such an operation *is* in fact an act, subordinate to other major sentence-constructing operations, which is carried out according to certain rules and with a certain intention, i.e. to create a new word form with a certain intended meaning and certain intended grammatical properties. By contrast, the application of a single morphophonological rule has no independent function; it is redundant from a communicative–functional point-of-view. While it is useful and necessary for speakers to include morphological operations in their repertoire of grammatical operations, it is completely useless to single out morphophonological rules proper as independent psychological or behavioral entities. Moreover, since MRPs are, or would be, obligatory, opaque and often extrinsically ordered rules,[21] one could argue that it would be extremely difficult or even impossible to learn them as such (Derwing 1973: 201, 310 and passim; Braine 1974; Vennemann 1974a). And whatever importance is assigned to such theoretical considerations, there is empirical evidence that speakers in fact do *not* learn and use separate MRPs (see ch. 10).

7.4.2 *Behavioral unity*

It is of course clear that in grammatical behavior morphological operations (or the abstract–phonological parts of derivations in an OGPh type theory) must be executed in their entirety, because ungrammatical forms would result if, say, only the morpholexical aspect or only morpholexis plus *part* of morphophonology is carried out. Preliminary studies of slips of the tongue reinforce this point. The sort of putative misapplications sketched above would often result in phonotactically incorrect forms, but it is a very typical property of slips that they always obey phonotactic constraints. Furthermore, there are very few slips in Fromkin's (1973) extensive data corpus (mainly English, to some extent German (Meringer)) which are best interpreted as misapplications of single morphophonological rules; such rules cannot apparently be manipulated separately. Slips involving morpho-

[21] On opacity and rule ordering, see §10.7.1.4.

phonological rules are in general either cases where the speaker has failed to apply the operation entirely or cases in which the speaker has applied the whole operation though it should not have been applied.[22]

Other kinds of studies also support the assumption that morphological operations are behavioral and psychological units. Thus, whole morphological formation patterns are sometimes productive, though they involve MRPs which are apparently non-productive as separate rules. Examples are morphological patterns involving umlaut alternations in Icelandic, (and also marginally in other Germanic languages)[23] vowel shift in English, Finnish assibilation ($/t/ \rightarrow /s/$) and $/e/$ raising (Skousen 1975a,b), Russian transitive softening, etc. (cf. §7.3). Several psycholinguistic experiments designed to investigate the alleged psychological reality of the English vowel shift rule (which is an MRP, ch. 10) (Moskowitz 1973; J. Ohala 1974a; Steinberg & Krohn 1975) also indicate that vowel shift is not a living rule but that speakers may know correspondences between surface vowels and apply certain morphological 'analogies' (Ohala 1974a) involving the rule.[24]

Thus, morphological operations are behavioral units. Since there is reason to believe that speakers' implicit *knowledge* of their language is heavily dependent on what they can *do*, particularly as regards those aspects which are not consciously attended (cf. §1.4.2), we may assume that they are also psychological competence units.[25] Consequently, the split-up of operations as in the examples of §7.3 has at best a very weak psychological significance. It may be needed to display differences in formal complexity of different operations, as was suggested in §7.3. Thus, languages tend to simplify their morphological operations over time (morphophonology proper tends to be eliminated, something

[22] See data in Fromkin (1973). (In a Swedish corpus of some 250 slips that I have collected the same generalizations are borne out.) There are some rather isolated errors in Fromkin's and Meringer's corpuses of English and German slips that may speak against the contention that MPRs cannot be independently manipulated. Thus, Celce-Murcia (1973: 199) explains *Sie haben längere Öhren* (for *Sie haben längere Ohren*) as a 'perseveration' of Umlaut (a typical MRP). However, one could also interpret this as a perseveration of the surface feature [− back].

[23] For example, children may sometimes inflect weak verbs according to strong patterns, etc.

[24] It is true that the results of these and other psycholinguistic experiments can be questioned on various methodological grounds (as in Kiparsky 1973a: 101–2; Kiparsky & Menn 1977, cf. also Linell 1974a: 139–41), but one can still say that the outcome of the experiments certainly does not support the OGPh theory. For some comments on the experiments pertaining to the English vowel shift rule, see p. 202, fn. 50.

[25] For some doubt in the applicability of this maxim in the present case, see §7.5.

which can make the morpholexical core transparent on the surface, §10.11). However, the 'derivations' of §7.3 should not be interpreted as amounting to a claim that speakers actually apply rules in a stepwise fashion, and the intermediate representations generated should be thought of simply as artifacts of linguistic description.

7.4.3 *Applicability of morphophonological rules proper*
There are also some interesting implications for the issue under discussion to be drawn from recent generative studies on rule ordering, derivational constraints, exceptionality and rule features, etc.

7.4.3.1 *Derivation-specific ordering.* In OGPh (Chomsky & Halle 1968) derivations proceed by letting different morpheme combinations pass through a system of rules ordered once and for all in a language-specific ('extrinsic') order. Rules apply to representations at a certain point in derivations, if they are obligatory and applicable; they cannot be applied at other points in derivations even if their structural conditions are met.[26] Other dialects may have other specific orderings of the same rules. This may suggest a picture of phonology, in which rules are independent and primary entities having definite language-general properties of application, and forms are completely subordinated to the rule system.

Several studies, internal to generative phonology, have shown that this picture cannot be upheld. These studies seem to have a common feature in that they claim that principles of rule application, in particular as regards the order(s) in which rules apply, are not tied to the rules as such but rather, at least to a greater extent than in OGPh, to forms, or types of forms, and to derivations.

For example, Anderson's (1974) theory of 'local ordering' means that certain forms must be marked for undergoing derivations in which rules apply in an unusual (marked) order. A rather different type of claim is embodied in the 'unordered rules hypothesis' of Koutsoudas, Sanders & Noll (1974) (and others, e.g. Iverson 1974). Here it is suggested that rules are unordered as such and may in fact apply in different combinations and orderings, but for each specific string the order of rule application is always predictable from universal principles. This, then, means there is no language-general ordering of rules, but rather the order of rule application is dependent on the properties of input forms.

[26] I disregard here disjunctive ordering and cyclical application.

The same is true of Anderson's theory, though there the properties of derivations are marked at input forms rather than universally predictable. One may argue that if ordering constraints turn out to be *derivation-specific*, either universally determined or marked for certain derivations, rather than language-specific and grammar-general (cf. OGPh), this speaks for the derivation, or in our theory: the whole morphological operation, as the primary unit.[27]

7.4.3.2 *Applicational dependence.* Other interesting generative findings concern cases of 'applicational dependence' between rules (see esp. Kiparsky 1973b; Iverson 1974: esp. 84ff; Miller 1975). Some rules (so-called global rules) apparently have to 'look back' at previous stages of the derivations in order to 'know' whether to apply or not (in addition, of course, their structural descriptions must be met). Such rules either (i) apply (or apply obligatorily rather than optionally) *or* (ii) do not apply only if another rule *has* applied, *or has not* applied earlier in the specific derivations. Some but not all of these conditions on rule applications can be accounted for in terms of rule ordering. (We have seen some examples of applicational dependence in §7.3.)

Applicational dependence also implies that properties of rule application are dependent on properties of specific derivations,[28] i.e. larger wholes such as morphological operations,[29] rather than of the separate rules themselves. Moreover, it turns out that applicational dependence is typical of MRPs (cf. Kiparsky's (1973b: 68) 'non-automatic neutralizing rules', cf. also §10.7.3.3) as opposed to phonotactic rules. This again points to the role of MRPs as being nothing but integrated aspects of morphological operations.

7.4.3.3 *Exceptionality of derivations with respect to rules.* In general, OGPh tries to formulate general natural-looking phonological rules which are supposed to account for morphophonological alternations. Counterparts of our MRPs are also treated as separate phonological

---

[27] In Linell (1974b) I also argue that the theory of Koutsoudas, Sanders & Noll (1974) (the unordered rules hypothesis) would make it probable that derivations take surface forms as inputs.

[28] Global rules are discussed in generative phonology also in terms of 'derivational constraints'.

[29] A morphological operation involves only 'obligatory' rules (see §10.5) and corresponds in most cases to a terminated generative–phonological derivation, since phonological rules proper that can be applied further 'down' in a generative derivation are typically optional and thus need not apply.

rules. However, such rules are never quite general and/or phonologically conditioned. Many forms fail to undergo the rules, although
they may well fit their structural descriptions. In order to prevent the
rules from applying to such forms, generativists have to invoke ordering
constraints (some aspects of which were discussed above) and various
diacritic markings of morphs, categories of morphs and specific morph
combinations (i.e. specific derivations), etc. I will now address myself to
some cases of the latter type.

Take, e.g., Russian transitive softening (cf. §7.3), according to which
stem-final /k,g,x/ are palatalized to /č,ž,š/ when followed by certain
derivational suffixes, e.g. in diminutives (see §7.3:(14) and p. 136, fn.
18). Historically, this palatalization goes back to a general rule turning
/k, g, x/ into palato-alveolars before front vowels. Although the
synchronic rule of modern Russian is a typical morphologically
conditioned MRP, generativists (e.g. Coats 1970) have tried to
formulate it in a general phonological form, essentially the same as that
of its ancient ancestor rule. To account for its limited applicability,
either morphemes which fail to trigger it (Coats 1970) or morphemes
which do trigger it (Iverson & Ringen 1977) must be diacritically
marked.[30] In effect, this leads to a rather abundant use of exception
features. However, the obvious generalization is that palatalization is
simply an aspect of a few specific formation patterns of derivational
morphology. Far from being a general separate rule it applies in specific
kinds of derivations.

Cases like the Russian example are quite common. For example,
Finnish /t/ → /s/ assibilation (again a rule which has been set up by every
orthodox generativist (§4.4)) is an MRP which partakes in at least one
productive morphological operation (preterite formation, §7.3:(12)).
Though the rule in question is involved in other (non-productive)
patterns too, it is hardly a separate rule; it is simply a property of the
preterite operation (and possibly a few other derivation types, cf. §4.4).
Another very typical MRP with similar properties is Southern Bantu
palatalization of labials (/pʰ + i/ → /tʃwʰ/, etc.) (Herbert 1977).

The fact that specific morphs or morph categories, or derivations in
which these morphs or morph categories are involved, are systematically
exempt from so many rules (corresponding to my MRPs) in OGPh

---

[30] In fact, neither of these solutions is sufficient for verbs, for which a generative
morpheme-based solution seems to need morphological (conjugation) features, cf. imp.
luži from *služit'* 'to serve' vs. imp. *peki* from *peč* 'to bake' (cf. Thelin 1975: 29).

treatments shows the inadequacy of these theories. It is entirely nonsensical to set up MRPs as if they were separate rules when they are actually never allowed to apply freely as separate rules. Instead, larger wholes, word forms and word-form constructing operations (i.e. counterparts of whole OGPh derivations)[31] must be posited as grammatical primes, and MRPs may be analytically abstracted as properties of such primes. Due to the productiveness of some such entire operations their constituent MRPs of course also apply to new forms *within* the operations (§7.4.2). Clearly, this case must be carefully distinguished from cases of productivity of independent phonological rules (§10.8).

7.5 The place of morphophonology

The theory of morphological operations suggests a treatment of morphophonology which is quite different from that of OGPh, where morphophonology goes with phonology proper into one monolithic phonological component. My considerations clearly imply that morphophonology rather belongs to morphology (Linell 1977a), which is also the traditional view (cf. Kuryłowicz 1968; Fischer-Jørgensen 1975: 41, 105 and passim). This is particularly obvious as regards morphophonological rules proper (MRPs), which are *by definition* postulated only to take care of morphophonological alternations. Yet, OGPh treats them as any other phonological rules, in spite of the fact that they are, as we will see in ch. 10, quite different from phonological rules proper on a large number of accounts. My conclusion regarding MRPs is that they are neither phonological nor living, separate rules at all. Karlsson (1974a: 25) has pointed out (following Kuryłowicz 1968) that MRPs are best regarded as non-functional complications of the grammar; they are nothing but synchronically unmotivated aspects of certain morphological operations.[32]

   Thus, there can hardly be any reasonable doubt about the complete integration of MRPs into morphological operations. However, the status of phonotactic rules (PhtRs), which, as we have seen (§7.3), may also account for morphophonological alternations,[33] is more am-

---

[31] Cf. p.140, fn. 29.
[32] On 'via rules', see §7.6.
[33] Roughly those which have traditionally been called 'automatic' alternations, e.g. Wells (1949).

biguous. We know that PhtRs perform other independent duties in the grammar (ch. 6), so there is no doubt that they are independent in *those* cases. The question is how to interpret their status within morphological operations. Are they integrated aspects, which would presumably be the view compatible with traditional analogy, or are they independent processes which are simply called for by certain morphological operations? It is tempting to make different choices dependent on whether we talk about behavior ('performance') or grammatical knowledge ('competence'), though this goes against what was said in §1.5, §7.4.2. Behavioral operations would obligatorily include the phonotactic adjustments (§7.4.2), but as a competence unit the morphological operation[34] could be construed simply as the core plus the adjustments performed by MRPs. This, however, is no major problem; it is not obvious to me that there could be any empirical consequences of making different options.

7.6 Complex morphological operations

I will now return for a moment to the grammatical description of morphological operations. What remains to be discussed is, among other things, the structure of *morpholexically complex* operations, i.e. cases in which several semantic–syntactic categories are expressed by single morphological elements (cf. portmanteau-morphs) or cases in which a certain semantically–syntactically defined operation involves a selection of different morphological expressions (cf. lexically conditioned allomorphy). To achieve this, however, a digression into the semantic and syntactic aspects of morphology is necessary.

I have argued (§2.2) that morphological operations are subacts subordinate to major sentence-forming operations. In traditional terms, we say that morphological operations express, or are governed by, semantic, syntactic and lexical categories. Some of these categories, e.g. number (in nouns) and tense, are semantically relatively well-defined, whereas others, e.g. case, sometimes have a direct relation to semantics (cf. 'roles' or 'deep cases' in the sense of e.g. Fillmore 1968) but are often dependent on (surface) syntactic relationships within the sentence or

---

[34] Note that I use the term 'operation' both for the grammar rule *type* and for the speech act *token* which is an application of the former. Sven Öhman (pers. comm.) has pointed out that it may be conceptually and terminologically preferable to reserve the term 'operation' for the latter concept and to use the term 'operator' for the former.

clause. Furthermore, there are categories like gender which may have a certain semantic motivation in some cases but are often quite arbitrary, and there are *totally* arbitrary lexical features such as declension and conjugation features (e.g. [±Strong] in Germanic inflectional morphology). There are reasons to arrange these various, possibly morphologically-expressed, categories in strength or markedness hierarchies in which the semantically best motivated categories are strongest and the completely arbitrary ones weakest or most marked. Some of the most common categories would be arranged roughly as follows:

(15) (a) *Nouns*:

Number > $\dfrac{\text{Species}}{\text{Case}}$ > Gender > Arbitrary declension categories

(b) *Verbs*:

$\dfrac{\text{Tense}}{\text{Aspect (form)}}$ > Mood > Person > Number (agreem.) >

Gender (agreem.) > $\dfrac{\text{Arbitrary conjugation categories}}{\text{(e.g. [±Strong])}}$

(> means 'stronger than' or 'less marked than')

Such hierarchies are supposed to represent universal tendencies (which means that some languages may, due to historical coincidences, deviate from them). Their reflections can be observed in many ways.[35] Thus, it may be the case

(16) (a) that strong categories are universally more common in various languages than weak ones
      (b) that strong categories tend to appear (and get systematic expressions) earlier in children's language development than weak ones
      (c) that strong categories resist aphasic aberrations better than weak ones
      (d) that when morphological systems are broken down in the historical developments of languages, strong categories stay in the language longer than weak ones

[35] Generalizations about strength hierarchies can be made particularly on the basis of works by Roman Jakobson and Joseph Greenberg, cf. Greenberg (1963, 1966). For some discussion, see Linell (1975).

(e) that there are implicational relations of the following kind: 'If a language has a certain weak category X (pertaining to a particular word class, e.g. nouns or verbs), then it also has the stronger category Y (in the same word class).' Thus, if for example, a language has number and person inflection in verbs, then it also has tense/mood inflection (but not vice versa).

It turns out that strength hierarchies also have repercussions on the ways in which the different categories are expressed by morpholexically complex morphological operations. In general, one may say that the stronger a category is, the more close is its relation of modification or determination to the semantico-syntax of the root or stem, and this is usually reflected in the surface order of the various morphological markers; strong categories are more 'stem-adherent' than weak ones.[36] Consider, e.g., a Finnish word form such as *kahviloissanikin* 'also in my cafés',[37] where the suffixes are further away from the root (to the right since Finnish is a suffixing language), the more indirect their relation of determination (with respect to the root) is:

(17)

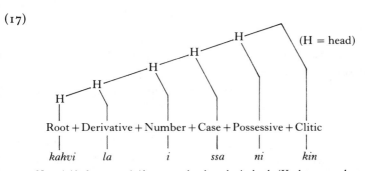

Note. /a/ in *la* goes to /o/ by a morphophonological rule (Karlsson 1974b: 112).

Here we can see the above-mentioned principle of stem-adherence rather beautifully illustrated. Thus, the derivative element *-la-* expresses together with the root a new and coherent concept (in fact, *kahvila* must be assumed to be a separate lexical item, as is usually the case with derived words). Number (plural, i.e. *-i-*) is a deep structure feature of the head constituent (*kahvila*). Case (inessive, expressed by

[36] This principle of morphological organization may be subsumed under a more general principle, recently 'rediscovered' by Bartsch & Vennemann (1972: 131) as the 'principle of natural constituent structure'.

[37] This example is from Karlsson (1974b: 54).

-*ssa*) also belongs to the deep structure[38] representation but, unlike number, it is clearly related to *other* constituents (outside the noun phrase) of the semantic deep structure. The possessive element (-*ni*), in its turn, is related to something outside the entire role structure of the descriptive phrase involved; it expresses a relation to the speaker. Finally, the clitic meaning 'also' is no doubt that determining element which is most loosely associated with the rest of the expression.

Of course, Finnish morphology is comparatively rich, but we can observe similar things in more restricted structures even in languages with a much poorer morphology, e.g. Swedish:

(18)

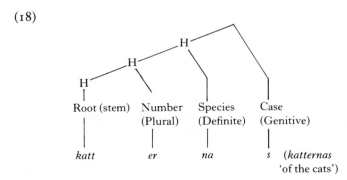

H			
Root (stem)	Number (Plural)	Species (Definite)	Case (Genitive)
katt	*er*	*na*	*s* (*katternas* 'of the cats')

In most cases, there seems to be a very simple relationship between the traditional dependency (or head-modifier) structure of an expression and its underlying operational structure. Thus, head expressions are the operands of operations, and the various modifiers are the overt signs of the operations that have been applied to the head expressions. However, for reasons that will soon become clear, I will assume that in most cases morphologically complex word forms (such as *kahviloissanikin* or *katternas*) are the resultants of *complex morphological operations* rather than sequences of simple morphological operations (one for each morphological category (or for each modifier-head relation)). Only certain simple forms, such as *katternas*, may, in principle, be operationally constructed in both ways.

Thus, the operation(s) underlying a word form like *katternas* may be either a series of simple morphological operations or one single complex operation. The former alternative would mean that each constituent operation is terminated before the next one begins; that is, the

---

[38] For convenience, I am using the concepts of standard generative transformational grammar here, despite the fact that some other model would be necessary (cf. §2.2).

pluralization operation gives first *katter* (from the lexical base form
katt), then the definitivization operation yields *katterna* (from *katter*),
and finally the genitivization operation gives *katternas* (from *katterna*).
In this model, each simplex operation includes the morphophonological
adjustments needed (in my example, these only concern prosodic
phenomena). The other alternative, one complex operation, would give
katternas from *katt* by means of one integrated operation, which would
be structurally analyzable as an application of all the morpholexical rules
(which are part of the various simple constituent processes), and after
that a joint morphophonological adjustment for the whole expression.
In my example, the morpholexical rules would first adjoin all affixes
(*-er*, *-na*, *-s*) before any morphophonological adjustment takes place.

While the first alternative is theoretically possible in some cases, and
does indeed fit the intuitive experience of speech production under some
unusual circumstances, e.g. hesitation, it is very reasonable to regard the
second alternative as the most viable one. Thus, it is easy to show that in
many cases the integrated compound operation is the only possible
alternative. The simple stepwise derivation of the first alternative is
possible only in more or less agglutinative languages where each
semantico-syntactic category corresponds to a simple expression
element (formative). Not even then is this alternative always open. In
the Finnish example (which in this respect is quite typical for Finnish)
the selection of the plural element *-i-* is dependent on the specification
for oblique case of the whole intended form. In the nominative (or
accusative) the plural allomorph would have been *-t*.

The stepwise model becomes completely impossible when several
semantico-syntactic categories are expressed by one and the same
morpholexical rule (which yields a so-called portmanteau morph).
Thus, it is well-known that in most Indo-European languages, number
and person have a common materialization in the verbal inflection, and
in many of these languages, e.g. Slavonic languages or Latin, the same
applies to number and case in the nominal inflection. Consider, for
example, the Latin paradigm of *bellum* 'war':

(19) nom. sg. *bellum*   nom. pl. *bella*
gen. sg. *bellī*   gen. pl. *bellōrum*
dat. sg. *bellō*   dat. pl. *bellīs*
acc. sg. *bellum*   acc. pl. *bella*
abl. sg. *bellō*   abl. pl. *bellīs*

Here no separate number or case morphs can be isolated. Evidently we have here morpholexical rules that materialize number and case expressions simultaneously.

Now, it is quite interesting to observe that the strength hierarchies discussed earlier (cf. (16)) have repercussions also in the morphology of such 'inflectional' languages as Latin. It turns out, as a result of structural studies, that the morpholexical rules that spell out portmanteau morphs are most conveniently and appropriately arranged in terms of systems where strong categories form the basis of united rule schemas and where weaker categories condition subrules. As far as nominal inflection is concerned, we would therefore expect that number conditions the main structure of the morpholexical system and that case accounts for specific subrules, rather than vice versa. In our Latin example this is reflected in the following manner. For each case there are always separate forms for the singular and the plural, whereas within each of the number categories there are not always different forms for all cases. If we want to write a complex morpholexical rule for the *bellum* declension in Latin, we would get something of the following kind:[39]

$$(20) \quad \begin{bmatrix} +\text{Noun} \\ +\text{Affix} \end{bmatrix} \rightarrow \left\{ \begin{array}{l} \left\{ \begin{array}{ll} -\bar{o}rum & / \quad \begin{bmatrix} +\text{Gen} \end{bmatrix} \\ -\bar{\imath}s & / \quad \begin{bmatrix} \begin{Bmatrix} +\text{Abl} \\ +\text{Dat} \end{Bmatrix} \end{bmatrix} \\ -a \end{array} \right\} \Bigg/ \begin{bmatrix} +\text{Plur} \end{bmatrix} \\[2em] \left\{ \begin{array}{ll} -\bar{\imath} & / \quad \begin{bmatrix} +\text{Gen} \end{bmatrix} \\ -\bar{o} & / \quad \begin{bmatrix} \begin{Bmatrix} +\text{Abl} \\ +\text{Dat} \end{Bmatrix} \end{bmatrix} \\ -um \end{array} \right\} \end{array} \right\}$$

(a)

(b)

(c)

(d)

(e)

(f)

If, on the other hand, we would try to write such a schema having single cases to the right, and number categories conditioning subrules, we would get a considerably more complex and intuitively less satisfactory rule.

In analogous ways the strength hierarchies tend to regulate the structure of morpholexical systems in other languages. These more or

[39] This rule could easily be generalized to cover masculines type *servus* and other declensions as well. For the notation, cf. Kiefer (1970).

less general properties of synchronic morpholexical systems correspond to the diachronic universal that when morphological systems are broken down – something which has occurred in most Indo-European languages – then this breakdown always affects weaker categories first. Distinctions are leveled out analogically in an order which is opposite to the strength hierarchies as displayed in (15). This means that the subrules of the rule schemas disappear while the main (strong) categories remain distinct (cf. Kuryłowicz 1966; Wurzel 1975).

As a result of the preceding discussion, we can add to the list of reflections of strength hierarchies (16) a couple of new generalizations. First, in as far as different semantico-syntactic categories have morphological expressions that can be isolated from each other (e.g. different affixes which are added agglutinatively), strong categories display a higher degree of adherence to the root (stem) than weak categories. The more vague term 'adherence' is chosen to cover also the fact that if the morphological operation consists in an internal modification of the root (e.g. ablaut or umlaut) – a mode of expression which is of course strongly 'root-adherent' – then we have to do with strong categories in most cases. For example, umlaut in Swedish or German may express number (i.e. plural) but not definiteness, and ablaut in Indo-European languages expresses tense distinctions rather than, say, person distinctions. Secondly, we have found that in as far as different semantic-syntactic categories have a joint morphological marker (portmanteau morphs), then the underlying morpholexical rule schema is founded on strong rather than weak categories.

7.7 Morpheme identity outside morphological operations

Morphological operations concern relations between phonologically cognate forms which are also morphologically, i.e. inflectionally or word-formationally, related. There are also phenomena in the morphology and morphemics of languages which do not meet all conditions of phonological and semantic similarity and grammatical relatedness. On one hand, there are true suppletions, i.e. forms which are phonologically quite heterogeneous but still related to each other as if they belonged to an inflectional paradigm or derivational system (e.g. *good – better, go – went*, etc., *old – age, big – size*, etc.). Obviously, these are different lexical items, but they are closely 'associated' in some way. Superficially, adult English speakers seem to use *go – went* in grammatical behavior in a way quite analogous to, e.g., *walk − walked.* That is, having invoked *go*, they *retrieve*, if necessary, *went* automatically, just as easily as they (presumably) *construct walked* having activated *walk*.[40] This indicates that suppletive forms are organized in *paradigms* in the lexicon.

Secondly, there are items which have some phonological similarity and also some (perhaps less systematic) semantic relatedness. Consider, e.g., forms like *foul − filth, beard − barber, labor − laboratory, moon − month* and many others (including some which are not etymologically related; *hide − hideous*, etc.). Of course, I do not deny that speakers sometimes discover or invent morpheme identities between such forms, and perhaps also extract some rule-like correspondences between single phonological segments in the respective forms (see §9.4). However, such associations are very peripheral in the grammar and normally nonfunctional, i.e. they are never used in productive grammatical processes. It seems to me that Vennemann's (1972a) notion of 'via rules' may be an appropriate device to account for these phenomena in a grammar.

---

[40] However, if our theory is correct, i.e. if under very similar surface manifestations there is an underlying difference between *retrieval* and *construction*, one should expect this difference to be manifested under pathological conditions, e.g. certain kinds of aphasia.

8 Word forms as primes

8.1 A brief recapitulation

In an OGPh type theory, word forms are treated as derived entities. Their properties are completely dependent on other more fundamental grammatical entities, primarily morphemes, and morphological and phonological rules, plus perhaps other properties of derivations such as derivational constraints (cf. §5.3). This of course also means that in as far as properties of word forms vary between speakers (of different times and/or dialects), this variation is in fact considered to be due to differences in these other primary grammatical entities. By contrast, in my theory word forms are assumed to be primary units of grammar. I have already given reasons for this hypothesis in the preceding chapters, and the purpose of the present chapter is to adduce some further supporting arguments and also to refute some counter-arguments. Let me first, however, briefly recapitulate some major conclusions of the preceding discussion:

(a) To explain invariance and variation in correct language-specific phonetic behavior, we need the notion of 'phonetic plan'. Such plans are plans for observable ('surface') behavior. Morphemes are not surface forms, but word forms are (ch. 3).

(b) There is evidence that lexical entries are a subset of word forms (stems, phrases, etc.), not abstract morphemes (ch. 4).

(c) Surface-phonemic contrast seems to be a fundamental and significant concept in phonology. Phonemic contrasts concern relations between different word forms, and other surface forms, not relations between abstract morphemes (ch. 5).

(d) Judgments of phonological correctness apply to surface forms, not to morpheme-invariants (ch. 6).

(e) New word forms are formed by analogical extensions of relations between surface forms, not by applying rules to abstract morphemes.

(f)   The word-form-constructing operations (i.e. morphological operations) are psychological and behavioral units. They have a clear function in a theory of communicative competence (ch. 2). On the other hand, OGPh type derivations which presuppose the independence of abstract representations and separate morpho-phonological rules (MRPs) are unjustified both on psychological-behavioral and on linguistic-functional grounds (ch. 7).

8.2   Further arguments for word forms as primary units

8.2.1   *Syntactically 'free' forms*

It has often been pointed out that word forms possess a syntactic freedom which does not pertain to the morphs which are the constituents of such forms (e.g. Ullman 1951: 43ff; Lyons 1968: 201–4). Word forms may sometimes constitute utterances of their own (Bloomfield's (1957: 27) 'minimum free forms'), and the ordering between word forms may often be varied to a considerable extent. Free forms are more plausible candidates for being grammatical primes than are bound forms (morphs).

Note, however, that there are a number of difficulties in defining word forms syntactically. I will return to this problem below (§8.3.1).

8.2.2   *Semantically 'free' forms*

The relative syntactic freedom of word forms is partly mirrored by a semantic freedom. Word forms are interpretable in a way that constituent morph(eme)s are not. Thus, one can talk about the meaning and reference of a nominal (word) form that is fully specified for number, case and species (or whatever nominal categories there are), whereas a single nominal stem cannot be assigned any such interpretation. Moreover, the meaning of grammatical morphemes such as derivatives and flexives is clearly syncategorematic and operational, i.e. it makes sense only if the morpheme is combined with a stem (i.e. when the meaning of the grammatical category is applied to the stem meaning). However, these arguments are quite weak, since (i) the meaning and reference of a specific word form (token) cannot be determined without considering the whole utterance context; (ii) whole phrases (noun phrases, etc.), i.e. not only word forms, may very well be referential units; and (iii) function words, such as particles and prepositions, are equally semantically syncategorematic as are grammatical affixes (cf. §8.3.1).

8.2.3 *Non-predictable features of meaning*

A much stronger argument pertaining to semantics is one which was brought to attention in my discussion of the nature of the lexicon (§4.3.3.2); many word forms (derived words and compounds) have idiosyncratic semantic properties which cannot be predicted from the meanings of the constituent morphemes and the grammatical structure of the forms. Moreover, there are many *morphological* features of lexicalized word forms which are not predictable (§4.3.3.2). This of course only shows that the lexicon must contain many ready-made polymorphemic structures, but indirectly it supports the importance of word forms (many of the lexical polymorphemic structures are formally single word forms, i.e. derived and compounded forms). In addition, there are also many lexicalized *phrases* in the lexicon (§4.3.3.2; cf. Anward & Linell 1975).

8.2.4 *The dependence of morphs on the word form context*

In ch. 7 I showed that in many cases the individual morpholexical and morphophonological rules cannot be set up as separate units; instead they are dependent on the context which is constituted by the morphological operation (cf. esp. §7.4). If we think in terms of forms instead of underlying operations, we can, not surprisingly, find a counterpart of this argument. Thus, the occurrence of constituent (allo)morphs is often dependent on the context constituted by the whole word form, rather than the other way around. For example, the occurrence of the plural allomorph $/+i+/$ after the stem in Finnish nouns indicates an oblique case and thus implies that another suffix (for case) will follow within the same word, whereas the allomorph $/+t+/$ signifies nominative (plural) and must be followed by a word boundary (e.g. *autot* 'cars' (nom.), *autoissa* 'in (the) cars' (iness.)). The allomorph $/+i+/$ may be said to have a semiotic syntagmatic function in that it contributes to the identity of the whole word form, thus possibly facilitating its identification (cf. Anttila 1975, 1976b). Or to look at it from another angle, the selection of the appropriate allomorph of the plural morpheme cannot be accomplished without considering properties of the whole word form (cf. morpholexically complex morphological operations, §7.6). Thus, the various Finnish plural forms cannot be exhaustively characterized as the result of independent(ly motivated) rules; rather, one must, e.g. in an OGPh type theory, adapt the rules to the entire word forms intended.

8.2.5 *Synchronic and diachronic variation and change*

One of the advantages of a 'concrete' theory working with word forms as phonetic plans and lexical items is that it provides a much more adequate and natural description (and of course, explanation) of synchronic variation and diachronic change in phonology than is the case with an OGPh type theory. All linguists would have to agree that change takes place *via* the surface level, and only a few would, like OGPh, argue that such change is necessarily reinterpreted as changes in underlying morphemes and morphophonology. In fact, such a view is not only far-fetched but in some cases even demonstrably inadequate.

One type of diachronic change pertains to borrowings from other languages. Then, surface forms, never abstract morphemes,[1] are borrowed. Their subsequent phonological nativization takes place within phonology proper. A closer inspection of change and productivity in phonology reveals that it concerns relations and properties of phonological rules proper (phonotactic rules, perceptual and articulatory rules, see ch. 10; cf. also ch. 11). As far as morphophonology proper is concerned, we seem to be faced with changes in whole morphological formation patterns (ch. 7). Moreover, phonological change spreads by lexical diffusion (Wang 1969; Chen & Wang 1975) from one lexical surface form to another. In language development, individuals learn lexical items, i.e. surface forms, one by one; much later morpheme identities are detected between forms (if they are detected at all, cf. §9.2). Similarly, individuals forget, and languages lose, surface forms one by one. There is no evidence that abstract morphemes exist and get lost, which would mean that all the different allomorphs in, perhaps, various scattered derived and compounded words would disappear at one and the same time.

Thus, idiosyncracies of change often concern specific lexical (surface) items. Synchronically, individual word forms have their own semantic and morphological idiosyncracies (§4.3.3.2). It is also probable that different speakers in the speech community differ with respect to these

---

[1] A possible exception would be, e.g., borrowing of Latin or Greek stems by linguistically conscious people who use them in coining new scientific terms, etc.

idiosyncracies. Moreover, differences among speakers of the same dialect seem to be greater concerning morphology and morpho-phonology than concerning phonology proper, which is hard, if not impossible, to explain for an OGPh type theory (§12.3.2.2).

Furthermore, if one studies synchronic variation in the pronunciation of word forms, one will find that speakers may often have a very detailed knowledge (intuition) about what variants are possible for each specific word form. (This applies to both phonemic and allophonic variation.)[2] Though there are some rule-like tendencies and implicational hierar-chies in the way different forms vary (having to do with, e.g., morphological category membership, stylistic value, familiarity, fre-quency of occurrence and other factors), speakers seem to be able to make item-specific ratings as for the extent to which many words are allowed to vary. Thus, e.g., Ralph (1977) has studied variation in a group of Swedish speakers with respect to Sw. /d/ deletion in adjectives (e.g. [bre:d] ~ [bre:] *bred* 'broad', [pry:d] ~ *[pry:] *pryd* 'prudish'), deletion of /-da/ in certain verbs (e.g. [spɛ:da] ~ [spɛ:] *späda* 'dilute', [pry:da] ~ *[pry:] *pryda* 'adorn'), variation in consonant length after the stressed vowel of nouns and adjectives with the structure of $C_0^3\acute{V}Cel$ (e.g. [dɑ:dəl] ~ [dad:əl] *dadel* 'date' (fruit), [ad:əl] ~ *[ad:əl] *adel* 'nobility'), etc. The items of the types involved are distributed, as it were, on scales ranging from those with much variation to those with little or no variation. (Thus, this is the synchronic counterpart of the diachronic phenomenon of lexical diffusion referred to above.) There are several studies of similar variation in other languages,[3] which all point to the same conclusions: (i) speakers have a detailed item-specific knowledge about lexical items which by far surpasses what is postulated in non-redundant structuralist or OGPh lexical entries; and (ii) lexical items are word forms rather than morphemes (i.e. variation is word form-specific rather than morpheme-specific).

8.2.6 *Phonetic gestalts*

I have suggested earlier (§3.7) that the sound shapes of word forms have gestalt properties and may even be phonological primes (i.e. competing with syllables and segments). Morphs, by contrast, are often not phonetic units but are merged with other morphs to make up word forms. Word forms, but not always morphs, may be separated by

---

[2] For these terms, see §3.4.
[3] Cf. for example, Bailey 1973; Paunonen 1973; Fidelholtz 1975.

intended pauses. (Of course, unintended pauses also occur more frequently at word boundaries than at morph boundaries or morph-internally.) There are also some experimental data indicating that word forms are primary units in the perceptual decoding of speech (§3.7) and also in reading (cf. Teleman 1974: 86).

8.2.7   *Intuitive plausibility*

Finally, we may point out that the analysis in terms of word forms seems intuitively much more intelligible to laymen than an analysis of utterances in terms of morphs. Most languages have a term for the concept of 'word' but no non-technical term for 'morph(eme)'. This may of course be an effect of cultural indoctrination and other more or less accidental factors. However, Sapir (1921: 33–5) notes that native illiterate speakers have no problems in identifying the words in an utterance, whereas morphemes are very hard for them to isolate. Similar results are reported in investigations of pre-school children's intuition (Teleman 1974).

8.3   Refuting some counter-arguments

One can imagine a considerable number of arguments against word form theory, and most of these have of course appeared in the literature. In this section I will briefly deal with a few of them.

8.3.1   *The definition of word forms*

It is commonplace that books on morphology discuss at length the difficulties in finding an exact definition of the notion of 'word form'. No semantic, syntactic or phonological criterion seems completely successful (Ullman 1951; Lyons 1968). Particular problems are connected with clitics (Zwicky 1977). While the number of word forms in a given utterance may be difficult to agree upon, the number of morph(eme)s may be easier to decide. However, while this may be true, a number of counter-arguments are justified.

(a)   While we may perhaps agree upon the number of morphs in most grammatical strings, there is another, more serious, problem with morphemes. It is hard, if not impossible, to state under what conditions morphs belong to the same morpheme (§9.4). There are no similar problems with word forms.

(b)   Any theory will be faced with the problem of distinguishing morphological from syntactic structures (as long as one admits that there are clear cases of such a distinction, which seems to be unanimously accepted). A morpheme-based theory cannot avoid this problem either.

(c)   Even if clitics are a problematic category, there is no case, as far as I know, where one has to have clitics in the lexical base forms. Clitics are always markers of grammatical operations, and it may perhaps turn out to be a less important problem whether clitic operations are morphological or purely syntactic.

8.3.2 *The selection of lexical forms*

A morpheme-based theory simply assumes that the lexicon contains all the morphemes of the language (whichever these are). A word-form-based theory, on the other hand, has to face a selection problem. If only a subset of all word forms are assumed to appear in the lexicon (§4.3.3), the problem arises how to define this subset. The standard answer would of course be that those forms which are semantically and/or syntactically (most) unmarked are likely to be(come) lexicalized. However, in many cases it is difficult to decide which are the unmarked forms. For example, in many Indo-European languages verbs are problematic; the infinitive and the (3. sg. or 1. sg.) present tense form are both undoubtedly relatively unmarked. Furthermore, one could opt for stems instead of word forms as lexical entries. So here we seem to have encountered a new case of indeterminacy. Again, I would argue that facts may well be indeterminate in themselves and that speakers may solve this indeterminacy in different ways. For example, analogical levelings in the history of verbal inflection of many Indo-European languages seem to support this point; sometimes infinitives, sometimes present forms have been used as operands. Thus, in modern French some verbs have generalized the vowel of the Old French infinitive (e.g. *lever, je lève* [*è* /ɛ/ being the stressed counterpart of *e* /ə/], cf. Old French: *lever*, 1. sg. pres. *lième*), other verbs have generalized the vowel of the present singular forms (*aimer, aime*, cf. Old French *amer, aime*). Similar examples are not hard to find in other languages or in other areas of inflectional morphology.[4] Thus, indeterminacy turns out to be a strength rather than a weakness in the word form theory, contrary to what many morpheme supporters argue.

---

[4]   Cf. e.g., Tiersma (1978) (data on Frisian verb inflection).

8.3.3   *The internal structure of word forms*

If the lexicon contains single morphemes, it means that lexical entries are always morphologically unstructured, and that all forms containing several morphological constituents are derived. My word form theory (§4.3.3) implies that both lexical items and derived forms are structured, and, more specifically, structured in very similar ways. This may look like a lost generalization, and it is indeed sometimes considered to be a drawback of the theory (cf. Matthews 1974: 72–5 and passim). However, this argument is purely formal and must be rejected, primarily because the first-mentioned morpheme-based lexicon is simply not a workable alternative (§4.3, chs. 8, 12). Furthermore, there is evidence for a distinction between unmarked base forms and derived forms. For example, analogical levelings are not randomly distributed; rather, the properties of some forms (i.e. base forms) are extended to other forms (i.e. derived forms) (e.g. Kuryłowicz 1966; Wurzel 1975).

8.3.4   *The loss of generalizations*

Linguists set up abstract morphemes mainly because they are thereby able to state a number of linguistic generalizations concerning morphology and morphophonology. These generalizations are sometimes lost in a word form theory, something which proponents of the morpheme theory adduce as evidence against it. However, the obvious rejoinder must be that such generalizations are neither natural nor necessary in a speaker's communicative competence (§2.2), and they do not seem to be extracted except by abstract-minded linguists (see, e.g. §4.2.2).

8.3.5   *Redundancy*

Connected with the last-mentioned point is the fact that the lexicon and rule system will be more redundant in a word form theory than in an OGPh type phonology. I have already dealt with this problem (§4.2); it is, in fact, much more probable that a speaker's lexicon and grammar are redundant than non-redundant.

8.3.6   *What the theory does not mean*

Some objections to 'concrete' phonological theories have been answered by Vennemann (1974b: 367–72), and I will postpone my own further counter-arguments to chs. 9, 12. In these chapters I will try to explain in more detail what my theory does *not* mean:

(a) Having surface forms, i.e. primarily word forms and stems, in the lexicon, does *not* mean that *all* word forms are lexicalized;[5] *some* forms are stored, but most forms are productively (re)created through morphological operations (§4.2, ch. 7).

(b) I do *not* argue that morphs and morpheme identities are non-existent but I *do* argue that they are wrongly dealt with in OGPh and, in particular, that morphemes are not phonological entities (chs. 9, 12).

[5] This was proposed by Vennemann (1974b). See for discussion §4.3.2.

9 Morphemes and morpheme identity

9.1 The nature of morphemes

Word forms may be analyzed in terms of smaller expression units, so-called *morphs*. There are often similarities in form and meaning between morphs contained in different word forms. This provides the basis for classifying morphs as variants of *morphemes*. A morpheme may be construed as a class of morphs, between which one and the same equivalence (or identity) relation ('*morpheme identity*') holds. Speaker's recognition of morpheme identity is of course a reality which cannot be denied. However, the history of contemporary phonology shows that we must be cautious in our interpretation of what this really means.

In structuralist linguistics, morphemes are often 'represented' in terms of invariant strings of symbols resembling phonetic symbols. These symbols stand for 'morphophonemes', and the morpheme-invariant representation is called a morphophonemic representation. Such representations may be constructed in such a way that the different concrete allomorphs can be generated by applying rules. This technique is typical of both Pāṇinian linguistics and OGPh. It was also used by some American structuralists, e.g. in Bloomfield's (1939) 'Menomini morphophonemics'. American structuralists generally thought of these 'hypothetical forms', i.e. the morpheme-invariants, as 'figments' or 'artifacts of linguistic description'.[1] However, when Chomsky, Halle (e.g. Halle 1959) and their followers (OGPh) took over the Bloom-fieldian descriptive technique they ascribed to it a completely different psychological interpretation. Due to their rejection of surface phonemic forms (cf. ch. 13), they regarded morphophonemic representations as *the phonological* forms. Morpheme-invariants were regarded as psycho-

---

[1] Cf. Bloomfield 1933: 213, 219, 1939: 105–6; Hockett 1961: 42, etc. See also Fischer-Jørgensen (1975: 110–12 and passim).

logically real, though abstract, representations of actual sound patterns. In spite of the obvious differences, mainly in terms of abstractness, morpheme-invariant representations[2] and phonetic representations were assumed to be objects of essentially the same sort.[3]

This generative interpretation is, I will argue, completely unfounded. It is a category mistake to represent a *relation* (that of morpheme identity) between forms (morphs) as a *'thing'* (i.e. in this case: as another linguistic *form*) (see ch. 12). Allomorphs may be phonetically (and hence phonologically, cf. §2.1) quite different, and it simply begs the question to argue that they are 'really' identical psychologically, which is what matters to the generativist. I argue throughout this book for much more concrete forms, i.e. phonetic plans, as 'phonological representations'. To regard morphemes as phonological invariants leads to a great number of insurmountable philosophical and empirical difficulties (see for further discussion ch. 12).

9.2 The establishment of morpheme identity

Morpheme identity is a relation between the members of a set of forms (word forms or parts of word forms, i.e. in general, morphs) which meet certain conditions of phonological, semantic and perhaps morphological similarity (cf. §9.4). In principle, for any such pair (or n-tuple) of morphs, a speaker can postulate a relation of morpheme identity. Such cases can be sporadic or seem far-fetched (from an adult's norm-governed point-of-view), e.g. *ear – hear, foul – filth*, or turn out to be systematic and generalizable, e.g. *ear – ears, loud – loudness, walk – walked*, etc. (with many intermediate cases such as *ring – rang, strong – strength*) (see §9.3).

Though allomorphs have phonetic (phonological) properties in common, nothing forces us to assume that there has to be a unique invariant (maybe abstract) set of phonological properties that is common to (or 'underlies') all the variants. This, in fact, would be a very weird way of interpreting a relation of class membership or invariance. A much more natural conception would be that of Wittgenstein's (1953: e.g. 32) 'family resemblance' which has, in fact, been applied to the morpheme.[4] I will discuss these issues more systematically in ch. 12.

---

[2] Usually termed 'systematic phonemic representations' in OGPh (e.g. Chomsky 1964: 76, 95–6; Postal 1968: xii).

[3] E.g. Postal 1968: 56; Anderson 1974: 50; Zwicky 1975a: 156, principle (G).

[4] See St Clair 1973; Anttila 1975, 1976b. It was also implicit in Linell (1974a: esp. 89ff).

9.3 Morpheme identity as a basis for reinterpretation and construction of forms

As soon as a speaker has established a morpheme identity relation (which may well be an unconscious process) this relation may in principle be extended ('by analogy') to new items (and pairs of items). Take, for example, *ear – hear*. Kiparsky (1974: 259) argues that its extension to *eye : heye* 'to see' would be an example of an 'analogical change which we do not find in the actual history of languages'. I am not at all convinced that such an analogical extension is impossible. After all, children frequently create new words analogically on the basis of postulated morpheme relations which are surprisingly outlandish. Recall, for example, Sturtevant's (1947) well-known example of *ear : irrigate = nose* : X which was resolved as X = *nosigate*.[5] Most such new creations and folk etymologies (a folk etymology can be defined as an etymologically unfounded recognition (postulation) of morpheme identity) are of course of very limited generalizability to additional forms and perhaps new situations of use. Moreover, they are very seldom accepted by the norm, which seems to be the main reason why we do not find them 'in the actual history of languages'.

Some morpheme identity relations may turn out to be much more useful to the language user. Pairs like *ear – ears, walk – walked* are instantiations of relations which are quite systematic and integrated within the grammar. Thus, classes of such forms provide the basis for regular analogies which prove to be generalizable and hence useful to the speaker. They lead to the development of morphological operations (ch. 7). Of course, I agree completely with Kiparsky (1965, 1974: 259 and passim) that the rule-governed character of these regular analogies must be adequately distinguished from the properties of sporadic analogies and that this *cannot* be done by simply using the traditional 'proportional formulas' (e.g. *ear : ears = eye* : X, where X = *eyes*). Any pair of forms used as the model in such a formula (e.g. *ear : ears*) would only be a more or less arbitrarily chosen *example* of a general type of relation between classes of forms. Regular analogies must be stated in

---

[5]   Sturtevant writes: 'One of my sons when a child suffered frequently from an ailment of the ear for which the standard treatment was irrigation with warm water. He reported the experience in the words, "I've been irrigated". Once he had some trouble with his nose, and warm water was poured into him by way of the nose. He reported "I've been nosigated"' (1947: 97).

terms of more or less general *rules*, which is done in the theory of morphological operations (ch. 7).[6]

There are of course more irregular cases of more or less grammatically motivated morpheme identities which remain outside morphological operations. These would instead be handled by suppletive forms arranged in paradigms, perhaps with 'via rules' associating properties of items of the paradigms (§7.7).

9.4 Conditions on morpheme identity

Morpheme identity can be established if certain conditions of phonological similarity and semantic affinity between forms are met. Integration in a systematic morphological pattern may strongly support morpheme identity recognition. Indeed, this may even make semantic affinity superfluous; consider, e.g., *-ceive* in Engl. *receive, deceive, conceive, perceive* or *-stå* in Sw. *stå* 'stand', *anstå* '1. wait, 2. be proper for', *avstå* 'give up, renounce', *bestå* 'last', *bistå* 'help', *förestå* 'manage, be in charge of', *förstå* 'understand', *påstå* 'claim', *tillstå* 'admit', *understå* (*sig*) 'dare to', *uppstå* 'arise', *utstå* 'endure'.[7] Some attempts

TABLE I (from Derwing 1973: 124)

Semantics				
III. OBSCURE	ear–irrigate four–formation wine–whine cold₁–cold₂	idiot–ideology labor–laboratory reside–residue month–menstrual	circle–Ku Klux Klan lead–plumber holy–Halloween moon–menstrual	
II. INTERMEDIATE	crypt–cryptic search–research hand–handle fond–fondle ray–radiate	moon–month louse–lousy tame–timid fable–fabulous wild–wilderness	candle–incandescent hand–handkerchief guise–beguile royal–regalia sister–sorority	
I. CLEAR	friend–befriend happy–happiness joy–joyous ride–rider sad–sadly	residue–residual save–salvation royal–regal various–variety joke–jocular	milk–lactate brain–cerebral brother–fraternity father–paternalism devil–diabolical	
Phonetic	A. CLEAR	B. INTERMEDIATE	C. OBSCURE	

[6] Nobody would assume that the single relationship *ear : hear* 'correspond(s) to a rule in English grammar', a view which Kiparsky (1974: 259), unjustifiably, considers to be an implication of the traditional notion of analogy.

[7] If we extend the concept of morpheme to cover the roots in true suppletivism too (*go – went, bad – worse*), morphological systematicity can be said to compensate for lack of phonological similarity too.

have been made to pinpoint the limits of morpheme identity. For example, Derwing (1973: 122–6) discusses the issue as 'the problem of lexical identity'[8] and gives examples of various pairs of items occupying different points on the scales of semantic and phonetic relatedness (p. 163). Derwing has also tried to approach the problem experimentally (Derwing & Baker 1976: 63–92).

In some recent papers by Ross (e.g. 1973) it has been contended that grammatical categories are fuzzy (or 'squishy' in Ross' wording). Something similar holds, it seems to me, for morpheme identity relations. Indeed, I would claim that it is completely futile to try to find any exact limits for morpheme identity recognition. There are obviously great differences between the lexica of different speakers and indeed within the same speaker's grammar at different times. As we have seen, these differences are not only due to the fact that some words are known by some speakers but not by others. Also within a given lexicon consisting of a specific set of items there are great variations concerning the extent to which morpheme identities are postulated. Most speakers have, now and then, conscious experiences of discovering or postulating a new morpheme identity between forms that they have known for long. Whether one sets up a putative morpheme identity relation is very much a matter of imagination and chance (except in the most obvious cases). One may simply happen to be confronted with specific situations in which it suddenly becomes quite natural to make an identity association which would normally be regarded as extremely far-fetched (compare, e.g., *ear – irrigate* of §9.3).

9.5 More on morpheme identity: inter- and intra-individual variation

I have claimed that language is indeterminate as to how far morpheme identities are or can be extended. This means that the variations between (and within) individual speakers' grammars are great.[9] This would be particularly true of those morpheme identity associations which are not supported by regular grammatical systems (see Derwing's table, p. 163). This indeterminacy[10] is both natural and harmless, since

---

[8]   This is obviously an unfortunate title, since we cannot possibly assume that morphemes are the only kind of lexical items (chs. 4, 8). The problem of what lexical items there are is a different one.

[9]   Cf. on this point also McCawley (1976: 156–7).

[10]   On indeterminacy, cf. also §1.5.6 and §5.2.9.

marginal morpheme identities are seldom or never exploited by speakers for communicative purposes. In fact, many clear morphophonological alterations between morphs that are obviously associated within common morphemes are not productively used and probably not extracted at all (cf. MRPs, ch. 10). Indeed, many historical changes in the morphology and morphophonology of languages would be hard to explain, unless speakers have only incomplete knowledge of morphophonology (or, at least, make very limited use of their knowledge). Careful studies of morphophonological change, e.g. Andersen's investigations of Ukrainian morphophonemics, reveals that 'the learner fails to exploit some of the more abstract regularities[11] observable in the corpus he is analyzing' (1969: 828). Likewise, studies of hypercorrections, e.g. Wurzel (1977) (§5.2.6), show that speakers do not have a maximally integrated OGPh type of phonology.

We can safely take inter- and intrapersonal variation regarding morpheme identities and abstract morphophonology to be a fact about linguistic communities. This is quite natural, given my theory in which (lexicalized) phonetic plans of word forms (which are obviously subject to much less variation) are the primary units. For OGPh, however, it is a very uncomfortable fact. Here morpheme-invariants are the *basic* units of phonology, and these invariants can only be postulated when morpheme identities have been established. Hence this implies that, according to OGPh, the very basis of phonology is considerably different for different speakers, and indeed for the same speaker at different stages of development. This is extremely implausible. One can hardly say that an OGPh type theory provides a natural account of the nature of interindividual competence variations or of the individual's competence development (see §12.3.2.2).

9.6 Further consequences

An adequate analysis of the nature of morpheme identity removes the fundament on which an OGPh type theory rests (unless one ascribes to morpheme-invariants and morphophonological rules a psychological interpretation of a kind that is quite different from the one now propagated).[12] In ch. 12 I will consider the OGPh theory of morpheme-

[11] I.e. in my taxonomy (ch. 10) morphophonological rules proper.
[12] In this case I would still argue that the generative formalism is very *misleading*, and therefore inadequate. See ch. 12.

invariant forms in more detail. We will note that my (traditional) theory does not share all the various conceptual, empirical and practical difficulties which are tied to the OGPh type theory. Moreover, we can avoid the whole abstractness controversy (which concerns conditions on morpheme-invariants) which is, I think, unsolvable within the OGPh framework (§ 12.2).[13]

---

[13] Of course, we will have an abstractness problem concerning the nature of phonetic plans instead. This, however, seems to be a problem of a kind that is much more liable to be solved in empirical terms.

10 *Typology of phonological rules*

Linguistics cannot, unless it wishes to become entirely circular or mathematical, afford to reject the use of external standards to give its relational data concrete validity in the real world. (Haugen 1951 : 359)

10.1 Introduction

I have already argued against some fundamental OGPh assumptions, e.g. that surface-phonemic contrasts are insignificant and that conditions on correct phonological strings are defined on a morphophonemic, rather than a surface phonemic, level. In ch. 12 I will, furthermore, show that the OGPh assumption that morpheme identity between morphs implies the existence of underlying morpheme-invariant phonological forms is unfounded. In the present chapter I will argue that an adequate theory of phonology will have to recognize several different *types of phonological rules*. Thus, we will find that there is ample evidence for rejecting yet another OGPh assumption, i.e. that there is no fundamental distinction between morphophonological and allophonic rules (i.e. according to OGPh, rules accounting for morphophonological alternations are similar in form and function to rules accounting for relatively low-level allophonics).[1]

10.2 Functions of rules

In §2.2 I argued for a general distinction between *construction* of forms (phonetic plans) and *execution* of forms, and thus, by implication, between rules pertaining to these two phases. In addition, in §2.3 I further specified a number of phonological capabilities that speakers may be assumed to possess. I tentatively identified three kinds of functionally different phonological rule types, i.e. phonotactic rules

[1] Cf. for example, Chomsky & Halle (1965 : 137).

(PhtRs), perceptual redundancy rules (PRRs) and articulatory reduction rules (ARRs). In addition, I posited morphological operations in which morphophonological rules proper (MRPs) are integrating aspects (see ch. 7). In this chapter, I will try to show that these rule types have indeed quite different formal (structural) and behavioral properties. However, we will also find that the category boundaries must be assumed to be sufficiently fuzzy. On some points, a further refinement of our taxonomy will be called for. Thus, e.g., I will add the category of sharpening and elaboration rules (§10.3.2) (cf. also §3.3.4).

10.3 Basic rule types[2]

I will now proceed to a preliminary characterization of the various phonological rule types. Many more details will emerge from the subsequent discussion in this chapter.

10.3.1 *Phonotactic rules*

(or constraints)[3] (PhtRs) express conditions on the structure of phonetic plans and careful pronunciations. For example, in Spanish an /e/ is predictable word-initially before /s/ followed by a consonant:

(1)   IF: #   s C

      THEN: ĕ

In many languages the location of word stress is predictable. For example, Polish has penultimate stress according to the following simplified PhtR:

(2)   IF: S   S #   (where S = syllable)

      THEN: [+stress]

Examples of somewhat more complex PhtRs were given in §6.4.1. For convenience the rule for the deletion and insertion of schwas in certain Swedish obstruent-plus-sonorant clusters is restated here:

---

[2]   The rest of this chapter is a revised version of Linell (1977b).
[3]   As for terminology, cf. §6.5.

(3) IF: $\quad X\ C_i \begin{bmatrix} \underline{\quad\quad} \\ -\text{stress} \end{bmatrix} \begin{Bmatrix} r \\ l \\ n \end{Bmatrix} Y$

THEN: (a) $\qquad \check{e}$ if $Y = \begin{Bmatrix} \# \\ C \end{Bmatrix}$

　　　(b) $\qquad \emptyset$ if $Y = V$

Conditions: X contains a stressed syllable and no word boundary. C_i is one of the consonant types occurring first in the cluster type in question (see p. 122).

As was noted in §6.2.2, the nature of speakers' judgments of pronounceability (what speakers believe are restrictions on pronounceability in their language, cf. Bjarkman 1975: 71) supports the assumption of having PhtRs refer to careful pronunciations. PhtRs concern directly extractable properties of real phonological–phonetic structurings (in contrast to MRPs, §10.3.5) and are valid for forms irrespective of whether they alternate morphophonologically or not (e.g. German final tensing applies to both non-alternating forms like *und*, *Alp*, *Werk* and alternating forms like *Bund* (cf. *Bunde*), *halb* (cf. *halbe*), *Berg* (cf. *Berge*). However, PhtRs also have an important function in morphological operations, where they account for 'automatic' morphophonological alternations (see §7.2–3). Some PhtRs must be assumed to be grammatically conditioned (several types, see §10.7.1.2).

10.3.2 *Sharpening and elaboration rules*
In §3.3.4 it was suggested that there are reasons to single out a special category of rules which govern certain kinds of sharpenings and (often 'stylistic' or artificial) elaborations in certain very articulated pronunciations.[4] Some such rules actually cause neutralizations which do not occur in natural connected speech. They typically apply in lexical pronunciation ('in isolation') and in phrase-final position and/or under emphasis. These rules are optional in the sense that they are not true of all tokens of the word forms in question (§10.5) though they may well be obligatory under certain syntactic and stylistic conditions. German final tensing would exemplify one type (§3.3.4.1). Other rules that I would tentatively place in this category are Sanskrit word-final sandhi rules, insertion of intervocalic /r/ in some varieties of English ([áĵdíərɪz] *idea*

---

[4] Cf. Dressler (1973c: 14) who talks about 'paradigmatic processes' (which are 'typically polarizing, dissimilative, or diphthongizing') and 'syntagmatic strengthening processes' (among which are some of the examples given below).

is), insertion of vowels in French syllabated speech ([sɛtə] *sept*, [avɛkə] *avec*), liaison in French, and also such exotic phenomena as /h/ and /ə/ epentheses in Tuscarora syllabated speech (Rudes 1976: 22). I am uncertain whether sharpening and elaboration rules should form a major category on a par with the others (MRPs, PhtRs, PRRs, ARRs) or not. For some rules, at least, a treatment under the general category of PhtRs seems motivated.

10.3.3 *Perceptual redundancy rules*

Consider the phonological structure of the English word *spoon*. It is possible to set up rules for the predictable features of /s/ and /p/; thus, e.g., (4) specifies the first consonant as /s/, whereas (5) states that /p/ is unaspirated:

(4)   IF: $\#$ [+ cons] [− son] (C) V

THEN: $\begin{bmatrix} -\text{voc} \\ -\text{son} \\ -\text{cont} \\ +\text{cor} \\ +\text{ant} \\ -\text{vce} \end{bmatrix}$

(5)   IF: s $\begin{bmatrix} -\text{son} \\ -\text{cont} \end{bmatrix}$

THEN: [− asp]

Condition: no intervening syllable boundary

These two rules are formally similar, and both specify predictable and articulatorily obligatory features. One could therefore argue that both represent exactly the same type of rule. Yet, some linguists would object to this. (4) could be regarded as a PhtR stating a syntagmatic restriction on the distribution of phonemes; no English-speaking person is probably unaware of the fact that the first consonant in *spoon* is an /s/, rather than simply a consonant. The aspiration of /p/, on the other hand, is not consciously known to native speakers; (5) would traditionally be called an 'allophonic' rule which specifies 'subphonemic', or subordinate, predictable ('redundant') features. One may therefore single out rules of type (5) as a kind of 'detail rule' which, unlike some PhtRs, may not have morphophonemic effects. It is, however, uncertain how these rules should be interpreted in a behavioral perspective. I will suggest the term *perceptual redundancy rules* (PRRs) assuming that perception (which is categorical) extracts certain features of phonetic strings as superordinate ('phonemic'), thus leaving out other subordinate, predictable features, which would then be specified by PRRs (§5.2.3). One *may* suggest that PRRs state relationships between perceptual structurings of different levels of detail. However, it may also be that the distinction between superordinate and subordinate features (in as far as it is a viable one at all) is not, at least not only, due to perceptual abstraction but rather depends on reorganization of percepts into memory-stored information. Thus, it may be suggested that PhtRs state redundancies over properties which are *present* in the lexical representations (i.e. phonetic plans of lexical forms), whereas PRRs specify properties which may be filled in, they too being part of the fully specified articulatory plans that determine idiomatic pronunciations. (Note that if, contrary to this, we conceive of the rules characterized here as PhtRs *also* as filling in properties *not* present in lexical forms, this is tantamount to having archi-segments (archi-phonemes) in the lexicon, something which has been proposed recently (by e.g. Hooper 1975; Rudes 1976; Ringen 1977).)

Another task which should perhaps be allotted to PRRs is to state relations of phonological equivalence between articulatorily heterogeneous sounds, e.g. between apical [r]-type and uvular (postvelar) [R]-type manifestations of /r/ (in a language or dialect where both types are accepted) (but see §3.4). Thus, on the invariant-defining level (subject to conditions of PhtRs but not PRRs) there would be one type (phoneme) /r/. However, articulatory plans involving coronal *r* vs. uvular *r* must clearly be regarded as distinct (cf. the different kinds of articulatory reductions possible) (§5.2.3). These divergent properties of fully specified plans would be filled in by PRRs. This would mean that in such a case all speakers of the language (dialect) would have the same 'kernel' set of superordinate (invariant) features defining the /r/ phoneme of the phonetic plans, whereas different speakers may add partly different, subordinate features, thus specifying their complete articulatory plans differently (i.e. for apical vs. uvular articulation).

Thus, even if there are some arguments for distinguishing PhtRs from PRRs, the boundary between the two categories cannot be too

172 Typology of phonological rules

sharp. Among many boundary cases one might mention the rule which regulates the /ç/ vs. /x/ distribution in Standard German:[5]

(6) IF: $\begin{bmatrix} +\text{son} \\ \alpha\,\text{back} \end{bmatrix}$ $\begin{bmatrix} -\text{son} \\ -\text{ant} \\ +\text{high} \end{bmatrix}$ (within morphs, mirror image)

↓

  THEN: [α back]

/ç/ and /x/ seem to be quasi-phonemes (term due to Korhonen 1969), on the verge of becoming phonemes. In fact, they do contrast marginally (if we disregard morphological differences), e.g. *Kuchen* /ku:xən/ – *Kuhchen* /ku: çən/ 'little cow'. Similarly, Russian /e/ (which palatalizes the preceding consonant) and /ɛ/ (which does not palatalize) may be developing into quasi-phonemes (cf. for example, Holden 1976).[6]

To summarize, there are, after all, some reasons to consider PhtRs and PRRs subcategories of one superordinate category.[7]

10.3.4 *Articulatory reduction rules*
(ARRs) express generalizations about differences between different pronunciations of the same word forms, i.e. differences in degree of reduction.[8] Such rules would state generalizations about such differences in segmentalization as between English (American) [wɪntəɹ] and [wĩɾ̃ə] for *winter*, French [ʒəsɛpɑ] and [ʃpɑ] for *je sais pas*, Swedish [ønɪværsɪté:t] and [øɳẙsté:t] for *universitet* 'university'.[9] Among general ARRs are language-specific variants of processes such as transfer of syllable-final consonants to the next syllable, deletion of unstressed vowels and assimilation and deletion of consonant clusters.

10.3.5 *Morphophonological rules proper*
(MRPs), finally, are a completely different kind of rules. They are such *not*-phonotactically-motivated rules as are needed to account for

---

[5] /r/ has to be considered as equivalent to a [−back] segment (cf. for example, *durch* 'through' pronounced as [dʊʁç], not *[dʊʁx]).

[6] For further examples, cf. §5.2.3.

[7] Later on I will show that the boundaries between MRPs and PhtRs and between PhtRs and ARRs are also fuzzy (see esp. §10.7.1.2 and §10.6.1, respectively).

[8] Cf. §3.5.

[9] See discussion of such rules for Swedish by Eriksson 1974; Gårding 1974; for German by Dressler et al. 1972; Kohler 1977; for English by Zwicky 1972a,b; Mansell 1973b; Cearley 1974; for Breton by Dressler 1972a; for Polish by Rubach 1977b; for Romanian by Rudes 1977.

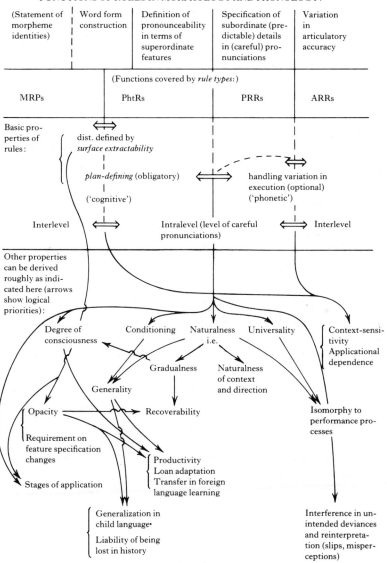

Fig. 10.1 Chart of logical dependencies within theory proposed

morphophonological alternations in the language. A good example is English vowel shift as, e.g., /ij/ ∼ /e/ in *serene – serenity*. The qualitative difference here is not a phonotactic necessity; [sɪrɪnɪtɪ] would be a perfect English noun (cf. *divinity*; cf. also alternations without vowel shift as in *caprice* /ij/ – *capricious* /ɪ/); however, it does not happen to be the noun connected with *serene*. In French, an MRP accounts for the relation /Ṽ/ ∼ /Vn (or Vm)/ in many morphologically related forms (e.g. masc. vs. fem.: *Jean – Jeanne, fin – fine, bon – bonne*).

In ch. 7 we have seen that PhtRs and MRPs account for morphophonological adjustments within morphological operations, the latter being unitary operations constructing phonetic plans on the basis of lexicalized plans. For MRPs, this is practically their only function in grammar.[10] Except when an MRP is the only overt expression of a morphological category, i.e. when it constitutes the morpholexical core (§7.2), as the /Ṽ/ ∼ /Vn/ alternation in the French case above, MRPs should be thought of as nothing but integrated and complicating aspects of morphological operations (§7.5).

10.3.6 *Summary : rule types and grammatical functions*

Thus, the general argument can be summarized as follows. Starting out from a certain theory of the lexicon (lexical items are concrete base forms and/or stems, see §4.3.3) and the utterance-producing grammatical devices, we argue for different functions of phonological rules in such a model of communicative competence of language users (§2.3). A fundamental distinction is between the 'cognitive' plan-constructing and plan-defining operations and the 'phonetic' plan-execution processes. If this model is adequate (which seems quite probable), then we would expect the different rule types to behave differently in a number of ways. This is indeed the case, as should be clear from the discussion below. The various properties of rules to be discussed and their mutual relationships are tentatively sketched in Fig. 10.1.

In Linell (1974a) I strongly emphasized the dichotomy between plan-defining rules (MRPs, PhtRs) and plan-execution rules (processes) (PRRs, ARRs) (NB: the latter, especially PRRs, are those which are traditionally termed 'allophonic' ('phonetic') as opposed to 'morphophonological' ('phonological')).[11] MRPs and PhtRs are those rules

---

[10] Cf. also their possible role as 'via rules', §7.7.
[11] Many people tend to talk about rules of sound patterns in terms of no more than two categories (e.g. 'morphological' vs. 'phonological', 'morphophonological' vs. 'allo-

which have or may have, respectively, morphophonemic effects, i.e. they map 'phonemes onto other phonemes' in traditional terminology. However, from other view-points there is no doubt a more radical difference between MRPs on one hand and the other types on the other. Indeed, MRPs should be thought of as belonging to morphology rather than phonology (§7.5).

10.4 Properties of rules: introduction

The rest of this chapter will be devoted to a discussion of the divergent properties of different phonological rule types. This discussion will obviously be dependent on many traditional insights as well as on several recent – mostly very brief – attempts to provide similar classifications.[12] It should be pointed out that my classification is not the only one possible, and this for several reasons. Thus, many dimensions are interdependent or reflexes of the same basic property (cf. Fig. 10.1). Furthermore, some classifications are meaningful only relative to the general framework proposed in this work. Note that some phonological rules can be assigned different properties depending on one's theory (e.g. with or without extrinsic rule ordering). In my survey, I will refer to several results attained within generative phonology; though I do not accept that theory as adequate, I still think that some results of research carried out in that framework may be of principled interest (and may perhaps be transferred to a more adequate framework).

I would also like to stress the *preliminary* character of my taxonomy. The exact properties of many specific phonological regularities are still uncertain or unknown. Likewise, many of the generalizations proposed will certainly have to be revised and corrected, once more data have been collected. Still, the existing data seem extensive enough for us to say with some confidence that the typology proposed must be basically correct.

phonic', 'phonological' vs. 'phonetic', 'rule' vs. 'process', etc.). I would prefer to avoid using these terms in this way, since they can be defined in many different ways. Moreover, just two categories will hardly make up an adequate typology (cf. also Dressler, 1977a).

[12] See, e.g., Andersen 1969: 826–8; Schane 1971; Stampe 1972; Vennemann 1972a: 236; Karlsson 1974a: 24ff, 43ff; Cearley 1974: 30–2; Linell 1974a: 98–100; Anderson 1975; Bjarkman 1975: 68–9; Skousen 1975b: 99ff; Brasington 1976; and, in particular, Dressler 1977a,b.

10.5 Invariance and variation: obligatoriness/optionality

It is commonplace in generative phonology to classify rules into *obligatory* and *optional* ones. In fact, what is at stake here is the assumption that for all tokens of the lexically and grammatically *same* utterance made up of the *same* word forms there is one underlying type or *invariant* phonological representation.[13] In my theory, these word-form invariants are the phonetic plans. One might then say that whenever a token occurs it is a logical necessity that its invariant (plan, type) occurs, since each manifestation must be a manifestation of some invariant or plan. The rules that define the properties of the invariant are then invariably[14] valid for all tokens since they define what underlies all tokens; they are 'obligatory'. There are also rules which account for the regular *variation between the tokens*. Such a rule is 'optional' since it is not true of *all* the manifestations. In the generative model the difference in obligatoriness is reflected in the obligatory application of the rules defining the invariants and in the optional application of the rules accounting for the variation.[15] This means that MRPs and PhtRs (except sharpening rules, §10.3.2) are obligatory plan-defining rules.[16] Sharpening rules, PRRs and ARRs, on the other hand, regulate the degree of perceptual accuracy (cf. however, §10.3.3) and articulatory segmentalization which is 'optional' and differentiates the various realizations.[17]

One should be aware of the possibilities of defining obligatoriness otherwise. For example, if we define it relative to fully specified phonetic structurings (fully specified articulatory plans) of fully

[13] This, of course, does not hold in cases of 'phonemic variation', cf. §3.4.
[14] Speakers may of course change their invariants in the development of their internalized grammars. This I disregard here.
[15] Labov (1969: 737ff, 1971: 179 and passim) has covered essentially this distinction with his concepts of 'categorical rule' vs. 'variable rule'.
[16] There are, however, cases where typical MRPs are optional in the sense that both the application and the non-application of such a rule would give rise to grammatical forms. For example, the Finnish t→s/__i rule (discussed at several places above, e.g. §4.4, §7.3) may or may not apply in the preterite formation of many verbs (cf. §7.3: (12)). Even the same speaker accepts and produces alternative variants such as *ylsi~ylti* 'he reached', *souti~sousi* 'he rowed' (see Paunonen 1973). However, these forms are conceived of as phonologically different forms (plans) (cf. §3.4); thus, application vs. non-application of the t→s rule define alternative plans. Such a case is obviously different from the variation resulting from varying applicability of ARRs.
[17] One can of course, with Dressler (1973a: 6), argue that the optionality of these rules lies in the choice of styles, while each style is characterized by having certain rules more or less obligatory (rules which do not apply in another style of speaking).

segmentalized pronunciations, then PRRs of course specify obligatory properties. However, our theory is based on the hypothesis that though this specification of articulatory details is 'articulatorily obligatory', it seems to be perceptually or cognitively 'optional' or at least subordinate (§10.3.3). Furthermore, note that a rule, e.g. an ARR, may have to apply obligatorily if another optional rule has applied (see applicational dependence, §10.7.3.3). Such a rule, or rule application, would also be termed 'optional' in the terminology chosen here.

As described here, obligatoriness/optionality is something of a defining criterion for phonetic plans and can therefore not be used as evidence for the typology. However, it can hardly be disputed that the distinction in question is fundamental in phonological theory. Thus, several other concepts, such as 'morphophonemic effect', 'neutralization' and 'opacity' should in my opinion be defined only with respect to the effects of *obligatory* rules. If, contrary to this, we insist on talking about 'optional neutralization' and 'optional opacity', one should bear in mind that

(a)   if a neutralization is not obligatory but only optional (i.e. if the morphophonemic merger is optional), then the speaker has access to non-neutralized forms in careful speech (which is important, cf. §3.3.4)

(b)   if a rule becomes opaque (§10.7.1.4) only by the optional application of other rules, then the speaker has access to a level (of careful pronunciations) on which the rule is transparent. Such 'optional opacity' may, unlike true, i.e. obligatory, opacity, be quite acceptable.

10.6 Use and validity of rules in normal regular speech

10.6.1 *Validity as a function of speech tempo*

I have already assumed that different pronunciations of an expression form have the same underlying phonetic plan (having certain specific grammatical and phonological properties) irrespective of the variations in the realizations. However, suppose we ask to what degree the *actually pronounced* phonetic strings conform to the restrictions defined by the various types of rules. It then appears that the degree of applicability of typical ARRs, e.g. supradentalization in Swedish, vowel reduction in many languages, etc., increases with rising speech tempo (casualness), whereas the same is not always true of PhtRs. In fact, the validity of some PhtRs *decreases* with increasing tempo and sloppiness. This category of rules comprises many restrictions on permitted segment clusters and segment types (the range of which is less restricted in casual speech, cf. §6.2.2), and sharpening rules (§10.3.2) (which are restricted to certain positions in careful speech styles); German final tensing (*gab er* [ga:pʔe:r]) fails to apply in casual speech ([ga:bər]). However, some PhtRs clearly tend to generalize their applicability with increasing tempo (sloppiness). Such rules usually have an assimilative character. For example, Swedish dental nasal assimilation acts as a PhtR morpheme-internally (e.g. *bank* 'bank' [baŋk], *bank]) but not over morpheme boundaries (*pannkaka* 'pancake' [˅pan:ˌkɑ:ka]); however, in casual speech we get [˅paŋ:ˌkɑ:ka]. Similarly, Sw. supradentalization may be obligatory morpheme-internally, at least for some speakers (e.g. *bord* 'table' [bu:ɖ)), and Pol. strident assimilation (e.g. s→ś/__ć) is in general obligatory within morph(eme)s (*list – liście* 'letter' (nom. loc.)) (Rubach 1977c); otherwise, these rules act as ARRs.[18] The increasing applicability of such rules in more casual speech has sometimes been accounted for in terms of boundary deletions (e.g. Dressler 1972a: 10, 1976a).

10.6.2 *Invocation in speech performance*

The distinction between obligatory and optional rules of §10.5 does not imply that the rules are obligatorily vs. optionally (respectively) utilized in actual speech performance, though generative phonology misleadingly may suggest this. Basically, phonological rules are correspondence formulas relating idealized phonological representations (structurings) (§1.4.3). Though some of them may be construed as conditions on operations and processes, it is unclear how and when they are invoked in actual speech performance. However, one may very well argue that the actual state of affairs is contrary to the generative suggestions. If phonetic plans do exist and if some of them are stored as lexicalized phonological information about words (chs. 3, 4), then *these* lexicalized plans need not be recreated (by application of rules) every time the words are used. Thus, MRPs and PhtRs would only be invoked if the utterance to be produced or recognized involves word forms which are not available to the speaker–listener (cf. morphological operations,

[18] Compare the two kinds of PhtRs to Schane's (1972) 'rules for maximum differentiation' and 'assimilative rules'. Cf. also Dressler (1973c).

ch. 7). PRRs and ARRs, on the other hand, are related to perceptual and articulatory dimensions, but this does not necessarily mean that such rules are actually used by listeners or speakers in every perceptual or articulatory act (Linell 1979b). Thus, it is hard to believe that the application of phonological rules in the grammatical derivation of forms corresponds in a step-by-step fashion to actually occurring performance processes (cf. proposals reviewed in §1.4.3). Although PRRs and ARRs *may* correspond in some way to real processes, our knowledge of the neurology of speech is still much too scant to allow any hypotheses concerning a possible isomorphy of rules to performance processes. This of course holds a fortiori for the rather subtle and abstract paradigmatic regularities covered by MRPs and PhtRs.

As is rather obvious, the points brought up under §10.6.2 are almost purely speculative. Hopefully, most of the other properties of rules to be discussed will prove to be more substantive.

10.7 Formal properties

I will first consider – under the provisos stated in §10.4 – a number of formal properties of phonological rules and their applications, and then, in §10.8–11, consider various kinds of 'external' evidence.

10.7.1 *Generality of rules with respect to the phonological constitution of strings*

10.7.1.1 *Context-sensitivity*. Rules of segmental phonology are based on the assumption that phonological (phonetic) strings can be adequately described in terms of sequences of *segments*, which, in their turn, are often thought of as simultaneous bundles of features.[19] Rules are then thought of as specifying or changing features of segments (or as inserting, deleting or permuting whole segments). It is customary to classify the rules into context-sensitive and context-free depending on whether they have to refer to a context outside the phonological segment affected or not. However, the concept of context-sensitivity may be defined in at least two ways. If we choose an inclusive interpretation, we may consider a rule context-sensitive if it refers to the phonological context outside the segment affected *and/or* to non-phonological features (e.g. lexical or morphological categories). It then appears that MRPs are always context-sensitive (they always map (or rather, partake in mapping) segments of forms onto segments of other forms), whereas

[19] This is clearly a considerable idealization. Cf. §3.7.

PhtRs (and presumably PRRs) may be context-free, i.e. they sometimes fill in features of segments which are predictable independently of the extrasegmental context. For example, a rule which states that all sibilants are voiceless in Swedish (PhtR or PRR?) is a case in point. Finally, ARRs are usually context-sensitive, although some are apparently context-free (e.g. a rule stating that all unstressed vowels are deleted at a certain level of reduction).

Some (e.g. Dressler 1977b) use a more restricted interpretation of context-sensitivity, according to which a rule is regarded as context-sensitive only if it refers to the *phonological* context outside the segment affected. This implies that more rules have to be regarded as context-free, including several MRPs (e.g. synchronic reflexes of umlaut in *foot* – *feet, man* – *men*, etc.)

10.7.1.2 *Conditioning.* Under this heading I will consider whether the structural description (the set of conditions defining possible input strings) of a rule can be exclusively defined in phonological–phonetic features or must contain other non-phonological features. This distinction applies only to context-sensitive rules, since context-free rules are by definition (10.7.1.1) (only) phonologically conditioned. (Related to conditioning are also the properties of generality, automaticity and transparency (§10.7.1.3–4). Observe, furthermore, that the characterization of a given rule in terms of these properties is clearly dependent on one's general theoretical framework (§10.7.1.4).)

It is often, but not always, true that PRRs and ARRs are 'automatic' and entirely phonologically conditioned, and that 'abstract' rules are morphologically conditioned or otherwise of restricted applicability. MRPs are always morphologically or morphophonologically conditioned – being dependent parts of morphological operations (§7.3) – whereas many PhtRs can be formulated in purely phonological terms (except, of course, for the reference to word boundaries). However, in many other cases PhtRs need more morphological specifications in their structural descriptions. Three main types may be distinguished among these latter PhtRs: (i) rules which need to refer to the morph structure (the localization of morph boundaries) within word forms, or to the distinction between roots and affixes, e.g. Turkish or Finnish suffix harmony, English PhtRs accounting for the regular plural, 3. sg. pres., genitive and preterite allomorphies;[20] (ii) rules which are restricted to

---

[20] See discussion in Linell (1976a: 14–6) and §7.3.

certain major lexical categories (e.g. in Swedish, a form like [ˇpam:ər] (tone 2) would be a perfectly good word, but a PhtR restricted to certain morphological classes excludes the possibility of its being a neutral noun, an adjective or a verbal present form, in which categories words of the given segmental structure always take tone 1); (iii) rules which are restricted to specific inflectional or derivational form classes, thus often defining the canonical phonotactic form of these classes. Such a constraint in Spanish demands that all plural forms end in /-s/ (cf. Linell 1976a: 16–17). For Swedish adjectives and past participles in *-en* there is a rule $n \rightarrow \emptyset / \_\_(+)t \#$ which deletes the /n/ in neuter forms (*mogen* 'ripe' – *moget* (**mogent*) (this rule is exceptionless for these categories, but it is not a general constraint in the language (cf. §7.3.(8)). Another similarly morphologically conditioned PhtR is Finnish $\emptyset \rightarrow k/s\_\_e +$ in the nominal declension (*kiitos* 'thanks' – *kiitoksen* (gen.)). Obviously, PhtRs of this type are those which are closest to MRPs (see §10.11).

Furthermore, 'concrete' rules (PRRs, ARRs) cannot simply be regarded as purely automatic phonetic processes. For one thing, they are by definition language-specific, i.e. they are part of the grammar of a specific language and determine the idiomatic pronunciations (and perhaps language-specific modes of perception). But they may also be grammar-dependent in a much more radical way. For example, differences in reduction may be due to syntactic or morphological categories.[21] A Swedish example is the following: The vowel of the definite plural morph *-en* in neutral nouns like *låren* 'the thighs' or *karen* 'the tubs' may not be syncopated (non-segmentalized), whereas the vowel of the otherwise identical non-neutral singular definite morph in *låren* 'the packing-case' or *karlen* /ka:r +en/ 'the fellow' may be (*lår'n* [lo:ɳ] and *kar'n* [kɑ:ɳ] respectively). In American English, the deletion of final /t, d/ is often suppressed if the /t, d/ is the only overt sign of the preterite (e.g. *mist* loses its /t/ more frequently than *missed*, similarly *told* with respect to *tolled*, see Labov 1971: 178–85). Dressler (1972a: 52–8) argues that there are principles of general validity involved here; deletion of unstressed vowels is possible in redundant endings (in e.g. participles and infinitives in Breton) but not in non-redundant endings (plural in Breton), furthermore it is prohibited in stems or 'full' words but not in 'form words' (articles, adpositions,

---

[21] This has been shown for English by Labov 1969, 1971; Zwicky 1970b, 1972b; and for Breton by Dressler 1972a.

pronouns, sentence adverbs etc.). Synchronic restrictions on rules of this type have their diachronic counterparts in that sound changes spread only *gradually* – and often starting with certain grammatical categories – through the lexicon ('lexical diffusion', Wang 1969; Chen & Wang 1975; cf. also Labov, Yaeger & Steiner 1973: 260–1).[22]

10.7.1.3 *Generality (freedom from exceptions)*. Irrespective of whether a given rule must be confined to certain grammatical categories or not (§10.7.1.2) it may, within its properly defined domain (among native, or nativized, items, cf. §10.8.2), be *general* or have *genuine exceptions*, i.e. exceptions which cannot be accounted for by another rule, or by constraining the rule itself in a principled way. With regard to this, it is clear that MRPs are typically loaded with idiosyncratic traits and exceptions of various kinds. Possibly, we must also allow some exceptions to PhtRs (§10.8.2, §10.11). PRRs and ARRs are probably general (disregarding the kinds of grammatical conditioning discussed in §10.7.1.2).

However, generality is always a relative matter. Most languages have considerable numbers of foreign words, some of which only gradually become nativized (i.e. subject to productive rules) (cf. Holden 1976). Some words resist some aspects of nativization, at least in the linguistic practice of speakers who know their foreign origin. Thus, e.g., there are some Greek loans in Swedish violating the native PhtR which prohibits [#Cs-] sequences (e.g. *psykologi* 'psychology', which, however, tends to become [sʏ-] when commonly used). Likewise, foreign words may resist quite general ARRs; with regard to supradentalization, some speakers prefer [rs] pronunciation to [ʂ] e.g. in *hirs* 'millet', and definitely so in a Latin phrase like *ars amandi* ([ars, *aʂ]).

Related to the notions 'phonological conditioning' and 'generality' is the term 'automaticity'. It seems that 'automatic' usually means

---

[22] Apart from what has been said here regarding non-phonological conditioning of ARRs, it is of course clear that the level of articulatory care in the various parts of specific utterances depends on factors such as the relative predictability of the content communicated and even of the words chosen. But there are also general (i.e. not utterance-bound) non-phonological conditions having an impact on the degree of reduction of word forms. Thus, reduction seems to be correlated with overall text frequency ('familiarity', cf. Fidelholtz 1975), and also with lexicalization (e.g. lexicalized compounds are generally more reduced than new formations), and certain syntactic functions (e.g. high degree of reduction in sentence adverbs). As for the factor of 'foreignness', see §10.7.1.3.

phonologically conditioned *and* general (free from exceptions) (e.g. Bloomfield 1957: 29; Hockett 1958: 279ff; Fischer-Jørgensen 1975: 108), though Kiparsky (1973b: 68) defines it simply as 'free from exceptions'. Thus, I will not treat automaticity separately.

Note that the extent to which properties like generality and automaticity are ascribed to rules is clearly dependent on the type of theoretical framework we are operating with. Thus, if – as in OGPh – we allow ordering of rules, especially language-specific (extrinsic) ordering, we can formulate certain rules in a more general way than would be possible if we had to define them directly relative to surface facts. (This is due to the fact that a rule may be followed by (an)other rule(s) in the derivations, this (these) rule(s) undoing some of the effects of the first-mentioned rule. Generative–phonological accounts are flooded with examples of this.) However, in this framework we will not characterize a rule as automatic and/or phonologically conditioned unless this is true on the surface.

10.7.1.4 *Transparency.* Related to automaticity is transparency. A transparent (= non-opaque) rule captures a surface regularity, i.e. its applicability (its SD and SC) can be read off from a mere inspection of surface forms (more exactly: careful pronunciations). In other words, it is directly extractable and presumably easily learnt. Kiparsky defines opacity (= non-transparency) as follows:

A rule P: A→B/C__D is opaque to the extent that there are phonetic forms [I believe one should say: careful pronunciations, see below, p. 184] in the language having either
(i)   A in the env. C__D
or [...]
(iia)   B *derived by the process P* in env. other than C__D
(iib)   B *not derived by the process P* (i.e. underlying or derived by another process) in env. C__D [C, D represent a morphological and/or phonological context] (1973b: 79).

Thus, we see that a rule P becomes opaque if

(7)   (a) it has (a sizeable number[23] of) exceptions (cf. (i))
        (b) its application is followed by a rule which 'counter-feeds' P and introduces new instances of A in env. C__D (cf. (i))
        (c) its application[7] is followed by other rules which either

---

[23] This is a relative matter. One should probably regard a rule as transparent even if it has a limited number of exceptions. Cf. §10.7.1.3 and §10.11.

obligatorily change some of the Bs to Es in env. C__D or obligatorily destroy the whole or part of the env. C__D (cf. (iia))

(d) it is obligatorily neutralizing (i.e. it is a neutralizing rule which *requires* feature changes according to §10.7.2.3) (cf. (iib)).

Thus, it is easily seen that PhtRs (and PRRs) are exactly the types of rules which are transparent, i.e. rules of the type:

$$\text{IF:} \quad C\left[\frac{+A}{\downarrow}\right]D \text{ (which is true on the surface)}$$

$$\text{THEN:} \quad B$$

(where A and B must not be incompatible, e.g. opposite specifications for the same feature). MRPs, on the other hand, are opaque (which follows from the definitions given in §7.2).

I have chosen to define opacity relative to the level of careful pronunciations (and phonetic plans) (cf. §10.5).[24] Of course, opacity of rules can be defined relative to the set of all possible phonetic strings in the language, and such a definition is used by some. However, this would make many PhtRs (and PRRs, ARRs) partially opaque since articulatory reduction may give rise to structures which do not obey these constraints (§6.2.2). Indeed, optionality of rules (cf. ARRs) implies the possibility of non-application even when the structural descriptions are met, and thus opacity according to type (i) above.

Returning to the case of obligatory rules, it should be noted again that a linguist's characterization of a given rule in terms of transparency depends to a considerable degree on his choice of theory. The same surface facts can often be generated either by an opaque but general and (morpho)phonologically conditioned rule in a theory allowing extrinsic ordering (e.g. OGPh) *or* by a transparent but less general and often diacritically (or morphologically) conditioned rule in a theory without extrinsic ordering. As a paradigm example, consider Kisseberth's (1969) and Vennemann's (1974a: 206) rules for suffix harmony in Yawelmani:

(8)   (a) (Kisseberth)

$$\begin{bmatrix} V \\ \alpha\,\text{high} \\ \text{Suffix} \end{bmatrix} \rightarrow [+\text{round}]/ \begin{bmatrix} V \\ +\text{round} \\ \alpha\,\text{high} \end{bmatrix} C_0 —$$

---

[24] Kiparsky (1973b: 85, fn. 9) also restricts himself to obligatory rules.

(b) (Vennemann)

$$\begin{bmatrix} V \\ \alpha \text{ high} \\ \text{Suffix} \end{bmatrix} \rightarrow [+\text{round}] / \left\{ \begin{bmatrix} \begin{bmatrix} -\alpha \text{ high} \\ HH \end{bmatrix} \\ [\alpha \text{ high}] \\ +\text{round} \end{bmatrix} \right\} C_0 -$$

(HH = 'high in harmony' – diacritic feature)

(Kisseberth's rule is followed by another rule which makes long high vowels non-high, thus making (8a) opaque according to (7c) above.)

Everyone seems to agree that obligatory opaque rules are (would be) more difficult to learn than transparent ones, but it is a matter of considerable dissent whether such rules (and extrinsic ordering) could be learnt at all.[25] There appears to be much evidence against the assumption of psychologically valid opaque rules (e.g. Derwing 1973; Braine 1974; Vennemann 1974a). I would conjecture that obligatory opaque rules, which only occur among MRPs, are *not* independently living rules but only integrating aspects of morphological operations (§7.4–5).

10.7.2 *Relations between inputs and outputs*

10.7.2.1 *Recoverability of inputs.* A typical property of MRPs and PhtRs as opposed to most concrete rules is that input segments are in most of the specific cases *not recoverable* from the outputs of the rules. For example, given a form as German sharpened [ra:t] one cannot determine from its phonological structure alone whether it is related to a form with /d/ (*Rade*) or /t/ (*Rate*) (final tensing is a PhtR, §10.3.2) or given a Finnish form as [kæsi] (*käsi* 'hand') you cannot tell whether the /s/ alternates with /t/ (as in *käsi, kätenä*) or not (as in *lasi* 'glass', *lasina*) (the /t/→/s/ rule is an MRP).[26] These rules are *neutralizing*, i.e. they obliterate distinctions present in inputs (cf. Kiparsky 1973b: 68).

ARRs may of course also ultimately neutralize distinctions present in careful pronunciations (e.g. German *Baumesse* vs. *Baummesse*). However, if phonetic details are investigated, one will often find that ARRs often produce gradual, rather than absolute, effects (§10.7.2.4). Thus, they often leave some trace of the input distinctions in their outputs (the [m] of *Baumesse* being shorter than that of *Baummesse*).

[25] For arguments that they can, see Kiparsky & Menn (1977).
[26] For discussion of aspects of this rule, cf. §4.4, §7.3, §7.4.3.3, §10.7.2.3, §10.8.1 and p. 176, fn. 16.

Compare in this respect the nasalization of French nasal vowels (*an* [ɑ̃] 'year', *bon* [bɔ̃] 'good') to nasalization in American English (produced by an ARR). In English, the nasalization of the vowel and the disappearance of the nasal consonant are gradual, whereas in French you always have a true, fully nasalized vowel (which is phonemically distinct from the corresponding oral vowel). Moreover, in English, the underlying nasal consonant is recoverable (being a nasal homorganous with the following stop);[27] vowel plus nasal is also an alternative pronunciation in English, e.g. [kæ̃t, kæ̃nt] *can't*, [kæ̃p, kæ̃mp] *camp*). In French, the alternating nasal is not generally recoverable, e.g. [œ̃] *un* alternating with /n/ ([yn] *une*), but [parfœ̃] *parfum* alternating with /m/ ([parfyme] *parfumer*).

10.7.2.2 *Segment inventories of inputs and outputs.* Another important difference between abstract and concrete rules is that MRPs and PhtRs *never introduce new types of segments*, i.e. segments which cannot occur in the inputs. This is so in the kind of model presupposed here since these rules either state generalizations of the structures of phonetic plans (careful pronunciations) (PhtRs) or map such plans onto other such plans (morphological operations of which MRPs (and sometimes PhtRs) are part, §7.3). In other words, MRPs always have and PhtRs sometimes have *morphophonemic effects*, i.e. they map segments ('phonemes') onto segments of the same types, sometimes obliterating input distinctions (§10.7.2.1) but never introducing new segment types. PRRs and ARRs, on the other hand, often introduce new segment types. Rule (5) above introduces the distinction of aspiration, which does not occur in phonetic plans (if PhtRs vs. PRRs is a valid distinction and if it is true that (5) is a PRR rather than a PhtR). ARRs very often introduce new segment types (and new cluster types, §6.2.2). Nasalized vowels in English (§10.7.2.1) or Swedish (e.g. [bɑ̃goːd] *bangård* 'railroad depot') are a case in point. Note that such new segment types, and cluster types, are generally not conscious to the native speaker (§10.9).

---

[27] Roger Lass (pers. comm.) has drawn my attention to some examples where this is not the case. Thus, for some speakers [hæːstɚ] is a possible pronunciation of *hamster* (careful speech: [hæ̃ːmstɚ]), where the labiality of the underlying nasal is not predictable (the homorganity requirement would predict underlying *hanster*). Note, however, that there is an alternative pronunciation [hæ ː(m)pstɚ] which may be regarded as somewhat less careful than [hæːmstɚ] and which does give the correct prediction.

10.7.2.3 *Requirement on feature specification changes.* A formal distinction between rules that state conditions on strings at a certain level of abstraction (i.e. PhtRs, PRRs) ('intralevel rules') and rules that partake in mapping forms onto other forms (MRPs) or relate different pronunciations (ARRs) ('interlevel rules') is that the latter may *require* changes of feature specifications (i.e. the structural description of at least some such rules contains a feature specification $[\alpha F_i]$ which is obligatorily changed by the rule to $[-\alpha F_i]$), whereas the former *must not require* such changes, though they may accomplish changes in some of their applications (i.e. within morphological operations). Consider, e.g., German final devoicing (9a) (a PRR?) and final tensing (9b) (a PhtR, 'sharpening rule', §3.3.4):

(9a) IF: $[-\text{son}]$ \$

  THEN: $[-\text{vce}]$

(9b) IF: $[-\text{son}]$ #

  THEN: $\begin{bmatrix} (-\text{vce}) \\ +\text{tns} \end{bmatrix}$

(under certain conditions, cf. §3.3.4.1)

These rules are valid for all German forms, whether alternating or not. Thus, they apply also to nonsense words and neologisms. However, if we had added the specification(s) $[+\text{vce}]$ (and/or $[-\text{tns}]$) to their SDs, they would only have been valid for alternating forms (e.g. [bunt] (or [bund̦]) *Bund* 'union' related to [bundə]), which would be counterintuitive, since non-alternating forms (e.g. [unt] *und*, or [bunt] *bunt* 'motley' related to [buntə]), including nonsense words ([krunt]) are clearly subject to the same restrictions.

Some rules among MRPs and ARRs, on the other hand, do require feature changes. As an example of a feature-change-requiring ARR, consider Swedish nasal assimilation, according to which only dental, not labial and velar, nasals assimilate; thus, some compounds with *panna* 'pan', *damm* 'pond' and *säng* /sɛŋ/ 'bed' are in casual speech: [ˇpam:bɪf:] 'hamburger', [ˇpaŋ:kɑ:ka] 'pancake', [ˇdam:trɛ:d̦, *dan:-] 'pond tree', [ˇdam:go:d̦, *daŋ:-] 'pond yard', [ˇsɛŋ:pal:, *sɛm:-] 'bed stool', [ˇsɛŋ:dy:na, *sɛn:-] 'bed cushion'.

There are certain types of structural changes which can be performed only by feature-change-requiring rules (i.e. interlevel rules), e.g. metatheses, which consequently occur only among MRPs and ARRs. Furthermore, there are the so-called exchange rules (§10.11) (only among MRPs). English vowel shift is sometimes formulated as an exchange rule (cf. Chomsky & Halle 1968); irrespective of whether this is correct or not,[28] the rule clearly requires feature specification changes. For each lax vowel, [ɪ, e] etc., there is one specific input vowel ([âɪ, îj], etc.). If [ɪ] alternates by means of vowel shift, it always alternates with [âɪ]. (There are in English also non-alternating instances of [ɪ] (e.g. *hiss*), and other alternating [ɪ]s which do not alternate via vowel shift (e.g. [ɪ] in *capricious* which alternates with [îj] in *caprice*).)

Not all MRPs require feature changes in their *formulations*. For example, Finnish assibilation ($/t/ \rightarrow /s/$) could be formulated as follows:

(10) IF: $\begin{bmatrix} -\mathrm{son} \\ +\mathrm{cor} \end{bmatrix}$ i / X
            ↓
      THEN: [+cont]
      (X = certain morphological categories, cf. Karlsson 1974b: 115–6)[29]

Note, however, that this rule (like all MRPs) always *performs* feature changes, since it only applies within morphological operations where it always turns /t/ to /s/. However, this property (which is typical of MRPs as opposed to PhtRs) simply follows from the definition of MRPs (§7.2).

10.7.2.4 *Discreteness/gradualness of change.* Chomsky & Halle (1968: 65) propose a distinction between 'phonological' rules which switch binary feature values, and 'phonetic' rules which are supposed to assign integer values to features along continuous phonetic parameters. In practice, the latter kind of rules has never been treated in orthodox (generative) phonology. It is clear, however, that many phonological regularities involve gradual, rather than discrete, adjustments of phonetic parameters. For example, the nasalization of the vowel and the disappearance of the nasal consonant in, e.g., a string type VNC (e.g. Engl. *can't, hint*) is a matter of many degrees (the nasal is, so to speak, gradually absorbed by the vowel),[30] though phonologists tend to describe it categorically in terms of binary choices (vowel is nasalized or not, nasal consonant deleted or not, etc.). Similarly, a stop subject to reduction in fast speech is often simply unreleased (though it may often

---

[28] Cf. discussion in Crothers & Shibatani (1975). See also p. 50, fn. 6.

[29] Cf. p. 185, fn. 26.

[30] For discussion of gradual nasalization processes in Polish and British English speech, cf. Rubach (1976, 1977c).

finally disappear in the articulation of allegro speech). Such a well-known ARR as American English flapping is usually considered to bring about a complete /t/–/d/ merger, but in fact there normally remain differences in vowel length and also in /t/–/d/ features (Fischer & Hirsh 1976). Many other ARRs pertaining to assimilation and simplification processes are gradual rather than absolute.

The status of PRRs is less clear. Perception tends to be categorical (cf. §3.3.5), but articulation is often a matter of degree (e.g. many degrees of aspiration of stops in different positions in English). All the fine details constituting a language-specific *basis of articulation* (cf. Drachman 1973), e.g. detailed specifics of timing and placement, would in a process-based phonology belong to the domain of gradual rules. In general, gradual rules have to be (at least mainly) phonologically/ phonetically conditioned (cf. §10.7.1.2; also, on naturalness, §10.10.2).

By contrast, rules with morphophonemic effects (MRPs and PhtRs) are clearly categorical. There is nothing gradual about umlaut in German (either the vowel is umlauted or not) or the /k/→/s/ rule in English (*electric* – *electricity*). As we know by now, MRPs and PhtRs partake in defining differences between plans of different words; thus, they have semantically relevant (grammatical or lexical) functions (which ARRs have not). There seems to be a tendency in perception to sharpen the physical correlates of grammatically relevant distinctions, and this in turn may lead to an increase also in the articulatory differentiation. Thus, I noted earlier (p. 99) the case of the Granada dialect of Spanish, in which laxing of vowels (e.g. [sElvA] *selvas* 'forests' vs. [selva] *selva* 'forest') is a morphologized rule (MRP) and where closed and open vowels (e.g. [e, a] vs. [E, A]) are described as very tense and very lax respectively, whereas the distinction is much less clear in those Spanish dialects in which laxing is merely conditioned by a following /h/ (aspirated /s/). Another case, this time from Finnish, is reported by Skousen. In dialects where schwa insertion is an ARR (*kylmä* 'cold' giving [kyləmæ]) the [ə] is

'weak' and is pronounced quickly [and] speakers are not aware of the extra syllable produced on the phonetic level [...] But in Savo dialects, the ə vowel has taken on the quality of the preceding vowel, giving [kylymæ]. Now the nonphonemic ə has been replaced by a y vowel, which is psychologically real. Surface y vowels occur in every possible environment, in stressed position (*syy* 'reason', *kysyn* 'I ask') and in nonstressed and final positions (*kysyy* 'he asks', *kieltäytyy* 'he refuses'). Speakers in Savo have changed the stress in forms like *kýlymässä* so that secondary stress is now applied to the third syllable, to give *kýlymässä*. These speakers, of course, consider the *y* in *kylymä* as an underlying vowel and apply the stress rules in accordance with the underlying representation. The important point, however, is that no speaker that has an inserted ə (which is not psychologically real) has reinterpreted stress to give forms like *kýləmässä*, where the ə vowel would be interpreted as phonemic. (1975b: 101–2)

10.7.3   *Application within derivations*

10.7.3.1 *Stage of application within generative derivations.* Suppose, for the sake of argument, that we regard MRPs, PhtRs, PRRs and ARRs all simply as 'phonological rules'. It will then probably turn out that rules form groups, possibly the four groups outlined here, applying at different places, or at different stages of derivations, in the grammar. Such results are probable, even if the analyst does not share the kind of functionally motivated theory of this book. Purely formal-structural studies seem to show this. Using a generative–phonological model, Koutsoudas (1977) argues that all rules with morphophonemic effects, i.e. obligatory neutralizing rules (mapping phonemes onto phonemes) (i.e. MRPs, PhtRs), apply in a block before all allophonic rules. A similar view seems to be part of Stampe's theories (Stampe 1972; Rhodes 1973: 536; Bjarkman 1975; cf. also Cearley 1974).

It is sometimes argued that there are cases when the application of an allophonic rule must precede the application of a rule with morphophonemic effects (the latter rule neutralizing a distinction which is contrastive in the language) (e.g. Anderson 1975: 52–6). An example of this type of situation would be the allophonic lengthening rule (PRR) which states that vowels are longer before voiced obstruents than before voiceless ones, and the flapping rule neutralizing the /t/–/d/ distinction in natural speech ([râɪDɚ] *writer* vs. [râɪːDɚ] *rider*) in many English dialects. However, as long as the 'morphophonemic' rule is not obligatory, it does not obliterate surface contrasts at the level of careful pronunciations (which should count most, §3.2.4) but only at a more reduced level. Moreover, the /t/–/d/ neutralization is seldom complete (§10.7.2.4). Thus, flapping is not morphophonemic in the strict sense (§10.5). It seems that the same is true for most of the cases when a 'morphophonemic' rule is said to follow an allophonic one.

10.7.3.2 *Ordering within blocks of rules.* I will now turn for a moment to the principles of ordering *within* subcomponents of rules. According to OGPh, phonological rules are ordered in a fixed language-specific sequence ('extrinsic ordering'). Recent research indicates that the view that rules are thus ordered once and for all is strongly overexaggerated. However, the *applications* of rules may interact in a number of ways ('feeding, counter-feeding, bleeding, counter-bleeding, non-affecting', see Kiparsky 1968a; Koutsoudas, Sanders & Noll 1974). It has been argued that the order of application in the specific cases is always derivable from universal principles (Iverson 1974; Koutsoudas, Sanders & Noll 1974). However, there is no unanimity among scholars that 'extrinsic ordering' can be completely dispensed with.[31]

The 'unordered rules' hypothesis has mainly been explored as far as MRPs and PhtRs are concerned, but it seems possible that PRRs and ARRs also follow universally preferred orders of reduction. In the theory proposed here, morphological operations (of which MRPs and some PhtRs are part) are assumed to be unitary wholes anyway (§7.4), so the question of ordering between independent rules is most important as regards true phonological rules, especially ARRs. I will return to their ordering below (§10.7.3.3). Note, however, that the frequent obligatory interaction dependencies between MRPs may be seen as an argument for the unity of morphological operations (§7.4.3.1).

10.7.3.3 *Applicational dependence between rules.* As was discussed earlier (§7.4.3.2) various generative–phonological studies have shown that there are interesting cases of applicational dependence between rules. Some rules (so-called 'global rules') apparently have to 'look back' at previous stages of the derivations, in order to 'know' whether to apply or not (in addition, their SDs must of course be met). Such rules *either* (i) *apply* (sometimes rather, apply obligatorily) *or* (ii) *do not apply* only if another rule *has* applied earlier in the specific derivations.

A subcase of (i) is termed 'phonological dependence' by Iverson and is defined as follows: 'A rule A is *dependent* on a rule B if the set of forms to which B is nonvacuously applicable includes the set to which A is nonvacuously applicable' (1974: 92). It is not difficult to find cases where the whole set of forms to which a rule (A) applies is a subset of the output forms of (an)other rule(s) (B, (B$_2$, B$_3$)). For example, the velar softening rule in Swedish (k→ç, g→j) only applies if the following front vowel is derived (cf. Kiparsky 1973b: 60–1). In Finnish, the assibilation rule (cf. p. 185, fn. 26) applies only if the /i/ is derived, most often by

---

[31] Compare, e.g., Dressler 1972c; Campbell 1973; Kaye 1975; Kiparsky & Menn 1977; Rubach 1977d; Vago 1977 who all argue in favor of extrinsic ordering.

the final /e/ raising rule (e→i/__#) (Kiparsky 1973b: 60). Sometimes, the set of forms to which the rules (A and B) are applicable are identical or almost identical. Thus, in English the qualitative vowel shift rule and the quantity change (tense-lax alternation) are mutually dependent in this way (except in cases like *caprice – capricious*).

Another case is at hand when we have rules which may apply freely in *different* derivations, but for certain derivations (operations), in which both rules would have applied if they were unordered and allowed to apply freely, there is a dependency such that if A applies, then B must not apply too (i.e. (ii) above).[32] Thus, Miller (1975: 129–31) argues that the rule of accent reduction in final syllables in Ancient Greek applies only to syllables which are underlyingly final, not to syllables which have become final through the interaction of another rule (corresponding to A in my discussion), i.e. a rule deleting certain final vowels.

Applicational dependence implies that properties of rule application are dependent on properties of specific derivations (i.e. larger wholes such as morphological operations) rather than of the single rules themselves (cf. §7.4.3). It turns out that applicational dependence is typical of MRPs as opposed to PhtRs. This again indicates that MRPs are not separate, independently living rules of languages.[33]

As for applicational dependence between concrete rules, we should note that these rules are in principle *optional*. However, some obligatory applicational relations clearly exist. Most common are probably obligatory feeding relations; a rule B applies always when another rule A has applied (A feeds B). Articulatory reduction seems to proceed in 'cycles' (Rudes 1976: 129–30); e.g. each deletion of an unstressed vowel is typically (obligatorily) followed by (feeds) various simplifications of consonant clusters (e.g. Gårding 1974; Rudes 1976).[34]

However, there occur also counter-feeding relations between ARRs,

---

[32] This is the case of counter-feeding ordering in generative–phonological descriptions. The cases under (a) above would be feeding or counter-bleeding depending on how the rules are formulated.

[33] Iverson (1974) takes the facts of 'phonological dependence' to imply that many instances of what has often been formulated as separate phonological rules (MRPs) should be coalesced to single rules (MRPs). My suggestion is that the relevant grammatical unit is the morphological operation (i.e. the whole morphological–morphophonological derivation) (see §7.4). Note that one of the rules in a relation of applicational dependence may well be the morpholexical rule of the operation (as in Miller's (1975) example of assibilation in Greenlandic).

[34] It would be interesting to find out whether these obligatorily fed rules are identical to PhtRs of the language.

i.e. if a rule A has applied, a rule B must *not* also apply. In many Bavarian and Austrian dialects of German, syncope + cluster reduction and vowel nasalization interact in this way (Mansell 1973c: 178–80; Dressler 1974):

(11)	Careful pronunciations:	/ba:n/ *Bahn* 'path, road'	/ba:dən/ *baden* 'bathe'
	Syncope + cluster reduction	—	ba:n
	Nasalization	bã:	—
	Natural, casual speech	[bã:]	[ba:n, *bã:]

Counter-feeding cases like this imply constraints not to destroy too much of the structure of careful pronunciations (cf. Kaye 1975).[35]

It is possible that there are also cases of obligatory bleeding and counter-bleeding relations among ARRs. In general, it may turn out that applicational dependence between rules is a property possible for 'interlevel rules' (cf. §10.7.2.3) (MRPs, ARRs) but not for 'intralevel rules' (PhtRs, PRRs). This again puts PRRs in an intermediate position, since these rules concern one level of pronunciation but several levels of perceptual accuracy.

10.7.4 *Domain of application*

It is evident that there are considerable differences between phonological rules as far as their domain of application is concerned, if by domain of application we mean the size and the nature of the string or constituent within which the regularity is defined (cf. Dressler 1976a). For example, PhtRs are defined within single morphemes (perhaps root morphemes, e.g. Swedish length regularities (cf. §3.3.5: (1–2)) see also Kaye 1974; Dressler 1977b: §29) syllables (e.g. German final devoicing (9a); for other examples, see Basbøll 1974, 1977b; Hooper 1976), or whole word forms (e.g. Swedish tonal accents, various stress rules in languages with fixed lexical stress). In many cases simple word forms rather than compounds constitute the correct domain (e.g. vowel harmony in Finnish). However, I know of no PhtRs that operate across word boundaries (leaving rhythm rules aside). ARRs, on the other hand, may apply across boundaries in fast speech, even if they, too, most often are restricted to 'phonological words' (which in careful speech are separated by short pauses). We have also seen (§10.6.1) that the applicability of ARRs increases with rising tempo and diminishing

---

[35] Such data may be used in arguing for extrinsic ordering (cf. p. 191, fn, 31). Here, nasalization would have to be ordered before syncope + cluster reduction.

articulatory carefulness, while the converse is true of some PhtRs.

The status of PRRs is unclear. Since perception can be assumed to aim at identifying lexical items in speech, it may be reasonable to assume that they are defined within the domain of words.

MRPs, finally, are of course restricted to the domain of words (and most often simple rather than compound words); they are defined as parts of morphological operations, the function of which is to construct word forms rather than syntactic syntagms. Chomsky & Halle (1968) are well aware of the fact that morphophonological rules belong to 'word-level phonology'; in fact, they make the general claim that phonological rules apply within the domain of words (unless special references to other kinds of boundaries are made, cf. 1968: 367). This position seems overstated, but Chomsky & Halle's claim becomes more reasonable, once it is realized that the authors hardly consider any concrete–phonological rules (PRRs, ARRs) at all in *The* SOUND *pattern of English* (my emphasis).

10.8 Extensions of rule applicability beyond normal use and standard norms

Productivity of a rule in a wide sense may be defined as the extension of the number of items or string types which are made subject to the rule. Such extension occurs in processes

(a) in the normal intentional use of language by fully competent speakers (creation of neologisms, nativization of loan words, etc., §10.8.1–2)

(b) in speakers' performance when talking other (secondary) languages (transfer, §10.8.3)

(c) in the use of language by children learning their mother tongue (§10.8.4)

(d) in specialized, artistic uses (linguistic games, §10.8.5)

(e) in speech performance under artificial (experimental) conditions (§10.8.6)

(f) in 'pathological' language performance (speech errors, aphasia, misperceptions, spelling mistakes, §10.8.7–10).

In other words, we are here faced with a rich array of divergent sources of evidence (though, unfortunately, very little of this potential evidence has so far been assembled).

10.8.1 *Productivity*

of a rule in a restricted sense manifests itself in the rule's being generalized to items that were earlier exceptions to it and in its application to new coinages. Various studies of such data have indicated that MRPs are typically non-productive. Examples are ablaut, umlaut and velar softening in Swedish, vowel shift and stop assibilation (/k/ ~ /s/ as in *electric – electricity*) in English (Moskowitz 1973; Ohala 1974a; Steinberg & Krohn 1975), /t/→/s/ assibilation (as in *käsi – kätenä*), consonant gradation,[36] final /e/ raising (again as in *käsi – kätenä*) in Finnish (Karlsson 1974b; Skousen 1975a,b) etc. PhtRs and concrete rules are, on the other hand, clearly productive (cf. for example, German final devoicing and tensing, Spanish /e/ epenthesis, Swedish supradentalization, etc.).

As far as productivity of MRPs is concerned, it is important to realize that some morphological operations, of which MRPs are part, may well be productive (see §7.4.2). In such cases, it is the whole morphological formation patterns which are productive, not the separate MRPs. To prove that MRPs are really productive as separate rules, one would have to adduce evidence that they are productive across the board (i.e. if an MRP belongs to several different morphological formation patterns, all these patterns are productive unless they also contain other un-questionably non-productive parts), that they generalize in child language and also eliminate their exceptions over time in the language as a whole. No such evidence has to my knowledge been found.

10.8.2 *Nativization of loan words*

Kiparsky (1973a: 103–13)[37] argues convincingly that the processes involved in the nativization of foreign words are phonetic approximation plus – sometimes, especially in cases of speakers having extensive knowledge of the lending language – preservation and transposition of surface phonemic contrasts of the lending language (if this is possible within the phonemic system of the target language, i.e. only sounds and contrasts which do not fit in are eliminated). This means that rules having directly to do with phonetic properties, i.e.

---

[36] The status of Finnish consonant gradation is somewhat unclear. Apparently, the subrule dealing with the quantitative alternation is, on the whole, productive, while the other subrules (qualitative cases) are not (see Kiparsky 1973a: 93–4; Groundstroem 1974; Karlsson 1974b; Skousen 1975a,b; Yli-Vakkuri 1976).

[37] Cf. also Weinreich 1968: 26–7.

PhtRs, PRRs and ARRs, apply to loans, whereas MRPs do not (cf. also Lovins 1974; Holden 1976).[38] However, especially in the practice of educated speakers, foreign words tend to lose their foreign traits only gradually (Holden 1976); thus, some PhtRs tend to accept violations by loans, thereby possibly allowing new, maybe foreign-sounding patterns to stay in the borrowing language (§10.7.1.3). For example, in Russian the palatalization of consonants before /e/ seems to accept an increasing number of violations (we get a 'foreign' type [Cɛ] contrasting with native [C'e]), whereas *akanje* ({o, a}→ʌ in pretonic syllables) has a stronger assimilating influence on loans (cf. Holden 1976). Sometimes, a new productive rule may emerge, which applies *only* to foreign words (Mathesius 1964). Furthermore, while loans may go on violating a PhtR in careful speech, they may be subjected to generalized versions of the same rule functioning as an ARR. Thus, loans in Polish such as *pensja* 'boarding-school', *sens* 'sense' have no nasal vowels in careful speech [pɛnsja, sɛns] but undergo nasalization in casual speech [pẽw̃sja, sẽw̃s] (Rubach 1977a).[39]

Dressler (1977b: 34) has argued that MRPs do sometimes apply to loan words. Again, however, we seem to be faced with productivity of morphological formation patterns rather than of single MRPs (cf. §10.8.1). Thus, if a loan word joins a particular morphological class, it will of course often be subject to the whole morphological operation including the adjustments performed by MRPs (though in many such cases there is a definite tendency for MRPs to be eliminated). As an example, consider Russian transitive softening (§7.3: (14)) which is productive in some morphological contexts (Ru. *bulldog* 'bulldog', augm. *bulldožina*).[40]

There are reasons to pronounce a warning against taking *all* 'nativization data' as relevant for determining the productivity of a phonological rule. Thus, loan words are very often conventionally taken over by the borrowing culture in the same orthographic form as they have in the source language. This means that we can get 'spelling

[38] An alternative theory of loan word adaptation (Hyman 1970), according to which foreign surface forms are treated in the nativization process as if they were underlying morphophonemic forms in the borrowing language and thus subject to all the morphophonological rules is clearly absurd (see Derwing 1973: 150–1; Kiparsky 1973a: 109–13; Linell 1974a: 130–1).

[39] For some discussion of problems having to do with borrowing from lento vs. allegro styles, heterolectal borrowing, etc., see Dressler (1973b).

[40] Dressler (1977b: 36). Cf. also p. 136, fn. 18.

pronunciations' in the borrowing language which are different from the foreign pronunciations. For Spanish loan words, English speakers may use both approximations to Spanish pronunciations [krέɪdow, armά:də, fəríjnə] (for *credo, armada, farina*) and more 'anglicized' versions ([kríjdow, armeídə, fəraínə] (see Nessly 1971). However, this must not necessarily be interpreted as evidence for the vowel shift rule in English (as Nessly thinks); indeed, other tests for productivity indicate that vowel shift is non-productive (§10.8: other sections). Instead, it shows that speakers know the main rules for pronouncing the letters in English,[41] which is something quite different (and hardly surprising).

10.8.3 *Transfer in foreign-language learning*

As one would expect, a difference between productive and non-

---

[41] Obviously, we must assume the existence of specific rules for how to pronounce orthographic strings (graphemes and graphemic sequences) which are either explicitly taught in reading instruction or implicitly discovered by the learner (when he 'breaks the code'). It is important not to confuse these *graphophonological* rules, which seem to be extrasystemic much like adaptive rules set up in secondary dialect acquisition (§5.2.6), with ordinary intrasystemic rules of phonology (i.e. MRPs, PhtRs, etc.). The relationship between orthography and phonological competence should be seriously considered. At the moment there seem to be some poorly supported hypotheses in this area. Thus, e.g., it seems quite improbable that phonological knowledge remains completely unaffected by the process of the speaker's becoming literate, as is sometimes assumed. (Note that many phonologists take a 'puristic' stand towards orthography; the possible influence of orthography on phonological competence is usually not even considered.)

Also unrealistic is the OGPh view that the rules used in reading are identical to the ('abstract', i.e. roughly morphophonological) rules posited independently in a generative phonology (for such a view, cf. Chomsky & Halle 1968: 49, 184, fn. 19; Schane 1971: 511; Chomsky 1972; and especially C. Chomsky (1970). For comments, see Steinberg 1971, 1973). There is no empirical evidence for such a view. Instead, it seems probable that graphophonological rules are added to the phonology as correspondence statements for relationships between phonemes (and phonotactic sequences) and graphemes (and graphotactic sequences) *without* being integrated into an overall expression component common to both speech and writing (cf. the nature of adaptive rules in secondary dialect acquisition, §5.2.6). (The 'optimal integration' view is propagated by e.g. Allén 1969; Bierwisch 1972. For some more moderate ideas, see Hellberg 1974: ch. 3. For some critical discussion of OGPh treatments of reading, see Steinberg 1971, 1973; Linell 1974a: 132ff).

The addition of graphophonological rules is probably not the only thing that happens to phonological competence when someone learns to read. For example, reading ability may also contribute to the discovery of new morpheme identity relations (§9.2–4) and new possible pronunciations of already known words (often these pronunciations will be more segmentalized than the usually reduced variants occurring in natural speech, cf. §3.4). However, it seems plausible that the core of the native speaker's phonological competence will remain largely unaffected by his becoming literate.

productive rules is discernible in the learning of foreign languages; concrete rules and PhtRs often transfer, i.e. they give rise to a 'foreign accent', whereas MRPs never do. That is, vowel alternations such as umlaut and ablaut in Swedish or English have obviously no influence on the speakers' pronunciations of foreign languages. Consider, as an example, what would happen to an Englishman's Swedish vowel productions, if Chomsky & Halle's (1968) vowel shift rule had the psychological validity of a productive phonological rule. Suppose he learns the word *bre* (alternative infinitive of *breda* 'to spread') a verb which shortens its vowel in the supine: *brett* [brɛt:]. Surface [bre:] is most similar to English [eɪ̯] as in *brain*, and hence the underlying representation would be /æ:/.[42] Since according to the English vowel shift rule vowels retain their underlying quality if they are shortened, the vowel in *brett* should become [bræt:]. There does not seem to be any tendency towards such a pronunciation in Swedish pronunciations by Englishmen. However, Englishmen do diphthongize long vowels in Swedish (diphthongization is a PhtR in (British) English), and they change the Swedish *r*-pronunciation into an English [ɹ] ([bɹeɪ̯]). Similarly, the Finnish /t/ ∼ /s/ assibilation rule does not transfer to Swedish in the pronunciations by Finns; *peti(g)* 'pedantic' does not become *[pe:si] for example. The reasons for this are that PhtRs and concrete rules define the 'basis of articulation' of a language ('pronounceability'), whereas MRPs have nothing to do with this (Karlsson 1974a: 34).

However, there are obviously exceptions to the rule that PhtRs transfer. For one thing, morphologically conditioned PhtRs (§10.7.1.2) do not transfer, except possibly when some close counterpart of the morphological conditions is present in the foreign language (in such cases morphological operations incl. MRPs transfer too), which is rare due to the language-specificity of morphology. But there are other PhtRs which seem to have no transfer effects either. Thus, for instance, the German rendition of Engl. *snob* is [snɔb̥] or [snɔp], not *[šno${}^{b}_{p}$}];

that is, the German PhtR prohibiting /s/ to occur initially before consonants does not transfer, whereas final devoicing and tensing ((9a,b)) do.[43] Furthermore, Spanish and Portuguese do not seem to

---

[42] As for Hyman's (1970) theory of the analysis of foreign words, see p. 196, fn. 38.

[43] These facts have been brought to my attention by Björn Hammarberg, to whom I am indebted for valuable discussion on transfer in general.

have the same difficulties in mastering foreign [#sC-]-combinations, although both languages have similar PhtRs (e.g. (1) above).[44] The explanation seems to reside in the fact that the two languages have quite different ARRs. Thus, in Spanish casual speech / #esC-/ tends to reduce to [#e{$^h_\emptyset$}C-], whereas in Portuguese the same structure reduces to [#{^š_s}C-]! Thus, transfer effects of PRRs/ARRS are usually clear, possibly because these rules largely concern unconscious (§10.9) habits pertaining to small and natural, phonetic (§10.10.2) tendencies which may be hard to overcome. (Compare in this respect what is sometimes referred to as 'basis of articulation' (Drachman 1973).) Some PhtRs, on the other hand, concern more conventionalized and clear sound distinctions (cf. §10.7.2.4) which may be more easily controlled by speakers (cf. §10.9).

On the whole, the area of phonological transfer is very little investigated.[45] The few data there are often indicate that rules, which are productive (ARRs) in the language according to other criteria, sometimes do *not* transfer. This seems to be true, e.g., of American flapping (at least when Americans speak Swedish, cf. Hammarberg 1967) and Swedish supradentalization. It is probably often inaccurate to characterize the transferability of a rule *in general*; possibly, transfer is also dependent on the sound system (the 'basis of articulation') of the target language.

Obviously, transfer effects are also dependent on a multitude of factors which have very little to do with the properties of the phonological rules of the source language, or the target language. For example, transfer effects may apparently be quite different depending on *how* the foreign language is acquired. For example, the amount of formal instruction received may vary a great deal, and quite different didactic methods may be used in different cases. Obviously, there is a great difference between, say, learning to speak a foreign language by having direct contact with speakers of the language in more or less natural speech situations, and, on the other hand, learning to speak by reading written texts. In general, one would expect more 'pure' transfer

---

[44] I am indebted to Lars Fant for providing this example and also for suggesting the explanation.

[45] Compare, however, Rubach (1977c) who demonstrates that formally similar but functionally dissimilar rules in English and Polish, e.g. prevocalic stop aspiration (PRR in English, sharpening rule in Polish) and vowel nasalization (ARR in English, PhtR/PRR(?) in Polish), behave in quite different ways in contact situations.

effects of ordinary phonological rules (PhtRs, PRRs, ARRs) in the former case, whereas the influence of 'graphophonological' rules (see p. 197, fn. 41) would probably be considered in the latter case. As evidence for this, consider the ways in which Swedes appear to learn Finnish length distinctions. In Swedish stressed syllables are either [V:C] or [VC:],[46] but not *[VC] or *[V:C:], whereas Finnish exhibits all four types of stressed syllables. Most Swedish-speaking persons seem to render Finnish /V̇C/ (as in e.g. *tuli* 'fire', *lima* 'glue', *pata* 'pot', etc.) as [VC:] (i.e. [tul:i], [lim:a], [pat:a]),[47] which would be only natural given that vowel length is apparently phonemic in Swedish (cf. §3.3.5). Thus, a Swede would tend to attend to the shortness of the Finnish *vowel* rather than that of the consonant and then apply the Swedish lengthening rule for consonants (§3.3.5: (1–2)) (a PRR?) and thus get [tul:i], (etc.) rather than [tu:li], (etc.). However, if Swedes are taught Finnish primarily by studying Finnish written texts, the opposite changes are most frequent (Karlsson 1977); thus, *tuli, lima, pata* are rendered as [tu:li], [li:ma], [pa:ta]. This should also be expected given the learning conditions involved, since there is a well-established graphophonological rule for Swedish stating that $\langle VC^1 \rangle$ (a vowel letter followed by at most one consonant letter) should be pronounced [V:C] (if the syllable is stressed).

10.8.4 *Overgeneralization in child language*

Studies of child language[48] have shown that certain rules are overgeneralized (restrictions and exceptions tend to be regularized), whereas other rules tend to be eliminated (i.e. there is no evidence for their being productively used). Again, it seems clear that PhtRs belong to the former category and MRPs to the latter.

However, there are naturally circumstances under which the facts are not as neat as I have pretended here. For one thing, we must note again that certain morphological operations, of which MRPs are part, e.g. some strong verb patterns in Germanic languages, may occasionally be productively applied by children, thus causing a certain generalization of the MRPs involved (§7.4.2). Furthermore, it must be emphasized that rule generalization is not the only principle that characterizes child

---

[46] Cf. rules (1, 2) of ch. 3.

[47] That this is the case has been confirmed by several Finnish linguists (pers. comm.).

[48] Some recent studies focusing on rules are Smith 1973; Ingram 1974; and Kiparsky & Menn 1977. Cf. also ch. 11.

language acquisition. Minimization of allomorphy (morphological transparency) (e.g. Kiparsky 1972a, 1974) is another one; that is, the child prefers to keep the phonological shapes of morphemes constant. Phonological rule generalization and allomorphy reduction sometimes conflict; if the latter principle wins, the generality of a PhtR may thereby be decreased rather than increased. For example, Swedish children sometimes fail to apply the schwa deletion rule (a PhtR, cf. §10.3.1:(3)) and form plurals of nouns such as *sadel* 'saddle', *cykel* 'bicycle' like [sà:dəlar], [sýk:əlar] instead of the correct forms [sà:dlar], [sỳk:lar].

10.8.5 *Linguistic games*

Another interesting way of studying productivity is to see what happens in linguistic games (Sherzer 1970, 1976; Campbell 1974; 276–7). Stampe (1972: 45–6) discusses, for example, the difference between the stop assibilation rule involved in the /k/ ∼ /s/ alternation in *electric – electricity* (an MRP) and the palatalization rule involved in the pronunciation [mɪšʲuː] for *miss you* (an ARR). The latter rule applies to Pig Latinized words (*yes*, in Pig Latin /esjeː/, is pronounced [ešʲeː]), but the former one does not (*yoke*, in Pig Latin /oːkjeː/, cannot become *[oːsjeː], *[oːšʲeː]). It seems probable that Stampe's observations can be generalized; MRPs do not apply in games, whereas PhtRs and ARRs do.[49]

10.8.6 *Psycholinguistic experiments*

Experiments are usually subject to more or less artificial conditions, and therefore the relevance and generalizability of results with respect to normal speech behavior can be questioned (cf. for example, Kiparsky & Menn's (1977) discussion). With due recognition of this fact, one can still claim that recent experiments devised to check the productivity of phonological rules support the general theory proposed in this paper. However, there appear to be some differences in the results of *production* tasks (in which persons, for example, are asked to produce new forms, e.g. *-ity* nouns on the basis of nonsense adjectives such as [mêɪz], [sîjp]) and *recall* tasks (in which persons are, for example, asked to recall forms, e.g. 'correct' pairs such as *grice* [grâɪs] – *gricity* [grɪsɪtîj] and 'incorrect'

---

[49] Sherzer (1976) says that morphophonemic rules *do* apply (at least sometimes) but as far as I can tell this is true only of such morphophonological adjustments which follow from PhtRs. I suspect the same would hold for Campbell's (1974) data on games in Kekchi (a Mayan language).

pairs such as [grâɪs] – [grâɪsɪtîj] some time after these test items were taught to them). In the former type of experiments (e.g. Ohala 1974a; Steinberg & Krohn 1975), MRPs tend to be dropped (i.e. answers such as [mélzɪtîj], [sîjpɪtîj] are given), whereas in the latter type (Myerson 1975 as reported by Kiparsky & Menn 1977) wrong morphophonological alternations tend not to be recalled as they were originally taught but rather they are corrected to normal alternations when recalled. However, this always happens within the appropriate morphological contexts, so there is no evidence for the productivity of MRPs as independent entities (cf. §10.8.1). However, the production tests *do* provide evidence *against* the productivity of MRPs.[50]

10.8.7 *Speech errors*
Linguistic games may be said to involve permutations of, and other operations on, phonemes rather than morphophonemes. Interestingly, the same seems to apply to slips of the tongue (cf. §5.2.13.1). Thus, Cearley (1974: 31) reports, with respect to the now familiar /k/~/s/ alternation in English, a slip where *a charge of electricity* was mispronounced as *sarge of electrichity*, i.e. not [kɑːdʒ] as we would expect if the morphophoneme /k/ had any significance here. Of course, phonological rules are only one of the factors involved in speech errors (others are contaminations of forms, substitutions of phonetically similar segments, and purely non-systematic confusions). However, an examination of the possible role of phonological rules in the description and explanation of the large corpus of slips discussed in Fromkin (1973) (and in Bond 1969; Roberts 1975, etc.) confirms the impression that MRPs are irrelevant.[51] By contrast, it is evident that slips always obey PhtRs, e.g. a *Freudian slip* because a *Shreudian flip*, not *Sreudian* which is phonotactically impossible in English.[52]

[50] Results similar to Myerson's have been obtained by R. Cena (Univ. of Alberta) (J. D. McCawley, pers. comm.). The net result of the various psycholinguistic tests of English vowel shift can perhaps be stated as follows. There is no evidence for the Chomsky & Halle (1968) type analysis in terms of abstract underlying vowels and applications of separate rules of quantity change, quality change and diphthongization (cf. §7.3). However, there *is* evidence that speakers know the correct pairings of particular tense and lax vowels ([âɪ] – [ɪ], [îj] – [e] etc.). At least, this is true of literate speakers (which is hardly surprising since the vowels of each pair constitute different pronunciations of the same vowel letter, cf. §10.8.2). There is also evidence that speakers can shift vowels correctly only in the appropriate morphological contexts (which is in accordance with my theory of morphological operations).

[51] Cf. however, p.138, fn. 22.

[52] This example is from Langacker (1972: 247).

10.8.8 *Aphasia*

The phonology of aphasic aberrations seems to vary very much, both inter- and intra-individually. There *are* some regularities in aphasic phonology but they are much less stable than in ordinary slips, and often less related to the rules of the specific language. As I argued in §5.2.13.2 it may be difficult to use aphasic data as evidence for or against hypotheses about normal language-specific phonological rules.[53]

10.8.9 *Misperceptions*

Another interesting but rather ethereal field of inquiry concerns misperceptions ('slips of the ear') (cf. §5.2.13.3). Garnes & Bond (1975) report results which at most points match those of studies of production slips. Thus, MRPs never seem to be involved, e.g. [s] in *electricity* is never perceived as /k/. On the other hand, slips of the ear conform to the phonotactic patterns of the language. The relationships between different levels of pronunciation, i.e. those accounted for by ARRs, often explain the nature of misperceptions (e.g. erroneous word divisions) (see 1975: 221–2).

In general, perceptual reinterpretation (§5.2.3) is subject to PhtRs and other concrete rules. The same applies to the percepts constructed in dichotic listening tests (§5.2.13.3). Note also that listeners also tend to perceive sounds, or sound combinations, in foreign languages in accordance with the PhtRs, and other concrete rules, of their own language. For example, Russians interpret Finnish [y] as /ju/ (Fi. *yksi* 'one' in common Russian rendition: /juksi/), Swedes interpret English [w] as /v/, etc. (cf. §5.2.3).

10.8.10 *Spelling mistakes*

Finally, the nature of spelling mistakes could also provide interesting evidence for a rule typology.[54] Again, it is commonly assumed that incorrect spellings generally deviate from the orthographic norm in the direction of a phonetically more accurate spelling.[55] This would confirm

[53] See Dressler (1973d, 1977b: §43–7). I cannot find that aphasic data provide evidence for abstract segments and an OGPh conception of phonology, as some scholars (Schnitzer 1972; Kehoe & Whitaker 1973) have argued. Cf. §5.2.13.2.
[54] On the relationships between phonology and spelling, cf. p.197, fn.41.
[55] This seems to hold for Swedish (for some data, see Husén 1950) as well as English (cf. Sampson 1970: 621–2). Derwing (1973: 128) points out that English-speaking children have very great difficulties in learning the English orthography (which is 'remarkably close' to underlying forms according to Chomsky & Halle, 1968: 49), while Russian

the importance of, especially, PhtRs and ARRs. The same holds very clearly for Read's (1971) data on English children's spontaneously invented spellings.[56]

However, spelling mistakes are of course rather equivocal, since the standard orthography of many languages may be determined by non-phonological principles too, e.g. morpheme-invariance by generalization of the spelling of one allomorph (in addition, spelling is of course often characterized by the *lack* of principles). Moreover, spelling mistakes are surely dependent on how reading and spelling are taught at school.

10.8.11 *Summary*

All types of external evidence available seem to reinforce the view that MRPs are non-productive and, indeed, not independently living phonological rules at all. Processes involved in games, speech errors, misperceptions and perceptual reinterpretation seem to take place at the level of phonetic plans; they are always in accordance with conditions on the structure of such plans.

10.9 **Degree of consciousness**

One insight underlying traditional phonological theory is that native speakers are much more aware of phonemic distinctions than of allophonic ones. For example, Swedes are generally entirely unaware of the existence of nasal vowels or of differences in aspiration between stop types in their own speech (both are the results of PRRs and/or ARRs). Similarly, Americans do not seem to perceive their nasal vowels as distinct types (instead they are variants of (oral) vowel plus nasal consonant), whereas French speakers do count *their* nasal vowels as segments clearly distinct from oral ones. If we formulate such observations in terms of phonological rules, we might say that the effects of incorrect applications of MRPs and PhtRs as compared to normal correct applications are in general consciously perceived by native speakers. Speakers are often able to state what distinct sounds there are at the level of phonetic plans. By contrast, they are to a large extent

children have minimal difficulties in learning to spell Russian (although Russian orthography is relatively 'phonetic' and quite remote from the underlying forms of at least one OGPh description, i.e. that of Lightner (1965)).

[56] See Linell (1974a: 136–9) for discussion.

unaware of variations in speech describable in terms of differences in the applications of PRRs and ARRs.[57]

On the other hand, there is always *some* kind of awareness of the existence of language-specific allophonic details (PRRs and ARRs). (The very notion of rule presupposes conventionality, which in its turn entails (potential) consciousness, §1.4.2, §1.5.5.) Thus, a low degree of consciousness is manifested in people's ability to register other speakers' deviant phonetic behavior, i.e. speech in which language-specific rules are violated. In most cases, people's awareness of the nature of deviations from habits defined by PRRs and ARRs is more diffuse than their awareness of deviations from phonemic patterns. Often there is simply a general impression of 'foreignness'. However, in some cases certain allophonic speech habits that deviate from the implicit norm espoused by the members of a certain speech community are socially stigmatized, which enhances their degree of consciousness (cf. for example, Labov 1971).

10.10 Relations to universal tendencies

10.10.1 *Universality*

Since MRPs are tied up to morphological operations – and such operations are often highly language-specific – there is little universal in them. (In so far as there are universal tendencies in them, this is due to their historical origin as articulatory rules, cf. §10.11). PhtRs also seem to display various language-specific restrictions but there is often a universal and natural basis for them (e.g. with regard to preferred syllable structures, cf. Hooper 1976). Concrete rules have a universal basis in principles of reduction and perceptual abstraction, but many details are language-specific. That is, though basic patterns of phonetic processes recur in most or all languages (nasal assimilation before obstruents, voicing assimilation within obstruent clusters, tendency towards devoicing of final obstruents, cluster reductions, etc.) (cf. Harms 1973), the various specific languages have particular *variants* of these processes. There are many language-specific restrictions on otherwise universal principles of coarticulation (e.g. Morin 1974). Some scholars,

[57] This, of course, is partly due to the fact that MRPs and PhtRs define physically discrete sound distinctions, while the effects of PRRs and ARRs are much more gradual (§10.7.2.4).

especially Stampe (e.g. Donegan & Stampe 1978), have argued that one could distinguish between 'learned rules' (roughly my MRPs and PhtRs) and inherited processes (ARRs?). Although Stampe recognizes various language-specific constraints on the latter 'processes', this position seems grossly overstated. The boundaries between different types of rules are not so neat (cf. p. 174, fn. 11). Moreover, with our definition of phonology (§2.1), *all* phonological rules (including Stampe's 'processes') contain at least some language-specific, and thus learned, aspects.

10.10.2 *Naturalness*

A 'natural' phonological rule is a rule which in its main features (direction and change effected) reflects the nature of some natural phonetic (articulatory or perhaps perceptual) process. (It would be pointless to require from a 'natural' rule that it be entirely predictable from purely phonetic processes, since such a definition would characterize all rules as 'unnatural', the reason being that all rules of phonology have some language-specific, i.e. arbitrary, ingredients, cf. §1.5.5.) All universal processes are presumably natural, but the converse is not true; there may be several natural alternative strategies in articulation and perception.

Naturalness of a rule can be decomposed into three subordinate conditions (cf. Dressler 1977a):

(a)   the change introduced must not be too great (cf. §10.7.2.4)
(b)   the environment must be a phonetically plausible (favoring) context
(c)   the direction of change must be phonetically plausible.

It seems reasonable to claim that PRRs and ARRs are necessarily 'natural' phonetic regularities since they appear to have some basis in articulatory or perceptual mechanisms (or perhaps in some mixture of the two). Rules that relate different 'strength variants' of the 'same' articulation, say coronal /r/ ([r, ɾ, ɹ, ʐ, ɽ, etc.]) are of the former type, whereas rules that state the perceptual equivalence of coronal [r] and uvular [R] are of the latter type (cf. §5.2.3).

PhtRs often have a natural phonetic basis. However, the 'change' effected (e.g. within morphological operations) may quite often involve 'quantal leaps' (Dressler 1977a) (§10.7.2.4). Historically, this corresponds to 'rule telescoping' : 'a sequence of diachronic rules may be telescoped into one single synchronic rule; i.e. A→B, B→C, and C→D go into just A→D if there is no synchronic motivation for positing B and C as intermediate stages' (Wang 1969: 23, fn. 23). Moreover, the environments of PhtRs are often generalized beyond phonetic plausibility. For example, in Eastern Standard Norwegian (especially as spoken in Oslo), the rule changing /s/ to /ʃ/ before /l/ (initially: *sla* 'to hit' [ʃlo:], and now also medially: *Oslo* [uʃlu]) is being generalized to apply also before /n/ (*snakke* 'to talk' [ᵛʃnak:ə]) (cf. discussion in Ohala 1974b: 254–6), and the rule is thus on its way to becoming something like the German PhtR (where /ʃ/ appears before all consonants).

MRPs express relations between segments in morphologically related word forms which may be phonetically quite heterogeneous: MRPs may make 'radical substitutions' (Bjarkman 1975: 68). Examples are vowels related by various vowel shift rules in English, German or Swedish (ablaut, umlaut), or /k/ and /s/ related by the assibilation rule in English. An even better example is the Spanish counterpart of the latter rule; in Spanish /k/ and /θ/ are alternating in, e.g. *eléctrico – electricidad*. As yet another beautiful example one may cite palatalization in Tswana (a clear MRP), in which alternations like /pʰ+i/ ∼ /tʃwʰ/, /b+i/ ∼ /dʒw/ occur (Herbert 1977).

Obviously, speakers are able to establish grammatical relations between forms parts of which are articulatorily and perceptually quite heterogeneous. There are, therefore, no compelling reasons why abstract rules must be natural. As a matter of fact, such rules are often formally *inversions* of natural rules. For example, in Classical Latin inverted rhotacism (/r/→/s/) occurred (cf. Vennemann 1974c: 146; Dressler 1977a).[58] Not only MRPs, but also PhtRs (at least those with morphological conditioning, cf. §10.7.1.2) may be inverted with respect to the historically original and phonetically natural rule. For example, the English article rule (/a/→/an/) could perhaps be seen as a morphologically conditioned PhtR (Vennemann 1972a, 1974c). A general discussion of how languages, as a result of various interacting historical processes, may develop 'crazy' rules in their morphophonological systems can be found in Bach & Harms (1972).

With regard to naturalness, so-called exchange rules are particularly confusing. They are of the form [αF$_i$]→[−αF$_i$]/X, i.e. a feature (F$_i$)

---

[58] For discussion and examples of rule inversion, see Vennemann (1972a,1974c). Examples of allegedly inverted rules also in, e.g., Karlsson (1974b) (Finnish) and Klausenburger (1978) (French).

changes its specification in a certain context (X) irrespective of the input value (+ or −). Thus, in a variant of Breton, there is, according to Dressler (1972b: 451), an exchange rule which is the 'crazy' result of two different sound changes:

$$(12) \quad \begin{bmatrix} +\text{cons} \\ \alpha\,\text{vce} \end{bmatrix} \rightarrow [-\alpha\,\text{vce}] \,/\, \begin{bmatrix} \alpha P \\ -\alpha L \end{bmatrix} \underline{\quad\quad}$$

(P, L are diacritic features)

This rule voices some obstruents in items with underlying voiceless obstruents, and devoices voiced obstruents in other items: /baːra/ 'bread' vs. [o̯ ˈpaːra] 'your bread', /pɛn:/ 'head' vs. [da ˈbɛn:] 'thy head'. Another example of an exchange rule regulates the change of vowels between the second and third radicals in Biblical Hebrew: (perfect:) *lamad* − (imperfect:) *yilmod* 'learn', (pf:) *qaton* − (ipf:) *yiqtan* 'be small' (Chomsky & Halle 1968: 326). Since exchange rules require feature specification changes, they cannot occur among PhtRs. Instead, they appear as parts of morphological operations, sometimes among MRPs and more typically among morpholexical rules (cf. Anderson & Browne 1973) (cf. §10.7.2.3).

10.11 Diachronic properties

The suggestion that MRPs need not be natural (§10.10.2) is sometimes objected to on the grounds that it *is* in fact *possible* to formulate many MRPs as homologous to natural phonetic processes. However, the explanation for this appears to be historical rather than synchronic; historically, these rules have developed out of natural living rules but are now 'fossilized' as abstract associations. A common history of phonological rules seems to be the following:

| (13) | Optional phonetically-based rule (ARR/ or PRR/) | $\xrightarrow{\text{Becomes}}$ obligatory, i.e. essential for defining invariants (phonetic plans)[59] | PhtR (Segments may be reinterpreted, generalization beyond phonetic naturalness) | $\xrightarrow{\text{Exceptions}}$ assemble. Rule becomes opaque and/or restricted to specific morphological categories. | MRP (no longer phonologically conditioned, the rule may become 'crazy')[60] | $\xrightarrow{\text{Eventually lost}^{61}}$ |

[59] This means that a phonetic feature which was present before (perhaps specified by a PRR) becomes interpreted as typical (essential) for a certain sound type ('phoneme') or for certain forms (phonetic plans), perhaps those belonging to specific morphological categories, i.e. the feature is reinterpreted as functionally more important (in my

Since rules no doubt migrate from one category to another over time, we cannot expect the categories to be completely distinct. There must be rules which are in the process of changing their typological status. Thus, many rules may function partly as PhtRs, partly as ARRs (e.g. Swedish nasal assimilation). Other rules are open to different interpretations. For example, many rules can be described either as PhtRs with exceptions (and perhaps morphological conditioning, §10.7.1.2) or as fairly general MRPs. Swedish velar softening and Finnish consonant gradation may be cases in point.

It may often be difficult or even impossible to determine which characterization is true of a rule at a given stage of development (if there has to be something like a uniquely true characterization). However, studies of productivity may often provide useful clues. We may, e.g. study the number of items which fit the structural description and yet do not undergo the rule (i.e. the exceptions). If this number is rising, the rule is probably an MRP, if it is falling, the rule is probably a PhtR. However, this criterion, like the others, must be used with care. If an MRP is tied to a productive morphological operation (cf. §10.8.1), then it may of course be extended to new cases (even if here too there is the opposite tendency for MRPs to be dropped). In particular, occasional extensions are not excluded; for example, Dressler (1977b: 25) draws attention to the extension of the palatalization in Spa. *dizes* ('you say') (cf. *digo* 'I say', *digas* 'you may say' (subj.)) to apply also in *fazes* 'you do' (cf. *fago* 'I do'). However, we do not expect MRPs to eliminate exceptions across the board, i.e. in all morphological and lexical contexts in which they occur (§10.8.1). PhtRs, on the other hand, do this (though sometimes gradually, §10.8.2).

It would be interesting to study what happens when a language is in the process of dying, i.e. when few speakers of the language are left and these speakers use the language more and more seldom, which presumably also leads to a decay in their competence(s). Dressler

model: specified by a PhtR). This usually also leads to an articulatory reinforcement of the distinction specified (cf. §10.7.2.4).

[60] What is one single MRP at this stage need of course not correspond to one single ancestor phonological rule. On the one hand, one single PhtR or MRP may correspond to several allophonic detail rules of an earlier stage (rule telescoping, §10.10.2). On the other hand, Dressler (1977a,b) argues (with several examples) that one single phonological rule may be split into several MRPs, once the rule(s) has (have) got tied to different specific morphological operations ('rule split').

[61] Possibly, rules can pass a stage of being minor 'via rules' (Vennemann 1972a) relating different items of the lexicon.

(1972b) has in fact studied the continuing disappearance of Breton; it appears, as we might suspect, that MRPs decay or disappear, whereas PhtRs, at least sometimes, tend to become generalized. Also, ARRs tend to eliminate their language-specific restrictions (see Dressler 1977b: 31–2).

Bjarkman (1975: 68) has argued that no rules migrate in the direction opposite to the one indicated in (13). Moreover, Kiparsky & Menn (1977: 73) argue that opaque MRPs are the only phonological rules that are known to be lost historically from grammars.[62] Possibly, this is a too strong hypothesis; rules which vacillate between being morphologically conditioned PhtRs and fairly general MRPs may perhaps get (re)established as PhtRs by some opacity-reducing mechanism (cf. Thomason 1976).

10.12 Summary

Studies of various properties of phonological rules strongly reinforce the view that there are important typological differences among these rules (see also the survey of properties in §10.13 and the classification of some specific rules in §10.14).[63] The traditional distinction between

---

[62] For another opinion, see Dressler (1972b: 449).

[63] Note that this classification must be regarded as coarse and preliminary. There are a number of serious difficulties involved in making such a classification, due to, among other things, lack of reliable data, possibilities of different analyses of the data, cases where subrules of a general rule behave differently, problems of dialect mixtures, etc. Dressler (1977b: 12) argues that the fact that so many rules cannot be uniquely classified in terms of discrete categories makes the whole typology untenable and that there would be a curious contradiction ('merkwürdiger Widerspruch') between having, on the one hand, discrete functional categories and, on the other hand, gradual and fuzzy properties of (many) specific rules. I do not find this to be too serious a problem. There *are* rules which behave very differently and do indeed seem to have quite different functions, and these rules provide enough motivation for assuming distinct types (barring some doubts about the PhtR–PRR distinction). Such a typology may be valid even if most, or even all, the various criteria discussed above fail to provide *absolutely* certain means for indicating the typological status of given rules. Likewise, the typology is not invalidated just because many specific rules in various languages are not functionally unambiguous (they cannot be since languages change). Not only phonological rule types but all linguistic categories seem to be fuzzy. But there is hardly any reason to give up distinctions such as noun vs. verb or noun phrase vs. predicate just because many forms and phrases lie between the categorical extremes (e.g. Ross 1973).

Incidentally, the theory of Dressler (1977a,b) seems to be in the same predicament as mine. Dressler argues that there are no distinct subtypes of phonological rules; all the rules are 'phonological' with miscellaneous combinations of specifications along

morphophonology and phonology proper gets a good deal of support, and, consequently, phonological theories (e.g. OGPh) that refuse to recognize this distinction are shown to be fundamentally inadequate.

On the other hand, facts do not support a very radical position in which one would claim that rules and regularities fall unambiguously into completely distinct categories.[64] In fact, such a view would be incompatible with facts about dialectal variation and historical change (cf. §1.5.6, §4.2.2). Furthermore, one cannot possibly claim that facts support a rigid level of 'autonomous' phonemics. While it seems clear that surface phonemic contrasts are important in phonetic plans, there is no reason to entertain the simplistic theory that human minds are tyrannically consistent in that they structure the sound shapes of words in such a way that all and only phonemic features are included in those plans.

gradual scales (pertaining to naturalness, productivity, etc.). Yet Dressler maintains that these different rules, to varying extents, are subsumed by, or belong to, different components of the grammar, notably lexicon, morphology and phonology proper. Each such component has its own specific character and function (cf. Dressler 1977b: 13ff). Does not this amount to claiming that phonological rules (with their gradual and non-variant properties) are assumed to fulfil quite different (discrete) functions?

[64] Among the works which discuss aspects of the rules tabulated here are the following (see reference numbers in §10.14, Appendix 2):

(1): Chomsky & Halle 1968; Moskowitz 1973; McCawley 1974; Ohala 1974a; Steinberg & Krohn 1975; Myerson 1975; Kiparsky & Menn 1977.

(2): Kiparsky 1973a; Paunonen 1973; Karlsson 1974b; Skousen 1975b; Kauppinen 1977.

(3): Karlsson 1974a,b; Groundstroem 1974.

(4): Vennemann 1972a, 1974b; Fromkin 1973; Skousen 1975b: 123-4.

(6): Kiparsky 1973a; Karlsson 1974b; Skousen 1975b; Groundstroem 1974; Kauppinen 1977; Yli-Vakkuri 1976.

(7): Karlsson 1974b; Campbell 1977.

(8): Karlsson 1974b; Campbell 1977.

(9): Eliasson 1972; Hellberg 1974.

(11): Wurzel 1970; Shibatani 1973; Kohler 1977.

(12): Thelin 1971; Holden 1976.

(13): Klausenburger 1974, 1978; Tranel 1974.

(14): Hellberg 1978.

(15): Elert 1970; Eriksson 1974; Hellberg 1974.

(16): Malécot 1960; Chomsky 1964.

(17): Chomsky 1964; Fischer & Hirsh 1976.

10.13 Appendix 1: survey of properties of phonological rules

PROPERTY	MORPHOPHONOLOGICAL RULES PROPER	PHONOTACTIC RULES	PERCEPTUAL REDUNDANCY RULES	ARTICULATORY REDUCTION RULES
1. Obligatoriness	Obligatory	Obligatory*	Obligatory but not invariant-defining†	Optional
2. Validity as a function of tempo	(Dist. not applicable)	Degree of correspondence between conditions defined by rules and actual manifestations decreases for some types and increases with increasing tempo		Applicability of rules increases with increasing tempo
3. Invocation in performance	Invoked in *some* speech acts		Related to processes in speech acts?	
4. Isomorphy to performance processes	No direct isomorphy?		Some kind of isomorphy???	
5. Context-sensitivity‡	Always sensitive to context outside segment affected	May be context-free		Context-sensitive (or sometimes context-free?)
6. Conditioning	Morphological or morphophonological conditioning	Sometimes grammatical conditioning, sometimes not	Usually phonologically/phonetically conditioned	
7. Generality	Many exceptions and idiosyncrasies	No or few exceptions	No genuine exceptions (among nativized words)	
8. Transparency	Opaque	Transparent		
9. Recoverability of inputs	Input segments often non-recoverable	Input segments usually recoverable	Input segments usually recoverable	(Dist. not applicable)
10. Segment inventories of inputs and outputs	Never introduce new segment types	May introduce new segment types	May introduce new segment types	May introduce new segment types
11. Requirement on feature specification changes	May require feature changes	Must not require feature changes		May require feature changes
12. Discreteness	Discrete		? (Depends on point-of-view)	Often gradual
13. Stage of application in a generative phonology	Before PhtRs (PRRs, ARRs)	Before PRRs, ARRs	Before ARRs	After other rules
14. Applicational dependence	May be applicationally dependent	No applicational dependence		Some types of applicational

17. Transfer in foreign language learning	No transfer	Some rules transfer, others do not		Usually more or less clear transfer effects
18. Overgeneralization in child language	Not generalized, tend to be eliminated	Tend to be overgeneralized		(Dist. not applicable, cf. 7)
19. Linguistic games	Do not interfere in games	Products of games obey PhtRs		Valid in games too
20. Psycholinguistic experiments	Not productive (whole morphol. operations may be)	Usually productive		Productive (?)
21. Speech errors	Are not elicited in slips	Slips obey PhtRs		Valid for slips too
22. Misperceptions	Do not interfere in misperceptions and perceptual reinterpretation	Misperceptions obey PhtRs and PRRs		Are involved in misperceptions
23. Degree of consciousness	Effects of erroneous applications consciously perceived by speakers as clearly distinct from correct forms			Speakers usually unaware of variations (but some variants are socially stigmatized)
24. Universality	Many language-specific traits	Considerable language-specific traits but universal basis		Main patterns may be universal, details language-specific
25. Phonetic naturalness of context	May be quite unnatural	Often generalized beyond phonetic plausibility. Also morphological conditioning	?	Natural
26. Phonetic naturalness in direction of change	No conditions of naturalness: often 'inverted'	May be inverted	?	Natural
27. Change in number of exceptions over times	Number of exceptions increases	Number of exceptions decreases		(Dist. not applicable, cf. 7)
28. Liability of being lost in history	May be lost	May not be lost (unless first developed into MRPs)		Very seldom (never?) lost
29. Language death	Decay or disappear	Some rules tend to be generalized		Tend to eliminate certain language-specific restrictions

* Except for 'sharpening rules' (§10.3.2).
† I.e. actually 'optional' in the sense adopted in §10.5.
‡ Context-sensitivity in the wide sense (§10.7.1.1).

10.14 Appendix 2: classification of some specific rules[62, 64]

	1. Optionality	2. Validity as a function of tempo	6. Conditioning (+ = only phonol.)	7. Generality	8. Transparency	9. Recoverability	10. Introduction of new segment types	12. Gradualness	14. Absence of applicational dependence	15. Domain of application (+ = unbounded)	16. Productivity in loan adaptation	17. Transfer	18. Overgeneralization in child language	21. Slips	23. Consciousness	25–6. Naturalness	27. Change in number of exceptions
1. Engl. vowel shift	–	(–)	–	–	–	–	–	–	–	–	–	–	– ?	–	–	–	–
2. Fi. assibilation (t→s /__i)	–	(–)	–	–	–	–	–	–	–	–	–	–	–	– ?	–	–	–
3. Fi. a→o/__i in certain suffixes	–	(–)	–	(+)	–	–	–	–	–	–	+	–	?	–	–	–	o(– ?)
4. Engl. a→an (indef. art.)	–	– ?	–	+	+	+	–	–	–	–	+	–	–	+	–	–	+
5. Sw. n→∅/__t (Adj., perf. part.)	–	(–)	–	(+)	+	+	–	–	–	–	+	–	–	– ?	–	–	o(– ?)
6. Fi. consonant gradation*	–	(–)	–(+)	–	–	–	–	–	–(+)	–	+/–	+ ?/–	–	– ?	–	+/–	–
7. Fi. root harmony	–	+ ?	–	–	–	–	–	–	+	–	–	–	–	?	–	–	–
8. Fi. suffix harmony	–	+ ?	–	+(–)	+	+	–	–	+	–	+	– ?	o	?	–	–/(+)	–
9. Sw. /e/ epenthesis/syncope	–	–	+	+	+	+/(–)	–	–	+	–	+	+	o	+	+/–	+	o
10. Spa. /e/ epenthesis	–	–	+	+	+	+	–	–	+	–	+	+	o	+	(+)/–	+/–	o
11. Germ. final tensing	+/–	–	+	+	+	–	–	–	+	–	+	+	o	+	+/(–)	+	o
12. Ru. akanje	+/–	+	+	+	+	–	+	+	+	?	+	+ ?	o	+	(–)/+	+	o
13. Fr. /ə/ deletion	+	+	+	+	+	–	–	+ ?	+	+	+	+ ?	?	?	+ ?	+	o
14. Sw. ɛ:→æ:/__[+alv.]	–	–	(–)/+	+	+	+	+	+ ?	+	–	+	+/–	o	+	(+)/–	+	o
15. Sw. supradentalization	+/(–)	+	+	(–)/+	+	+	+	+	+	+	+	+/–	– ?	+	(–)/+	+	o
16. Engl. vowel nasalization	+	+	+	+	+	+	+	+	+	?	+	+	o	+	+	+	o
17. Engl. flap formation	+	+	+	+	+	+(–)	+	+	+	+	+	+/–	o	+	(–)/+	+	o
18. Germ. postvocalic /r/ vocalization	+	+	+	+	+	+	+	+	+	+ ?	+	+	o	+	(–)/+	+	o

* Qualitative subcase tends to be unproductive, quantitative subcase may still be productive.
\+ = property typical of 'concrete' rule.
– = property typical of 'abstract' rule.
? = lack of information.
o = distinction not applicable.

11 *The child's acquisition of phonology*

11.1 Introduction

In this chapter I will discuss some aspects of the child's acquisition of phonology in the light of the theoretical framework outlined in this book. The treatment will be very sketchy, and the proposals have to be regarded as tentative and partly speculative. As elsewhere in this book I will concentrate on levels of representation and types of rules. Thus, the important issues of the child's development of specific phonetic contrasts will be ignored.[1]

11.2 Levels of representation in adult phonology

I have argued earlier for a model of adult phonology in which levels of representing the sound structure of forms and the various types of rules are related approximately as follows:

(1)

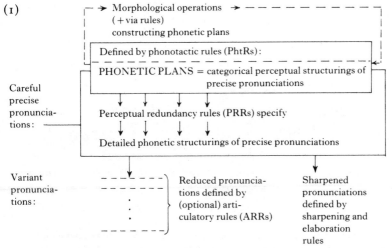

---

[1] Compare, on this issue, especially Jakobson 1941; Smith 1973; Ferguson & Farwell 1975; Ingram 1976b.

Thus, careful and precise pronunciations are the basic variants to which speakers' phonetic plans relate. If we are justified in distinguishing phonotactic rules (PhtRs) from perceptual redundancy rules (PRRs) (cf. §10.3.3), then we can speak of at least two levels of representing these, i.e. categorical forms (= phonetic plans) and maximally specified phonetic representations. Variant pronunciations are derived from the latter by means of articulatory rules and sharpening rules.[2] Morphological operations map phonetic plans onto other phonetic plans (and, similarly, via rules (§7.7) represent associations between such (lexicalized) plans).

11.3 Levels of representation in child phonology

The model sketched in §11.2 refers to the competence of a fully fluent speaker (i.e. normally adults or older children). When it comes to young children who are still in the process of developing their competence, trying to approach the norm represented by adults and older peers, the situation gets more complicated, since we must deal with both the child's imperfect competence and (the child's apprehension of its relation to) the target adult competence.[3] Therefore, we have to consider the relations between the following representations:[4]

(2) (a) AdPhPl adult's phonetic plan (adult-type structuring of careful pronunciations)

    (b) AdPro (representation of) adult's actual pronunciations

    (c) ChPS child's perceptual structuring of adult's spoken forms

    (d) ChPhPl child's phonetic plan

    (e) ChPro (phonetic representation of) child's actual pronunciations

Many treatments of child phonology discuss only the relationship between adult 'correct' forms (2a) and the child's spoken forms (2e), apparently assuming that (2a), (2b), (2c) and (2d) can be assumed to be identical. This is hardly a realistic hypothesis, however.

---

[2]   In the remainder of this chapter sharpening rules (cf. §10.3.2) will be disregarded.
[3]   Something similar of course holds for other cases of speakers having imperfect knowledge of target languages.
[4]   Cf. Ingram (1974, 1976a,b).

11.3.1 *The relationship between adult norms and the forms to which the child is actually exposed*

The relationship between (2a) and (2b) may perhaps be ignored in many cases, since adults often (consciously or unconsciously) try to articulate clearly when talking to children. If so, the forms to which the child is exposed are the most segmentalized forms, i.e. those which display the full phonological structure of words, that which the child must learn in order to gain knowledge of what the norm takes to be the full phonetic structure of the words in question (§3.3.4). However, there are no doubt also many cases of word forms which are almost always spoken in reduced variants. This is true particularly if we compare them to certain styles of speech ('received' pronunciation, language on the stage, etc.) which occur very seldom in ordinary speech situations with people speaking in the vernacular. In such cases, it may take considerable time before the child becomes acquainted with the most precise pronunciations.

11.3.2 *The relationship between the adult's spoken form and the child's perceived form*

In several theories of child phonology it seems to be taken for granted that the child, from the very beginning, perceives adults' spoken forms accurately (and also that these perceived forms function as the child's phonetic plans, i.e. (2b), (2c) and (2d) are assumed to be identical). This, e.g., seems to apply to Stampe's (1969) account.[5] This view is probably not correct. What seems to be true is that children's perceptual structurings are well ahead of their articulatory achievements (§11.3.4). There is evidence, however, that young children do not attend to all the crucial details of adults' pronunciations from the very beginning. Ingram (1974: 53) argues that there is 'noise' in children's perception, and that such parts of the adult words are never represented in children's utterances. Golick (1974) has adduced some data supporting the view that children's perceptual capacity is not fully developed at a very early age. In experiments specifically designed to test children's perceptual discriminative capacity, Eilers & Oller (1976) found that certain phonological distinctions are harder to perceive than others; thus, two-year-old children easily confused $/f/$ and $/\theta/$ and $/\tilde{V}N/$ and $/V/$ while, e.g., $/k^h/ - /k/$ or $/p^h/ - /t^h/$ were quite easy to keep apart. Salus &

[5] E.g. (1974: 446).

Salus (1974), in a paper reviewing the literature on the order of children's acquisition of phonological distinctions, argue that the reason for the later appearance of, e.g., some fricative consonants is that they are not perceptually discriminated by an immature nervous system.[6]

Finally, we may refer to Braine's (1974: 283–4) argument that segments ('phonemes') are auditory gestalts for children before features are systematically perceived and controlled. It may be added to this that syllables and whole word forms are perhaps even more probable as 'auditory gestalts' than segments (§3.7). Anyway, it is commonly assumed that children may perceptually reinterpret adult forms, i.e. their ChPSs are not equal to adult AdPhPls, which may be a source of phonological change.[7]

11.3.3 *The relationship between the child's perceived forms and the child's phonetic plans*

Ingram (1974) argues that (2c) and (2d) cannot be considered identical either. Thus, he discusses the following forms spoken by a girl at 1,6 years (from Holmes 1927):

(3)   (a) *kitty* [tɪti]   (d) *book* [bu.k:] or [buki]

     (b) *bib*   [bɪbi]   (e) *duck* [dʌ.k:]

     (c) *walk* [waki]   (f) *Tuck* [tʌ.k:]

Here, the child is using, on occasion, the diminutive ending such as in the word *kitty*. There are other cases where this is generalized to other forms that typically do not take it, such as *bib* and *walk*. Others, such as *duck* and *Tuck*, do not show this. In the cases of *kitty*, *duck* and *Tuck*, we can say that the child's perceived form [my ChPS] is the same as the child's underlying form [my ChPhPl]. For *bib* and *walk*, however, the child's underlying form is distinct from the perceived form in that it has additional information to qualify it for the application of the DIMINUTIVE rule. (1974: 52)

In my terminology, *bib* and *walk* have child-specific phonetic plans derived, as it seems, by an obligatory application of a diminutive morphological operation.[8]

---

[6]   See also Waterson 1971; Drachman 1975: 239–40, and the literature cited in Salus & Salus 1974.

[7]   E.g. Andersen 1973, Ohala 1974a. For some critical comments on such a theory, cf. Dressler 1976b: 5.

[8]   A similar and quite common type of operation in child language is *reduplication* (cf. Ingram 1974: 54ff).

11.3.4 *The relationship between the child's phonetic intentions and his actually produced forms*

The gap between children's assumed phonetic intentions and their actually spoken forms, i.e. between (2d) and (2e),[9] is a favorite subject of studies of child phonology. Thus, it is a well-known fact that the perceptual structurings of the child appear to be much more developed than its articulatory achievements.[10] This is shown, for example, by the child's way of acquiring a new phonemic contrast in its pronunciations. This contrast will often be applied correctly in all words immediately.[11] For example, a child often uses /t/ for both the /t/ and the /k/ of adult language, but when it once has acquired /k/ as a separate articulatory unit, then this sound will often be used correctly and only in those words which should have /k/ (not in those which should have (retain) /t/). Another proof of the comparatively highly developed perception of children is their well-known tendency to correct adults when these try to use child language, in spite of the fact that the children themselves do not master the 'errors' in their own speech.[12]

11.3.5 *Representations and rules in young children's phonological competence*

We may summarize part of the preceding discussion in the following diagram of levels and rules in early child phonology seen in relation to adult target phonology (1):

(4)

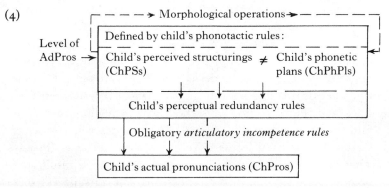

[9] Or if (2a), (2b), (2c) and (2d) are not properly kept distinct, between any of these and (2e).

[10] E.g. Jakobson 1968: 17; Smith 1973: 134; Braine 1974: 284.

[11] Cf. Stampe 1969: 446; Smith 1973: 139–40; Drachman 1975: 239–40. However, there is also evidence in child language data for *gradual* adoption of new distinctions by lexical diffusion (Olmsted 1971; Hsieh 1972; Itkonen 1977).

[12] For discussion of related observations, see Stampe (1972: 134ff).

Though ChPSs and ChPhPls need not be identical (§11.3.3) they may be assumed to lie at the same level of abstraction, i.e. the level of adults' actually spoken forms. The relations between the child's internalized forms and its actual pronunciations are handled by 'articulatory incompetence rules'. Morphological operations are quite simple (morpholexis preferably transparent, no morphophonology).

11.4   The development into adult competence

In terms of the models outlined earlier, we may sketch the development from an ontogenetically early competence (§11.3.5: (4)) to adult competence (§11.2: (1)) as comprising at least the following aspects:

(a)   The gradual development of additional and more complex morphological operations.

(b)   The discovery of more articulated pronunciations, which moves the level of phonetic plans upwards (from more reduced forms to maximally careful forms).

(c)   The refinement of perceptual habits; eventually, the child's sets of phonotactic rules and perceptual redundancy rules will develop into the adult's corresponding sets of rules.

(d)   The development of the child's articulatory capacity, which eventually will move the child's level of maximal articulatory accuracy up to that of the adult, which is also the level of the child's phonetic (articulatory) plans. Thus, articulatory incompetence rules will be eliminated. Instead, the adult's system of optional reduction rules is developed. There are obvious similarities between children's (obligatory) articulatory incompetence rules and adults' (optional) articulatory reduction rules. The former seem to derive from various natural phonetic processes. Gradually, the child learns to suppress these processes (in ways which are at least partly language-specific). As a result, they become optional; the mature speaker is able to suppress these tendencies – as a result of his efforts to speak carefully – or need not care about it, in which case his pronunciation is reduced.[13]

---

[13] This theory is essentially due to Stampe (1969, 1972). For comments on Stampe's theory that the adult's phonological system is 'largely the residue of an innate system of phonological processes' (Stampe 1969: 443), see Linell 1974a: 121–3; Kiparsky & Menn 1977.

According to (b), the child's phonological forms gradually become more abstract relative to its original phonetic forms. Consider as an example the English word *writer* (in American pronunciation) where part of the developing series of forms may perhaps be something like this:

(5) $\ldots \rightarrow /\text{ra\^iDa}/ \rightarrow /\text{ra\^iD}ʒ/ \rightarrow /\text{ra\^iD}ər/ \rightarrow /\text{ra\^itər}/$

Can this development be extended to yield an OGPh type (Chomsky & Halle 1968) underlying form /ri:ter/? This seems extremely implausible. The transition /ra\^itər/→/ri:tər/ would involve a very drastic change leading from a possible phonetic structuring (with /a\^i/ (and /t/)) to a much more abstract entity. There is no evidence that such changes occur (cf. §12.3.2.1). Smith (1973), in an extensive case study based on generative phonology, finds no convincing examples indicating that the child's phonological structuring can be more abstract than adult surface forms (1973: 180–1). And more importantly, there is evidence that adult speakers operate with surface forms (chs. 3–8), and the assumption of abstract morpheme-invariant forms is open to a large number of criticisms (ch. 12).[14]

As far as (a) is concerned, we know that children, when they come to grips with the semantic–syntactic categories to be morphologically expressed, tend to use simple morphological operations, preferably such that they involve the addition, or deletion, of a salient (and, if possible, unambiguous) morph (Slobin 1973: 202ff), and require a minimum of morphophonological adjustment. The effects of morphophonological rules proper (MRPs) tend to be ignored by children. This is also true of languages in which morphophonology is of quite fundamental importance in the morphological system, e.g. Hebrew (Barkaï 1975). Only gradually children learn to use morphological patterns involving MRPs properly. There are some experimental results that seem to show that at least some older children may productively apply patterns involving English vowel shift (cf. §10.8.6). However, nothing indicates that this involves generative-type derivations from morpheme-invariant representations (as, e.g., Kiparsky & Menn (1977) are still inclined to think). In fact, the abstract morpheme-theory involves some rather absurd implications for a theory of phonology acquisition (see §12.3.2).

[14] Less OGPh-minded generativists are also subject to this criticism. Thus, Kiparsky & Menn (1977) clearly believe in the child's acquisition of abstract morphemes. Stampe (1969), too, assumes some abstract structurings, e.g. Latin *nepo :s* as /nepo:ts/ (cf. gen. *nepo :tis*), Greek *himas* as /himants/ (cf. gen. *himantos*).

11.5 On children's perceptual accuracy

I would like to return for a while to topics related to those of §11.3.2. As was noted, there is some evidence that children's early perceptual structurings may be rather diffuse and imperfect. This is only natural, since the child's perceptual and cognitive capacities can be assumed to be immature, the child's linguistic experience is scanty and does not allow him or her to decide what features in the signal should be especially attended to. Moreover, the child's short-term memory span is small, and long-term memory allows only a limited access to past linguistic experiences. However, soon the child's perceptions will become more accurate. The child will recognize the recurring patterns in the different appearances of the same word and abstract from irrelevant, non-linguistic details. It will learn to distinguish words from other words; there is evidence that surface phonemic contrasts may be important (§5.2.12).

But children's perceptual structurings exhibit a detailedness which by far transcends that of a phonemic level. Thus, children who have mastered the essential points of the phonological system of their language, soon become very skilled in phonetic listening. They almost invariably observe all the fine details which determine idiomatic pronunciations. This is most conspicuous in their own articulatory achievements, but these of course presuppose (at least) a similarly detailed perception. During adolescence many persons lose their ability to master the idiomatic pronunciations of foreign dialects and languages. Probably, perception suffers from a less extensive loss of accuracy than articulation, but many persons still seem to experience an inability to hear distinctions of foreign languages which are said to be there. Moreover, Labov[15] has shown that people may be unable to hear distinctions in their *own* speech (of their primary dialect) although these distinctions are being consistently pronounced by themselves. As was mentioned in §2.4.2, Drachman has explained this by the hypothesis that young children may make very fine perceptual differentiations which then determine distinct articulations of near-homophonous words. These articulatory habits would then be retained through life while the ability of perceptual differentiation (or at least identification) is diminished.

---

[15] Cf. Labov (1972), etc.

12 On the fallacy of regarding morphemes as phonological invariants

The argument 'if [ɔ̃y] can be /ɔ̃ɛ/, then the vowel shift rule will cover it' reminds me a bit of the argument type 'if my aunt had wheels she'd be a bicycle'. (Lass 1976: 28)

12.1 Morphemes as phonological invariants

Syntactic structures, and their behavioral manifestations, i.e. strings of grammatical behavior, can be divided up into smaller semantically and formally motivated parts, e.g. phrases and word forms. The smallest parts, which are semantically and formally isolatable, are *morphs*. Morphs are classified by linguists and, though presumably to a somewhat more limited extent, by language users in terms of *morphemes*. The concept of morpheme may be defined as follows (§9.1):

(1)   A morpheme defines a class of words or parts of words, in general: morphs, which are semantically and grammatically equivalent and phonologically similar.

The relationship between the morphs of a morpheme may be referred to as *morpheme identity*. For example, most English speakers know that *divine* and *divinity* (or rather its stem /dɪvɪn-/) are related in terms of morpheme identity. The number of phonologically distinct (allo)morphs within the same morpheme may be quite large, especially in morphologically complex languages. For example, the Russian morpheme /v'ert/ 'to turn' has thirty phonemically distinct (allo)morphs.[1]

Normally, the relations between the specific (allo)morphs of mor-

---

[1] Worth (1967: 2280, fn. 29).

phemes may be specified by more or less general morphophonological and phonological rules. In generative phonology, particularly in its orthodox variant (OGPh), the following fundamental assumption is made:

(2)   In each case of a morpheme having allomorphs which can be related by morphophonological rules (i.e. in all cases except suppletion), there is one underlying invariant phonological form.

Often, the *morpheme* is said to be *identical to this* underlying invariant phonological *form*. I will refer to (2) as the *phonologically invariant morpheme (PhIM) hypothesis*[2]. For example, *divine* and *divinity* are, according to Chomsky & Halle (1968), derived from an underlying form /divīn/[3] which is common to both allomorphs. The allomorphs are derived by means of independently motivated rules, i.e. vowel shift, diphthongization, and trisyllabic laxing (plus low-level phonetic rules) (see Chomsky & Halle 1968: 178–86). The generative model therefore captures two types of generalizations, i.e. morpheme identities within classes of morphs and (morpho)phonological regularities. Though these generalizations may perhaps also be expressed within other types of models, OGPh claims that its kind of model is most likely to be psychologically true. This is the point which I will argue against in some detail in this chapter. In fact, I consider the above-mentioned assumption ((2) = PhIM hypothesis) that morphemes are phonological invariants to be the most fundamental mistake of OGPh (and other theories that are similar to OGPh on this point).

Before I discuss this, a few points should perhaps be clarified.

First, one should be aware that the method of expressing morpheme identities by means of deriving allomorphs by rules from underlying morpheme-invariants has a respectable tradition in linguistics.[4] I will make no attempt to trace this history. One should note, however, that what is my subject matter here is not this formal model as such but rather the specific OGPh interpretation of it, i.e. that morpheme-invariants are *really existing*, memory-stored *phonological forms*. Other linguists belonging to other schools have often interpreted underlying

---

[2]   There are various other designations current in the literature, e.g. the 'uniqueness criterion' (Schane 1972: 226).

[3]   See p. 9, fn. 21.

[4]   E.g. Sanskrit grammarians, Robins 1967: 146–7; Bloomfield 1939, cf. also 1933: 213ff; several post-Bloomfieldians (cf. Newman 1968: 508–9 for references, see also Anderson 1974: ch. 3).

morpheme-invariants in other ways, e.g. as purely 'hypothetical forms' or as historically original (but synchronically non-existent) forms.

The key-words of the OGPh interpretation are 'psychologically real', 'phonological' and 'form'. Psychological reality is something I will not quarrel about. It seems clear that speakers do perceive or discover morpheme-identity relations between forms. However, I would contend that there are many cases where such identities are in principle synchronically recoverable, at least if one reflects over the items of the lexicon, but where speakers still do not discover them (since they play practically no role in the speakers' (or listeners') linguistic practice, e.g. they are not needed in the inflection or derivation of forms, cf. §9.4). OGPh, on the other hand, is concerned with an idealized speaker–listener who knows his language perfectly (cf. Chomsky 1965: 3) and hence probably establishes all morpheme identities that are synchronically detectable.[5]

The second point is crucial. Underlying morpheme-invariants, are according to OGPh, *phonological* forms, i.e. they are made up of phonological–phonetic features organized in terms of sequences of segments, precisely as phonetic representations.[6] Thus, they are entities of the same sort as phonetic representations,[7] i.e. mental structurings of sound signals (cf. for example, Anderson 1974: 50), although, of course, the morpheme-invariant forms are normally not phonetic representations of those strings of speech which they underlie. Since OGPh does not recognize the significance or existence of any other phonological representation than the morpheme-invariant one, this amounts to claiming that the mentally real phonological representations of grammatical speech may be quite abstract, i.e. remote from what can occur phonetically. I will argue that this position is untenable. I will also return to the generative abstractness controversy below.

The third important point, the conception of morpheme-invariants as *forms*, is of course implied by the second one. Thus, morpheme-

---

[5] Some generativists have gone very far in arguing for synchronic morpheme identities. For example, Lightner (1971: 543–6) declared that there is no principled reason not to assume (synchronically valid) morpheme identity in cases like *father – paternal, eight – octagonal, behead – decapitate.*

[6] I will not here discuss the question whether phonetic representations are adequately characterized as segment strings. Cf. §3.7.

[7] Thus, we find generativists arguing as, e.g., Hyman: 'it is claimed that a child need not *hear* the *phonetic* shape of an underlying segment [i.e. of a morpheme-invariant form] to have stored it in his brain' (1970: 76) (my italics).

invariants are forms in the same way as phonetic morphs or words are, they are not simply a linguistic–technical means of stating the morpheme-identity *relations*. I will argue that OGPh here commits a category mistake.

There are some parts of (1) and (2) above which may need additional comments. Thus, the morphs to be considered as allomorphs of the same morpheme must be sufficiently similar, both semantically and phonetically (cf. (1)). There have been some attempts recently to specify these conditions of similarity more exactly.[8] I suspect that no such exact conditions can be defined (cf. §9.4). However, this point is immaterial to the discussion, since it is quite clear that as soon as a morpheme identity has been established (and thereby new cases of alternating morphemes) by the speaker, this – ipso facto – implies that the speaker tacitly sets up an underlying morpheme-invariant to account for it (cf. the PhIM hypothesis).

Another debatable point may be the meaning of suppletion in the PhIM hypothesis. However, it seems clear that generativists would treat only cases with no (or almost no) phonetic similarity between (allo)morphs under suppletion. That is, suppletion would be exemplified by cases like *go – went, good – better*, etc. and by morpholexically conditioned allomorphs such as English plurals /-z/, /-ən/ (*oxen*), /-∅/ (*sheep*) etc.[9]

12.2 The abstractness controversy in generative phonology

If (2) is assumed to hold throughout (except in cases of genuine suppletion), it means that many morpheme-invariant forms will be quite remote from their corresponding derived phonetic forms, since the phonological discrepancy between allomorphs may be very great (even in cases of indubitable morpheme identities). Moreover, OGPh also assumes that non-alternating morphemes may undergo morphophonological rules; as soon as these rules are independently motivated, such morphemes may get a 'free ride'.[10] Thus, rules apply to a maximum number of forms.[11] For example, *moss, spa*, and *boy* are assumed to be

[8] Cf. for example, Schane 1968: xvii–xx; Derwing 1973: 122–6; Derwing & Baker 1976: 63–92.
[9] These aspects would be handled by a 'readjustment component' outside phonology according to Chomsky & Halle (1968: 10–11).
[10] Zwicky (1970a, 1975a: 158: (Q)).
[11] This is presumably backed up by an empirically unmotivated assumption that the lexicon and grammar of a language are maximally integrated (cf. §4.2.2).

underlyingly /mos/, /spæ/ and /bɔe:/, respectively, and the former two undergo at least seven and five rules respectively (Chomsky & Halle 1968: 211, 215). Thus, this also significantly adds to the total abstractness of the lexicon.

Since morpheme-invariants are assumed to be *the* psychologically real *phonological* forms of the language, it is hardly surprising that their phonological abstractness has been felt as a problem by many generativists. Thus, starting with Kiparsky (1968b), a very ardent controversy concerning what kinds of abstractness should be allowed has developed.[12] Though I think that this discussion is based on an erroneous assumption (= PhIM hypothesis), I will briefly comment on some of the conditions on abstractness proposed in this debate.

12.2.1 *Naturalness conditions*

Several authors in the late 1960s (Kiparsky 1968b; Postal 1968) assert that morpheme-invariant representations in OGPh must not be arbitrary or totally abstract forms (as in variants of glossematics, stratificational grammar, etc.); after all, they are representations of the *sound* structure of spoken forms. Accordingly, Postal (1968: 55) proposed the *naturalness condition*, which seems to imply that under-lying phonological representations should be mechanically computable onto phonetic representations by means of universally interpretable phonetic principles, *unless* there are well-motivated language-specific facts, i.e. morpheme identities and morphophonological rules, which make the assumption of more abstract underlying forms necessary. This claim is very weak, since the requirements of naturalness are suspended as soon as there is a well-motivated (and perhaps phonologi-cally unnatural) relation between allomorphs to be accounted for.

It may be suggested that a stronger naturalness condition be accepted, to the effect that *all* rules that partake in mapping underlying phonological representations onto phonetic ones must be natural phonetic rules, i.e. they must reflect the direction and change of some articulatorily (or perceptually) natural process. But this is inadequate for at least two reasons:

(a)   It is a mistake to assume that morphophonological rules – which are functionally very different from e.g. articulatory reduction

---

[12] Kiparsky's important contributions can be found in Kiparsky (1973a). Other papers of principal interest are Crothers 1971; Jensen 1974; Crothers & Shibatani 1975. See these for further references.

rules – must be phonetically natural. For example, ablaut rules cannot be formulated as natural rules. On the other hand we cannot exclude these alternations, unless the PhIM hypothesis is abandoned. (One can hardly deny that a paradigm like *drink – drank – drunk* involves morpheme identity.)

(b)　Naturalness conditions on rules will not automatically exclude all kinds of abstractness (or unnaturalness) of underlying forms.[13] In fact, underlying forms may still be quite remote from phonetic forms, since many rules may be involved in the mapping, or some rules may apply several times. Thus, imagine a language with the two simple and natural rules $V \to \emptyset/C\_\#$ and $C \to \emptyset/\_\#$.
$$[-low]$$

With these rules we could derive [kipa] from, say, underlying /kipamikutefisoku/. (Thus, in such cases, we would also need at least conditions on derivations and/or rule applications.)

12.2.2　*The alternation condition*

A rather different type of condition is Kiparsky's (1968b) *alternation condition*, which was primarily devised to exclude abstract representations of non-alternating morphemes. Thus, the strong version of this condition states that only morphophonologically alternating morphemes are assigned abstract underlying forms, whereas non-alternating morphemes are assigned roughly surface-phonemic forms (Kiparsky 1973a: 18).[14] This condition is insufficient for primarily the following two reasons:

(a)　Unless supplemented with other conditions, it puts no restrictions at all on the phonological representations of alternating morphemes. These, then, may still be as abstract as may be required by (2) above to account for all morpheme identities.

(b)　It introduces a radical difference between alternating morphemes (which may have very abstract phonological forms) and non-alternating morphemes (which are phonologically represented by phonetic forms). Thus, adapting Chomsky & Halle (1968) to this

---

[13] Some types of abstractness of underlying forms may perhaps be eliminated. For a discussion of different kinds of abstractness, see Jensen (1974).

[14] The weak version of the condition simply makes abstract representations of non-alternating morphemes marked.

condition, *meat* would be /mīt/ and *meet* /mēt/, and *bite* /bīt/ would be 'rhyming' on the phonological level with *meat*. Moreover, the alternation which motivates an abstract representation of a morpheme may be quite peripheral in the language (whereas the word form affected may be quite common). For example, *line* would be phonologically /lâɪn/ for a speaker who does not know the word *linear* or who has not assumed a morpheme identity relation between it and *line*. However, when (if) this happens, *line* would change from /lâɪn/ to /līn/. There is no evidence that anything of this corresponds to any psychologically or behaviorally valid state of affairs.

12.2.3 *The revised alternation condition*
Kiparsky (1973b) proposed a revised condition which is rather a condition on the application of certain kinds of rules and only indirectly on underlying forms. Thus, Kiparsky proposed that 'non-automatic, neutralizing' rules, i.e. roughly morphophonological rules proper (MRPs) (see ch. 10, especially 10.7.3.3), may only apply to derived forms (note that all morphophonologically alternating morphemes must occur in at least some derived contexts). While this condition captures important properties of MRPs (as opposed to other phonological rules), it is, in principle, open to the same objections as the original alternation condition (see §12.2.2).

12.2.4 *The surface allomorph condition*
If we want to constrain the abstractness of the underlying forms of alternating morphemes, we need another kind of condition. A candidate for being such a condition is what we may call the *surface allomorph condition*: One of the concrete allomorphs (in phonemic representation) is selected as morpheme-invariant.[15] However, this condition introduces concreteness only for those surface forms which contain the allomorph chosen as invariant, while the underlying form may still be quite abstract relative to the other allomorphs. Thus, for *divine* – *divinity*, essentially two options exist; either *divine* is /dɪvɪn/ (and *divinity* /dɪvɪnɪtɪ/) or *divinity* is /dɪvâɪnɪtɪ/ (and *divine* /dɪvâɪn/). I

---

[15] Essentially this condition is part of Vennemann's 'Strong Naturalness Condition': 'Lexical representations of roots are identical to one of the radical "allomorphs" of the paradigm plus an (often empty) set of suppletion rules' (1974b: 347). The position is of course not new. For example, McCawley (1967a: 80) attributed it to D. W. Whitney.

would still argue that both /dɪvɪn/ and /dɪvâɪnɪtɪ/ are unacceptable as phonological representations of *divine* and *divinity* respectively.

It should be pointed out that there is some similarity between this and the theory proposed in this work, in which word forms, not morphemes, are lexical and phonological primes. Thus, I would propose that words of the type *divinity* may indeed be derived from words of the type *divine* (at least this is true for some speakers). Suppose, for the purpose of this discussion, that also the word *divinity* itself is derived in this manner. Then, one operates on the lexical representation(s) /dɪvâɪn/ (and /ɪtɪ/) to get /dɪvɪnɪtɪ/. However, the phonological form of *divinity* is of course /dɪvɪnɪtɪ/, not /dɪvâɪnɪtɪ/ (as in a natural generative theory). /dɪvâɪn/ and /ɪtɪ/ are the phonological structures of *other* forms, i.e. the word *divine* and the suffix *-ity* (see §7.3).

12.2.5 *'Homing in' from concrete allomorphs*

A weaker condition on alternating morphemes is discussed by Derwing (1973: 190ff) under the name of 'Jakobson's principle' (after Jakobson 1948). In essence this means that the morpheme-invariant need not be a specific actual allomorph but that it must be composed exclusively of properties which occur in the different concrete allomorphs.[16] Further-more, it should be composed in such a way that it allows the derivation of all concrete allomorphs entirely by means of rules which are extractable on the surface, i.e. so-called transparent (Kiparsky 1971, 1973b) rules, the application of which is inferrable from a simple inspection of 'surface forms' (in my terminology: phonotactic rules (PhtRs), cf. §10.3.1). Some argue that these rules must also be completely general and entirely phonologically conditioned, i.e. the alternations should be 'automatic'.[17] Furthermore, we could require that non-alternating morphemes be simply assigned (their) surface representations.

Some variant of this theory has no doubt been espoused by most structuralists (except the most radical neo-Bloomfieldians). Thus, Jakobson (1948) has it, and one variant was countenanced by Sapir (cf. McCawley 1967b). Recently, 'concrete-minded' critics of OGPh have opted for it (Crothers & Shibatani 1975: 510ff).

Despite its popularity, this condition is, it seems to me, open to some objections. It is both too strong and too weak:

[16] This procedure is called 'homing in' by Zwicky (1975a: 157).
[17] In the sense of, e.g., Bloomfield (1957: 29).

(a) There are certain problems in drawing a sharp boundary between transparent phonotactic rules (PhtRs) and morphophonological rules proper (MRPs). It may be difficult to apply the conditions of phonological conditioning and freedom from exceptions (§10.7).

(b) Where an alternation condition is included, it assumes differing degrees of abstractness for alternating and non-alternating morphemes (cf. §12.2.2).

(c) If the theory is interpreted as requiring that all morphophonological alternations be handled by PhtRs, it seems too strong. It would presumably mean that all alternations which require the interaction of opaque rules (MRPs) would be left unexpressed (i.e. all such morpheme identities would be handled by suppletion). Though MRPs are not living phonological rules (§7.3–5, §10.3.5 and passim), there are of course many productive morphological operations that involve MRPs as aspects (consider, e.g., vowel alternations in Semitic languages to be discussed presently, §12.2.6). Thus, a theory including the conditions under consideration has to be supplied with some equivalent of my morphological operations.

(d) Finally, and perhaps most importantly, conditions on rules may not be enough as conditions on underlying forms (§12.2.1). The conditions considered allow for at least some of the abstract forms permitted by the surface allomorph condition and are therefore partly open to the same objections as stated in §12.2.4. Its weaker variants (e.g. Derwing 1973) (which do not require all rules to be completely general and phonologically conditioned) seem to permit representations such as /dɪvâɪnɪtɪ/ (§12.2.4). Stronger variants also allow for some arbitrariness and abstractness of underlying forms. Thus, though reliance on archi-phonemes and the principle of selecting the allomorph occurring in the most unconditioned environment may guarantee unique underlying forms in many cases (e.g. Crothers & Shibatani 1975: 510ff), there remain cases where almost arbitrary decisions must be made. For example, Swedish morphemes involving obstruent-plus-sonorant clusters (and some sonorant-plus-sonorant clusters /lr, nl, nr/, etc.) alternate according to the complex PhtR discussed in §6.4.1 and repeated here for convenience:

(3)   IF: X C_i $\begin{bmatrix} \overline{\phantom{-\text{stress}}} \\ -\text{stress} \\ \downarrow \end{bmatrix} \begin{Bmatrix} r \\ l \\ n \end{Bmatrix}$ Y

 THEN: (a)   e if Y = $\begin{Bmatrix} \# \\ C \end{Bmatrix}$

        (b) $\emptyset$ if Y = V

In standard generative descriptions[18] singular forms such as *fågel* and *nyckel* are normally assigned underlying forms /fogl/ and /nykkel/, respectively, although both are always phonetically bisyllabic [fóg:əl, nỳk:əl]. (The reason for positing different kinds of underlying forms is the desire to derive their distinct tonal accents, but notice that this is ad hoc, there being no independent motivation, in this type of words, for the assumption of the absence vs. presence of underlying /e/.) The corresponding plural forms would be /fogl+ar/ and /nykkel+ar/, respectively, although all such forms obligatorily lack the /e/ on the surface. Any other solution faithful to the PhIM hypothesis would likewise have to assign either /e/s to allomorphs, where they cannot occur, or the absence of /e/s to allomorphs, where they obligatorily occur, or both. However, if we leave the PhIM straitjacket, we can propose a much more straightforward solution, in which we admit that tonal accents are sometimes unpredictable and in which forms are assigned their real structures (e.g. /fó:gel, fò:glar, nỳk:el, nỳk:lar/).

12.2.6 *The surface phonotactics condition*

On the basis of his well-known data on Maori passive formation (§4.3.3.4), Hale (1973) proposed a condition on underlying forms of the following kind: 'There is a tendency in the acquisition of a language for linguistic forms to be analyzed in a way which minimizes the necessity to postulate underlying phonological representations of morphemes which violate the universal surface canonical patterns of the language' (1973: 420). Thus, Hale proposes that underlying forms should be phonotactically similar to surface forms. Of course, this condition would rule out only certain kinds of abstractness (cf. Jensen 1974), so it would only constitute a partial remedy of the abstractness problem. Moreover, if such a condition were accepted, it would mean that many well-motivated morphemes could not be set up. For example, in most Semitic languages root morphemes consist in general only of three-

---

[18] E.g. Öhman 1966; Teleman 1969, Linell 1972.

consonantal combinations, while the vowels of specific forms are due to morphological processes. Thus, the root meaning 'to write' would be /ktb/ in Arabic.[19] Of course, such a structure is not only phonotactically impossible in Arabic; it is universally unpronounceable. Yet, one can hardly avoid considering /ktb/ to be the root morpheme (unless one adopts some new definition of 'morpheme'). Examples like this, however, show the difficulty in maintaining the hypothesis that morphemes are phonological invariants (2).

12.2.7 *Conclusion*

The proposals discussed here are only a small portion of the conditions on abstractness that could be invented within a generative phonology. However, the sample of proposals given illustrates quite well the difficulties involved. In fact, one may conclude that it is impossible to retain both assumption (2) that morphemes are phonological invariants, *and* the hypothesis that these underlying phonological forms must be reasonably concrete. Is it then necessary to assume that phonological forms are concrete? Is there any empirical evidence for this? It has been pointed out that many of the rejections of abstract forms made by 'natural' generativists and others are simply due to the fact that the abstractists criticized have transgressed the limits of tolerance of these scholars (Roberts 1976:279, fn. 2). While this is true to some extent, I would still argue that one can hardly assume (without any reliable confirming evidence and contrary to a considerable amount of negative evidence) that speakers do structure phonetic signals on very abstract levels.[20] Thus, there should reasonably be restrictions on the abstractness of psychologically valid phonological forms. The only non-arbitrary way to constrain abstractness seems to be to demand that phonological structurings must be phonetic representations, i.e. representations of pronunciations or percepts of phonetic signals. Thus, I have argued that phonological forms should be conceived of as

---

[19] Some forms related to the root are:

kataba	'he wrote'	uktub	'write!'
katabtu	'I wrote'	kattaba	'he wrote a lot'
jaktubu	'he writes'	kita:b	'book'
jaktub	'may he write'	kutub	'books'

[20] Moreover, the burden of proof reasonably rests on those who argue for abstract, psychologically real phonological forms. Of course, one could save oneself by interpreting 'psychological reality' and 'phonological' in some sufficiently abstruse manner, but this hardly provides any real explanations. Cf. §1.4.

phonetic plans having certain specific properties (see especially chs. 3, 4). This is also supported by empirical evidence of many kinds (see chs. 3–10, §12.3.1). This, then, implies that the thesis of morphemes as phonological invariants (2) must be abandoned.

12.3 Arguments against morphemes as phonological forms

Most of the arguments to be given below (12.3.2–8) are of a fairly general, sometimes philosophical character. I would argue that these general considerations strongly support my linguistic suggestions. However, it is important to realize that there are quite strong arguments in favor of my thesis which are based upon linguistic, psychological and behavioral facts too. I would therefore like to recapitulate some of this evidence first (§12.3.1).

12.3.1 *Arguments for the primary significance of word forms and phonemic contrasts*

The OGPh theory of morphemes as phonological invariants assumes that morphemes, rather than word forms, are lexical and grammatical primes, and that the significant level of phonological representation is morphophonemic, rather than (surface) phonemic.[21] Therefore, if, contrary to this, there is evidence that word forms are lexical and grammatical primes and that surface phonemic contrasts are of primary importance, this would also be evidence against the OGPh theory.

There is indeed plenty of such evidence, as has been demonstrated at considerable length earlier in this work. Here, only a small fraction will be mentioned:

(a)   To explain invariance and variation in correct language-specific phonetic behavior, we need the notion of 'phonetic plan'. Phonetic plans are plans for observable ('surface') behavior. Word forms, but not morphemes, are such surface forms.

(b)   Word form constructing (morphological) operations operate on word forms (or stems) as inputs and are psychologically and behaviorally unitary processes.

(c)   Many polymorphemic structures have semantic and grammatical properties which cannot be derived from the properties of their

---

[21] More recently, some generativists have admitted that surface phonemic contrasts may be important, without, however, denying the primary significance of the morphophonemic level.

constituent morphemes. Thus, the latter cannot be independent primes.

(d) Word forms and word form constructing operations have clear functions within a theory of communicative competence, something which is not true of morphemes and OGPh type phonological derivations.

(e) Judgments of phonological correctness and of identity and similarity of phonological strings apply to surface forms.

(f) Studies of properties of morphophonological rules show that they are clearly different from phonological rules proper. To define the difference between morphophonology and phonology proper we need a level of word forms in roughly phonemic representations.

(g) Surface phonemic contrasts are indispensable in the explanation of phonological changes (e.g. preservation of contrasts under phonetic changes, the loss of non-distinctive features, transition of forms to new paradigms, allomorphy reduction, transfer of allophones to new positions).

(h) Surface phonemic contrasts are also essential in the explanation of, e.g., secondary dialect acquisition, child language, speech errors, misperceptions, etc.

12.3.2 *Unsupported implications for language ontogenesis*

The theory that a speaker's organization of his knowledge of phonology is based upon morpheme-invariants and rules for deriving phonetic representations has of course implications for the theories of how language is acquired and for what mechanisms operate in linguistic performance. I will argue that some of these implications are absurd or, at least, implausible and empirically unsupported (§12.3.2–3). As regards language ontogenesis, there are at least two different aspects to discuss.[22]

12.3.2.1 *Change of strategy.* When a child starts to acquire language, he/she has to learn to recognize word forms and phrases in the speech of his/her elders. Gradually the child will become more and more attentive and capable of identifying the salient phonetic features of the various

---

[22] I will not here discuss Chomsky & Halle's (1968: 331–2) idealization that language acquisition may be regarded as instantaneous ('a reasonable first approximation', Chomsky 1967b: 441, fn. 41), since few generativists would defend it. Instead, we will concentrate on the more realistic (generative) theory that language acquisition is a constant restructuring process. See McCawley 1968b; Linell 1974a: 119ff.

forms. These will be stored and used as phonetic plans, i.e. the child will use them to develop his/her own productions (ch. 11). Thus, the child structures speech in terms of word forms and phrases and associates these with meanings. The recognition of abstract morphemes is of course excluded as long as the child has not discovered the various morpheme identity relations and the often quite intricate morpho-phonological regularities accounting for allomorphic variation. OGPh theory must therefore claim that, at some point in time, the child will, perhaps gradually, change strategies and start using abstract morphemes in the process of analyzing speech. This would also mean that meaning becomes associated with morphemes rather than with surface forms. But this is impossible in countless cases of polymorphemic words, the meaning of which is not completely derivable from the meanings of constituent morphemes (§4.3.3.2). Furthermore, Steinberg argues that 'the postulation of a continuing near phonetic-meaning association can significantly contribute to an accounting of rapid speech production and understanding, for there would be a great reduction[23] in the amount of psychological work involved in relating meaning to sound' (1973: 246). Steinberg (1973: 247) also notes another remarkable implication of OGPh theory, i.e. that the amount of processing needed for accurate speech production and recognition will constantly *increase* as the child acquires more knowledge, since new morpheme identities will lead to more abstract morpheme-invariants (see §12.3.2.2). Thus, implications are obviously highly improbable, if not absurd. Besides, there is no behavioral evidence that the above-mentioned type of strategy change ever takes place.

It should also be recalled that an OGPh type theory does not only assume that very abstract phonological forms are set up. It also assumes that speakers are able to posit opaque rules, i.e. rules which are not extractable from surface regularities but rather frequently contradicted by surface facts, and, furthermore, that ordered systems of such rules, perhaps with considerable depth of ordering, are 'internalized'. This puts very great demands on the learner; well-known human capacities of discrimination, generalization and regularity-extraction from the physically present environment would not suffice at all (cf. Derwing 1973: 201, 310). As Braine puts it,

[23] I.e. in comparison with what a 'morpheme theory' would have to assume.

The learner must be assumed [. . .] to possess an extremely powerful and subtle hypothesis-testing mechanism – one that is able to hypothesize features in underlying forms for which there is no support in the surface forms; able to construct series of hypothetical rules for converting underlying to surface forms, and test the rules for empirical adequacy; and finally, able to compare different combinations of possible representations and rules for their relative simplicity in the content of the entire set of representations and rules for the language (1974: 297).

Plainly, such learning mechanisms are virtually unknown in learning theory. To Chomsky, however, this is no serious memento.[24] Instead, to save the hypothesis that speakers do internalize generative trans-formational syntax or OGPh, Chomsky has invoked the assumption of rather special innate abilities for internalizing complicated linguistic structures. But this invocation is ad hoc and unnecessary.[25] There is no empirical support that OGPh type phonologies (or generative trans-formational grammars in general) are psychologically valid at all. Rather, most linguistic, psychological and behavioral evidence indicates that speakers operate with word forms and relationships between such forms (§12.3.1). Moreover, such a theory would not necessitate any extraordinary types of learning principles (cf. above).

Thus, to return to the main theme of this section, there is evidence

---

[24] Commenting on Braine (1974), Chomsky (1975a: 232, fn. 3) finds him representing 'the dogmatism that has so impeded psychological theory in the past'.

[25] For a critique of Chomsky's innateness hypothesis, cf. Sinclair-de-Zwart 1969; Putnam 1971; Derwing 1973; summary in Linell 1974a: 123–4. Some relevant points of this critique can be summarized as follows:

(a) The assumption seems ad hoc, motivated by the need to save Chomsky's competence as a theory of psychological realities.

(b) None of the various proposed formal universals used to motivate the hypothesis have been proved to be true.

(c) Some of the assertions made by Chomsky about the primary linguistic data available to the child are highly debatable (e.g. the claim that data are 'degenerate' in quality).

(d) The innateness hypothesis is methodologically inferior. What one does is simply to postulate innate features ad hoc (claims about innateness cannot be tested in practice) thereby admitting that one is incapable of finding a more illuminating kind of explanation.

(e) The assumption that the capacity to learn and use language possesses highly specific (ad hoc) features serves to isolate language from other cognitive and perceptual capacities in man. It precludes the possibility of giving unitary descriptions and explanations of different forms of learning, perception and cognition. Such explanations could be sought, e.g., in a Piagetian developmental scheme (cf. for example, Sinclair-de-Zwart 1969) or in a general theory of the ontogenesis of communicative behavior (cf. for example, Bruner 1975).

that concrete words continue to function as phonological building-blocks also in the mature speaker. This of course is not to deny that there are important differences in the child's and the adult's ways of perceiving, processing and producing language. For example, a skilful speaker is surely capable of integrating many operations into blocks and shortcuts of various kinds (cf. for example, Piaget's learning theory). But there is no evidence that this involves the processing of abstract entities like morpheme-invariants.

12.3.2.2 *The representation of marginal changes as basic.* There is reason to believe that morpheme identity relations are established by different speakers to quite different extents (§9.4). This is true especially of forms which are related by means of derivation rather than inflection. By contrast, variations in other parts of the grammar are much less extensive. For example, speakers of the same dialect often differ little in the articulation of word forms (and, hence, these speakers' phonetic plans are presumably also similar) or in the inflection of words (their underlying morphological operations are presumably similar). From the view-point of speakers' communicative competence, i.e. their linguistic knowledge enabling them to produce, perceive and understand grammatical speech, these last-mentioned phenomena are quite central, whereas morpheme identities which go beyond inflectional processes and the most productive processes of word formation are marginal. This is adequately reflected in a model in which phonetic plans are phonological primes and morphological operations apply to such plans, while more peripheral morpheme identities are accounted for by a network of associations ('via rules', etc., cf. §7.7) assumed to be rather fragmentary for most speakers. By contrast, OGPh employs abstract morphemes as lexical building-blocks and phonological primes, whereas concrete word forms ('phonetic representations') are always derivatives. Whereas the 'word form theory' assumes that paradigmatic knowledge, such as morpheme identities, may be added to the grammar *without* necessarily being fully integrated,[26] i.e. they do not cause restructurings

---

[26] Note that incomplete and varying integration of received information is typical of most learning. L. Anderson has objected to generative learning theory and maintained that 'learning is redundant' and 'inductive: statistical and additive' (1972: 422) to a considerable extent. In the same vein, McCawley argues against the hypothesis that children constantly restructure their grammars in order to arrive at the maximally simple and general system (which can be shown to be an unrealistic notion on many other accounts, cf. §4.2.2). McCawley argues that there is reason to believe that, to a

of the very base of phonology, OGPh must assume that a constant restructuring process (affecting base forms) characterizes language acquisition; since the nature of morpheme-invariants is crucially dependent on the number and nature of morpheme identity relations discovered or invented by the speaker, this means that the addition of a new relation (which may be of quite peripheral importance) may, perhaps drastically, change the basic phonological form of a morpheme underlying many word forms. Consider, e.g., the case of Sw. *bära* (strong verb, 'to carry'). Assuming that a child first learns forms like the imperative (*bär*), the infinitive (*bära*) and the present tense (*bär*), he will probably start out with an underlying form /bɛːr/. However, this underlying invariant will soon become abstract relative to several forms, even if only the oblique forms (*bar, burit, buren*) are taken into consideration. When new abstract morpheme identity relations are recognized, the underlying invariant will become still more abstract and the number of word forms with abstract underlying forms will increase. Thus, predictable regularities within the strong verb system as a whole contribute to this (on this basis Linell (1973b) proposed /bir/ as morpheme-invariant!). More abstractness results if morpheme identity is extended to include *börda* ('burden'). Some speakers might associate *bår* ('barrow, stretcher') and even *bord* ('table'), and via *börda* we might get to *börd* ('birth, lineage'), *boren* (vowel [uː] or [oː]) ('born') (and why not *barn* 'child'?), etc.

Similarly, the acquisition of learned vocabulary (which normally takes place only after several years at school) would, according to OGPh, often cause drastic restructurings of the phonological forms of many everyday words. This situation typically holds for most instances where English vowel shift is involved (cf. discussion in e.g. Moskowitz 1973), and for several of the vowel alternations and other regularities in French learned vocabulary which were posited as phonological rules of modern French by Schane (1968) (see Walker 1975).

To summarize, every time a new morpheme identity relation is added to the grammar, it is possible, and very likely, that the basic units in phonology, the underlying morpheme-invariant forms, are changed in

large extent, children follow the principle of least effort, which would presumably involve additive learning and only *partial* integration instead of constant drastic restructurings. And 'the result of successive applications of a least effort principle typically involve "detours" that have served to minimize effort but which add up to a convoluted path; in fact, the meandering of rivers has been shown to be a consequence of the least effort principle that determines how water flows' (1976: 162).

an OGPh type model. That is, generative phonology does in fact claim that radical changes occur in speakers' competences rather often, i.e. they regularly occur when the speakers learn new words and regularities, even if these words and regularities have little or no significance for speech performance.[27] Furthermore, since morpheme identities are probably forgotten now and then (and then perhaps learnt again) generative theory implies that the very base of a speaker's phonological knowledge of forms is rather unstable. All these consequences of the generative theory are clearly absurd. Since one must obviously demand from a theory which makes claims for psychological validity that it provide a natural account of competence development and interindividual competence variation, we must conclude either that OGPh cannot be interpreted as a theory of psychological realities or that OGPh makes fallacious claims about competence ontogenesis and variation.

12.3.3 *Demand for excessive computing*

Though many generativists are notoriously equivocal concerning the relationship between competence and performance (as these notions are used in the theory of generative transformational grammar)[28] many of them seem to agree that in some way or another the length of derivations corresponds to the amount of psychological work needed in the production or recognition of the forms involved.[29] Hence, if the phonological forms stored in the lexicon (memory) are quite abstract morphemes, the language user must perform a great amount of computing (go through long 'derivations') to convert these internalized forms to their overt phonetic form. Moreover, this happens in every single act of speech production or speech recognition, since, according to OGPh, no more concrete structurings (such as phonemic–phonetic plans) are available that would make short cuts possible. In other words, the language user must always make use of *all* his grammatical (paradigmatic) knowledge about the specific utterance (e.g. about peripheral morpheme identities, §12.3.2.2) since this knowledge is, so to speak, built into the psychologically real lexical structurings and the

---

[27] This is especially remarkable since many generativists are assuming very far-reaching morpheme identities. See, e.g., Vennemann 1968: 69–70; Lightner 1971: 543–6 (see p. 225, fn. 5). For some pertinent remarks on this practice, see Maher (1969).

[28] Compare on this issue especially Derwing (1973: ch. 8); Steinberg (1975).

[29] Cf. Fodor & Garrett 1966: 141; Kiparsky 1968a: 171; Watt 1970 and discussion in §1.4.1.

rules applied in the derivation. The undesirability of this consequence of the morpheme theory is immediately evident. Also simple and frequent forms, which may often have long derivations (cf. §12.2), become difficult to operate with. A moment's reflection reveals further absurdities. Since the abstractness of morpheme-invariants normally increases when more morpheme-identity relations between forms are discovered (§12.3.2), this means that the more one knows about one's language the more difficult will well-known forms be to handle![30] Furthermore, since, according to OGPh, polymorphemic words must always be derived anew, there will be no difference between the case of using a well-known (maybe frequently occurring) derivative and the case of creating a new derivative by means of the rules of derivational morphology and phonology.

12.3.4 *Morphemes as grammatical non-phonological units*

The morpheme was defined in §12.1 as a class of grammatically equivalent morphs. That is, the morpheme 'is a syntactic–semantic unit, not necessarily a phonological unit' (Hooper 1975: 536); what is constant in a morpheme are its grammatical (and semantic) properties, whereas its phonological manifestations vary (except, of course, for non-alternating morphemes). OGPh, however, explains away allomorphic variation by postulating an underlying phonological invariance. Yet, allomorphs may be said to have a semiotic function of their own (§8.2.4), and they clearly play a role in historical changes (§5.2.10.4). Morphemes, on the other hand, need not be manifested phonologically at all (cf. zero morphemes), and several morphemes may share one single phonetic expression (cf. portmanteau morphs).

12.3.5 *Category mistake : relations represented as 'things'*

Abstract morphemes cannot be thought of as representations of sound signals.[31] Nor can they be phonetic plans since it would be absurd to talk about plans of behavior which cannot be executed as such under any conditions (cf. §3.2). Perhaps they can be regarded as historically earlier phonetic representations of the forms involved,[32] but such an

---

[30] As observed by Steinberg (1973 : 247).

[31] When arguing against morphemes in the following sections, I am referring to abstract (=non-phonetic) invariant forms of alternating or non-alternating (cf. §12.2) morphemes.

[32] Some scholars, e.g. Sampson (1970: 613ff); Ladefoged (1971b: 50), have argued that this is the only possible interpretation of abstract morphemes.

interpretation would be completely irrelevant in a synchronic competence model. How, then, *should* they be understood?[33] Let us consider the possibility of interpreting a morpheme-invariant as an *imagination*, i.e. as a model of speakers' way of (tacitly!) imagining or construing a sound shape common to all the morphs of the morpheme. Under this interpretation, the morpheme would be some kind of smallest common denominator of the allomorphs (concrete forms), an invariant which embodies the phonological *similarities* between the morphs. Perhaps the speaker (tacitly!) abstracts these similarities and imagines them as embodied in one single underlying form?

This argument appears to be thoroughly unsound. A *relation* of similarity is not a 'thing' (or even 'a property of a thing'). It is a gross *category mistake* to believe that the fact that two or more things are involved in an equivalence, identity or similarity relation implies that there is some kind of real physical link between them (cf. Harré 1972: 28). If one sees two persons A and B who are similar in their outlook and behavior, one may possibly form an idea X of a person who would incarnate the 'similarities' and lack the differences between A and B. But this idea or imagination has no real referent. True, the similarities between A and B can be explained by the possibility that they have a common parent, and the idea X can be understood as referring to that parent. But surely the parent does not exist simply because the idea X can be formed. That the parent may actually exist has not the slightest significance for the 'synchronically' perceived similarity relation between A and B. Similarly, as was just noted, that underlying phonological forms can be interpreted as actual forms at previous stages of the historical development of the language in question is likewise completely irrelevant for a synchronic competence model.

Thus, it seems impossible to defend the existence of an underlying form as a mental thing by the alleged fact that it can be imagined. Anything could be the object of an imagination. If all objects in the contents of imaginations are regarded as 'existing entities', then it is surely not that kind of 'existence' which is relevant for us here (cf. Quine 1952). Using sufficient fantasy and perversion we can probably imagine the phonology of words in many different ways. Those who defend the existence of underlying forms would probably not be prepared also to acknowledge the 'existence' of all these queer imaginations of the phonology of words. What we might possibly be interested in are

[33] On the possibility of interpreting morphemes as as-if representations, see §12.4.3.

spontaneous or *natural* imaginations of the phonology of words, such as show up in memory recall, for example. Underlying morpheme-invariant forms have no such properties. Rather, an adherent of the 'theory' criticized here would have to assume the existence of referents of 'tacit' imaginations, which seems extraordinarily outlandish (cf. §1.4.2, §1.5.5).

In general, morphemes interpreted as reified sums of properties common to allomorphs are similar to universal ideas, and thus they are subject to all absurdities which characterize these. Bishop Berkeley already in the eighteenth century objected to the alleged existence of a 'universal human being' as an imagination (idea). What properties would this imagined human being possess? Would he, for example, have long or short hair, or would he be bald perhaps? Would his eyes be blue or brown? Would he be tall or short, fat or lean, etc.? None of these properties are universal among human beings. Yet every human being must possess a specific configuration of properties. A universal idea of a human being cannot be devoid of all properties. But any concretization of the idea would necessarily imply the assignment of non-general properties.

Something similar holds for underlying morpheme-invariants. In a generative–phonological description underlying forms may well leave crucial features unspecified, since these properties are derived by phonological rules. How then can they be understood as normal imaginations? What is a form which lacks vowels completely (e.g. Arabic /ktb/, cf. §12.2.6)? Similarly, vowels without backness or vowel height values, consonants with no other features than [+consonantal], words without any kind of prosody[34] are not imaginable. The basic reason behind all this is that morpheme-invariants are not things (forms) at all. They are artifacts of linguistic description which summarize configurations of observed properties of concrete word forms (e.g. their phonological interrelations, membership in morpheme classes and grammatical categories).

Instead of 'explaining' the similarities between allomorphs by assuming the existence of an underlying morpheme-invariant, it is surely much better to invoke Wittgenstein's (1953) well-known notion of 'family resemblance'. This has in fact been done in the case of morphemes by, e.g., St Clair (1973: 25) and Anttila (1976b).

---

[34] On this point, cf. the discussion of §3.3.5.

12.3.6 *Ontological eliminability*

The 'abstract' part of OGPh is devised to account for morpheme identities between forms and the ways in which new word forms (i.e. inflected forms, derived words, compounds) are derived. We have seen that these phenomena can be alternatively accounted for by a theory which assumes a lexicon of concrete phonetic plans and a set of operations which operate on these to give new word forms (see especially chs. 7, 9).[35] Moreover, there is substantial evidence that this theory is more adequate than OGPh.

The concrete theory is built upon the assumption that concrete word forms, or rather phonetic plans (ch. 3), are psychologically real. In fact, such an existential assumption must be made by OGPh too.[36] However, the latter theory assumes *in addition* that morpheme-invariants exist as phonological forms. Since apparently 'direct' evidence for the existence of these underlying forms (e.g. introspective evidence) is lacking (cf. §12.3.5, §12.3.7), an assumption of existence must be based on 'indirect evidence'. In the available literature there are several instances of arguments which explicitly attempt to establish such indirect evidence for the psychological reality of morpheme-invariants. Such evidence may have to do with historical changes, psycholinguistic tests, aphasia, speech errors, etc.[37] However, it always seems possible to show that this evidence is actually either irrelevant or rather supports the theory proposed here (see chs. 5–10, 13). Consequently, the explanatory force of a model of phonology is not increased by the addition of an assumption of reality for morpheme-invariants. At best, OGPh has the same descriptive extension as my theory,[38] and by Occam's razor we can remove morpheme-invariants from our ontology.

12.3.7 *Introspective inaccessibility*

As I have already pointed out, one can raise serious suspicions that abstract morpheme-invariants have no psychological reality on the basis of the fact that they are completely inaccessible to introspection (cf. §1.4.2, §1.5.5). Moreover, considered as phonological forms they often

---

[35] In addition, 'via rules' may be needed, cf. §7.7.

[36] Cf. arguments in favor of allomorphs and phonemes, §5.2–3.

[37] For a list of different kinds of external evidence used by generativists, see Zwicky (1975a).

[38] Actually, its descriptive extension is much smaller if we seriously consider psychological and behavioral facts.

seem strange and counter-intuitive (at least to those who are not fully convinced generativists). Admittedly, many aspects of grammatical competence are not directly available to consciousness and introspection, but some aspects clearly are fully or subsidiarily conscious or could be promoted to some level of consciousness. For example, speakers may become conscious of many details of the pronunciation of word forms and phrases. (The concepts of phonetic and articulatory plans would be needed to explain this, ch. 3.) Also speakers may be conscious of morpheme identities as relations between words. By contrast, abstract morpheme-invariants never show up in the native speaker's conscious mind. Not even professional phonologists who have practised much in refining their linguistic intuitions can mobilize morpheme-invariants spontaneously. We know of course – not least from the psychoanalysis by Freud – that many subconscious entities cannot be reached by means of normal introspection. But also from subconscious entities, we normally require that they reveal themselves through some kinds of indirect effects which cannot be explained without assuming their existence. Various techniques, like electrical stimulation of the brain, drugs, hypnosis, etc., have occasionally brought otherwise inaccessible information into consciousness. Such techniques have not been tried in the case of linguistic constructs, but nothing indicates that morpheme-invariants would ever get any support from this kind of research.

There are some additional objections to our discussion of introspective inaccessibility. These objections are also based on the hypothesis that psychologically real entities need not be introspectively accessible or intuitively plausible. This line of defense is of course taken by Chomsky and other generativists.[39]

Thus, one may argue that morphemes may well turn out to be real when – in some remote future – we finally gain sufficient insight into the neurophysiological correlates of linguistic competence. This is, of course, true in principle, but the argument may still be considered as ad hoc and irrelevant. It is ad hoc to the extent that it is advanced to save the theory in a situation where the theory is confronted with important counter-arguments and unfavorable evidence. It is irrelevant since there is general agreement (also among generativists) that linguistic theory (and much of psychological theory, for that matter) is and must be

[39] Cf. Chomsky 1957: 93–4, 1964: 56–9, 1965: 8–19, 1969: 82; Katz 1966: 179–81; Fodor 1976: 52–3.

carried out on a 'molar' level[40] (whether this is 'mentalistic' or 'phenomenological', as most linguists would say,[41] or 'behavioristic', e.g. Skinner (1957)), since at present next to nothing is known about neurophysiology. On this level, there is no convincing support for the idea of morphemes as phonological invariants (as I have tried to argue here). Moreover, it seems quite improbable that morphemes could have neurophysiological counterparts, since behavioral data concerning speech performance, aphasia, etc., seem to speak against it. (However, as long as neurophysiological mechanisms cannot be more directly observed and manipulated, this argument cannot be conclusive.)

Another argument which may be used to support the assumption of morphemes as introspectively inaccessible units, claims that a language user need not know anything about the inner structure of his language, just as one does not have to know the theory of combustion engines in order to drive a car or a theory of locomotion to be able to walk. It has even been suggested that just as one needs no theory of the biochemical processes involved in food digestion in order to digest one's dinner, one needs no knowledge of linguistic rules in order to speak a language. However, this argument[42] completely. overlooks the fundamental difference between natural processes that happen to people (cf. digestion) and complex voluntary (consciously monitored, rule-governed, purposive, symbolic) behavior (cf. language use). There is also a very great difference between driving a car and producing or comprehending grammatical speech acts (for which many rules are constitutive, not only regulative). Though most aspects of linguistic competence are normally not consciously attended to, people do have intuitions about linguistic structures, and they can promote other aspects to some level of consciousness or intuitive understanding as was noted earlier. Moreover, one would require special reasons to prefer a theory of psychological reality that is introspectively and intuitively unsupported (the morpheme theory), when there is an alternative theory which is clearly compatible with or supported by intuitive understanding (the word form theory).

Some generativists have suggested that common-sense conceptions of phonological structure of a kind that an observant and intelligent

---

[40] Cf. Taylor (1970: 63ff).
[41] For an argumentation that linguistic analysis should be 'phenomenological' rather than 'psychoanalytic', see §1.4.2.
[42] Attributed to Postal by Itkonen (1974: 194).

layman may arrive at are deceptive and artificial[43] and that the true nature of grammar is systematically inaccessible to introspection and consciousness. These suggestions are not corroborated by any convincing evidence. Rather, they seem to be adopted ad hoc to protect the theory from negative evidence (of introspective or other kind) (cf. §1.4.2).[44]

12.3.8 *Practical inapplicability*

In connection with the preceding arguments, one may also draw attention to the fact that generative phonology (and generative grammar in general) has – at least as regards its most abstract parts – proved to be quite useless in applied linguistics, language teaching, etc. No one has, to my knowledge, performed any revealing contrastive analysis in terms of underlying morpheme-invariants and abstract morphophonological rules. Several critics (e.g. Wardhaugh 1967; Kohler 1971) have argued that such studies would be unrealizable or meaningless. This is hardly surprising, if, as I argue, morpheme-invariants are psychologically invalid and morphophonological rules proper are not living independent phonological rules.[45] Of course, generative grammars are written for quite other purposes than possible pedagogical or other applied aims and cannot be criticized for not meeting all the requirements of various branches of applied linguistics. But generative theory is supposed to be a representational model of the actual knowledge of the native speaker, and as such it must also have something to give applied linguistics. The fact that it actually fails to give anything is therefore a severe criticism.

12.3.9 *General lack of plausible and intelligible interpretations*

We have already observed (see especially §12.3.5, §12.3.7) the great difficulties in finding a reasonable conceptual, psychological or behavioral interpretation of what morpheme-invariants really are. I would not claim that it is impossible to make some sense out of morpheme-invariants, but I would argue that such interpretations would

---

[43] This artificial and misleading 'knowledge' would then probably be more 'superficial' than is real grammar (according to OGPh). As for phonology, this may imply that the analyst (erroneously) comes up with, say, an 'autonomous' phonemic analysis instead of a morphophonemic one. There are some indications that some generativists may argue along these lines (cf. Anderson 1973: 11). Cf. p. 13, fn. 34.

[44] For yet another objection to the reasoning of this section, see §12.3.9.

[45] For this latter point, see §7.4–5, ch. 10.

be well compatible with the theory of morpheme identity as a *relation* (§12.4). It should be noted that generativists themselves have done very little as far as the clarification of the nature of morpheme-invariants is concerned. Characterizations as, e.g., 'abstract two-dimensional matrices in which the columns represent the strings of segments and the rows different features' (Chomsky & Halle 1968: 331) do not explain how 'segment', 'feature', etc. should be understood in this context. Usually, generativists simply refer to the role of underlying morpheme-invariants within the generative–phonological model; they are those representations from which one must start in order to get the right phonetic representations as outputs from the phonological rule system.[46] Thus, they are not intuitively understandable in themselves and 'justified solely because they simplify the description in the sense of reducing the number of grammatical rules needed for generating correct sentences' (Itkonen 1974: 187). This is certainly not incompatible with the interpretation of morpheme-invariants as artifacts of linguistic description. In fact, such an interpretation is invited, as long as the theoretician leaves his abstract 'explanatory principles' as entirely formal, non-understood entities.

But are we not now demanding too much from linguistic theory? Is it not true that there are successful and generally accepted theories in other sciences, e.g. modern physics, which involve non-comprehended constructs? If so, one may argue, there is nothing odd or indecent about postulating the existence of mental things that are unobservable and difficult to grasp. But this argument is not very convincing either. For one thing, physical theory has very often been able to demonstrate the reality of unobservable entities, either by being able to observe them directly by means of new types of instruments or by discovering new previously unobserved effects of the entities in question, whereas there is no general ambition to seek positive evidence for generative constructs of underlying competence. Rather these constructs are made systematically inaccessible and largely unempirical, since the Chomskyan notion of 'competence' is, at least sometimes,[47] depicted as having at most a very indirect relation to actual performance, and

---

[46] Cf. Anderson: 'The phonemic [i.e. morphophonemic] representation is intended to present the ideal phonetic form of the element in question, the form it would take if no other principle of the language were to dictate otherwise' (1974: 47).

[47] The relationship between 'competence' and 'performance' has been described in quite ambiguous and inconsistent terms in different works by Chomsky. See especially Derwing (1973: ch. 8); Steinberg (1975).

therefore, unfavorable psychological and behavioral evidence may be discarded as being irrelevant.

Moreover, the fact that there may exist queer little particles according to physical theory can hardly justify the postulation of such mental things as underlying morphemes, when this postulation runs counter to all psychological realism and introspective evidence and leads to a clear violation of the principle of Occam's razor.

12.4 Some abstract interpretations of the notion of 'morpheme-invariant form'

There are some rather reasonable (synchronically relevant) interpretations of the concept of 'morpheme-invariant form' which have not been considered so far. These interpretations, I will argue, are either non-psychological or are at least not incompatible with my ontology, which treats the relation of morpheme identity as basic (cf. §12.1).

12.4.1 *Morphemes as values*

Most linguists who have utilized morphemes and morphophonemic representations as linguistic units have refrained from giving precise explications of their ontological status. However, at least in European structuralist traditions (Saussure, Trubetzkoy, etc.), one often finds the concept of 'value' (German: *Wert*, Fr. *valeur*) in this context. Thus, e.g., Trubetzkoy (1958: 37–41) discusses the definition of the 'phoneme'. Discarding psychological and physical interpretations he argues: 'Da das Phonem zum Sprachgebilde gehört und das Sprachgebilde eine soziale Institution ist, ist das Phonem ein *Wert* und besitzt dieselbe Art von Existenz wie alie Werte' (1958: 41, his italics). If phonemes are values, and not physical or psychological entities, the same would hold a fortiori for morphophonemes.[48] Values are social 'abstractions' along with entities like theories (as such), propositions (principles, norms, rules, etc.), arguments, facts, reasons, etc. These entities lack time and space coordinates and are neither physical nor psychological (they belong to a 'third world', Popper (1972)). Whatever kind of existence is assigned to these entities, they are different from things with time and/or space coordinates. However, one may argue that

---

[48] Trubetzkoy uses explications for the notion of morphophoneme such as 'idée complexe ... de deux ou plusieurs phonèmes' or 'ein im Sprachbewusstsein existierendes Korrelat jeder Alternation' (cf. Ďurović, 1967: 557, 559).

'third world' phenomena, such as norms, may be internalized in a person's mind and they may therefore be (become) psychologically real. What then seems crucial is the form in which they are internalized. I would assume that phonetic plans and other phonetic representations have a status that is different from morphophonemic representations (=morpheme-invariant forms).[49] The former are 'forms', structurings of sound signals, whereas the latter partake in expressing *relations* between such forms.

12.4.2 *Morphemes as functional information*

Let us suppose that a morpheme is defined as a set of items of *functional information* (these items being organized, say, in terms of feature matrices, cf. the quotation from Chomsky & Halle in §12.3.9) such that it allows the speaker to form or deduce the various allomorphs. This seems to be a reasonable explication which may avoid some of the conceptual difficulties discussed above. It is certainly true that the existence of various kinds of information concerning e.g. associations between cognitive or linguistic structures must be somehow mentally stored. Like so many brain processes and information-processing functions, these are or need not be introspectively accessible (Pylyshyn 1973). (Pylyshyn (1972) has argued in this vein in a defense for Chomskyan tacit competence.)

One may certainly concede that positing morpheme-invariants may be interpreted as a way of expressing some sort of functional information which allows the speaker to associate allomorphs (though this information is often of limited communicative importance, §7.7). However, the concept of functional information is deliberately quite vague and is certainly compatible both with my assumption of the morpheme identity *relation* as basic and with the generative PhIM hypothesis. Moreover, I would characterize my lexicalized phonetic plans also as 'functional information'; the lexicon is not assumed to store some kind of copy of auditive impressions (cf. §4.1). So if abstract morphemes are regarded as representing functional information, phonetic plans do so just as much. But the latter are of course much more directly related to what phonological structurings are used for (i.e. their function), i.e. in the encoding and decoding of linguistic structure

---

[49] This is by no means an uncommon opinion. Cf. for example, Wells: 'Whatever a morphophonemic formula does mean, it does not mean any actual morph, and in this way [it] differs essentially from a phonemic formula' (1949: 113).

in speech. Furthermore, if we focus specifically on morpheme identity relations, I maintain that it is misleading or at least unwarranted to disguise the nature of this kind of functional information in terms of abstract phonological forms.

12.4.3 *Morphemes as 'as-if' representations*

Still another, perhaps not unrelated, kind of interpretation of abstract morphemes is that of *as-if representations*. By this I mean that the underlying morpheme-invariants simply express features of the phonological behavior of concrete word forms. Surface forms behave in some respects *as if* they had the phonological properties of their OGPh-type morpheme-invariant representations.[50] This seems to be tantamount to saying that word forms do not actually have the phonological–phonetic properties of their underlying forms and that underlying forms are non-existing entities.

Let us take a few examples of what an as-if interpretation of underlying forms means. One might, for example, regard /j/ and /v/ in Swedish as underlying semi-vowels, because these sounds (phonemes) occur phonotactically *as if* they belonged to the category of 'liquids and semi-vowels' (Linell, Svensson & Öhman 1971: 96). One might perhaps even say that the speaker knows that /j/ and /v/ in certain respects *are similar to* semi-vowels, though they are phonetic fricatives. However, in cases like this, generative jargon prefers to say that they *are* semi-vowels, which is misleading.

In Swedish, English and other Germanic languages there are strong arguments for deriving /ŋ/ from underlying /ng/ in a generative phonology (Sapir 1925: 49; Chomsky & Halle 1968: 85–6; Sigurd 1970; Vennemann 1970; Linell, Svensson & Öhman 1971: 98–9; Bonebrake 1973, etc.). This does not necessarily mean that /ŋ/ *is* bisegmental or *consists of* /n/ + /g/. But the speaker might *'know' about* /ŋ/ that it is different in certain respects from /m/ and /n/ and that it has certain properties (or intrasystematic relationships) which are lacking in the other nasals.

Consider finally a much more extreme example. S. Anderson (1972) advances a number of structural arguments for regarding a 'pluralizing infix -*ar/l*-' in Sundanese as an underlying prefix. A form like [nãriʔis] 'to cool oneself (subj. plural)' would be underlying /ar#niʔis/, and the prefix of /ar/ would be 'moved' and 'inserted' after the initial consonant

---

[50] The as-if interpretation is at least hinted at by Crothers (1971: 8).

of the root by means of a metathesis rule (1972: 263). In this case, it seems totally absurd to claim that an infix in (the phonological) reality is found at another place in the string and that it *is* a prefix. One might possibly go as far as to admit that the infix in question in certain respects (namely relative to Sundanese nasalization) behaves *as if* it were absent from its proper place in the string.

Examples like these are countless. In fact, *all* abstract morpheme-invariants that are distinct from possible perceptual structurings of possible pronunciations must be interpreted in the as-if mode. Thus, underlying forms are generally not what they seem to be; they are liable to be subject to category mistakes. One might of course object that abstract morphemes – as they have been conceived of in generative practice – are not totally abstract. Some features of underlying forms *can* be interpreted literally, i.e. underlying $[\alpha F_i]$ specifications may have articulatory or perceptual $[\alpha F_i]$ counterparts. But the trouble is that such features cannot be directly differentiated from those features which are open only to as-if interpretations. Ideally we would like the as-if features to be formally marked off in contrast to the real phonological properties which are part of the phonological structurings of the word forms in question.[51]

Remarkably enough, some generativists hold that an as-if representation of underlying forms is compatible with an assumption of reality. It has been said that underlying forms represent that pronunciation which the words would have unless the phonological rules existed.[52] If all phonological rules are supposed to be real processes which the form goes through before being realized as sounds, it follows that the underlying forms must be real too. However, there is no evidence that morphophonological rules proper are on a par with phonological rules proper (ch. 10). Rather, they are either integrated as aspects of morphological operations or paradigmatic associations ('via rules') between word forms (cf. §7.7).

It is also rather odd that generative phonologists combine their 'contrary-to-phonetic-fact' solutions with claims of empirical status. Thus, it is often claimed that underlying feature specifications like $[\alpha F_i]$ are 'empirical' in spite of the fact that in phonetics and concrete phonology the corresponding specification is $[-\alpha F_i]$. Such descriptions normally result from a heavy exploitation of structural gaps. For

[51] Compare the role of morphophonological features as discussed in §4.4.
[52] Cf. p. 248, fn. 46.

example, Wurzel (1970: 3–4) knows that German [ə] is non-front and non-back; still he regards it as back, which is possible because the place of a non-round, non-high back vowel is free. Chomsky & Halle feel free to set up /x/ in *right* /rixt/ (1968: 233–4), /+i/ in *bile* /bīl+i/ (1968: 130), /ɔ̃ː/ in *boy* /bɔ̃ː/ (1968: 215), etc. There seem to be no obvious limits to what kind of as-if representations may occur. In fact, Chomsky & Halle have also advocated solutions which are admittedly 'wrong' or 'incorrect', but acceptable (in their opinion) because they are 'not harmful'. Botha (1971: 219–20) has observed the consequences of such notions for the degree of empiricalness of the theory. On the whole, the theory that morphemes are phonological invariants, yields *very misleading statements about phonetic–phonological facts of various languages.*

12.5 Can the generative 'morpheme theory' be justified by reference to elegance, simplicity, coherence, etc.?

Linguists usually do not indulge in trying to make their metaphysics (cf. §12.6) explicit, and generativists follow this tradition. In fact, the notion of morpheme is probably regarded as entirely uncontroversial by many scholars in the field. It is taken for granted that they may well be psychologically real entities. The advantages of the 'morpheme theory' (based upon PhIM) over other theories are often discussed in terms of 'elegance', 'simplicity', 'coherence', 'explicitness', etc. Could one argue for the theory in these simple metatheoretical terms? I will briefly consider three attempts to save the theory in this way. All of these arguments will be found to be unsound.

12.5.1 *Pragmatic success*

Is it possible to argue that morphemes are probably real phonological forms, since the 'morpheme theory works well'? The answer is no. For one thing, one can hardly agree – in view of all the counter-evidence based upon linguistic performance, language acquisition, historical changes, etc. – that an OGPh type theory 'works well', but let us, for the sake of the argument, assume that it does. Even then, however, one would not be entitled to argue that, since constructs like morpheme-invariants, morphophonemes, etc., function well or even appear to be necessary as descriptive units in an adequate grammar, they must have real existing referents. Botha (1971: 125–7) discusses such fallacious arguments under the name of 'how else' arguments. Here it may suffice to point out that the idea that descriptive units which 'work well' must be true and real is founded on a pragmatic theory of truth which hardly any serious philosopher of science would accept.

12.5.2   *Coherence and explicitness*

Chomsky and other generativists have criticized previous 'taxonomic' linguistics for only classifying data and for failing to provide explicit definitions of basic units, axioms and rules of derivation. Therefore, the exact logical consequences of the system could not be determined. It seems clear that OGPh meets such requirements far better (though Botha (1971: ch. 5) has shown that there are still important insufficiencies). It is sometimes suggested that a model of phonology which is to meet the methodological requirements of a theory that aims at descriptive and explanatory adequacy, *must* be constructed as the generative one, i.e. with morpheme-invariants as axioms and phonetic representations as derived theorems. Of course, such arguments are groundless. It is clearly possible to build a theory of phonology (or syntax) in which *some* word forms (or surface structures, respectively) are chosen as axioms, from which *other* possible word forms (or surface structures) are derived by means of rules.[53]

12.5.3   *Simplicity and elegance*

Quite often alternatives to OGPh are discarded by generativists as being 'insignificant', 'not interesting', 'inelegant', or 'uneconomical'.[54] However, scientific theories cannot be turned down simply because they do not appeal to someone's sense of 'elegance' or 'interestingness' (cf. §4.2.1). As far as simplicity is concerned, there is no guarantee that what seems simple in a certain linguistic description is also simple for the language user (cf. §4.2.2). Moreover, the general notion of simplicity has proved to be hard to apply in science in general, and also in linguistics.[55] Very often arguments of simplicity bear an arbitrary character of an unmotivated article of faith. For example, it is sometimes said that it would be 'incomprehensible' if there were no morpheme-invariant

---

[53] Cf. Vennemann (1974b). In my theory, the former task is carried out by morphological operations.

[54] Cf. for example, Kisseberth (1969); Vago (1977: 26).

[55] Cf. Bunge (1963); Harré (1972) and others and, concerning linguistics, Chomsky & Halle (1968: ch. 9); Wang (1968); Chen (1973a,b); Derwing (1973: 135–55, 243–7); Lass (1976), etc.

forms in view of the fact that many morphemes have a considerable number of allomorphs. But this is no more incomprehensible than the fact that there are tables with highly varying shapes, sizes and colors without there necessarily being any 'universal table' or 'table invariant'!

The myth that an OGPh type theory is 'simple' or 'economical' is evidently based upon an assumption that morphemes are stored in the memory and that the memory has to be economical. There are at least three rejoinders to this proposal (see also §4.2):

(a)   There is no empirical support for this type of economy require-
      ments on the memory.
(b)   Even if, with morphemes in the memory, the number of items would
      be minimized, they would also be abstract and difficult to
      retrieve, and the necessary computing in speech production and
      recognition would increase very much (§12.3.8). And it seems that
      the brain favors ease of retrieval more than economy of storage.
(c)   Even if an alternative theory based on phonetic plans of concrete
      word forms would presuppose a storage of more items in the
      memory, it need not suppose that all (inflected and derived) forms
      have to be stored.

12.6 Conclusion

The question of the reality of morphemes as phonological invariants clearly involves conceptual and philosophical problems. It is, at least partly, a metaphysical problem; it concerns the most general assump-tions which underlie our theories and which are consciously or unconsciously adopted by the scientists as unprovable axioms.[56] Obviously, all scientific theories are necessarily based on some metaphysical presuppositions, and the metaphysics adopted generally plays an important role in determining the ways of scientific thinking.[57] Scientists should not leave their metaphysics unconscious and unclear, for if they do, their 'empirical' theories and results will rest on confused assumptions. Metaphysical statements cannot be tested, but they can nevertheless be critically discussed. One may compare the arguments for and against them so that metaphysics which seems most

[56] Cf. for example, Alston (1964: 1); Botha (1968: 50, 1971: 106); Harré (1972: 100, 180); Harré & Secord (1972: 78).
[57] On this issue, see e.g., Agassi (1964); Wartofsky (1967); Masterman (1968) (some interpretations of Kuhn's (1962) concept of paradigm); Harré (1972).

fruitful can be selected. In this vein, I have examined the assumption that morphemes are inaccessible phonological invariants. Both linguistic facts (cf. § 12.3.1) and more philosophical arguments lead us to conclude that the generative assumption is a most unfortunate one.[58] It is true that the non-existence of abstract morphemes cannot be proved, but in view of all the arguments that can be raised against the generative assumption, it seems extremely difficult to maintain it.

[58] In fact, this assumption is only one among many infelicitous metaphysical assumptions underlying the theory of generative transformational grammar. The following ideas may also be mentioned:

(a)   The adoption of a natural-science-based methodology as the only suitable explanatory paradigm for linguistics (cf. Itkonen 1974; Ringen 1975). This adoption is unfortunate also for the explanation of linguistic behavior (§1.4.3, Linell 1978a).

(b)   The mind as a paramechanistic system (cf. Linell 1974a: 144–6, 1979a).

(c)   Linguistic structure and competence as relatively independent of linguistic performance (use of language) (cf. §1.5.2).

(d)   (as a consequence of (c)) Meaning as 'ideas underlying mental images' (cf. Katz 1966: 177–85; Chafe 1970: 75) rather than rules of use.

(e)   Language and linguistic communication as independent of other forms of communicative acts (cf. Bruner 1975; Allwood 1976).

(f)   Language as independent of general cognitive and perceptual capacities (and, instead, as due to a very specific innate endowment for language learning (cf. p. 237, fn. 25)).

(g)   The functioning of the memory as dependent almost exclusively on economy of storage rather than ease of retrieval (cf. §4.2.2).

(h)   The speaker's internalized grammar as a closed and maximally integrated system (cf. p. 75, fn. 9).

(i)   (a subcase of (h)) Spoken language and written language as two manifestations of one common integrated linguistic system (cf. p. 197, fn. 41).

(j)   A language, i.e. its range of correct structures, as an infinite set of *sentences* (cf. McCawley 1976); this assumption involves two pernicious aspects: (i) that the primary data are sentences abstracted from contexts of use rather than, say, utterance types used in certain situation types; and (ii) that the only proper unit of linguistic analysis is the sentence (rather than, say, macrosyntagms, larger discourse units, turns of a language game, etc.).

(k)   Language as independent of culture (Anttila 1976d).

(l)   Language acquisition by the child and grammar construction by the linguist as equivalent sorts of activities (Derwing 1973: 80–2, 1977).

(m)   Speech communities as highly homogeneous (cf. p. 75, fn. 9).

(n)   Language acquisition as a constant restructuring process in which purely additive processes and oblivion play no role (cf. ch. 11).

13 The concreteness and non-autonomy of phonology

13.1 On the insufficiency of structuralist phonology

Some people seem to have interpreted Linell (1974a) as implying a return to pre-generative structuralist phonology. It is true that the theory proposed here in important respects stands closer to structuralist (and more 'traditional') phonology than OGPh. However, in other respects it clearly rests upon ideas and goals formulated in generative phonology, particularly its more recent 'natural' variants.[1] I hope that this emerges clearly from the preceding chapters of this book. However, it may perhaps not be out of place to mention some points where, broadly speaking, structuralist phonology seems to be insufficient. Obviously, these points do not apply equally to all variants of structuralism; it applies most typically to the mainstream of American post-Bloomfieldian structuralism.

13.1.1 Relationship between phonology and phonetics

It seems to me that many structuralists make the distinction between phonology and phonetics much too radical. Similarly, the distinction between distinctive and irrelevant (redundant) features is overstated. From a psychological or behavioral point-of-view, distinctive features do not form a sharply defined structure distinct from all allophonic or phonetic facts. In many cases, it is not clear what aspects are most essential for phonology. Different speakers may make different interpretations, thus structuring sound signals perceptually in partly different ways. Moreover, there is more linguistic (e.g. grammatically

---

[1] In general, classifications such as 'structuralist' and 'generativist' should be avoided as descriptive terms, since they may mean so many things. In fact, almost all linguists are (have to be) structuralists in some senses and generativists in some senses. Cf. Anttila (1972b).

defined) structure to allophonic (phonetic) regularities than is admitted by many linguistic theories (cf. ch. 10). In short, phonology should be seen as language-specific phonetics (§2.1), and 'form' and 'substance' cannot fruitfully be construed as different entities belonging to different worlds,[2] nor can they be studied independently of each other.

Obviously, OGPh shares, in this and other respects,[3] many features with classical structuralism. Though phonetic features were introduced into phonology, they have mostly been treated in very formal terms. The amount of interest invested in truly phonetic regularities or in phonetic explanations has been quite limited.

13.1.2 *The concept of rule*
The second point to be raised against structuralist phonology is its lack of an explicit and illuminating treatment of the role of rules in languages and linguistic competences. Obviously, generative linguistics here counterbalanced the structuralist preoccupation with item-and-arrangement. However, OGPh may have made the pendulum swing over too far in the other direction. The power of rules was overexploited and, in particular, different types of rules were not adequately kept distinct (ch. 10).

13.1.3 *Autonomous phonology*
Structuralist linguistics was 'autonomous' in the sense that it tried to keep phonetic, psychological and social facts and theories out of linguistics. But it also argued for a neat separation of levels within the grammar. Thus, according to some American structuralists, phonological analysis should be carried out independently of any assumption pertaining to structure on 'higher' levels of grammar ('autonomous phonology', Postal (1968)). This attitude seems entirely unrealistic,[4] and in practice it was hardly maintained.[5] A few (cf. Pike 1947, 1952) explicitly argued for the necessity of 'grammatical prerequisites'. OGPh

[2] It is my impression that many structuralists inspired by Saussure and Hjelmslev have used these notions too simplistically. For a more perceptive treatment, see Coseriu (1954).
[3] OGPh, with its inclination not to consider external evidence and its goal of expressing all linguistic generalizations as economically as possible, is in fact an extreme form of American structuralism.
[4] As most classical structuralists (Saussure, Trubetzkoy, Bloomfield, Sapir, Jakobson, etc.) would have argued. Cf. for example, Haas (1967); Ohlander (1976).
[5] Some, e.g. Hockett (1942: 20–1, 1955: 45), pretended to be radical 'autonomous phonologists'.

abandoned autonomous phonology, but again it went too far astray, failing to sort things out properly. To generativists, non-autonomy implied that phonology must be abstract and non-phonetic (§13.2–3).

13.2 The concreteness and non-autonomy of phonology

Phonology is not autonomous. Obviously, if phonemic contrasts are important for perceptual structurings of speech and for phonetic plans (which they most probably are, ch. 5), then these structurings and plans cannot be constructed without reference to the organization of the lexicon and to semantic considerations regarding potential meaning differentiation. Reference to grammatical boundaries is also mandatory. Furthermore, phonological rules of different kinds are very often dependent on grammatical, semantic and/or lexical categories (cf. ch. 10, especially 10.7.1.2). That is, phonology is grammar-impregnated. This is of course only natural; consider, e.g., language acquisition where phonology and grammar are developed simultaneously and as a consequence of the child's demand for and development of a larger lexicon and a more varied communicative competence.

Thus, phonology cannot be fully analyzed without information about morphological (and other) categories, morpheme identities and morphophonological regularities. However, OGPh builds part of this non-phonetic information into the phonological forms themselves, thus making phonology abstract, i.e. phonological representations become morpheme-invariant and morphophonological rules are regarded as phonological rules proper. But this kind of abstractness does not follow from non-autonomy. OGPh confuses the matter by treating such morphological and morphophonological information which is necessary in predicting the phonetic structure of forms (and in creating new forms, i.e. in the construction of phonetic plans) as being *contained* in the phonological forms.[6] This category mistake has been promoted by another related error, i.e. the assumption that morpheme-invariants are

---

[6] Cf. Halle: 'A phonological description must provide a method for inferring (deriving) from every phonological representation the utterance symbolized, without recourse to information not contained in the phonological representation' (1959: 21). It may be pointed out that when OGPh *builds in* morphological, morphophonological and lexical information into the underlying phonological forms (§4.4), this in fact amounts to an attempt to fulfil this condition (i.e. utterances must be inferrable from the phonological representations exclusively), i.e. in a way phonology remains 'autonomous', though of course the content of this OGPh phonology is partly (what other linguists would consider to be) morphological and morphophonological.

phonological forms. We have seen that this assumption is unwarranted and leads to numerous conceptual and empirical problems (ch. 12). Furthermore, there are very good reasons to regard phonological representations as phonetic (of a certain kind, cf. ch. 3). Thus, we can claim that phonology should be considered as non-autonomous *and* concrete.[7]

13.3 On some classical arguments against structuralist phonology

At the beginning of the 1960s some leading generativists launched a number of criticisms against structuralist phonology, particularly against a rigid 'autonomous phonemic' level.[8] To judge from the phonological debate since then, or rather from the *lack* of debate on these specific issues, these arguments have commonly been considered as devastating to structuralist phonology and the classical phoneme. It would now seem appropriate to reconsider some of these arguments in the light of the preceding discussion. (Note, however, that I am not advocating the significance of an 'autonomous' or 'taxonomic' phonemic level (cf. above, especially chs. 3, 5). However, even a less rigid model (like mine) would be called into question if the generative arguments to be discussed were really conclusive).

13.3.1 *The superfluousness of a phonemic level in a maximally general phonology*

OGPh may be regarded as an extreme variant of structuralism in which the phonologist, released from the requirements of invariance, bi-uniqueness and linearity (Chomsky 1964), tries to account for contrast vs. non-contrast, distributional constraints (complementary distribution, structural gaps, etc.), free variation, morpheme identities and morphophonological alternations while aiming at maximal economy, generality and elegance. Postal (1968) argued, in essence, that a phonology starting from a morphophonemic[9] level from which the various phonetic representations are derived by rules (cf. OGPh) will meet these requirements most adequately. It can, according to him,

---

[7] I.e. concrete relative to what OGPh proposes (see §3.3.3).

[8] See especially Halle 1959, 1961; Chomsky 1964; Bach 1964; Chomsky & Halle 1965; Postal 1968. For some early counter-attacks, see esp. Householder (1965, 1966).

[9] The term used by Postal and other generativists is 'systematic phonemic'.

account for everything that can be accounted for by a phonology which *in addition* has an 'autonomous phonemic' level. Moreover, his model makes the description more economic and powerful; it can also account for other things which cannot be handled by 'autonomous phonology'. The addition of a phonemic level would only repeat regularities which can be described without it, and it would make otherwise possible generalizations impossible to express (cf. §13.3.2).[10]

Postal's argumentation is hardly convincing. First of all, we are not primarily interested in making all possible structural ('significant') generalizations about phonology, which is, after all, Postal's ultimate goal. Instead, we are interested in those generalizations that a speaker–listener may reasonably make. This will make a considerable difference, as we have seen earlier. Secondly, Postal's argument crucially presupposes the presence of a morphophonemic (i.e. morpheme-invariant) level in phonology; otherwise the autonomous phonemic level would not 'duplicate' regularities. But this assumption is far from well-motivated. On the contrary, there are all kinds of reasons to reject it (ch. 12).[11] Moreover, it is not quite true that OGPh can account for all linguistic, psychological and behavioral facts that have to do with the presence or absence of surface phonemic contrasts (ch. 5). It seems that OGPh would have to be patched up with derivational constraints or some equivalent device (§5.3).

13:3.2 *The impossibility of a phonemic level in a significant phonology*

Halle (1959, 1961) presented an argument against the phoneme level which is something of a corner stone of generative argumentation against 'autonomous phonology'.[12] Halle argued for the impossibility of maintaining a phoneme level (meeting the conditions of invariance, bi-uniqueness and linearity defined by Chomsky (1964)) which would separate the set of morphophonological rules (mapping morpho-phonemes onto phonemes) from the set of allophonic rules (mapping

[10] Cf. similar argument in Chomsky (1967a: 114).

[11] Similarly, Postal's (1968: 208–16) 'argument from phonotactics' ('phonotactic conditions on a phonemic level would for the most part only duplicate conditions on the morphophonemic level') must be refuted. (In fact, Clayton (1976) has reversed Postal's type of argument saying that phonotactic conditions on the morphophonemic level are unnecessary, since they would mostly only duplicate phonotactic conditions on a phonemic level (which are psychologically valid, cf. ch. 6)).

[12] It has been repeated several times, e.g. by Chomsky 1964: 88ff; Postal 1968: 39ff; Anderson 1974: 34ff.

phonemes onto (allo)phones). The impossibility of such a level could be demonstrated in two ways.

In one case, utilized by Halle himself, it is shown that a unitary regularity must be split up into two rules: a morphophonological one and an allophonic one, if a sharp distinction must be retained between the two rule types. Halle (1959) used the example of Russian obstruent assimilation; autonomous phonology must describe this as a morpho-phonological process, in which all paired voiceless obstruents are mapped onto the corresponding voiced phonemes, *and* an allophonic process, in which the unpaired voiceless obstruent phonemes /c, č, x/ are mapped onto voiced allophones [dz, ǰ, ɣ], in spite of the obvious unity of the assimilation process. Such examples can easily be multiplied; Chomsky (1964: 90–1) discusses English vowels, Bach (1964: 128) obstruent assimilation in a German dialect, Anderson (1974: 37–8) a common pattern of nasal assimilation before obstruents, and Kiparsky (1965: 3–4) umlaut (as a historical development) in Old High German.

The other type of examples shows that rules that are allophonic according to 'taxonomic phonology' must sometimes precede a morphophonological rule, which shows that the phoneme level cannot be regarded as a boundary line between two non-overlapping rule systems. An example can be drawn from a common variant of Swedish[13] in which the phoneme /r/ has at least three clearly different allophones; (i) trilled (or sometimes flapped) [r] is possible in all positions (where /r/ occurs) in very careful pronunciation and is common also in normal speaking style in syllable-onsets, especially after obstruents (at least before stressed vowels) and when /r/ is long; (ii) fricative [ʐ] which is common prevocalically; and (iii) [ɚ], a semi-vocalic *r*-colored sound which occurs postvocalically in casual speech. It turns out that [ɚ] is the only variant of /r/ which triggers supradentalization, i.e. the process which turns coronals into alveolars (supradentals), cf. e.g. [faʂː] /fars/ *fars* 'farce' as opposed to [barːs] /barr + s/ *barrs*, gen. of *barr* 'fir needle', etc. If we stick to the strict variant of 'autonomous phonemics' (as characterized by Chomsky 1964) supradentalization must be regarded as a morphophonological rule (though very few structuralists have maintained the linearity condition in this case, cf. Elert 1970: 72ff); cf. many examples of contrasts between dental and supradental: *fat* [-t] 'plate' – *fart* [-ţ] 'speed', *bod* [-d] 'shop' – *bord* [-ḍ] 'table', *ton* [-n] 'tone' – *torn* [-ṇ] 'tower', etc. But the /r/ variant rule (/r/→[ɚ]) is an allophonic

---

[13] I am indebted to Håkan Eriksson for bringing my attention to these facts.

rule, since [r] and [ɹ̩] never contrast.[14] In spite of this it must precede supradentalization. Consider the following derivations:

Examples:	*ba*ʀ*a*	*ba*ʀʀ*a*	*va*ʀ*d*ɑ	*a*ʀᴛ	*ba*ʀʀᴛ*räd*
	'only'	'shed its needles'	'become'	'species'	'conifer'
Morphophon. repr.:	/r/	/rr/	/rd/	/rt/	/rr+t/
/r/→[ɹ,ʐ]:	ʐ		ɹ̩d	ɹ̩t	
Supradentalization:			ɖ		
				t	
Phonetic repr.:	[bɑːʐa]	[bàr:a]	[vàːɖa]	[ɑːʈ]	(bàr:trɛːd)
Phonemic repr.:	/bàːra/	/bàr(ː)a/	/vàːɖa/	/aːʈ/	/bàr(ː)trɛːd/

Obviously, there is no unique level where the phonemic forms can be directly read off.

Halle's argument is, however, not as devastating as generativists like to think. First, we may of course make partly the same objections as with Postal (§13.3.1); if phonemic contrasts are of primary psychological significance, this should be brought out in some formal way even if the result would look more uneconomical. Halle's argument also presupposes the underlying morpheme-invariant level; it would not go through if, e.g. morphophonological rules are instead thought to map phonemes onto other phonemes (cf. chs. 7, 10).

But there are more weaknesses in Halle's position. Thus, it crucially depends on the assumption of the linear ordering of rules. If, as some phonologists have argued (especially Koutsoudas, Sanders & Noll 1974), only rule applications, but not rules as such, are ordered, Halle's arguments become void (Hutchinson 1972: 36ff).[15] Furthermore, we may very well allow one and the same rule to have different functions in different contexts (cf. Russian obstruent assimilation). To return to my Swedish example, pronunciations with supradentals are obligatory morph-internally (e.g. *bord* [buːɖ, *buːrd] 'table', [*art* [ɑːʈ, *ɑːrt] 'species') but not in other cases (e.g. across word boundaries: *bor du här?* 'do you live here?' [buːr dʉː...], [buːɖʉː...]). In the former case, the supradentalization rule acts as an obligatory phonotactic rule, in the latter case as an articulatory rule (§10.6.1).[16]

---

[14] The distinction between e.g. *barr* [bar:] and *bar* [bɑːɹ̩] 'bar' is normally attributed to length.

[15] Hutchinson (1972: 35–6) also argues (on the basis of Schane 1971) that it is possible to order all rule applications with morphophonemic effects before all rule applications with allophonic effects, so that in between we would have a phonemic representation. (Cf. also §10.7.3.2). For objections, see e.g. Mansell (1973a).

[16] Most speakers would agree, however, that an overprecise [r]+dental pronunciation is

To return to the Russian example (and similar examples), we also notice that the phonemic contrast between voiced and voiceless obstruents is not distinctive in the position under consideration, i.e. before other (voiced) obstruents (cf. Johns 1969: 395; Derwing 1973: 186). The rule involved is a PftR of the following type:

$$[F_i] \rightarrow [\alpha F_i] \ / \ A \begin{bmatrix} — \\ \beta F_j \end{bmatrix} B \qquad \text{(i.e. irrespective of input value, } F_i \text{ is specified as } \alpha \text{ in the context involved)}$$

This means that the distinction $\begin{bmatrix} \alpha F_i \\ \beta F_j \end{bmatrix} \leftrightarrow \begin{bmatrix} -\alpha F_i \\ \beta F_j \end{bmatrix}$ is absent in the context

of A__B; according to archi-phoneme theory there is only one archi-phoneme which is unspecified for [F_i]. Thus, as observed by Karlsson (1974a: 20–1), Halle's argument does not apply to archi-phoneme theories, e.g. Trubetzkoy (1958). Halle's argument is built on the principle of 'once a phoneme, always a phoneme' (absolute invariance condition), for which there is no clear empirical support. The really convincing case would be one in which the distinction $\begin{bmatrix} \alpha F_i \\ \beta F_j \end{bmatrix} \leftrightarrow \begin{bmatrix} -\alpha F_i \\ \beta F_j \end{bmatrix}$

exists (is phonemic) in the context of A__B in spite of a rule that assigns the value α to F_i. This seems possible only in a situation in which there are two kinds of morphemes: (i) morphemes which are $\begin{bmatrix} -\alpha F_i \\ \beta F_j \end{bmatrix}$ in a

context C__D other than A__B and are subject to the rule in question in the latter position; and (ii) morphemes which do not participate in the above-mentioned alternation and are $\begin{bmatrix} -\alpha F_i \\ \beta F_j \end{bmatrix}$ in the context of A__B (for

example, as a consequence of another rule). I doubt that such cases exist.[17] Cases involving so-called exchange rules come close, but it is generally denied that such rules occur as purely phonological rules (cf. §10.10.2).

13.3.3 *The non-transitivity of free variation*

Postal (1968: 216–28) presents another argument against autonomous phonemics based on the 'non-transitivity of contrast', which is,

always available. This, then, means that supradentalization is not morphophonemic in the strict sense (§10.5) and that Halle's argument is irrelevant for this case. The same kind of situation actually holds for many cases where 'morphophonological' rules are said to follow 'allophonic' rules. (Cf. some cases mentioned by Anderson 1975).

[17] Pettersson (1975: 142–3) discusses the case of Czech /g/ vs. /k/, which, however, as he himself recognizes, fails to constitute a genuine counter-example to my proposal.

according to him, 'the strongest argument showing the incorrectness of the autonomous assumption that there is a significant, independent level (of autonomous phonemes)' (1968: 227–8). Postal claims that the autonomous phoneme level, where phonemic contrasts and hence also – by comparison with the corresponding phonetic representations – free variation can be read off, implies that phonemic contrast and free variation must be transitive, symmetrical and reflexive, i.e. equivalence relations in the technical sense. However, Postal's claim is incorrect as for phonemic contrast. Contrast between phonetic segments cannot be a transitive relation, and one can therefore not claim that transitivity is some kind of logical consequence of the autonomous phoneme level (Hurford 1971: 27–9). If contrast were a transitive relation, then, e.g., if [ɛ:] and [o:] are in contrast, and [o:] and [æ:] are in contrast, then [ɛ:] and [æ:] must also be in contrast, which need not be true at all (cf. Swedish). However, as far as free variation is concerned, Postal's argument is more to the point. Thus, his argument should actually be concerned with the 'non-transitivity of free variation'.

Two segments are in free variation (in a certain position) if they do not contrast phonemically. Then they must also have one common invariant representation on the phonemic level. Now if X_1 and X_2 are in free variation (have the same phonemic representation), and if X_2 and X_3 are likewise in free variation (in the same position), then X_1 and X_3 must also be in free variation. However, this requirement on transitivity is not a reasonable condition on phonological representations. Consider examples of 'phonemic overlapping' (Bloch 1941); in English, for example, [ə] is in free variation with various full vowels while these latter vowels contrast mutually, i.e. they are *not* in free variation. Thus, [ə] varies with [ʌ] in U*nless*, [ɪ] in I*ntentional*, [e] in E*ntire*, [æ̈:] in A*nticipate* and [æ] in A*morphous* (Postal 1968: 219). [ədíʃn] may be a variant of E*dition* [e-] and A*ddition* [æ-], [əféktɪv] similarly of E*ffective* [e-] and A*ffective* [æ-], etc. (1968: 220). Postal concludes that free variation is not a transitive relation, an insight which would be incompatible with autonomous phonemics. Generative phonology, on the other hand, makes no assumption of transitivity, since it accounts for contrast and free variation only indirectly (1968: 218).

Postal's argument seems to focus on a difficulty in phoneme theory. However, a moment's reflection reveals the root of the problem; Postal considers several levels of pronunciation at the same time. The [ə]-type vowels are reduced counterparts of several different vowels that are clearly distinct at the level of careful pronunciation. Obviously, free variation must be a relation within sets of items of the same type or at the same level. Thus, free variation must concern phonetic variants at the same level of pronunciation, not the relation between phoneme and phones, or between phonetic variants of different levels. If, e.g., we consider only the level of the most careful pronunciations, then free variation between units (to the extent that it exists) is certainly transitive. (I.e. for certain words, [âı] and [iː] are variants, as in [âıðə] vs. [iːðə], §3.4.)[18] Moreover, free variation in phonology is concerned only with relations between surface forms, and nothing hinges on assumptions of reality for abstract morpheme-invariants.

13.3.4 *Conclusion*

Though I have only considered a few generative arguments against the phonemic level (most other arguments are variants of these), we have clearly seen that they are far from conclusive. Leaving details aside, the following points are the most important counter-arguments:

(a)   The arguments under consideration attack only a particularly rigid version of structuralist phonemics, one in which the phoneme level is defined by Chomsky's (1964) conditions of linearity, invariance, bi-uniqueness and local determinacy. This version has not been practised by many phonologists.

(b)   Critics fail to recognize that several of the problems ascribed to phonemics stem from the fact that several levels of articulatory accuracy are being considered at the same time. If Chomsky (1964: e.g. *writer–rider* example, cf. fn. 18) and Postal (1968: Engl. full and reduced vowels in connection with the argument concerning the 'non-transitivity of free variation') had concentrated on one level, e.g. that of the most precise pronunciations, these problems would have dissolved.[19]

(c)   For the critics the goal of a phonological theory is to offer the most general, simple, coherent and elegant descriptions of the phonology of languages that are formally possible. It is *not* to provide a model that may be psychologically valid (despite the fact

---

[18] Chomsky (1964: 82ff), in arguing against 'taxonomic phonemics', also fails to sort out different levels of pronunciation, e.g. in the case of Engl. *writer – rider*. Incidentally, the *writer – rider* case is not a very good example, since the /t/↔/d/ distinction is seldom completely merged in casual speech either (Fischer & Hirsh 1976).

[19] Obligatory vs. optional rules is a very important distinction, §10.5.

that some lip service is paid to the latter goal). Thus, the generative model defended by the critics is nowhere made subject to empirical testing. External evidence is never used. As I have argued earlier, such evidence clearly supports a theory based on phonetic plans and phonemic contrasts.

(d) The generative arguments presuppose the existence of morpheme-invariant representations as an underlying phonological level. This is an untenable idea (ch. 12). Hutchinson (1972), in his (already quoted) critical discussion of Chomsky's & Halle's arguments against the phoneme, argued that 'it has not been demonstrated that we are forced to reject it [i.e. the phoneme]. Rather, we are only forced to reject it as the appropriate entity for representing morphemes' (1972: 24). I agree completely. Since morphemes are not phonological forms (ch. 12), we thus conclude that Chomsky and Halle have not demonstrated that the phoneme must be relegated from phonology.

(e) The arguments correctly assume that phonology is non-autonomous, a point on which many structuralists would agree, but they erroneously conclude that non-autonomy implies abstractness of phonological representations.

Obviously, the classical generative arguments against the phoneme and the phoneme level are not valid counter-arguments against the kind of phonological theory propagated in this book.

Epilogue

Chomsky has correctly identified the subject matter of linguistics as psychological in nature, but he[. . .]has taken positions[. . .]which presuppose an autonomy for linguistics which it cannot have if it is to be a 'branch of cognitive psychology'. (McCawley 1976 : 163)

The proposals made in this study are not new, and my considerations have led me to a view which, I think, may be regarded as rather traditional. Yet the preliminary character of many of the proposals must be emphasized. Our knowledge of the psychological and behavioral aspects of phonology is still very sketchy. I would therefore like to conclude with a few summarizing comments on the state of the art in phonological theory and some desiderata for the future.

In the generative heyday it was often asserted that linguistics was overwhelmed by data, and that the most strongly felt insufficiency was the lack of explicit, adequate and interesting theories. Now there has been an enormous proliferation of new theories documented in countless books and articles published in the last one or two decades. Yet, I suppose many scholars in the field still think that the greatest progress can be expected from new theoretical works. But this is an unfortunate attitude. Certainly theoretical work is still necessary, but if really interesting and empirically well-supported theories are to be developed, there is an enormous need of *data*, especially data concerning detailed and systematic observations of actual speech performance, language acquisition, interindividual variation, errors in speech production and perception, etc. Such data must cover a sufficient number of typologically different languages. Furthermore, phonology-based experimental work has hardly begun.[1] There is also a great need

---

[1] Some work has recently been done by scholars such as Derwing, Lindblom (e.g. Liljencrants & Lindblom 1972), J. Ohala, Steinberg, Wang, and others. In addition, there is of course a very extensive body of experimental data in *phonetics*, and my impression is that these data have too often been neglected by phonologists.

for insightful theories of the pragmatics of language, and works which attempt to set language in a wider psychological and sociological perspective. In theoretical studies one should take a closer look at the general metaphysical and methodological assumptions behind the theories. As is often remarked, a theory is only as sound as its basic assumptions.

Bibliography (and citation index)

Abbreviations

In the bibliography the following abbreviations for names of journals, reports, etc. have been used.

ALH	Acta Linguistica Hafniensia (Copenhagen)
ANF	Arkiv för Nordisk Filologi (Lund: Gleerups)
AP	American Psychologist (Washington, DC)
ARIPUC	Annual Report of the Institute of Phonetics of the University of Copenhagen
AS	American Speech (New York)
BSPS	Boston Studies in the Philosophy of Science (Dordrecht: Reidel)
ChJL	Chicago Journal of Linguistics (Chicago)
CJL	The Canadian Journal of Linguistics (Toronto, Ont.: Canadian Linguistic Association)
CLHU, NSF	The Computation Laboratory of Harvard University (Mathematical Linguistics and Automatic Translation): Report to the National Science Foundation (Cambridge, Mass.)
CLS	Papers from the (n:th) Regional Meeting of Chicago Linguistic Society (Chicago Linguistic Society, Chicago, Ill.)
CP	Cognitive Psychology (New York: Academic Press)
FL	Foundations of Language (Dordrecht: Reidel)
FoL	Folia Linguistica (The Hague: Mouton)
FUF	Finno-Ugrische Forschungen (Helsinki)
Gl.	Glossa (Burnaby)
GMSLL	Georgetown Monograph Series on Languages and Linguistics (Washington, DC)
GPTL	Gothenburg Papers in Theoretical Linguistics (Göteborg: Department of Linguistics)
FIPhSKUM	Forschungsberichte, Institut für Phonetik und sprachliche Kommunikation der Universität München
HER	Harvard Educational Review (Cambridge, Mass.)
IF	Indogermanische Forschungen (Berlin: de Gruyter)
IJAL	International Journal of American Linguistics (Baltimore)

IULC	(Paper reproduced by) Indiana University Linguistics Club (Bloomington, Ind.)
JASA	The Journal of the Acoustical Society of America (Lancaster, Pa.)
JChL	Journal of Child Language (Cambridge)
JIPA	Journal of the International Phonetic Association (London: International Phonetic Association)
JL	Journal of Linguistics (Cambridge: Cambridge University Press)
JP	The Journal of Philosophy (Lancaster, Pa.)
JPh	Journal of Phonetics (London: Academic Press)
JPR	Journal of Psycholinguistic Research (New York)
JSFOu	Journal de la Société Finno-Ougrienne (Helsinki)
JVLVB	Journal of Verbal Learning and Verbal Behavior (New York)
LA	Linguistic Analysis (New York)
LB	Linguistische Berichte (Braunschweig)
Lg.	Language (Baltimore)
LI	Linguistic Inquiry (Cambridge, Mass.)
Ling.	Linguistics (The Hague)
LS	Language Sciences (Bloomington, Ind.)
MWPL	Montreal Working Papers in Linguistics (Montreal: Dept. of Linguistics)
NJL	Norwegian Journal of Linguistics (Oslo)
OPUE	Occasional Papers, University of Essex (Language Centre)
PB	Psychological Bulletin (Washington, DC)
PEP	Probleme und Ergebnisse der Psychologie (Berlin)
Ph.	Phonetica (Basel, etc.)
PILUS	Papers from the Institute of Linguistics, University of Stockholm
PL	Papers in Linguistics (Edmonton, Alberta)
POLA	Project on Linguistic Analysis. (Report from) Phonology Laboratory, Department of Linguistics, University of California, Berkeley.
PR	The Philosophical Review (Ithaca, New York)
PsR	Psychological Review (Washington, DC: American Psychological Association)
RRL	Revue roumaine de linguistique (Bucarest)
RUUL	Reports from Uppsala University Department of Linguistics (Uppsala: Dept. of Linguistics)
SAL	Studies in African Linguistics (University of California, Los Angeles: Department of Linguistics and the African Studies Center)
SB	Förhandlingar vid sammankomst för att dryfta frågor rörande Svenskans Beskrivning (edited by different departments of linguistics in Sweden)
SBL	Salzburger Beiträge zur Linguistik (Salzburg: Institut für Sprachwissenschaft)

SG	Studia Grammatica (Berlin: Akademie-Verlag)
SJA	Southwestern Journal of Anthropology (Austin, Texas)
SL	Studia Linguistica (Lund: Gleerups)
STL-QPSR	Quarterly Progress and Status Report, Speech Transmission Laboratory, Royal Institute of Technology, Stockholm.
TCLP	Travaux du Cercle Linguistique de Prague (Prague)
WLG	Wiener Linguistische Gazette (Vienna: Institut für Sprachwissenschaft)
WPL-CISRC	Working Papers in Linguistics, Computer and Information Science Research Center, The Ohio State University (Columbus, Ohio)
WPLH	Working Papers in Linguistics, University of Hawaii (Honolulu)
WPPLL	Working Papers, Phonetics Laboratory, Lund University
WPP-UCLA	Working Papers in Phonetics, University of California at Los Angeles
ZPhSK	Zeitschrift für Phonetik, Sprachwissenschaft und Kommunikations-forschung (Berlin)

Citations: After each entry, references are given [within brackets] to the pages where it is cited.

Agassi, J. (1964) 'The nature of scientific problems and their roots in metaphysics'. In Bunge, M. (ed.) *The critical approach to science and philosophy*. London: Macmillan. [255]

Ahlgren, I. (1975) *Interaction between form and content in linguistic perception*. (MILUS 3) Stockholm: Dept. of Linguistics. [68]

Allén, S. (1969) 'Lingual expression and generative grammar'. In *Actes du Xe Congrès International des Linguistes* (Bucarest: Éditions de l'Academie de la République Socialiste de Roumanie), 235–9. [197]

Allwood, J. (1976) *Linguistic communication as action and cooperation: a study in pragmatics*. (Gothenburg Monographs in Linguistics 2, Dept. of Linguistics). [13–16, 24, 32, 46, 50, 256]

Alston, W. P. (1964) *Philosophy of language*. Englewood Cliffs, NJ: Prentice-Hall. [255]

Andersen, H. (1969) 'A study in diachronic morphophonemics: the Ukrainian prefixes'. *Lg.* 45: 807–30. [75, 165, 175]

– (1972) 'Diphthongization'. *Lg.* 48: 11–50. [67]

– (1973) 'Abductive and deductive change'. *Lg.* 49: 765–93. [8, 95, 218]

Anderson, J. & Jones, Ch. (1974) *Historical linguistics 2*. Amsterdam: North-Holland

Anderson, L. B. (1972) 'Explanation, abstractness and language learning'. *CLS* 8: 416–30. [238]

Anderson, S. R. (1972) 'On nasalization in Sundanese'. *LI* 3: 253–68. [251–2]

- (1973) 'U-umlaut and Skaldic verse'. In Anderson, S. R. & Kiparsky, P. (1973), 3–13. [13, 93, 247]
- (1974) *The organization of phonology*. New York: Academic Press. [139–40, 161, 224–5, 248, 261–2]
- (1975) 'On the interaction of phonological rules of various types'. *JL* 11: 39–62. [81, 175, 190, 264]
- & Browne, W. (1973) 'On keeping exchange rules in Czech'. *PL* 6: 4. [208]
- & Kiparsky, P. (1973) (eds.) *A festschrift for Morris Halle*. New York: Holt, Rinehart & Winston
Anttila, R. (1972a) *An introduction to historical and comparative linguistics*. New York: Macmillan. [18, 41, 104]
- (1972b) 'Who is a structuralist?' Ms., University of California, Los Angeles. [75, 257]
- (1975) 'The indexical element in morphology'. *Innsbrucker Beiträge zur Sprachwissenschaft*. Reihe Vorträge 12. [153, 161]
- (1976a) *Analogy*. The Hague: Mouton. [129]
- (1976b) 'The metamorphosis of allomorphs'. In Reich, P. (ed.) *The Second Lacus Forum 1975*. Columbia: Hornbeam Press, 238–48. [153, 161, 243]
- (1976c) 'The reconstruction of Sprachgefühl: a concrete abstract'. In Christie, W. (ed.) *Current progress in historical linguistics*. Proceedings of the Second International Conference on Historical Linguistics (Tucson, Arizona, January 1976). Amsterdam: North-Holland, 216–34. [28]
- (1976d) 'Child language, abduction, and the acquisition of linguistic theory by linguists'. In von Raffler-Engel, W. & Lebrun, Y. (eds.) *Baby talk and infant speech*. Amsterdam: Swets & Zeitlinger, 24–37. [256]
Anward, J. (1979) 'On communicative functions of syntactic constructions: evidence from Swedish'. Uppsala: Dept. of Linguistics. [8]
- & Linell, P. (1975) 'Om lexikaliserade fraser i svenskan'. (*SB* 9) *Nysvenska studier* 55: 77–119. [78, 153]
Bach, E. (1964) *An introduction to transformational grammars*. New York: Holt, Rinehart & Winston. [10, 260, 262]
- & Harms, R. (1968) (eds.) *Universals in linguistic theory*. New York: Holt, Rinehart & Winston
- & Harms, R. (1972) 'How do languages get crazy rules?' In Stockwell, R. & Macauley, R. (1972), 1–21. [207]
Bailey, Ch.-J. (1970) Review of Mulder, J. W. F. (1968). *Lg.* 46: 671–87. [96]
- (1972) 'The integration of linguistic theory: internal reconstruction and the comparative method in descriptive linguistics'. In Stockwell, R. & Macauley, R. (1972), 22–31. [21, 101]
- (1973) 'Variation and linguistic theory'. Arlington, Va.: Center for Applied Linguistics. [155]
- (1976) 'Phonology since generative phonology'. *Papiere zur Linguistik* 11: 5–19. [30, 88]
Bannert, R. (1974) 'Kvantiteten i svenskan: En av de fonetiska mekanismerna med betydelseskiljande funktion.' *SB* 8: 31–47 (Lund: Inst. f. nordiska språk). [59, 60]

Barkaï, M. (1975) 'On phonological representations, rules, and opacity'. *Lingua* 37: 363–76. [221]

Bartsch, R. & Vennemann, Th. (1972) *Semantic structures : a study in the relation between semantics and syntax.* (Athenäum-Skripten Linguistik 9) Frankfurt am Main: Athenäum. [145]

Basbøll, H. (1974) 'The phonological syllable with special reference to Danish'. *ARIPUC* 8: 39–128. [53, 68, 123, 193]

– (1977a) 'The structure of the syllable and a proposed hierarchy of distinctive features'. In Dressler, W. U. & Pfeiffer, O. E. (1977), 143–8. [123]

– (1977b) 'On the function of boundaries in phonological rules'. In Goyvaerts, D. L. (forthcoming). [53, 68, 193]

Becker, D. A. (1967) 'Generative phonology and dialect study: an investigation of three modern German dialects'. Unpublished PhD thesis. University of Texas at Austin. [101]

von Bertalanffy, L. (1968) *General system theory.* Harmondsworth: Penguin Books. [75]

Bever, T. G. (1970) 'The cognitive basis for linguistic structures'. In Hayes, J. R. (1970), 279–352. [20, 38, 75]

Bierwisch, M. (1967) 'Syntactic features in morphology: general problems of so-called pronominal inflection in German'. In *To honor Roman Jakobson.* The Hague: Mouton, 239–70. [127]

– (1972) 'Schriftstruktur und Phonologie'. *PEP* 43: 21–44. [197]

Bjarkman, P. (1975) 'Toward a proper conception of processes in natural phonology'. *CLS* 11: 60–72. [124, 169, 175, 190, 207, 210]

Black, M. (1962) *Models and metaphors.* Ithaca, New York: Cornell University Press (fourth printing 1968). [22–3]

Blesser, B. (1969) 'Perception of spectrally rotated speech'. Unpublished PhD thesis, MIT. [52]

Bloch, B. (1941) 'Phonemic overlapping'. *AS* 16: 278–84. Reprinted in Joos, M. (1957), 93–6. [265]

Bloomfield, L. (1933) *Language.* London: Allen & Unwin. [102, 160, 224]

– (1939) 'Menomini morphophonemics'. *TCLP* 8: 105–15. [160, 224]

– (1957) 'A set of postulates for the science of language'. In Joos, M. (1957), 26–31 (also in *Lg.* 2 (1926), 153–64). [152, 183, 230]

Bond, Z. (1969) 'Constraints on production errors'. *CLS* 5: 302–5. [110–11, 202]

Bonebrake, V. (1973) 'The role of syllabification in Swedish nasal assimilation. Part 1: Competence study.' *SB* 7 (*Folkmålsstudier* 23), 80–102. [251]

Botha, R. P. (1968) *The function of the lexicon in transformational generative grammar.* (*Janua Linguarum*, Series Maior 38) The Hague: Mouton. [1, 8, 10, 255]

– (1971) *Methodological aspects of transformational generative phonology.* The Hague: Mouton. [xiv, 13, 78, 253–5]

– (1973) *The justification of linguistic hypotheses.* The Hague: Mouton. [xiv, 2, 13, 26–7]

Braine, M. (1967) 'On the basis of phrase structure: a reply to Bever, Fodor, and

Weksel'. In Jakobovits, L. & Miron, M. (eds.) *Readings in the psychology of language*. Englewood Cliffs, NJ: Prentice-Hall, 274–84. [73]
- (1974) 'On what might constitute learnable phonology'. *Lg.* 50: 270–99. [54, 56, 74, 137, 185, 218–19, 236–7]
Brame, M. (1972) (ed.) *Contributions to generative phonology*. Austin: University of Texas Press
Bransford, J., Barclay, J. R. & Franks, J. (1972) 'Sentence memory: a constructive versus interpretive approach'. *CP* 3: 193–209. [46]
Bransford, J. & McCarrell, N. (1974) 'A sketch of a cognitive approach to comprehension: some thoughts about understanding what it means to comprehend'. In Weimer, W. & Palermo, D. (eds.) *Cognition and the symbolic processes*. New York: John Wiley, 189–229. [46]
Brasington, R. W. P. (1976) 'On the functional diversity of phonological rules'. *JL* 12: 125–52. [175]
Brown, G. (1977) *Listening to spoken English*. London: Longman. [120]
Brown, R. & McNeill, D. (1965) 'The tip of the tongue phenomenon'. *JVLVB* 5: 325–37. [58]
Bruck, A., Fox, R. & LaGaly, M. (1974) (eds.) *Papers from the parasession on natural phonology*. Chicago: Chicago Linguistic Society
Bruner, J. (1975) 'The ontogenesis of speech acts'. *JChL* 2: 1–19. [237, 256]
Bunge, M. (1963) *The myth of simplicity*. Englewood Cliffs, NJ: Prentice-Hall. [73, 254]
- (1964) 'Phenomenological theories', in Bunge, M. (ed.) *The critical approach to science and philosophy*. London: The Free Press of Glencoe (Collier-Macmillan), 234–54. [10]
Campbell, L. (1971) Review of King, R. D. (1969). *Lg* 47: 191–209. [101]
- (1972) 'Is a generative dialectology possible?' *Orbis* 21: 289–98. [101]
- (1973) 'Extrinsic ordering lives!' *IULC*. [191]
- (1974) 'Theoretical implications of Kekchi phonology'. *IJAL* 40: 269–78. [83, 201]
- (1977) 'The psychological and social reality of Finnish vowel harmony'. To be published in Vago, R. (ed.) *Issues in vowel harmony*. Amsterdam: John Benjamins. [211]
Campbell, R. & Wales, J. A. (1970) 'The study of language acquisition'. In Lyons, J. (ed.) *New horizons in linguistics*. Harmondsworth: Penguin Books, 242–60. [19]
Cazden, C. (1967) 'On individual differences in language competence and performance'. *The Journal of Special Education* 1: 135–50. [19]
Cearley, A. (1974) 'The only phonological rule ordering principle'. In Bruck, A., Fox, R. & LaGaly, M. (1974), 30–42. [172, 175, 190, 202]
Celce-Murcia, M. (1973) 'Meringer's corpus revisited'. In Fromkin, V. (1973), 195–204. [111, 138]
Chafe, W. (1970) *Meaning and the structure of language*. Chicago: University of Chicago Press. [256]
Chen, M. (1973a) 'On the formal expression of natural rules in phonology'. *JL* 9: 223–49. [73, 254]

- (1973b) 'Predictive power in phonological description'. *Lingua* 32: 173–91. [73, 254]
- & Wang, W. (1975) 'Sound change: actuation and implementation'. *Lg.* 51: 255–81. [154, 182]

Chomsky, C. (1970) 'Reading, writing and phonology'. *HER* 40: 287–309. [197]

Chomsky, N. (1957) *Syntactic structures*. The Hague: Mouton. [13, 245]
- (1961) 'On the notion "rule of grammar"'. *Proceedings of the Twelfth Symposium in Applied Mathematics 12*: 6–24. (Also in Fodor, J. A. & Katz, J. J. (1964), 119–36). [23]
- (1964) *Current issues in linguistic theory*. The Hague: Mouton. [xiii, 13, 43, 88, 91, 101, 161, 211, 245, 260–2, 266]
- (1965) *Aspects of the theory of syntax*. Cambridge, Mass.: MIT Press. [12–13, 28, 75, 225, 245]
- (1967a) 'Some general properties of phonological rules'. *Lg.* 43: 102–28. [88, 261]
- (1967b) 'The formal nature of language'. Appendix A, 397–442. In Lenneberg, E. (1967). [6, 235]
- (1968) *Language and mind*. New York: Harcourt, Brace & World. [8, 13]
- (1969) 'Linguistics and philosophy'. In Hook, S. (1969), 51–94. [13, 22–3, 54, 245]
- (1972) 'Phonology and reading'. In Levin, H. (ed.) *Basic studies in reading*. New York: Harper & Row. [197]
- (1975a) *Reflections on language*. Glasgow: Fontana/Collins. [4, 10, 22–3, 25, 76–7, 237]
- (1975b) (1955) *The logical structure of linguistic theory*. New York and London: Plenum Press. [6]
- & Halle, M. (1965) 'Some controversial questions in phonological theory'. *JL* 1: 97–138. [66, 167, 260]
- & Halle, M. (1968) *The sound pattern of English*. New York: Harper & Row. [xiv, xv, 6, 9–10, 50–2, 54, 66, 73–4, 92, 101, 112, 118, 127, 133–4, 139, 188, 194, 197–8, 202–3, 208, 211, 221, 224, 226–8, 235, 248, 250–1, 253–4]

Clayton, M. (1976) 'The redundance of underlying morpheme-structure conditions'. *Lg.* 52: 295–313. [118, 126, 261]

Coats, H. (1970) 'Rule environment features in phonology'. *PL* 2: 1: 110–40. [136, 141]

Cohen, D. & Wirth, J. (1975) (eds.) *Testing linguistic hypotheses*. New York: John Wiley.

Collinder, B. (1938) 'Lautlehre und Phonologismus'. In *Actes du Quatrième Congrès International des Linguistes*. 122–6. [47]

Coseriu, E. (1954) *Forma y sustancia en los sonidos del lenguaje*. (Revista de la Faculdad de Humanidadas y Ciensías 12) Montevideo. [258]
- (1974) *Synchronie, Diachronie und Geschichte*. Translation by Sohre, H. of Coseriu, E. (1958) *Sincronía, diacronía e historia* (Montevideo). Munich: W. Fink Verlag. [1, 3, 75]

de Courtenay, B. (1895) *Versuch einer Theorie phonetischer Alternationen*. Strasbourg. [49, 88]

Crothers, J. (1971) 'On the abstractness controversy'. *POLA* 12: CR 1–29. [227, 251]

– & Shibatani, M. (1975) 'On some fundamental concepts of phonology'. In Goyvaerts, D. L. & Pullum, G. E. (1975), 505–35. [114, 188, 227, 230–1]

Cutting, J. (1975) 'Aspects of phonological fusion'. *Journal of Experimental Psychology : Human Perception and Performance* 104: 2: 105–20. [114]

Dahl, Ö. (1974a) (ed.) *Papers from the First Scandinavian Conference of Linguistics* (Kungälv, 1974). Göteborg: Dept. of Linguistics

– (1974b) 'Can Phonemes be reduced to features?' In Dahl, Ö. (1974a), 57–69. [66]

Dahlstedt, K.-H. (1970) 'The dilemmas of dialectology'. In Benediktsson, H. (ed.), 158–84. [62]

– (1975) (ed.) *The Nordic languages and modern linguistics* 2. Proceedings of the Second International Conference of Nordic and General Linguistics (Umeå, 14–19 June 1973). Stockholm: Almqvist & Wiksell

Darden, B. (1971) 'Diachronic evidence for phonemics'. *CLS* 7: 323–31. [98, 103, 105]

– (1976) 'On abstraction'. *CLS* 12: 110–21. [56]

Dell, F. (1970). 'Le e muet et la morphologie dérivationelle du français'. MIT dissertation. [91]

Derwing, B. (1973) *Transformational grammar as a theory of language acquisition.* (Cambridge Studies in Linguistics 10). Cambridge: Cambridge University Press. [xiv, 5, 6, 12–13, 19, 21, 23, 27, 31, 54, 56, 65, 73–4, 76, 104, 124–5, 137, 163–4, 185, 196, 203, 226, 230–1, 236–7, 240, 248, 254, 256, 264]

– (1975) 'English pluralization: a testing ground for rule evaluation'. To appear in Prideaux, G. D., Derwing, B. & Baker, W. J. (eds.) *Experimental linguistics.* [27]

– (1977) 'Is the child really a "little linguist"?'. In Macnamara, J. (1977), 79–84. [256]

– & Baker, W. (1976) 'On the learning of English morphological rules'. (Report to the Canada Council). University of Alberta, Edmonton: Dept. of Linguistics. [5, 43, 77, 130, 164, 226]

Dingwall, W. O. (1971) (ed.) *A survey of linguistic science.* Linguistics Program, University of Maryland

Donegan, P. J. & Stampe, D. (1978) 'The study of natural phonology'. Forthcoming in Dinnsen, D. (ed.) *Current approaches to phonological theory.* Bloomington: Indiana University Press. [49, 206]

Drachman, G. (1972) 'On the notion "phonological rule"'. *WLG* 2: 2–16. [16, 51, 112–13]

– (1973) 'Phonology and the basis of articulation'. *Die Sprache* 19: 1–19. [189, 199]

– (1975) 'Generative phonology and child language acquisition'. In Dressler, W. U. & Mareš, F. V. (1975), 235–51. [218–19]

– (1977) 'On the notion "phonological hierarchy"'. In Dressler, W. U. & Pfeiffer, O. E. (1977), 85–102. [xv]

Dressler, W. U. (1971) 'Some constraints on phonological change'. *CLS* 7: 340–9. [105]

278   *Bibliography (and citation index)*

- (1972a) *Allegroregeln rechtfertigen Lentoregeln : Sekundäre Phoneme des Bretonischen.* Innsbruck: Institut für Sprachwissenschaft. [56, 172, 178, 181]
- (1972b) 'On the phonology of language death'. *CLS* 8: 448–57. [208–10]
- (1972c) 'In support of extrinsic ordering: German /ng/'. *WLG* 2: 17–20. [191]
- (1973a) 'On rule ordering in casual speech styles' *WLG* 4: 3–8. [176]
- (1973b) 'Zum Aussagewert der Lehnwortphonologie für die Abstraktheitsdebatte. *Die Sprache* 19: 125–39. [196]
- (1973c) 'For a socio-psycho-linguistic theory of phonological variation'. *SBL* 1: 13–23. [169, 178]
- (1973d) 'Die Anordnung phonologischer Prozesse bei Aphatikern'. *WLG* 4: 9–19. [113, 203]
- (1974) 'Phonologische Prozesstypologie'. Prag: Acta Universitatis Carolinae. Philologica 5 (Linguistica Generalia 1), 135–46. [193]
- (1976a) 'Können Morphemfugen die Domäne phonologischer Prozesse begrenzen ?' In Pohl, H. D. & Salnikow, N. (eds.) *Opuscula Slavica et Linguistica.* Festschrift für Alexander Issatschenko. Klagenfurt: J. Heyn, 123–38. [178, 193]
- (1976b) 'How much does performance contribute to phonological change?' *WLG* 13: 3–18. [218]
- (1977a) 'Morphologization of phonological processes. (Are there distinct morphonological processes ?)'. Ms. for Juilland, A. (ed.) *Linguistic studies offered to Joseph Greenberg,* vol 2. Saratoga, California: Anma Libri. [175, 206–7, 209–11]
- (1977b) *Grundfragen der Morphonologie.* Vienna: Verlag der Österreichischen Akademie der Wissenschaften. [99, 126–7, 175, 180, 193, 196, 203, 209–11]

Dressler, W. U., Fasching, P., Chromec, E., Wintersberger, W., Leodolter, R., Stark, H., Groll, G., Reinhart, J. & Pohl, H. D. (1972). 'Phonologische Schnellsprechregeln in der Wiener Umgangssprache'. *WLG* 1: 1–28. [172]
- & Mareš, F. V. (1975) *Phonologica 1972.* (Akten der zweiten Internationalen Phonologietagung, (Vienna, 5–8 September 1972). Munich: W. Fink Verlag
- & Pfeiffer, O. E. (1977) *Phonologica 1976.* (Akten der dritten Internationalen Phonologie-Tagung, Vienna, 1–4 September 1976). Innsbruck: Innsbrucker Beiträge zur Sprachwissenschaft 19

Ďurovič, L´. (1967) 'Das Problem der Morphonologie'. In *To honor Roman Jakobson.* The Hague: Mouton, 556–68. [249]

Eilers, R. & Oller, K. (1976) 'The role of speech discrimination in developmental sound substitutions'. *JChL* 3: 319–29. [217]

Elert, C.-C. (1957) 'Bidrag till en fonematisk beskrivning av svenska.' *ANF* 72: 35–60. [7]
- (1970) *Ljud och ord i svenskan.* Stockholm: Almqvist & Wiksell. [107, 211, 262]

Eliasson, S. (1972) 'Unstable vowels in Swedish: syncope, epenthesis or both?' In Firchow, E., Grimstad, K., Hasselmo, N., O'Neill, W. (eds.) *Studies for Einar Haugen.* The Hague: Mouton, 174–88. [122–3, 211]
- (1973) 'Generativ fonologi, morfofonemik och svenskans [š] och[ç]. *SB* 7 (*Folkmålsstudier* 23, Abo 1973), 195–213. [102–3, 107]

- (1975a) Review of Vandamme, F. J. (1972). *Zeitschrift für Dialektologie und Linguistik* 17: 53–62. [39]
- (1975b) 'On the issue of directionality'. In Dahlstedt, K.-H. (1975), 421–45. [124]
- (1977) 'Inferential aspects of phonological rules'. In Dressler, W. U. & Pfeiffer, O. E. (1977), 103–10. [103]
- & La Pelle, N. (1973) 'Generativa regler för svenskans kvantitet' *ANF* 88: 133–48. [59]
Emery, F. E. (1969) (ed.) *Systems in thinking*. Harmondsworth: Penguin Books. [75]
Eriksson, H. (1974) 'On word reduction'. In Dahl, O. (1974a), 87–92. [97, 172, 211]
Ferguson, Ch. & Farwell, C. (1975) 'Words and sounds in early language acquisition'. *Lg.* 51: 419–39. [104, 215]
Fidelholtz, J. (1975) 'Word frequency and vowel reduction in English'. *CLS* 11: 200–13. [155, 182]
Fillmore, Ch. (1968) 'The case for case': In Bach, E. & Harms, R. (1968), 1–88. [143]
Firth, J. R. (1957) *Papers in linguistics* (1934–51). Oxford: Oxford University Press. [68–9]
Fischer, W. & Hirsh, I. (1976) 'Intervocalic flapping in English'. *CLS* 12: 183–98. [189, 211, 266]
Fischer-Jørgensen, E. (1975) *Trends in phonological theory*. Copenhagen: Akademisk Forlag. [xv, 30, 100, 105, 142, 160, 183]
Fodor, J. A. (1976) *The language of thought*. Hassocks: Harvester Press. [11, 13, 24, 26, 71, 245]
Fodor, J. A., Bever, T. & Garrett, M. (1974) *The psychology of language*. New York: McGraw Hill. [11, 14, 17, 46, 110]
- & Katz, J. J. (1964) (eds.) *The structure of language: readings in the philosophy of language*. Englewood Cliffs, NJ: Prentice-Hall
- & Garrett, M. (1966) 'Some reflections on competence and performance'. In Lyons, J. & Wales, R. J. (eds.) *Psycholinguistics Papers*. Edinburgh: Edinburgh University Press, 135–79. [11, 240]
Foss, D. & Swinney, D. (1973) 'On the psychological reality of the phoneme: perception, identification and consciousness'. *JVLVB* 12: 246–57. [68]
Fraser, C., Bellugi, U. & Brown, R. (1963) 'Control of grammar in imitation, comprehension and production'. *JVLVB* 2: 121–35. [43]
Fromkin, V. (1973) (ed.) *Speech errors as linguistic evidence*. The Hague: Mouton. [66, 77, 110–12, 137–8, 202, 211]
- (1975) 'When does a test test a hypothesis, or, what counts as evidence?' In Cohen, D. & Wirth, J. (1975), 43–64. [6]
Fudge, E. (1970) 'Phonological structure and "expressiveness"'. *JL* 6: 161–88. [102–3]
- (1973) (ed.) *Phonology*. Harmondsworth: Penguin Books
Fujimura, O. (1973) (ed.) *Three dimensions of linguistic theory*. Tokyo: TEC Company

Ganz, J. (1971) *Rules : a systematic study.* The Hague : Mouton [23]

Gårding, E. (1974) 'Sandhiregler för svenska konsonanter'. *SB* 8 : 97–106 (Lund : Inst. f. nordiska språk). [121, 172, 192]

Garnes, S. & Bond, Z. (1975) 'Slips of the ear : errors in perception of casual speech'. *CLS* 11 : 214–25. [113, 203]

Geis, M. & Zwicky, A. (1971) 'On invited inferences'. *LI* 2 : 561–6. [45]

Gilbert, J. H. (1972) (ed.) *Speech and cortical functioning.* New York : Academic Press

Goldsmith, J. (1976) 'An overview of autosegmental phonology'. *LA* 2 : 23–68. [69]

Golick, M. (1974) 'Phonological development : does misperception play a role in children's misarticulations ?' *MWPL* 1 : 109–21. [217]

Goyvaerts, D. L. (forthcoming) (ed.) *Phonology in the 1970s.* Ghent : Story-Scientia. Also issued as a volume of the journal *Communication & Cognition*

– & Pullum, G. E. (1975) (eds.) *Essays on the sound pattern of English.* Ghent : Story-Scientia. [30, 52]

Greenberg, J. (1963) 'Some universals of grammar with particular reference to the order of meaningful elements'. In Greenberg, J. (ed.) *Universals of language.* Cambridge, Mass. : MIT Press, 73–113. [144]

– (1966) *Language universals.* The Hague : Mouton. Also in Sebeok, Th. (1966) (ed.) *Current trends in linguistics 3.* The Hague : Mouton, 61–112. [144]

– (1973) 'The typological method'. In Sebeok, Th. (ed.) *Current trends in linguistics 11.* The Hague : Mouton, 149–93. [4]

Grice, H. P. (1975) 'Logic and conversation'. In Cole, P. & Morgan, J. (eds.) *Syntax and semantics 3 : speech acts.* New York : Academic Press, 41–58. [15, 32, 35, 45]

Grossman, R. E., San, J. & Vance, T. G. (1975) (eds.) *Papers from the parasession on functionalism.* Chicago : Chicago Linguistic Society

Groundstroem, A. (1974) *Finnische Flexionslehre. Ein Vorläufiger Überblick.* University of Stockholm : Finska institutionen. [195, 211]

Haas, W. (1967) 'Grammatical prerequisites of phonological analysis'. In Hamm, J. (ed.) *Phonologie der Gegenwart.* Graz : Hermann Böhlaus, 227–41. [258]

Haber, L. (1975) 'The muzzy theory'. *CLS* 11 : 240–56. [26, 77]

Hale, K. (1973) 'Deep-surface canonical disparities in relation to analysis and change : an Australian example'. In Sebeok, Th. (ed.) *Current trends in linguistics 11.* The Hague : Mouton, 401–58. [73, 75, 82–3, 232]

Halle, M. (1959) *The sound pattern of Russian.* The Hague : Mouton. [74, 88, 160, 259–64]

– (1961) 'On the role of simplicity in linguistic descriptions'. In Jakobson, R. (ed.) *Structure of language and its mathematical aspects : Proceedings of Symposia in Applied Mathematics 12.* Providence, RI : American Mathematical Society, 89–94. [88, 260]

– (1962) 'Phonology in generative grammar'. *Word* 18 : 54–72. Also in Fodor, J. A. & Katz, J. J. (1964), 334–52. [66, 101, 104]

– (1963) 'Phonemics'. In Sebeok, Th. (ed.) *Current trends in linguistics 1 : Soviet and East European linguistics.* The Hague : Mouton, 5–21. [100]

- (1969) 'How not to measure length of lexical representations and other matters'. *JL* 5: 305–8. [66]
- (1973) 'Prolegomena to a theory of word formation'. *LI* 4: 3–16. [124]
- & Stevens, K. (1959). 'Analysis by synthesis'. In Wathen-Dunn, W. & Woods, L. E. (eds.) *Proceedings of the seminar on speech compression and processing 2.* AFCRC-TR-59-198, USAF Cambridge Research Center paper D 7. [46, 54]

Hammarberg, B. (1967) 'Interference in American English speakers' pronunciations of Swedish'. *SL* 21: 15–36. [199]

Hamp, E., Householder, F. & Austerlitz, R. (1966) (eds.) *Readings in linguistics 2.* Chicago: University of Chicago Press

Harman, G. (1967) 'Psychological aspects of the theory of syntax'. *JP* 64: 75–87. [23]

Harms, R. (1968) *Introduction to phonological theory.* Englewood Cliffs, NJ: Prentice-Hall. [66]
- (1973) 'Some on-rules of English'. *IULC.* [205]

Harré, R. (1972) *Introduction to the philosophies of science.* Oxford: Oxford University Press. [10, 73, 242, 254–5]
-& Secord, P. (1972) *The explanation of social behaviour.* Oxford: Basil Blackwell. [14, 16, 23, 255]

Haugen, E. (1951) 'Directions in modern linguistics'. *Lg.* 27: 211–22. Also in Joos, M. (1957), 357–63 (page ref. to Joos). [167]

Hayes, J. R. (1970) (ed.) *Cognition and the development of language.* New York: John Wiley

Hebb, D. O. (1949) *The Organization of behavior : a neurophysiological theory.* New York: John Wiley. [48]

Hellberg, S. (1974) *Graphonomic rules in phonology : studies in the expression component of Swedish.* Göteborg: Acta Universitatis Gothoburgensis. [59, 100, 122, 197, 211]
- (1978) 'Unnatural phonology'. *JL* 14: 157–77. [211]

Hempel, C. (1966) *Philosophy of natural science.* Englewood Cliffs, NJ: Prentice-Hall. [10]

Herbert, R. (1977) 'Morphophonological palatalization in Southern Bantu: a Reply to segmental fusion'. *SAL* 8: 143–71. [141, 207]

Hockett, Ch. (1942) 'A System of descriptive phonology'. *Lg.* 18: 3–21. Also in Joos, M. (1957), 97–108. [258]
- (1955) *A Manual of phonology.* Indiana University publications in anthropology and linguistics, Memoir 11, *IJAL.* [xv, 258]
- (1958) *A Course in modern linguistics.* New York: Macmillan. [183]
- (1961) 'Linguistic elements and their relations'. *Lg.* 37: 29–54. [160]

Holden, K. (1976) 'Assimilation rates of borrowing and phonological productivity'. *Lg.* 52: 131–47. [172, 182, 196, 211]

Holmes, U. (1927) 'The phonology of an English-speaking child'. *AS* 2: 212–25. [218]

Hook, S. (1969) (ed.) *Language and philosophy : a symposium.* New York University Press/University of London Press

Hooper, J. (1974) 'Rule morphologization in natural generative phonology'. In Bruck, A., Fox, R. & LaGaly, M. (1974), 160–70. [99]

282   *Bibliography (and citation index)*

- (1975) 'The archi-segment in natural generative phonology'. *Lg.* 51 : 536–60. [71, 126, 171, 241]
- (1976) *Aspects of natural generative phonology.* New York: Academic Press. [53, 68, 99, 193, 205]
- & Rudes, B. (1977) 'Archisegments: a reply to Bolozky'. *Gl.* 11 : 106–14. [87]
Hörmann, H. (1971) *Psycholinguistics.* Translation by Stern, H. of Hörmann, H. (1970) *Psychologie der Sprache.* Berlin: Springer-Verlag. [75]
Householder, F. (1965) 'On some recent claims in phonological theory'. *JL* 1 : 13–34. [260]
- (1966) 'Phonological theory: a brief comment'. *JL* 2 : 99–100. [97, 260]
Hsieh, H. I. (1970) 'The psychological reality of tone Sandhi rules in Taiwanese'. *CLS* 6 : 489–503. [76]
- (1972) 'Lexical diffusion: evidence from child language acquisition'. *Gl.* 6 : 89–104. [219]
Hudson, G. (1974) 'The representation of non-productive alternation'. In Anderson, J. & Jones, Ch. (1974), 205–30. [78, 83, 87]
- (1975a) *Suppletion in the representation of alternations.* Unpublished PhD thesis, UCLA. [87]
- (1975b) 'Formal and functional explanation of diachronic evidence for phonemics'. In Grossman, R. E., San, J. & Vance, T. G. (1975), 213–22. [106]
Hurford, J. R. (1971) 'The state of phonology'. *Ling.* 71 : 5–41. [265]
Husén, T. (1950) *Rättstavningsfrågans psykologi.* (Pedagogiska Skrifter 207–9). Stockholm: Svensk Läraretidnings Förlag. [203]
Hutchinson, L. (1972) 'Mr. Chomsky on the phoneme', *IULC.* [91, 263, 267]
Hyman, L. (1970) 'How concrete is phonology?' *Lg.* 46 : 58–76. [196, 198, 225]
Hymes, D. (1971) 'Competence and performance in linguistic theory'. In Huxley, R. & Ingram, E. (eds.) *Language acquisition : models and methods.* New York: Academic Press. [19, 22]
- (1972) 'On communicative competence'. In Pride, J. B. & Holmes, J. (eds.) *Sociolinguistics.* Harmondsworth: Penguin Books, 269–93. [19, 22]
Ingram, D. (1974) 'Phonological Rules in young children'. *JChL* 1 : 49–64. [200, 216–18]
- (1975) 'Surface contrast in phonology: evidence from children's speech'. *JChL* 2 : 287–92. [109]
- (1976a) 'Phonological analysis of a child'. *Gl.* 10 : 1 : 3–27. [216]
- (1976b) *Phonological disability in children.* London: Edward Arnold. [215–16]
Itkonen, E. (1974) *Linguistics and metascience.* Studia Philosophica Turkuensia. Fasc. 2. Kokemäki. [xiv, 11, 15, 20, 22–3, 25, 28, 75, 246, 248, 256]
- (1976) 'Linguistics and empiricalness: answers to criticisms'. Report 4, University of Helsinki, Dept. of General Linguistics. [28]
Itkonen, T. (1977) 'Huomioita lapsen äänteistön kehityksestä' (Notes on the acquisition of phonology). *Virittäjä* 3 : 279–308. [219]
Iverson, G. (1974) 'Ordering constraints in phonology'. Unpublished PhD dissertation, University of Minnesota, Minneapolis. [139–40, 191–2]
- & Ringen, C. (1977) 'On constraining the theory of exceptions'. In Brown, R. L., Houlihan, K., Hutchinson, L. & MacLeish, A. (eds.) *Proceedings of the*

1976 Mid-America Linguistics Conference. Minneapolis: University of Minnesota. 155–63. [141]

Jakobson, R. (1941) *Kindersprache, Aphasie und allgemeine Lautgesetze*. Uppsala. English translation: Keiler, A. R. (1968) *Child language, aphasia and phonological universals*. The Hague: Mouton. [215]

– (1948) 'Russian conjugation'. *Word* 4: 155–67. [230]

– (1968) 'The role of phonic elements in speech perception'. *ZPhSK* 21: 9–20. [40, 219]

Jakobson, R., Fant, G. & Halle, M. (1952) *Preliminaries to speech analysis*. Cambridge, Mass.: MIT Press. [xv, 41, 52]

– & Halle, M. (1956) *Fundamentals of language*. The Hague: Mouton. [40, 52]

Jensen, J. (1974) 'How abstract is abstract?' *Gl*. 8: 247–60. [227–8, 232]

Johns, D. A. (1969) 'Phonemics and generative phonology'. *CLS* 5: 374–81. [88, 264]

Johnson-Laird, P. N. (1970) 'The perception and memory of sentences'. In Lyons, J. (ed.) *New horizons in linguistics*. Harmondsworth: Penguin Books. [46]

Jonasson, J. (1971) 'Perceptual similarity and articulatory reinterpretation as a source of phonological innovation'. *STL-QPSR* 1/1971: 30–42. [97]

Joos, M. (1957) (ed.) *Readings in linguistics*. Chicago: University of Chicago Press

Karlsson, F. (1974a) 'Phonology, morphology, and morphophonemics'. *GPTL* 23. [106, 142, 175, 198, 211, 264]

– (1974b) 'Centrala problem i finskans böjningsmorfologi, morfofonematik och fonologi'. *Suomi* 117: 2 (Helsinki). [85, 123, 135, 145, 188, 195, 207, 211]

– (1977) 'Några anteckningar om svenskans kvantitet'. Unpublished ms. Turku: Dept. of General Linguistics. [59, 200]

Katz, J. J. (1964) 'Mentalism in linguistics'. *Lg*. 40: 124–37. [11, 16, 23, 25, 33]

– (1966) *The philosophy of language*. New York and London: Harper & Row. [13, 245, 256]

Kauppinen, A. (1977) 'Mikon kielioppia: Navaintoja 3 vuoden 4 kuukauden ikäisen pojan kielen kehityksestä vuoden aikana'. Unpublished Master's thesis, University of Helsinki: Dept. of Finnish. [87, 211]

Kavanagh, J. & Mattingly, I. (1972) (eds.) *Language by ear and by eye. The relationships between speech and reading*. Cambridge, Mass.: MIT Press

Kaye, J. (1974) 'Morpheme structure constraints live!' *MWPL* 3: 55–62. [126, 193]

– (1975) 'A functional explanation for rule ordering in phonology'. In Grossman, R. F., San, J. & Vance, T. G. (1975) 244–52. [191, 193]

Kehoe, W. & Whitaker, H. (1973) 'Lexical structure disruption in aphasia: a case study'. In Goodglass, H. & Blumstein, Sh. (eds.) *Psycholinguistics and aphasia*. Baltimore and London: Johns Hopkins University Press, 267–79. [16, 84, 112, 203]

Kiefer, F. (1970) *Swedish morphology*. Stockholm: Skriptor. [73, 127, 148]

Kim, Ch.-W. (1971) 'Experimental phonetics'. In Dingwall, W. O. (1971), 16–128. [63, 67]

King, R. D. (1969) *Historical linguistics and generative grammar.* Englewood Cliffs, NJ: Prentice-Hall. [101, 105, 129]
- (1973) 'Rule insertion'. *Lg.* 49: 551–78. [114]
- (1975) 'Integrating linguistic change'. In Dahlstedt, K.-H. (1975), 47–65. [75]
Kintsch, W. (1974) *The representation of meaning in memory.* Hillsdale, NJ: Lawrence Erlbaum. [79]
Kiparsky, P. (1965) *Phonological change.* MIT dissertation. Reproduced in 1971 by *IULC* (page references to IULC version). [51, 104, 129, 162, 262]
- (1968a) 'Linguistic universals and linguistic change'. In Bach, E. & Harms, R. (1968), 170–202. [11, 104–5, 191, 240]
- (1968b) 'How abstract is phonology?' In Kiparsky, P. (1973a), 5–56. [227–8]
- (1968c) 'Metrics and morphophonemics in the Kalevala'. In *Studies presented to Roman Jakobson by his students.* Cambridge, Mass.: Slavica Press, 137–48. [93]
- (1971) 'Historical linguistics'. In Dingwall, W. O. (1971), 576–649. [83, 106, 230]
- (1972a) 'Explanation in phonology'. In Peters, S. (1972), 189–227. [106, 201]
- (1972b) 'Metrics and morphophonemics in the Rigveda'. In Brame, M. (1972), 171–200. [93]
- (1973a) 'Phonological representations'. In Fujimura, O. (1973), 1–136. [85, 138, 195–6, 211, 227–8]
- (1973b) 'Abstractness, opacity and global rules'. In Kiparsky, P. (1973a), 57–86. [114, 140, 183–5, 191–2, 229–30]
- (1974) 'Remarks on analogical change'. In Anderson, J. & Jones, Ch. (1974), 257–75. [79, 129, 162–3, 201]
- & Menn, L. (1977) 'On the acquisition of phonology'. In Macnamara, J. (1977), 47–78. [104, 138, 185, 191, 200–2, 210–11, 220–1]
Kisseberth, Ch. (1969) 'On the abstractness of phonology: the evidence from Yawelmani'. *PL* 1: 2. [83, 184, 254]
- (1970) 'On the functional unity of phonological rules'. *LI* 1: 291–306. [121]
Klausenburger, J. (1974) 'Rule inversion, opacity, conspiracies: French liaison and elision'. *Lingua* 34: 167–79. [211]
- (1978) 'French linking phenomena: a natural generative analysis'. *Lg.* 54: 21–40. [207, 211]
Klima, E. (1972) 'How alphabets might reflect language'. In Kavanagh, J. & Mattingly, I. (1972), 57–80. [75]
Koerner, E. F. K. (1975) (ed.) *The transformational-generative paradigm and modern linguistic theory.* Amsterdam: John Benjamins
Kohler, J. (1971) 'On the adequacy of phonological theories for contrastive studies'. In Nickel, G. (ed.) *Papers in contrastive linguistics.* Cambridge: Cambridge University Press, 83–8. [247]
- (1977) 'Investigating coarticulation'. In Dressler, W. U. & Pfeiffer, O. E. (1977), 243–7. [56, 172, 211]
Korhonen, M. (1969) 'Die Entwicklung der morphologischen Methode im Lappischen'. *FUF* 37: 203–62. [98, 172]
Koutsoudas, A. (1977) 'On the necessity of the morphophonemic–allophonic

distinction'. In Dressler, W. U. & Pfeiffer, O. E. (1977), 121–6. [190]

Koutsoudas, A., Sanders, G. & Noll, C. (1974) 'The application of phonological rules'. *Lg.* 50: 1–28. [139–40, 191, 263]

Kozhevnikov, V. A. & Chistovich, L. A. (1965) *Speech, articulation and perception.* (Revised) (Joint Publications Research Service 30.543). Washington, DC: US Department of Commerce. [67]

Kuhn, T. (1962) *The structure of scientific revolutions.* Chicago: University of Chicago Press. [255]

Kuryłowicz, J. (1966). 'La nature des procès dit "analogiques"'. In Hamp, E., Householder, F. & Austerlitz, R. (1966), 158–74. (First printed in *Acta Linguistica* 5 (1945–9): 121–38). [149, 158]

– (1968). 'The notion of morpho(pho)neme'. In Lehmann, W. P. & Malkiel, Y. (1968), 65–81. [142]

Labov, W. (1969) 'Contraction, deletion and inherent variability of the English copula'. *Lg.* 45: 715–62. [176, 181]

– (1971) 'The study of language in its social context'. In Fishman, J. (ed.) *Advances in the sociology of language 1.* The Hague: Mouton, 152–216. (Originally in *Studium Generale* 23: 30–87 (1970)). [94, 176, 181, 205]

– (1972) 'On the use of the present to explain the past'. In *Preprints of the 11th International Congress of Linguists* (Bologna, 28 August–2 September 1972), 1110–35. [41, 222]

– (1975) 'The quantitative study of linguistic structure'. In Dahlstedt, K.-H. (1975), 188–234. [105]

Labov, W., Yaeger, M. & Steiner, R. (1973) 'A quantitative study of sound change in progress'. NSF Report printed and distributed by The US Regional Survey, Philadelphia. University of Pennsylvania. [42, 104, 182]

Ladefoged, P. (1967) *Three areas of experimental phonetics.* Oxford: Oxford University Press. [40]

– (1971a) *Preliminaries to linguistic phonetics.* Chicago: University of Chicago Press. [xv, 52]

– (1971b) 'The limits of phonology'. In Hammerich, L. L., Jakobson, R. & Zwirner, E. (eds.) *Form & substance.* Phonetic and linguistic papers presented to Eli Fischer-Jørgensen. Copenhagen: Akademisk Forlag, 47–56. [31, 53, 64, 241]

Lakoff, G. (1971) 'On generative semantics'. In Steinberg, D. & Jakobovits, L. (eds.) *Semantics. An interdisciplinary reader in philosophy, linguistics, and psychology.* Cambridge: Cambridge University Press, 232–96. [33]

Langacker, R. (1972) *Fundamentals of linguistic analysis.* New York: Harcourt Brace Jovanovich. [202]

Lashley, K. S. (1951) 'The problem of serial order in behavior'. In Jeffress, L. A. (ed.) *Cerebral mechanisms in behavior.* New York: John Wiley, 112–36. [8, 51, 63]

Lass, R. (1976) *English phonology and phonological theory.* Cambridge: Cambridge University Press. [5, 53, 223, 254]

Laver, J. (1970) 'The production of speech'. In Lyons, J. (ed.) *New horizons in linguistics.* Harmondsworth: Penguin Books. [67]

Leben, W. & Robinson, O. (1977) 'Upside-down phonology'. *Lg.* 53: 1–20. [77]

Lehmann, W. P. (1953) 'A note on the change of American English /t/'. *AS* 28: 271–5. [100]

– & Malkiel, Y. (1968) (eds.) *Directions for historical linguistics*. Austin: University of Texas Press

Lenneberg, E. (1967) *Biological foundations of language*. New York: John Wiley. [40, 62]

Liberman, A. M., Cooper, F. S., Shankweiler, D. P. & Studdert-Kennedy, M. (1967) 'Perception of the speech code'. *PsR* 74: 431–61. [44]

Lightner, Th. (1965) 'Segmental phonology of Modern Standard Russian'. Unpublished PhD thesis, MIT. [106, 136, 204]

– (1971) 'Generative phonology'. In Dingwall, W. O. (1971), 498–575. [6, 78, 225, 240]

Liljencrants, J. & Lindblom, B. (1972) 'Numerical simulation of vowel quality systems: the role of perceptual contrast'. *Lg.* 48: 839–62. [268]

Linell, P. (1972) 'Remarks on Swedish morphology'. *RUUL* 1. [xiv, 58–9, 73, 110–11, 122, 127, 232]

– (1973a) '/ʉ/. On the phonology of the Swedish vowel system'. *SL* 27: 1–52. [xiv, 90, 97]

– (1973b) 'The phonological character of umlaut and ablaut in Swedish'. *RUUL* 2: 7–28. [xiv, 239]

– (1974a) *Problems of psychological reality in generative phonology: a critical assessment*. *RUUL* 4. [xiii, xiv, xv, 5, 13, 16, 19, 21, 27, 48, 56, 78, 84, 104, 113, 138, 161, 174–5, 196–7, 204, 220, 235, 237, 256–7]

– (1974b) 'Surface forms and the unordered rules hypothesis'. In Dahl, Ö. (1974a), 203–20. [xiii, 56, 59, 140]

– (1975) 'Markering – om mellanspråkliga likheter och skiljaktigheter i morfologi och syntax'. *Publication* 10. Umeå University: Dept. of General Linguistics. [144]

– (1976a) 'Phonemes, derivational constraints or what?' *Lingua* 38: 263–80. [xiii, 43, 56, 80–1, 83–4, 90, 105, 115, 180–1]

– (1976b) 'On the structure of morphological operations'. *LB* 44: 1–29. [xiii, 78–80, 122, 130]

– (1976c) 'Is linguistics an empirical science? Some notes on Esa Itkonen's "Linguistics and metascience"'. *SL* 30: 77–94. [28–9]

– (1977a) 'Morphophonology as part of morphology'. In Dressler, W. U. & Pfeiffer, O. E. (1977), 9–20. [xiii, 80, 142]

– (1977b) 'Evidence for a functionally-based typology of phonological rules'. In Goyvaerts, D. L. (forthcoming). [xiii, 168]

– (1978a) 'Notes on the relation between linguistics and psycholinguistics'. In Drachman, G. (ed.) (forthcoming) *SBL* 5. [14, 256]

– (1978b) Vowel length and consonant length in Swedish word level phonology'. In Gårding, E., Bruce, G. & Bannert, R. (eds.), *Nordic Prosody*. Lund: Dept. of Linguistics. 123–136. [59–60]

– (1979a) 'On the similarity between Chomsky and Skinner'. In Perry, Th. (ed.) *Evidence and argumentation in linguistics*. Berlin: de Gruyter. [4, 16, 33, 256]

– (1979b) 'The concept of phonological form and the activities of speech production and perception'. Mimeo, Uppsala: Dept. of Linguistics. [48, 65, 71, 179]

Linell, P., Svensson, B. & Öhman, S. (1971) *Ljudstruktur*. Lund: Gleerups. [102, 120, 251]

Lovins, J. (1974) 'Why loan phonology is natural phonology'. In Bruck, A., Fox, R. & LaGaly, M. (1974), 240–50. [196]

Luelsdorff, Ph. (1971) 'A segmental phonology of Black English'. Unpublished dissertation, Georgetown University. [75, 102]

Lyons, J. (1968) *Introduction to theoretical linguistics*. Cambridge: Cambridge University Press. [152, 156]

Macnamara, J. (1977) (ed.) *Language learning and thought*. New York: Academic Press

Maher, P. (1969) 'The paradox of creation and tradition in grammar: sound pattern of a palimpsest'. *LS* 7: 15–24. [240]

Malécot, A. (1960) 'Vowel nasality as a distinctive feature in American English'. *Lg.* 36: 222–9. [91, 211]

Malmberg, B. (1968) *Svensk fonetik* (fourth edition). Lund: Gleerups. [107]

– (1969) 'Sakkunnigutlåtande över de sökande till professuren i fonetik i Uppsala'. Mimeo, University of Uppsala. [7]

Mandelbaum, D. G. (1949) (ed.) *Selected writings of Edward Sapir*. Berkeley and Los Angeles: California University Press (fourth impression 1963). [91]

Mansell, P. (1973a). 'Phonemes, rule relatedness or what?' *FIPhSKUM 1*: 75–100. [90, 105, 115, 263]

– (1973b) 'A new proposal for defining allophones'. *FIPhSKUM 1*: 103–31. [31, 172]

– (1973c) 'Counter-feeding and rule ordering'. *FIPhSKUM 1*: 163–83. [193]

Martinet, A. (1955) *Économie des changements phonétiques*. Bern: Francke. [99, 104–5]

– (1962) *A functional view of language*. Oxford: Oxford University Press. [4]

Masterman, M. (1968) 'The nature of a paradigm'. In Lakatos, I. & Musgrave, A. (eds.) *Criticism and the growth of knowledge*. Cambridge: Cambridge University Press, 59–90. [255]

Mathesius, V. (1964) 'Zur synchronischen Analyse fremden Sprachguts'. In Vachek, J. (ed.) *A Prague School reader in linguistics*. Bloomington: Indiana University Press, 398–412. [196]

Matthews, P. H. (1972) *Inflectional morphology. A theoretical study based on aspects of Latin verb conjugation*. (Cambridge Studies in Linguistics 6). Cambridge: Cambridge University Press. [125]

– (1974) *Morphology*. Cambridge: Cambridge University Press. [78, 80, 158]

McCawley, J. D. (1967a) 'The phonological theory behind Whitney's Sanskrit Grammar'. In *Language and areas : studies presented to George V. Bobrinskoy*. University of Chicago: Division of Humanities, 77–85. [229]

– (1967b) 'Sapir's phonologic representation'. *IJAL* 33: 106–11. [230]

– (1968a) *The phonological component of a grammar of Japanese*. The Hague: Mouton. [74]

- (1968b) 'Can you count pluses and minuses before you can count?' *ChJL* 2: 51–6. [73, 235]
- (1974) Review of Chomsky, N. & Halle, M. (1968). *IJAL* 40: 50–88. Also in Goyvaerts, D. L. & Pullum, G. E. (1975). [51–2, 211]
- (1976) 'Some ideas not to live by'. *Die Neueren Sprachen* 75: 151–65. [26, 164, 238–9, 256, 268]

McNeill, D. & Lindig, K. (1973) 'The perceptual reality of phonemes, syllables, words and sentences'. *JVLVB* 12: 419–30. [69]

Mead, G. H. (1950) *Mind, self and society*. Chicago: University of Chicago Press. [65]

Mehan, H. (1972) 'Language using abilities'. *LS* 22: 1–10. [19]

Meringer, R. (1908) *Aus dem Leben der Sprache. Versprechen. Kindersprache. Nachahmungstrieb*. Berlin: Behr's Verlag. [111, 137–8]

- & Mayer, K. (1895) *Versprechen und Verlesen*. Stuttgart

Miller, G. (1975) 'On constraining global rules in phonology'. *Lg.* 51: 128–32. [140, 192]

Miller, G. A., Galanter, E. & Pribram, K. H. (1960) *Plans and the structure of behavior*. New York: Holt, Rinehart & Winston. [48]

Miner, K. (1975) 'English inflectional endings and unordered rules'. *FL* 12: 339–65. [130]

Morgan, J. (1972) 'Verb agreement as a rule of English'. *CLS* 8: 278–86. [26]

Morin, Y.-Ch. (1974) 'Règles phonétiques ou règles phonologiques?' *MWPL* 1: 45–7. [31, 205]

- (1975) La phonétique est- elle abstraite?: le cas du bourouchaski'. *MWPL* 5: 175–80. [126]

Moskowitz, A. (1973) 'On the status of vowel shift in English'. In Moore, Th. (ed.) *Cognitive development and the acquisition of language*. New York: Academic Press, 223–60. [133, 138, 195, 211, 239]

Mulder, J. W. F. (1968) *Sets and relations in phonology*. Oxford: Clarendon Press

Murdock, B. (1974) *Human memory : theory and data*. New York: John Wiley. [74]

Myerson, R. (1975) 'A developmental study of children's knowledge of complex derived words in English'. Mimeo, Harvard Graduate School of Education. [202, 211]

Nagel, Th. (1969) 'Linguistics and epistemology'. In Hook, S. (1969), 171–82. [23]

Neisser, U. (1967) *Cognitive psychology*. New York: Appleton-Century-Crofts. [65]

Nessly, L. (1971) 'Anglicization in English phonology'. *CLS* 7: 499–510. [197]

Newman, P. (1968) 'The reality of morphophonemes'. *Lg.* 44: 507–15. [224]

Nordenfelt, L. (1977) *Events, actions and ordinary language*. Lund: Doxa. [15]

Nyman, M. (1977) 'The Family resemblance of Latin *caput* and *capillus* (and what can be gleaned from it)'. *IF* 82, 163–90. [53]

Ohala, J. (1974a) 'Experimental historical phonology'. In Anderson, I. & Jones, Ch. (1973), 353–89. [129, 133, 138, 195, 202, 211, 218]

– (1974b) 'Phonetic explanation in phonology'. In Bruck, A., Fox, R. & LaGaly, M. (1974), 251–74. [207]

Ohala, M. (1974) 'The abstractness controversy: experimental input from Hindi'. *Lg.* 50: 225–35. [76]

Ohlander, S. (1976) *Phonology, meaning, morphology.* (Gothenburg Studies in English 33) Göteborg: Acta Universitatis Gothoburgensis. [258]

Öhman, S. (1966) 'Generativa regler för det svenska verbets fonologioch prosodi'. *SB* 3: 71–88 (Göteborg: Inst. f. nordiska språk). [232]

– (1972) 'Discussion paper on acoustics of speech: linguistic theory and speech research'. In Gilbert, J. H. (1972), 177–85. [19]

– (1975) 'Modelling linguistic interaction in terms of lexical operators: preliminary considerations'. In Dahlstedt, R. H. (1975), 304–52. [33, 35, 37, 41, 45]

– (1976) 'Competence and performance as theory and practice'. Ms., Uppsala: Dept. of Linguistics. [19]

Olmsted, D. (1971) *Out of the mouths of babes.* The Hague: Mouton. [219]

Paunonen, H. (1973) 'On free variation'. *JSFOu* 72: 285–300. [85, 155, 176, 211]

Peters, S. (1972) (ed.) *Goals of linguistic theory.* Englewood Cliffs, NJ: Prentice-Hall

Pettersson, Th. (1975) 'In favour of the archiphoneme'. *WPPLL* 10: 139–54. [264]

Picard, M. (1974) 'Reexamining phonological rules: examples from French'. *MWPL* 1: 123–32. [92]

Pike, K. (1947) 'Grammatical prerequisites to phonemic analysis'. *Word* 3: 155–72. Also in Fudge, E. (1973), 115–35. [258]

– (1952) 'More on grammatical prerequisites'. *Word* 8: 106–21. [258]

Polanyi, M. (1969) *Knowing and being. Essays by M. Polanyi.* Grene, M. (ed.). Chicago: University of Chicago Press. [44]

Popper, K. (1972) *Objective knowledge.* Oxford: Oxford University Press. [18, 249]

Postal, P. (1968) *Aspects of phonological theory.* New York: Harper & Row. [73, 90, 115, 161, 227, 258, 260–1, 264–6]

Putnam, H. (1971) 'The "innateness hypothesis" and explanatory models in linguistics'. In Searle, J. (ed.) *The philosophy of language.* Oxford: Oxford University Press, 130–9. [237]

Pylyshyn, Z. (1972) 'Competence and psychological reality'. *AP* 27: 546–52. [250]

– (1973) 'What the mind's eye tells the mind's brain: a critique of mental imagery'. *PB* 80: 1–24. [71, 250]

Quine, W. V. (1952) 'On what there is'. In Linsky, L. (ed.) *Semantics and the philosophy of language.* Urbana: University of Illinois Press, 189–206. [242]

– (1970) 'Methodological reflections on current linguistic theory'. *Synthèse* 21: 386–98. [10, 23]

Ralph, B. (1977) 'Individuell och kollektiv variation: Fonologisk-lexikaliska aspekter'. *SB* 10 *Nysvenska studier* 57: 19–30. [155]

Read, Ch. (1971) 'Pre-school children's knowledge of English phonology'. *HER* 41: 1–34. [204]

Rhodes, R. (1973) 'Some implications of natural phonology'. *CLS* 9: 530–41. [190]

Ringen, C. (1977) 'Vowel harmony: Implications for the alternation condition'. In Dressler, W. U. & Pfeiffer, O. E. (1977), 127–32. [171]

Ringen, J. (1975) 'Linguistic facts: a study of the empirical scientific status of transformational generative grammars'. In Cohen, D. & Wirth, J. (1975), 1–41. [xiv, 1, 11, 28]

– (1976) 'On evaluating data concerning linguistic intuition'. Ms., Dept. of Philosophy, Indiana University, South Bend. [14]

Roberts, W. (1975) 'Speech errors as evidence for the reality of phonological units'. *Lingua* 35: 263–96. [110–11, 202]

– (1976) 'Phonological theory, absolute neutralisation and the case of Nupe'. *Gl.* 10: 241–87. [7, 104, 233]

Robins, R. H. (1967). *A short history of linguistics*. London: Longman. [224]

Rommetveit, R. (1972) 'Deep structure of sentences versus message structure'. *NJL* 26: 3–22. [19]

Ross, J. R. (1972) 'A reanalysis of English word stress'. In Brame, M. (1972), 229–323. [121]

– (1973) 'Nouniness'. In Fujimura, O. (1973), 137–257. [26, 164, 210]

Rubach, J. (1976) 'Feature invasion'. *JIPA* 6: 23–8. [188]

– (1977a) 'Nasalization in Polish'. *JPh* 5: 17–25. [196]

– (1977b) *Changes of consonants in English and Polish. A generative account.* Wrocław: Polska Akademia Nauk. (Prace Językoznawcze 87). [172]

– (1977c) 'Contrastive phonostylistics'. In *Papers and Studies in Contrastive Linguistics* 6: 63–72. [178, 188, 199]

– (1977d) 'Rule ordering and concrete derivations in phonology'. *Linguistica Silesiana* 2: 77–90. [191]

Rudes, B. (1976) 'Lexical representation and variable rules in natural generative phonology'. *Gl.* 10: 111–50. [77, 170–1, 192]

– (1977). 'A note on Romanian fast-speech'. *RRL* 22: 87–97. [172]

Salus, P. & Salus, M. (1974) 'Developmental neurophysiology and phonological acquisition order'. *Lg.* 50: 151–60. [218]

Sampson, G. (1970) 'On the need for a phonological base'. *Lg.* 46: 586–626. [74, 203, 241]

Sapir, E. (1921) *Language*. New York: Harcourt, Brace & World. [5, 70, 75, 156]

– (1925) 'Sound patterns in language'. *Lg.* 1: 37–51. Also in Mandelbaum, D. G. (1949), 33–45, and Fudge, E. (1973), 101–14. [112, 251]

– (1933) 'La réalité psychologique des phonèmes'. *Journal de Psychologie Normale et Pathologique* 30: 247–65. Also in Mandelbaum, D. G. (1949), 46–60. [91]

de Saussure, F. (1964) *Cours de linguistique générale*. Paris: Payot. (First published 1916)

Savin, H. (1972) 'What the child knows about speech when he starts to learn to read'. In Kavanagh, J. & Mattingly, L. (1972), 319–26. [69]

- & Bever, T. (1970) 'The nonperceptual reality of the phoneme'. *JVLVB* 9: 295–302. [68–9]

Schane, S. A. (1968) *French phonology and morphology*. Cambridge, Mass.: MIT Press. [xv, 83, 92, 226, 239]

- (1971) 'The phoneme revisited'. *Lg.* 47: 503–21. [88, 92, 99, 105–6, 115, 175, 197, 263]
- (1972) 'Natural rules in phonology'. In Stockwell, R. & Macauley, R. (1972), 199–229. [178, 224]
- (1973) *Generative phonology*. Englewood Cliffs, NJ: Prentice-Hall. [91]
- (1974) 'How abstract is abstract?' In Bruck, A., Fox, R. & LaGaly, M. (1974), 297–317. [56]

Schnitzer, M. (1972) 'Aphasiological evidence for the tense–lax distinction for underlying vowels in English'. *Preprints of the 11th International Congress of Linguists* (Bologna, 28 August–2 September 1972), 278–90. [16, 84, 112–13, 203]

Schwartz, R. (1969) 'On knowing a grammar'. In Hook, S. (1969), 183–90. [23]

Searle, J. (1969) *Speech acts*. Cambridge: Cambridge University Press. [22–3]

Sherzer, J. (1970) 'Talking backwards in Cuna: the sociological reality of phonological descriptions'. *SJA* 26: 343–53. [75, 201]

- (1976) 'Play languages: implications for (socio)linguistics.' In Kirshenblatt-Gimblett, B. (ed.) *Speech play*. Philadelphia: University of Pennsylvania Press, 19–36. [201]

Shibatani, M. (1972) 'The phonological representations of English inflectional endings'. *Gl.* 6: 117–27. [131]

- (1973) 'The role of surface phonetic constraints in generative phonology'. *Lg.* 49: 87–106. [118–19, 125, 211]

Sinclair-de-Zwart, H. (1969) 'A possible theory of language acquisition within the general framework of Piaget's developmental theory'. In Elkind, D. & Flavell, J. (eds.) *Studies in cognitive development*. Oxford: Oxford University Press, 326–36. [237]

Sigurd, B. (1965) *Phonotactic structures in Swedish*. Lund: Uniskol. [117]

- (1970) 'The status of ŋ, ç and ʃ in Swedish'. In Benediktsson, H. (ed.) *The Nordic languages and modern linguistics*. Proceedings of the International Conference of Nordic and General Linguistics, Reykjavík, 1969. Reykjavík: Vísindafélag Íslendinga, 481–97. [102, 251]

Skinner, B. (1957) *Verbal behavior*. New York: Appleton-Century-Crofts. [4, 246]

Skousen, R. (1975a) 'On the nature of morphophonemic alternation'. In Koerner, E. F. K. (1975), 185–232. [76, 85, 129, 138, 195]

- (1975b) *Substantive evidence in phonology. The evidence from Finnish and French*. (*Janua Linguarum*, Series Minor 217) The Hague: Mouton. [76, 83, 85, 135, 138, 175, 189–90, 195, 211]

Slobin, D. (1971) (ed.) *The ontogenesis of grammar*. New York: Academic Press

- (1973) 'Cognitive prerequisites for the development of grammar'. In Ferguson, Ch. & Slobin, D. (eds.) *Studies of child language development*. New York: Holt, Rinehart & Winston, 175–208. [221]

Smith, N. (1973) *The acquisition of phonology. A case study*. Cambridge:
Cambridge University Press. [200, 215, 219, 221]

Sommerstein, A. (1974) 'On phonotactically motivated rules'. *JL* 10: 71–94.
[118, 125]

Stampe, D. (1969) 'The acquisition of phonetic representation'. *CLS* 5: 433–44.
[217, 219–21]

– (1972) 'How I spent my summer vacation.' Mimeographed dissertation. Ohio
State University and MIT. [111, 175, 190, 201, 219–20]

Stanley, R. (1967) 'Redundancy rules in phonology'. *Lg*. 43: 393–436. [124]

St Clair, R. (1973) 'The independency principle in dialectology'. *LS* 27: 23–6.
[21, 75, 102, 161, 243]

Steinberg, D. (1971) 'Would an orthography based on Chomsky and Halle's
underlying phonological representations be optimal?'. *WPLH* 3/71: 1–18.
[92, 197]

– (1973) 'Phonology, reading and Chomsky and Halle's optimal orthography'.
JPR 2: 239–58. [197, 236, 241]

– (1975) 'Chomsky: from formalism to mentalism and psychological invalidity'.
Gl. 9: 218–52. [xiv, 5, 11–13, 19, 21, 25, 27, 240, 248]

– & Krohn, R. (1975) 'The psychological validity of Chomsky & Halle's vowel
shift rule'. In Koerner, E. F. K. (1975), 223–59. [138, 195, 202, 211]

Stevens, K. (1960) 'Toward a model for speech recognition'. *JASA* 32: 47–55.
[46]

– & Halle, M. (1967) 'Remarks on analysis by synthesis and distinctive
features'. In Wathen-Dunn, W. (ed.) *Models for the perception of speech and
visual form*. Proceedings of a symposium, Boston, 11–14 November 1964.
Cambridge, Mass.: MIT Press, 88–102. [54, 101]

Stich, S. (1975) 'Competence and indeterminacy'. In Cohen, D. & Wirth, J.
(1975), 93–109. [20, 26]

Stockwell, R. & Macauley, R. (1972) (eds.) *Linguistic change and generative
theory*. Bloomington: Indiana University Press

Straight, S. (1976) 'Comprehension versus production in linguistic theory'. *FL*
14: 525–40. [39]

Studdert-Kennedy, M. (1976) 'Speech perception'. In Lass, N. (ed.)
Contemporary issues in experimental phonetics. New York: Academic Press,
243–93. [42, 67]

Sturtevant, E. (1947) *An introduction to linguistic science*. New Haven: Yale
University Press. [162]

Tatham, M. (1969) 'Classifying allophones'. *OPUE* 3. [31, 64]

Taylor, C. (1964) *The explanation of behaviour*. London: Routledge & Kegan
Paul. [23]

– (1970) 'The explanation of purposive behaviour'. In Borger, R. & Cioffi, F.
(eds.) *Explanation in the behavioural sciences*. Cambridge: Cambridge
University Press, 49–95. [14, 16, 246]

Taylor, R. (1966) *Action and purpose*. Englewood Cliffs, NJ: Prentice-Hall. [23]

Teleman, U. (1969). 'Böjningssuffixens form i nusvenskan'. *ANF* 84: 163–208.
[122, 232]

- (1974) 'Ordklasser och satsdelar – finns dom ?' In Teleman, U. & Hultman, T. (eds.) *Språket i bruk*. Lund: LiberLäromedel, 72–98. [156]
- (1977) 'How to be concrete in linguistics'. In Weinstock, J. (ed.) (1977). [39]

Thelin, N. B. (1971) *On stress assignment and vowel reduction in Contemporary Standard Russian*. (Studia Slavica Upsaliensia 9). Uppsala: Almqvist & Wiksell. [211]

- (1975) *Towards a theory of verb stem formation and conjugation in Modern Russian*. (Studia Slavica Upsaliensia 17). Uppsala: Almqvist & Wiksell. [141]

Thomason, S. (1976) 'What else happens to opaque rules ?' *Lg.* 52: 370–81. [210]

Tiersma, P. (1978) 'Bidirectional leveling as evidence for relational rules'. *Lingua* 45: 65–77. [157]

Tranel, B. (1974) 'Le cas de l'effacement facultatif du schwa en français: quelques implications théoriques'. *MWPL* 1: 1–11. [92, 211]

Troike, R. (1969) 'Receptive competence, productive competence and performance'. *GMSLL* 22: 63–4. [41]

Trubetzkoy, N. S. (1958) *Grundzüge der Phonologie* (third edition). Göttingen: Vandenhoek & Ruprecht. [xv, 49, 249, 264]

Tulving, E. & Donaldson, W. (1972) (eds.) *Organization of memory*. New York: Academic Press. [74]

Twaddell, W. F. (1935) 'On defining the phoneme'. Language monographs published by the Linguistic Society of America, 16. Also in Joos, M. (1957), 55–79. [4]

Ullman, S. (1951) *The principles of semantics*. Oxford: Basil Blackwell. [152, 156]

Ureland, S. (1972) 'Observations on Texas–Swedish phonology'. *SL* 25: 69–110. [101]

Vago, R. (1977). 'In support of extrinsic ordering'. *JL* 13: 25–41. [191, 254]

Vandamme, F. J. (1972) *Simulation of natural language : a first approach. (Janua Linguarum*, Series Maior 50). The Hague: Mouton. [39]

Vennemann, Th. (1968) 'Die Affrikaten in der generativen Phonologie des Deutschen'. *Ph.* 18: 65–76. [240]

- (1970) 'The German velar nasal: a case for abstract phonology'. *Ph.* 22: 65–81. [251]
- (1972a) 'Rule inversion'. *Lingua* 29: 209–42. [150, 175, 207, 209, 211]
- (1972b) 'Sound change and markedness theory: on the history of the German consonant system'. In Stockwell, R. & Macauley, R. (1972), 230–74. [68]
- (1974a) 'Phonological concreteness in natural generative grammar'. In Shuy, R. & Bailey, Ch.-J. (eds.) *Towards tomorrow's linguistics*. Washington, DC: Georgetown University Press, 202–19. [83, 137, 184–5]
- (1974b) 'Words and syllables in natural generative grammar'. In Bruck, A., Fox, R. & LaGaly, M. (1974), 346–74. [76–8, 158–9, 211, 229, 254]
- (1974c) 'Restructuring'. *Lingua* 33: 137–56. [207]

Walker, D. (1975) 'Lexical stratification in French phonology'. *Lingua* 37: 177–196. [239]

Wang, W. (1968) 'Vowel features, paired variables and the English vowel shift'. *Lg.* 44: 695–708. [22, 73, 254]

– (1969) 'Competing changes as a cause of residue'. *Lg.* 45: 9–25. [75, 104, 154, 182, 207]

Wardhaugh, R. (1967) 'Three approaches to contrastive phonological analysis'. *CJL* 13: 3–14. [247]

Warren, R. M. (1970) 'Perceptual restoration of missing phonemes'. *Science* 167: 392–3. [65]

Wartofsky, M. (1967) 'Metaphysics as heuristics for science'. *BSPS* 3. Dordrecht: Reidel. [255]

– (1968) *Conceptual foundations of scientific thought*. New York: Macmillan. [10]

Waterson, N. (1971) 'Child phonology: a prosodic view'. *JL* 7: 179–211. [218]

Watt, W. C. (1970) 'On two hypotheses concerning psycholinguistics'. In Hayes, J. R. (1970), 137–220. [11, 240]

Weigl, E. & Bierwisch, M. (1970) 'Neuropsychology and linguistics: topics of common research'. *FL* 6: 1–18. [112]

Weinreich, U. (1954) 'Is a structural dialectology possible?' *Word* 10: 388–400.

– (1968) *Languages in contact*. The Hague: Mouton. [195]

Weinreich, U., Labov, W. & Herzog, M. I. (1968) 'Empirical foundations for a theory of language change'. In Lehmann, W. P. & Malkiel, Y. (1968), 95–195. [26, 75, 104]

Weinstock, J. (1977) (ed.) *The Nordic languages and modern linguistics 3*. Proceedings of the Third International Conference of Nordic and General Linguistics. Austin, Texas: University of Texas Press

Weitzman, R. S. (1972) 'Lacuna in generative phonology: contrast and free variation'. *PL* 5(3): 354–65. [90]

Wells, R. (1949) 'Automatic alternation'. *Lg.* 25: 99–116. [142, 250]

Whitaker, H. (1969) 'On the representation of language in the human brain'. *WPP-UCLA* 12 (September 1969). [11]

Winch, P. (1958) *The idea of a social science and its relation to philosophy*. London: Routledge & Kegan Paul. (Sixth impression 1970). [23]

Wittgenstein, L. (1953) *Philosophical investigations*. Translation of the author's 'Philosophische Untersuchungen' by Anscombe, G. E. M. Oxford: Basil Blackwell. [20, 243]

Witting, C. (1959) *Physical and functional aspects of speech sounds*. Uppsala Universitets Arsskrift 1959: 7. Uppsala: Almqvist & Wiksell. [7, 59]

– (1962) 'On the auditory phonetics of connected speech: errors and attitudes in listening'. *Word* 18: 221–48. [64]

– (1977) *Studies in Swedish generative phonology*. Uppsala: Almqvist & Wiksell. [59, 60]

Worth, D. S. (1967) 'The notion of "stem" in Russian flexion and derivation'. In *To honor Roman Jakobson*. The Hague: Mouton, 2269–88. [223]

von Wright, G. H. (1971) *Explanation and understanding*. London: Routledge & Kegan Paul. [15]

Wurzel, W. U. (1970) *Studien zur deutschen Lautstruktur. SG* 8. [73, 127, 211, 253]

– (1975) 'Morphologische Regeln in historischer Sicht'. In Dahlstedt, K.-H. (1975), 119–45. [149, 158]

- (1977) 'Adaptionsregeln und heterogene Sprachsysteme'. In Dressler, W. U. & Pfeiffer, O. E. (1977), 175–82. [101–2, 165]
- & Böttcher, R. (1977) 'Konsonantenkluster: Phonologische Komplexität und Aphasische Störungen'. To appear in Bierwisch, M. (ed.) *Psycholinguistik*. Berlin: Akademie-Verlag. [113]
Yli-Vakkuri, V. (1976) 'Onko suomen kvalitatiivinen astevaihtelu epäproduktiivinen jäänne?' *Sananjalka* 18: 53–69. [195, 211]
Zimmer, K. (1969) 'Psychological correlates of some Turkish morpheme structure conditions'. *Lg.* 45: 309–21. [73, 76]
Zwicky, A. (1970a) 'The free-ride Principle and two rules of complete assimilation in English'. *CLS* 6: 579–88. [226]
- (1970b) 'Auxiliary reduction in English'. *LI* 1: 323–36. [181]
- (1972a) 'Note on a phonological hierarchy in English'. In Stockwell, R. & Macauley, R. (1972), 275–301. [172]
- (1972b) 'On casual speech'. *CLS* 8: 607–15. [172, 181]
- (1975a) 'The strategy of generative phonology'. In Dressler, W. U. & Mareš, F. V. (1975), 151–66. [2, 161, 226, 230, 244]
- (1975b) 'Settling on an underlying form: the English inflectional endings'. In Cohen, D. & Wirth, J. (1975), 129–85. [130]
- (1977) 'On clitics'. In Dressler, W. U. & Pfeiffer, O. E. (1977), 29–39. [156]